The Princeton Review

Cracking the

AP® HUMAN GEOGRAPHY EXAM

2015 Edition

Jon Moore

PrincetonReview.com

PENGUIN RANDOM HOUSE

Random House, Inc. New York

The Princeton Review

The Princeton Review
24 Prime Parkway, Suite 201
Natick, MA 01760
E-mail: editorialsupport@review.com

Published in the United States by Random House LLC, New York,
and simultaneously in Canada by Random House of Canada Limited,
Toronto.

A Penguin Random House Company.

ISBN: 978-0-8041-2534-5
ISSN: 1948-2205
eBook ISBN: 978-0-8041-2535-2

AP and Advanced Placement Program are registered trademarks of
the College Board, which does not sponsor or endorse this product.

The Princeton Review is not affiliated with Princeton University.

Editor: Selena Copock
Production Editor: Emily Epstein White
Production Artist: Craig Patches

Printed in the United States of America on partially recycled paper.

10 9 8 7 6 5 4 3 2 1

2015 Edition

Editorial
Rob Franek, Senior VP, Publisher
Casey Cornelius, VP Content Development
Mary Beth Garrick, Director of Production
Selena Coppock, Managing Editor
Calvin Cato, Editor
Colleen Day, Editor
Aaron Riccio, Editor
Meave Shelton, Editor
Alyssa Wolff, Editorial Assistant

Random House Publishing Team
Tom Russell, Publisher
Alison Stoltzfus, Publishing Manager
Dawn Ryan, Associate Managing Editor
Ellen Reed, Production Manager
Erika Pepe, Associate Production Manager
Kristin Lindner, Production Supervisor
Andrea Lau, Designer

ACKNOWLEDGMENTS

I would like to thank the following people for their input, advice, and support for this book: Barbara Hildebrant, David Lanegran, John Trites, Paul Gray, Ken Keller, Dan Berry, Tim Strauss, Adrian Bailey, Catherine Lockwood, Lawrence A. Brown, Keith Snedegar, Katherine Macpherson, Fernando Bosco, Chuck Monroe, Linda Barrett, Kevin Butler, and the extraordinary people of Alternate Room. In addition, I would also like to thank the editorial staff at The Princeton Review for their assistance and hard work. Finally, I give special appreciation to my wife, Amy, and son, Sutter, for their love and humor during the writing of this book.

This book is dedicated in memory of Ginger and Dublin.

Thank you to top-notch Princeton Review tutor Bryan Cunningham for his content review of the 2015 edition of this book.

CONTENTS

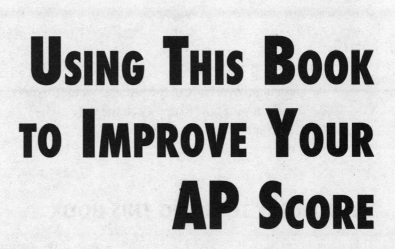

PART I

USING THIS BOOK TO IMPROVE YOUR AP SCORE

PREVIEW: YOUR KNOWLEDGE, YOUR EXPECTATIONS

Your route to a high score on the AP Human Geography Exam depends a lot how you plan to use this book. Respond to the following questions.

1. Rate your level of confidence about your knowledge of the content tested by the AP Human Geography Exam:
    A. Very confident—I know it all
    B. I'm pretty confident, but there are topics for which I could use help
    C. Not confident—I need quite a bit of support
    D. I'm not sure

2. If you have a goal score in mind, circle your goal score for the AP Human Geography Exam:

    5   4   3   2   1   I'm not sure yet

3. What do you expect to learn from this book? Circle all that apply to you.
    A. A general overview of the test and what to expect
    B. Strategies for how to approach the test
    C. The content tested by this exam
    D. I'm not sure yet

YOUR GUIDE TO USING THIS BOOK

This book is organized to provide as much—or as little—support as you need, so you can use this book in whatever way will be most helpful to improving your score on the AP Human Geography Exam.

*   The remainder of **Part I** will provide guidance on how to use this book and help you determine your strengths and weaknesses

*   **Part II** of this book will:
    *   provide information about the structure, scoring, and content of the AP Human Geography Exam
    *   help you to make a study plan
    *   point you towards additional resources

- **Part III** of this book will explore various strategies:
  - how to attack multiple choice questions
  - how to write high-scoring free-response answers
  - how to manage your time to maximize the number of points available to you

- **Part IV** of this book covers the content you need for the AP Human Geography Exam.

- **Part V** of this book contains practice tests.

You may choose the use some parts of this book over others, or you may work through the entire book. This will depend on your needs and how much time you have. Let's now look how to make this determination.

HOW TO BEGIN

1. **Take a Test**
   Before you can decide how to use this book, you need to take a practice test. Doing so will give you insight into your strengths and weaknesses, and the test will also help you make an effective study plan. If you're feeling test-phobic, remind yourself that a practice test is a tool for diagnosing yourself—it's not how well you do that matters but how you use information gleaned from your performance to guide your preparation.

   So, before you read further, take Practice Test 1 starting at page 299 of this book. Be sure to do so in one sitting, following the instructions that appear before the test.

2. **Check Your Answers**
   Using the answer key on page 319, count how many multiple choice questions you got right and how many you missed. Don't worry about the explanations for now, and don't worry about why you missed questions. We'll get to that soon.

3. **Reflect on the Test**
   After you take your first test, respond to the following questions::

   - How much time did you spend on the multiple-choice questions?

   - How much time did you spend on each essay?

   - How many multiple-choice questions did you miss?

   - Do you feel you had the knowledge to address the subject matter of the free response questions?

- Do you feel you wrote well-organized, thoughtful free responses?

- Circle the content areas that were most challenging for you and draw a line through the ones in which you felt confident/did well.

4. **Read Part II of this Book and Complete the Self-Evaluation**

As noted in the Guide section above, Part II will provide information on how the test is structured and scored. It will also explain the areas of content that are tested.

As you read Part Two, re-evaluate your answers to the questions above. At the end of Part II, you will revisit and refine the questions you answered above. You will then be able to make a study plan, based on your needs and time available, that will allow you to use this book most effectively.

5. **Engage with Parts III and IV as Needed**

Notice the word *engage*. You'll get more out of this book if you use it intentionally than if you read it passively, hoping for an improved score through osmosis.

Strategy chapters will help you think about your approach to the question types on this exam. Part III will open with a reminder to think about how you approach questions now and then close with a reflection section asking you to think about how/whether you will change your approach in the future.

Content chapters are designed to provide a review of the content tested on the AP Human Geography Exam, including the level of detail you need to know and how the content is tested. You can review key terms at the end of each chapter.

6. **Take Test 2 and Assess Your Performance**

Once you feel you have developed the strategies you need and gained the knowledge you lacked, you should take Test 2, which starts at page 345 of this book. You should do so in one sitting, following the instructions at the beginning of the test.

When you are done, check your answers to the multiple-choice sections beginning on page 365. See if a teacher will read your essays and provide feedback.

Once you have taken the test, reflect on what areas you still need to work on, and revisit the chapters in this book that address those deficiencies. Through this type of reflection and engagement, you will continue to improve.

7. **Keep Working**

   As discussed in Part II, there are other resources available to you, including a wealth of information at the AP Central website. You can continue to explore areas that can stand improvement and engage in those areas right up to the day of the test.

PART II

ABOUT THE AP HUMAN GEOGRAPHY EXAM

THE STRUCTURE OF THE AP HUMAN GEOGRAPHY EXAM

The AP Human Geography Exam is divided into two sections: multiple-choice questions and free-response essays. Section I of the test consists of 75 multiple-choice questions to be answered in 60 minutes. There is a five-minute break following Section I. Section II of the test contains three essay-format free-response questions (FRQs) that are all to be completed within a 75-minute period.

THERE'S A LOT OF GEOGRAPHY OUT THERE

The AP Human Geography Exam is based upon seven knowledge areas. The material draws examples from all over the world, and there is a limited historical timeframe with which you must be familiar. On the multiple-choice section the distribution of questions is as follows:

Multiple-Choice Question Distribution

	Question Types	Percent of Questions	Approximate Number of Questions
Content Areas:			
	Geography: Its Nature and Perspectives	5–10%	4–8
	Population and Migration	13–17%	10–13
	Cultural Patterns and Processes	13–17%	10–13
	Political Organization of Space	13–17%	10–13
	Agriculture, Food Production, and Rural Land Use	13–17%	10–13
	Industrialization and Economic Development	13–17%	10–13
	Cities and Urban Land Use	13–17%	10–13

Keep in mind that geography is an academic field, and these knowledge areas overlap quite often. Still, as you can see from the table, the six subject areas are each about one-sixth of the test and the general geographic foundations questions are scattered throughout the test. So don't spend too much study time on the foundations section versus the other six subject areas.

FREE-RESPONSE QUESTIONS (AKA THE ESSAYS)

There is not a strict rule about the types of essay questions presented in the AP Human Geography Exam, nor are there requirements that any particular subject area be covered from year to year. However, there are some things you can expect in the free-response section:

- At least one question will have a **map, table, diagram, or model** that you must analyze to answer part of the question or the entire question. It is possible that all three questions have some sort of visual element that you will have to analyze to some degree.
- Another essay question will likely require you to make a **critical argument** regarding a theory, principle, or issue in human geography. Basically, you will have to explain what is right and wrong about the subject of the question.
- Another common occurrence are **process** questions, for which you have to describe the details of a geographic theory, principle, or issue. In other words, how does something work in a particular order—factor affects people and causes them to migrate to place Z.
- Be aware that there are **hybrid questions** that may ask you to do all of these in a single essay.

BE READY FOR ANYTHING

The questions do not come in any particular order, so be ready to jump from subject to subject throughout the exam. For example, when you take the multiple-choice portion of the exam, there may be a population question, then a city model question, and then one on religions. The essay questions are presented in random order, and we never know from year to year which three subjects will fall into the essay section. This is why practice tests are so important. You mind has to shift gears many times in the course of the exam. Think about it: Your teacher has presented your AP class in an ordered manner, subject by subject. Yet you are going to be tested in a disorganized manner. Thus, you need to be mentally prepared to link subjects and jump around in order to do well.

This book will help you. If you know how the test works, then there will be far less of a chance that the randomness of the subject matter will be a problem.

HOW SHOULD I STUDY?

To figure out what to study, you need to know what is on the test and what the test writers are looking for.

WHAT DO THEY WANT FROM ME?

What is the AP Human Geography Exam really testing? In a nutshell: They want to know if you can use the different models, theories, principles, and issues in human geography to explain how we organize the inhabited surface of the earth.

The course is meant to help you see the world around you in a new way. For example, you shouldn't just see a city with streets and buildings. Instead, by using urban models, you can divide cities by their component parts: a central business district (CBD), industrial land use, housing zones differentiated by income, ethnicity, age, or architecture. And you need to know how cities got that way. What are the forces that shape the theoretical place? How do principles such as site and situation matter? Are contemporary issues such as urban sprawl a problem for expanding cities? These are the types of questions you should ask yourself as you walk around each day to prepare for the test.

HERE'S YOUR GAME PLAN

To show what you know about human geography, keep the categories of and in mind as you study and prepare for the exam. Also, be ready to produce real-world examples to explain how something works, or even to explain why a theory may not be correct. To help you do this, here are a few overall strategies to prepare for the exam:

- Always look for linkages between the seven subject areas. If you can build associations in your mind between what may seem at first to be unrelated subjects (for example, population and economy,) then you will remember it far better than if you studied those areas separately.
- Know **only** the relevant history required for the test (the industrial revolution is important, the French Revolution is not). Start approximately at 1800 C.E. and go all the way to the present.
- Ask yourself what innovative theories were developed by geographers and related scientists. Who were these people and why were their ideas important?
- Examine the component parts of models and know the details about those parts. Consider why a model is organized in a particular way. How and why do parts of different models change over time?
- Keep a personal glossary of key principles in addition to the lists we provide you with in this book. The glossary should include general terms like *space* and *place*, and specific ones like the *Zone of Peripheral Squatter Settlements*. Knowing your vocabulary and the names of important concepts helps in the multiple-choice section. Using these terms will earn you many points in the essay section.

SCORING

The scores that you receive for the AP Human Geography Exam are very different from the grades that you get in school. The report that you receive from ETS sometime around early July will give you a 1 to 5 point score rating your performance:

5 points	Extremely well qualified
4 points	Well qualified
3 points	Qualified
2 points	Possibly qualified
1 point	Not recommended

These qualifications are the recommendation of ETS to colleges and universities as to whether you should receive credit for the course. Although ETS associates these scores with certain levels of grade performance by college students, you should not attach an A, B, C, D, or F grade to these scores. Why? It's a difficult standardized test—good students can do poorly and mediocre students can score highly, if they are good at this type of exam. Nonetheless, **your goal is a score of 4 or 5**. A score of 3 sounds okay, but it probably won't earn you college credit. Each year somewhere between 25 percent and 27 percent of students will earn the 4 or 5 score. Be in the top 75 percent or above and you've achieved the goal.

HOW DO THEY DECIDE ON THE SCORES?

Contrary to rumor, ETS does not use magic to score AP test performance. In fact, AP scoring is a highly regulated and statistics-driven process. The overall exam score is divided evenly between the two sections:

Section Number	Section Name	Percent of Score
Section I	Multiple Choice	50%
Section II	Free Response (essays)	50%

That seems simple enough, but it's important to realize that in Section I there are 75 questions and that you write three essays in Section II. Likewise, the way points are accumulated in each section is very different. On the next page and in Part III of this guide you'll get the details of how scores are earned in each section and how you can use an AP Human Geography–specific test-taking strategy to maximize your score.

MULTIPLE-CHOICE SECTION SCORING

As in other standardized tests, answers to the multiple-choice section are filled out by the student on a bubble sheet. Scores from these sheets are tabulated by scanning machines at ETS headquarters in Princeton, New Jersey.

In the end, a raw score is tabulated and then compared to the performance of all the other students who took the exam. This comparison may result in a scaled score that will then be combined, at equal weight (fifty-fifty), with the score on the essay section. How points are scaled may seem like magic, but scaling scores are done under traditional rules set by ETS statisticians using normalized distribution, or "bell-curve."

What's a Good Multiple-Choice Score?

Depending upon how scaled scores are divided by statisticians, the number of correct answers needed to get a 4 or 5 score can vary from year to year. Set yourself a target of at least 50 correct questions out of 75 on the multiple-choice section to ensure a 4 or 5 score for the exam.

FREE-RESPONSE "ESSAY" SECTION SCORING

You must attempt to answer each of the three essay questions on the exam. Leaving an essay question blank will make it nearly impossible to get a 4 or 5 on the AP Human Geography Exam. What to do if you are stumped by an essay question is covered in Chapter 2 of this guide.

The three essays are scored by "readers" who are experienced AP Human Geography high-school teachers and university-level geography instructors or professors. Readers are organized into three teams that each focus on reading only one of the questions. All of the readers on a team are trained simultaneously to score their essay questions, and they all use the same training materials. This is done to maintain consistency in the scoring process. In addition, each reader uses a scoring "rubric," or table, that divides up the possible number of points from each section of the essay and indicates how points are given. Readers must follow the rubric on each and every essay. This is good news for AP students. There are clear and standardized ways to score points no matter who reads your essay.

Readers do not give your essay an A, B, C, D, or F grade. Instead, each essay score begins with 0 points, and you earn points along the way as you construct your answer and provide the correct information. You are not penalized if you write incorrect information. Point totals for each essay can range from 6 to 12. Understand that the official exam will not tell you whether the question is a six-, eight-, or eleven-point question. It wouldn't matter if it did, as the number of points available for each essay has more to do with the structure of the question and the anticipated answer than it does with the level of difficulty or weighted value of the question.

What's a Good Essay Section Score?

Like the multiple-choice scaled score, how the essay section is scored varies each year depending on overall student performance. To ensure a 4 or 5 exam score, set the goal of averaging at least 60 percent of the available points on the three essays. Be sure to score at minimum two points on your lowest scoring essay.

HOW AP EXAMS ARE USED

At the several hundred institutions of higher education that accept AP, your score of 4 or 5 will earn you three semester credit hours for a number of introductory geography classes or fulfill a general education requirement (and possibly both). These equivalent classes fall under several names at different universities. You can look online or in the college's official course catalogue for class names or titles similar to

- Introduction to Geography
- Introduction to Human Geography, Principles of Human Geography
- World Regional Geography, Survey of World Regions, The World Around Us
- (The Geography of) Peoples and Places (of the World)

Look at the general education requirements (aka liberal arts or distribution requirements) of the university to see if the class for which you receive credit also fulfills a requisite in an area such as social science, cultural diversity, or global education. At some universities, an introductory geography or world geography class can fulfill two of these general education requirements simultaneously—known as "double-dipping."

Make sure to speak to an academic advisor at the colleges or universities to which you are applying or have been accepted about how they issue credit for the 4 or 5 AP score. If they don't know or if the college does not have a policy concerning AP Human Geography Exam credit, there are a number of resources you can contact to help make sure that you are rewarded for your work. To resolve AP Human Geography Exam credit issues, you or your high school AP teacher should contact

- the geography department or a geography faculty member at the university
- the dean's office of the university's school or college where geography is housed
- the Geographic Alliance office for the state where you are enrolled in college
- the Association of American Geographers in Washington, D.C.: www.aag.org
- a regional ETS field office: www.ets.org

One or two of these resources should be able to resolve any AP Human Geography credit issues. Realize that AP Human Geography is a relatively new test with a limited number of students. As a result, you may be the first person to ever try to receive AP Human Geography credit at your university. Be the first to get it!

Any 4 and 5s earned before you have applied for college are great to highlight on your college applications. By maximizing your score on this test in ninth, tenth, or eleventh grade, you can move up in the world of college admissions and be accepted at a more prestigious institution.

OTHER RESOURCES

There are many resources available to help you improve your score on the AP Human Geography Exam, not the least of which are your **teachers**. If you are taking an AP class, you may be able to get extra attention from your teacher, such as obtaining feedback on your essays. If you are not in an AP course, reach out to a teacher who teaches AP Human Geography and ask if the teacher will review your essays or otherwise help you with content.

Another wonderful resource is **AP Central**, the official site of the AP Exams. The scope of the information at this site is quite broad and includes:

- Course Description, which includes details on what content is covered and sample questions
- Sample questions from the AP Human Geography exam
- Free response question prompts and multiple choice questions from previous years

The AP Central home page address is: **apcentral.collegeboard.com**.

For up-to-date information about the ongoing changes to the AP Human Geography Exam Course, please visit: apcentral.collegeboard.com/apc/public/courses/teachers_corner/8154.html

Finally, **The Princeton Review** offers tutoring and small group instruction. Our expert instructors can help you refine your strategic approach and add to your content knowledge. For more information, call 1-800-2REVIEW.

DESIGNING YOUR STUDY PLAN

In Part I, you identified some areas of potential improvement. Let's now delve further into your performance on Test 1, with the goal of developing a study plan appropriate to your needs and time commitment.

Read the answers and explanations associated with the Multiple Choice questions (starting at page 319). After you have done so, respond to the following questions:

- Review the topic chart on page 8. Next to each topic, indicate your rank of the topic as follows: "1" means "I need a lot of work on this," "2" means "I need to beef up my knowledge," and "3" means "I know this topic well."

- How many days/weeks/months away is your exam?

- What time of day is your best, most focused study time?

- How much time per day/week/month will you devote to preparing for your exam?

- When will you do this preparation? (Be as specific as possible: Mondays and Wednesdays from 3:00 to 4:00 P.M., for example)

- Based on the answers above, will you focus on strategy (Part III) or content (Part IV) or both?

- What are your overall goals in using this book?

PART III

TEST-TAKING STRATEGIES FOR THE AP HUMAN GEOGRAPHY EXAM

PREVIEW ACTIVITY

Review your Test 1 results and then respond to the following questions:

- How many multiple choice questions did you miss even though you knew the answer?
- On how many multiple choice questions did you guess blindly?
- How many multiple choice questions did you miss after eliminating some answers and guessing based on the remaining answers?
- Did you find any of the free-response questions easier or harder than the others—and, if so, why?

HOW TO USE THE CHAPTERS IN THIS PART

For the following Strategy chapters, think about what you are doing now before you read the chapters. As you read and engage in the directed practice, be sure to think critically about the ways you can change your approach.

1

How to Approach Multiple-Choice Questions

WHAT YOU NEED TO KNOW

Before you begin to prepare for the multiple-choice questions, let's review the critical information about the section that we covered in the introduction:

SECTION 1: MULTIPLE CHOICE QUESTIONS

Number of Questions:	75
Time Allowed:	60 minutes
Writing Instrument:	No. 2 pencil
Needed for a 4 or 5:	Minimum 50 correct answers

Now that you have that in mind, to do well on this part of the AP Human Geography Exam you need to know your human geography and how to answer multiple-choice AP questions. You may know the material from class and your textbook very well, but if you don't know *how to take the test* then you won't get the credit you deserve.

Let's consider two possible scenarios:

Josh is a student getting good grades in high school AP Human Geography all year and then gets a low score on the AP exam because he's not ready for these types of questions. On the other end of the spectrum, Jessica is a student who is not very comfortable with all the various topics in the AP Human Geography course. However, because she knows how to effectively answer the multiple-choice questions, she winds up getting a 4 on the exam—much to the chagrin of Josh.

You may be wondering, How can I do well on the exam and not end up like Josh? *You need a strategy*. The key is to get inside the head of the people testing you. In this section we will show you how Educational Testing Service (ETS) and their test authors put you under pressure and how they write the questions to trick you into choosing the wrong answer. Along the way, I will give you several strategies and practice opportunities to crack the multiple-choice section.

MULTIPLE-CHOICE STRATEGY

In this section we'll go over the rules of effective multiple-choice test-taking, discuss time management, and teach you how to use the Process of Elimination. Combined, these strategies will improve your AP multiple-choice test-taking skills and score.

RULES OF EFFECTIVE AP TEST TAKING

To score your best on the multiple-choice section of this test, you will first need to remember the following rules:

- Finishing is not the real goal; accuracy is.
- Keep in mind you have limited time.
- Four out of every five answer choices are wrong.

PACING

Guessing also raises your score because it saves you time. Wasted time is your enemy. Seventy-five questions in 60 minutes is a lot. In practical terms, it's about 45 seconds per question. How can you possibly answer all the questions in such a short time period? Two ways: Guess and Go, or Don't.

GUESS AND GO

Consider the thought process of two AP Human Geography test takers as it relates to the following question:

The international treaty that laid the interior political boundaries of Sub-Saharan Africa was

(A) Treaty of Ghent
(B) Potsdam Agreement
(C) Camp David Accords
(D) Treaty of Versailles
(E) Berlin Conference

Josh

The political boundaries of Africa—I know this was decided by European colonial powers, and not Africans. It was in the late 1800s or early 1900s, so that eliminates (A). Potsdam was at the end of World War II, and Camp David was much more recent. So that gets rid of (B) and (C). Now, what were the other two? Versailles was the home of the French kings. But, they were gone at the end of the French Revolution, in the late 1700s. Berlin is near Potsdam. Here it's a "conference" and not a "treaty" like in (D)...Hmmm...Both sound possible. Was it in France? The French had a lot of colonies in Africa. I think the Germans had colonies in Africa too, but I'm not sure how many or where. Which country would be most likely to host such an international treaty? The Germans were really powerful in the early twentieth century and defeated France a few times. But the French were the larger colonial power around the world. Hmmm...Which one is more likely to be the location of this treaty? Well, (D) sounds great but so does (E). I put (D) for the last answer so maybe this one should be (E), or maybe that last one was wrong. Maybe I should read and rephrase the question again...

Jessica

The political boundaries of Africa—these were divided by European colonial powers around the late 1800s. Africa was the last part of the world to become colonized by Europeans. And the last part of the world to gain independence. Ghent was part of American history, so cross off (A). Potsdam and Camp David were about World War II and Israel, respectively, so cross off (B) and (C). Versailles is in France and Berlin is in Germany. So it's either (D) or (E). Versailles was the home of Louis XV, who lived in the 1700s. And it's a museum today. Thus, (D) doesn't sound right. I'll guess (E).

Next question.

> The central business district within that concentric zone model is found...

In the scenario above, Josh continues to deliberate between (D) and (E) while Jessica goes on to the next question. What's the difference? Jessica did all the work she could considering the remaining options, then took a smart guess and moved on. Josh did all the work he could, and got stuck trying to make a decision between the two remaining options. As the test goes on, Josh will lag further and further behind Jessica, not because he knows less human geography, but because he is less willing to take that guess and move onward, and *save time*. To do well on the AP Human Geography Exam, you'll need to do what you can, then be willing to *take your best guess and move on* to the next question.

...Or Don't

This is not to suggest that speeding through the test is your goal. In fact, focusing on finishing the section is the wrong goal altogether. You should work accurately and efficiently on the questions you *can* answer correctly so that you earn a solid raw score. To do so, you might not even attempt some of the questions. If you truly cannot eliminate even one answer choice, then you're better off randomly guessing, which costs you nothing. Or, if you prefer to save the question for later, put a circle around the number of the question you're skipping in the test booklet—not on the answer sheet! This way you know also to skip bubbling in an answer for that question. Additionally, you'll be able to take another look at those questions if you have time after you answer all the ones that are easier for you.

Rushing to finish the test only to make a bunch of careless mistakes won't get you a good score. Instead, as you practice for the exam, you need to find the pace at which you can work efficiently and effectively without sacrificing accuracy. Don't waste extra time with a question once you've done all that you can to solve it, and don't rush and misread and rephrase the question or the answer choices.

You Set the Pace

After you study your geography notes, textbook, and content review chapters of this book, practice your multiple-choice strategy by using the full-length practice tests in this book to determine your optimal pace. Can you answer 75 questions in 60 minutes and get most of them right? If so, you can very well receive 60 or more raw score points, and likely score a 4 or above depending on your essays. Are you able to answer only about 60 questions and maintain accuracy? If so, you can still get nearly 60 raw score points by being accurate. In the end, being accurate can be far more important than finishing.

Process of Elimination

Every time you read a multiple-choice question, remember that four of the five answer choices are wrong. Use the Process of Elimination (POE) method to get rid of what you know is wrong as you go through the answer choices (use a diagonal slash through the letter—(E)—in the question booklet, *not on the bubble-sheet!*). Then deal with any answer choices that remain.

For most questions, you'll be able to eliminate two or three answer choices relatively quickly. That leaves you with two choices to consider. Don't forget about the guessing reward. We'll talk more about POE throughout the rest of this chapter. Just remember that all the answer choices are "wrong until proven right," and you'll be on your way to showing what you know on the multiple-choice part of the test.

What If I Can't Eliminate ANYTHING?

If you can't eliminate any answers, it's best to pick a letter of the day and move on. There is no penalty for incorrect answers; your score is based on the number of questions you answer correctly, so you have nothing to lose by guessing. Always keep in mind that the multiple-choice section is difficult if not impossible for most students to finish on time. Your goal is to end up with a minimum of 50 correct answers. If you did that on a regular test at school that had 75 questions, you'd see a score of 66 percent and most likely have a "D" next to your name. But that's not how the AP exam works, fortunately. And if you do reasonably well on the essay section, you'll earn that 4 or 5 that you are working to achieve.

"EXCEPT" Questions

Occasionally, the multiple-choice question is inverted. When you see a question with the word "EXCEPT" or "NOT" in it, then you know four out of five answers are correct. Your job is to uncover the wrong one. Often these are comparison questions where the two things being compared have a lot in common. In the question booklet, put a check mark next to each answer that is true, or not an exception. Then use Process of Elimination (POE) to work through the other possibilities and find the one that doesn't fit.

THE STEPS TO CRACKING A QUESTION

Now we'll show you a step-by-step method to solving multiple-choice questions. The best way to learn this process is to practice on an AP Human Geography Exam question.

5. The purpose of the European Coal and Steel Community and the European Economic Community (Common Market), which later lead to the European Union, was to form supranational organizations based upon the concept of

(A) open border policies
(B) a single European currency, or Euro
(C) nuclear disarmament
(D) military cooperation with the United States and Canada
(E) free-trade policies

STEP 1: READ AND REPHRASE THE QUESTION

First you must make sure that you understand what the question is asking. Rephrase the question so that it is clear to you. Read the sample question again; what is it really asking?

> What was the purpose of the organizations that
> preceded the European Union?

STEP 2: WHEN? WHO AND WHERE? WHAT?

Before you read the answer choices, you must get an idea of the historical period or the political or economic context you are in (the when), who is involved and where, and what the question is asking you. Answer these questions in your mind or even in the question booklet before you read the answer choices. For example, in the above question about European supranationalism, you can answer in the following way:

> **When?** Post-World War II Europe
> **Who and Where?** The original members of the European Union, Western Europe
> **What?** Supranational organizations

Once you've answered these questions, take a moment to call up the relevant economic geography that you know. If it's a topic you know, it should be easy to find the correct answer. If not, you can still use what you know to get rid of the wrong answer choices using Process of Elimination.

STEP 3: PROCESS OF ELIMINATION

Even if you don't exactly know the history of the formation of the European Union, you can still use strategy to eliminate wrong answer choices. Remember to read each answer choice with a critical eye, looking for what makes it wrong. Cross off the choices that you know are wrong; leave ones that you are uncertain about or those you think may be correct.

Let's review what we know so far about the question:

> **When?** After World War II
> **Who and Where?** Western European countries
> **What?** Supranational organizations

Ask yourself what you know about the European Union and its predecessors. You probably know that it's mainly an organization based upon economic policy, unlike NATO, which has a military-strategic purpose. Armed with this information, let's take a look at the answer choices.

Learn more about the EU in Chapter 6

5. The purpose of the European Coal and Steel Community and the European Economic Community (Common Market), which later lead to the European Union, was to form supranational organizations based upon the concept of

(A) open border policies
(B) a single European currency, or Euro
(C) nuclear disarmament
(D) military cooperation with the United States and Canada
(E) free-trade policies

Take a look at answer choice (C). Do coal and steel have anything to do with nuclear arms? No. Cross off (C). How about (D)? Again, none of the names of these groups imply anything to do with the military. However, many of the countries that we're talking about, but not all, were members of the North Atlantic Treaty Organization (NATO). NATO and the EU are two different types of the same thing. So scratch off (D). You may not be sure about (A), (B) or (E). All of these are major functions of the European Union today. Thus, you have to ask which of these was the *purpose* of these precursor organizations. You may know that the Euro was only recently introduced, in the year 2000. Therefore, you should feel confident and scratching off (B).

If you're stuck between (A) and (E), what should you do? Take a guess.

STEP 4: GUESS AND GO

Once you've narrowed down the choices as much as you can, take a guess. As you learned, the *guessing reward* benefits students who are willing to take smart guesses throughout the test. If you use Process of Elimination (POE) to get rid of choices that you know are wrong, and then take a smart guess from among the remaining choices, you will score your personal best on this test.

> The European Coal and Steel Community and the Common Market were established as free-trade zones that removed tariffs on goods moving across international borders between member states. This reduced production costs and made European steel and other products cheaper on international markets. This was an attempt to create a comparative advantage for European Steel companies.

After using POE, you have a fifty-fifty shot of guessing the right answer on our sample question, so just pick one if you can't get any further.

Let's look at answer choice (A). Open-border policies are something that Europeans enjoy, because they no longer have to stop at the border for customs or immigration officers. This does not seem directly linked to coal and steel or larger markets. And coal and steel are commodities that are directly *traded* between countries. Thus, (A) is not likely the answer, and (E) is the correct answer.

Can you see how taking a moment to frame the question can help you find the right answer quickly and easily? Knowing just some of the information can be enough to make a smart guess. This does not mean that you should not learn as much of the material on supranational organizations as possible. The more you know, the easier it will be to eliminate wrong answer choices and zero in on the correct answer. However, using the steps and POE will help you get the right answer quickly by making the most of the information you know.

Step by Step by Step by Step

Let's go through the four steps again by working on another AP Human Geography multiple-choice question.

19. The population statistic that uses the difference between crude birth rates and crude death rates, and estimates the annual percentage growth rate of a country's population, is known as the

    (A) total fertility rate (TFR)
    (B) replacement rate
    (C) rate of natural increase (RNI)
    (D) doubling time
    (E) total life expectancy

Step 1: Read and Rephrase the Question

What statistic is used to measure a country's population growth?

Step 2: When? Who and Where? What?

When? This is not a question that requires a historical, political, or economic context. However, there is an important context clue in the word "annual." The question is asking about a statistic that is calculated each and every year.

    Who and Where? The whole country's population. Nothing in the question tells us that we're dealing with a specific group or place.

    What? A population statistic that measures "annual" growth.

Step 3: Process of Elimination

You know that doubling time (D) and total life expectancy (E) are both statistics that are measured over a long period time. So cross them off. You know that the replacement rate is a TFR of 2.1. So cross off (B). However, you are not sure how the TFR is calculated so leave (A).

Step 4: Guess and Go

Now you have (A) and (C) left. Guess and go or reason it out a little more. You think fertility has something to do with births, but not deaths. So cross off (A). And (C) is your answer. Move on to the next question....

PRACTICE THE STEPS

Now it's your turn. Use the four steps to solve the following multiple-choice question by filling in the blanks below.

14. Which of the following countries is the best example of a current theocracy?

    (A) China
    (B) Greece
    (C) Great Britain
    (D) Iran
    (E) Turkey

Step 1: Read and rephrase the question.

_____

_____

_____

_____

Step 2: When? Who and Where? What?

When? _____

Who and Where? _____

What? _____

Step 3: Process of Elimination

_____

_____

_____

_____

Step 4: Guess and Go

_____

_____

_____

_____

HERE'S HOW TO CRACK IT

First, ask yourself this question: What is a theocracy and what is a current example of one? So there's your what and your when. But, who, as a whole country, can be labeled a theocracy? Let's go through the possible answers.

First, *theocracy* has something to do with religious leaders running a country. You know that Saudi Arabia was the example of a strong theocracy used in class or your textbook. However, it's not on the list of choices.

(A) China can be crossed off immediately, as a formal religion rarely exists under Communism.

(B) Greece may be a possibility. Theocracy is a Greek word, but the Greeks have a long tradition of democracy. So cross off this answer.

(C) Great Britain is also a possibility. The monarch of Great Britain is also the head of the Church of England. Before you decide on this answer, take a look at the other answers to see if there is a better one—remember the word "best" in the question.

(D) Iran is a strong possibility. The country has been ruled by ayatollahs, Muslim clerics who have ruled the country since the fall of the Shah.

(E) Turkey is a possible choice. Turkey is mostly Muslim; however, the nation is applying to become part of the European Union. Keep this point in mind: A theocracy like the one in Saudi Arabia would not be what Europeans had in mind for the EU. Thus, Turkey must not be a theocracy.

Now you have to guess between Great Britain and Iran. The monarch in Great Britain (currently Queen Elizabeth II) is the head of the Church of England. But, in Britain people seem to have a lot of religious freedom. However, in Iran there is not much religious freedom at all. Therefore, Iran (D) is the best answer (and is correct).

SO FAR, SO GOOD, EXCEPT...

Not all questions are going to be factual (such as names of treaties), historical (such as the history of European free-trade), definition (such as fertility rates), or definition-example (such as theocracy in Iran). Some questions are going to require you to *interpret* theories that you have learned in the course. When theory questions come up, you have to make sure that you understand the question. This step becomes even more critical, as we will see in the example on the next page.

33. The relationship between Thomas Malthus's theory of population and the Green Revolution is best historically characterized by the following.

(A) Green Revolution agricultural technologies have increased food production, thus extending global carrying capacity and decreasing the overpopulation predicted by Malthus.

(B) Green Revolution theorists ideologically rejected Malthus's theory, and his ideas were not accepted until the late twentieth century by Neo-Malthusian scholars.

(C) As part of the Green Revolution, Malthus predicted many of the environmental problems that emerged in the twentieth century, such as famine and global warming.

(D) Malthus predicted the coming of the Green Revolution, where new agricultural technologies, such as pesticides, hybrids, fertilizers, and mechanization would play an important role increasing agricultural production.

(E) Malthus invented several Green Revolution technologies such as chemical fertilizers and pesticides. He predicted that his inventions would allow for larger global population.

STEP 1: READ AND REPHRASE THE QUESTION

Your first inclination is to ask, what's the link between Malthus and the Green Revolution? However, you should step back and ask yourself what you know about these two bodies of theory. Malthus makes a warning against overpopulation, and the Green Revolution feeds more people. The two theories are, in a way, contradictory. Therefore, you should ask, how might the Green Revolution contradict Malthus, or vice versa?

Malthusian theory is presented in the population section of the course, and the Green Revolution is presented in the agriculture section of this book.

STEP 2: WHEN? WHO AND WHERE? WHAT?

This step is still important for the theory question. Divide up these questions and ask yourself what you know about each theory.

When? Malthus was in the early 1800s. The Green Revolution was in the twentieth century.

Who and Where? Malthus was concerned that the world would become overpopulated and not be able to feed itself. The Green Revolution benefitted farmers in the Third World.

What? Malthus used mathematics to model population growth and food production. The Green Revolution was a collection of agricultural technologies that made for large increases in global farm production.

STEP 3: PROCESS OF ELIMINATION

From your answers in Step 2 you can automatically eliminate some of the multiple-choice answers. Choices (B), (C), and (E) should be obvious eliminations based on what you know about the two theories. They are factually wrong. This leaves you with (A) and (D). Both list the Green Revolution and Malthus's theory in the correct chronological order.

STEP 4: GUESS AND GO

What was Malthus's prediction? Did he just worry about too many people and not enough food, or did he also predict the solution? Go back to your reformulation of the question. Malthus (and later Neo-Malthusians) *warned* about the dangers of overpopulation. He predicted gloom and doom, not the bounty of new farming technologies. Thus (A) is the best answer.

In addition to being a theory question, this example was also a comparison question. Comparison questions ask you to examine the relationships between two concepts or phenomena. Let's look at another comparison question where there may be two answers to each of the when, who, where, and what's in Step 2.

21. In an examination of the Burgess Concentric Zone model of the Anglo-American city and the Ford Griffin Model of the Latin American city, what differences are found in the location of poor residential areas?

(A) In the Concentric Zone model the poor are in the CBD and in the Latin American city model the poor are in the Zone of Maturity.

(B) In the Concentric Zone model the poor are in the periphery and in the Latin American city model the poor are in the inner city.

(C) In the Concentric Zone model the poor are in the periphery and in the Latin American city model the poor are in Zones of Disamenity.

(D) In the Concentric Zone model the poor are in the inner city and in the Latin American city model the poor are in the Zone of *in situ* Accretion.

(E) In the Concentric Zone model the poor are in the inner city and in the Latin American city model the poor are in the periphery.

STEP 1: READ AND REPHRASE THE QUESTION

Again, we have two theories being compared. You might first be inclined to ask, how are the two urban models different in structure and where are poor residential areas found in each? However, a more basic question can be asked: Where do poor people live in U.S. cities versus those in Latin American cities? Remember that urban models try to generalize the average city in a region. In relative terms, locations should be roughly the same in most cities.

STEP 2: WHEN? WHO AND WHERE? WHAT?

Divide up these questions to ask yourself what you know, basically, about each region and theory.

When? In the models, Concentric Zones are from the 1920s; the Latin American city model is contemporary and updated.

Who and Where? Poor in cities. In Anglo-America (the United States and Canada), they have been there for a while. In Latin America, many are immigrants from the rural areas.

What? Residential space (homes) of the poor in cities

STEP 3: PROCESS OF ELIMINATION

The Concentric Zone model doesn't necessarily say where the poor live. Yet, you do know that many poor people in the United States and Canada live in the inner city. The Latin American city model says that there are peripheral squatter settlements. Squatters are typically poor and cannot afford to buy land. Having said this, we can eliminate (A), (B), and (C). Choice (A) is wrong since in the Latin American city model, they aren't in the zone of maturity. Choice (B) is wrong because of the first part of the answer, and (C) is wrong because of both parts of the answer. You're left with (D) and E).

STEP 4: GUESS AND GO

Looking at (D), the poor in the United States and Canada could be in the CBD (downtown), and you may not be sure what *in situ* accretion means. Choice (E) seems to fit better with "inner city" and the poor being located in peripheral squatter settlements. We'll go with (E), even though (D) appears to be a parallel answer (E is correct).

This question required you to visualize two graphical models. Knowing the models is very important in the AP Human Geography Exam, as sometimes the questions will show you the models, and sometimes they won't—you need to be able to visualize them in your head. Therefore, we advise you to pay close attention to the Know the Models sections of the review chapters in Part IV of this book.

MAPS

There are going to be a number of questions on the multiple-choice section that require you to identify a region, read the pattern on a map, or analyze a graph or table of data.

For the map questions, you'll need to be able to identify the places and examples that you have learned in class. One way to test yourself is to get blank maps and fill in the locations of regions, migration patterns, and example countries and cities as you study your class notes.

You might be saying to yourself, "my teacher said there isn't a map quiz on the exam!" On the AP Human Geography Exam there aren't any map questions that ask you to simply identify a point or a country. Nor would you be asked to name the capital of a country. These questions are too simple. It is assumed that you have learned where most places are on the map as part of the course. However, you are expected to answer map questions that involve geographic principles and theories. Often these questions ask you to identify examples of the concepts you have learned, and for that you'll need the background knowledge and map practice.

Many map questions are like simple definition questions. Either you know where something is or you don't. However, as we just learned with the definition and definition-example questions, there are ways to eliminate some of the possible answers and increase your chances of guessing correctly even when you don't have the concrete knowledge.

Let's go through a map question together and see.

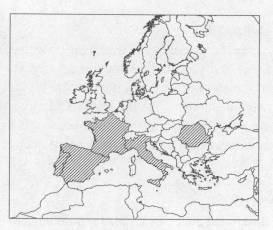

32. The shaded area on the map depicts areas in Europe where

(A) Roman Catholicism is the most popular religion
(B) Romance languages are the dominant linguistic group
(C) the Euro is the only accepted currency
(D) agriculture represents more that 50 percent of the economy
(E) constitutional monarchy is the form of government

STEP 1: READ AND REPHRASE THE QUESTION

Read the map to rephrase the question:

> What do southwestern Europe and Romania have in common?

STEP 2: WHEN? WHO AND WHERE? WHAT?

When? Recognize that the map is contemporary Europe.

Who and Where? The two areas, which include Portugal, Spain, France, Italy, and Romania, but also southern Belgium and parts of Switzerland. Also notice the parts of Europe not included in the two areas.

What? A common regional characteristic or trait common to both areas?

STEP 3: PROCESS OF ELIMINATION

With little to go on from the printed question, let's go through the answers one by one. (A) All of the areas in the western area appear to be Catholic-dominated. Is Romania? No. But if you weren't sure, ask yourself if there are other Catholic-dominated areas in Europe. One in particular should stick out, Ireland—it's not shaded. Therefore, (A) is probably not the answer.

Choice (B), Romance languages include Portuguese, Spanish, French, Italian, and (as you might guess from the name) Romanian. But what about Belgium and Switzerland? So far, (B) looks like a good answer, but we should go through the rest to make sure it's the *best* answer. The Euro, choice (C), is not accepted in Great Britain, true. But it is the only currency in Germany, Denmark, Austria, Sweden, and Finland. So (C) is not likely. Choice (D) is very unlikely, because even in the peripheral regions of Europe (e.g., Portugal and Romania), services and manufacturing dominate economic productivity. Choice (E) is like (D) and (A). There are constitutional monarchies outside of the shaded area (e.g., Great Britain, the Netherlands, Denmark, and Sweden). Also, consider that in France and Italy, monarchy has long since vanished. Cross that one off too.

STEP 4: GUESS AND GO

No need to guess here; (B) is the only answer that fits. Here are the details. The southern half of Belgium, referred to as Wallonia, is French speaking. Likewise, French and Italian are two of the four regional languages within Switzerland (along with German and Romansch).

GRAPHS AND TABLES

Another common type of question involves reading graphs or tables. In the AP Human Geography course, you are expected to be able to read and analyze numerical data—what geographers refer to as "quantitative" data. Why? A lot of geographical analysis work involves number crunching. Being able to read the numerical results of analysis is a necessary skill.

WHAT DO THEY ASK?

Most of the numerical data in the exam is drawn from the *population* and *economic* geography sections of the course. As will be discussed in Part IV of this book, knowing what is a **high, low,** and **normal** or a **stable rate** (like RNI, or rate of natural increase), **indicator** (like GNP, or gross national product), or **index** (like HDI, or human development index) score is important to your ability to answer such questions correctly. A graph will often show you two types of data and ask about the relationship between them. For example, a population pyramid shows the total population by gender and age cohort—the bottom bar shows the number of males age 0 to 4 on the left and females age 0 to 4 on the right, then moves up in age from there—5 to 9, 10 to 14, and so on. A table shows you groupings of data, often in rows and columns. The categories of data will be across the top and the place names will be the first column on the left, like in the example in the following table:

Name	Population	RNI	Total Life Expectancy
Country X	10,000,000	1.2%	64
Country Y	40,000,000	−0.2%	78
Country Z	50,000,000	2.3%	53

You are then going to be asked one or more questions about what you see in the data. Sometimes not all of the data is relevant, but it's likely that you are going to have to read the entire table to get the gist of the question.

Furthermore, *if you know the theory or principle behind the question, the actual numbers may be irrelevant*. You will need to be able to identify one example as being in a specific category, versus another example being in a separate category. For example, in the table above, Country Z is likely a Third World agricultural-based economy, versus Country Y, which is a First World nation in Europe. How do you know? The numbers are indicative of these categories and places. A negative RNI (shrinking population) with a high life expectancy is a combination found only in highly developed nations with service-based economies and good social services. A high RNI (strong population growth) and low life expectancy is expected only in agriculturally based Third World regions.

Mastering the basic skills of numerical analysis is not only possible for every student, but is a necessity for the AP Human Geography Exam. These tables are essentially puzzles with basic rules required to solve them. The rules are determined by the theories and principles behind the data. *Know the theories and principles, and you will know the rules.*

Let's look at a graph question to apply the principles we know to answer the puzzle.

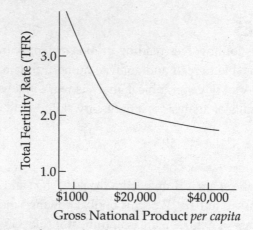

18. Using the graph above, what would be the expected total fertility rate (TFR) of a Third World, agriculture-based country?

   (A) 1.8
   (B) 2.0
   (C) 2.4
   (D) 3.2
   (E) 6.0

Now let's practice those steps again.

STEP 1: READ AND REPHRASE THE QUESTION

What is a TFR that would be found in your average Third World agricultural country?

STEP 2: WHEN? WHO AND WHERE? WHAT?

When? This is not a question that requires a historical or political context.

   Who and Where? However, the economic context of "Third World" and "agricultural" are critical here. The question is <u>not</u> asking you about newly industrialized countries (NICs). Instead, think about poor Third World countries where agriculture is the primary source of economic production.

   What? Fertility in poor countries, which we expect to be high, just as fertility in wealthier countries tends to be low.

STEP 3: PROCESS OF ELIMINATION

Reading the curved trend line on the graph, (A) and (B) show TFRs that are too low, as they represent GNP *per capita* at very high levels of production—per capita dollar amounts found only in manufacturing- and service-based economies. Cross out (B). Choice (C) is unlikely because on the trend line, a TFR of 2.4 would be around $6,000 to $8,000 per year, which is what you would find in many NICs. To help you visualize it, use the straight edge on the side of your pencil to measure what GNP *per capita* would be for a particular TFR. Cross out (C). Now you're left with (D) and (E).

STEP 4: GUESS AND GO

Note that the question says "Using the graph above"; 6.0 does not appear on the graph, even though the trend line could, in theory, reach that level. Choice (D) is your best choice since a TFR of 3.2 is around $1,000 in GNP *per capita*, which is representative of the economic productivity of agriculture-based economies.

   Okay! That was a lot of practice. Now you'll do some problems on your own, score yourself, review, then move on to the next chapter and learn about essays.

PRACTICE QUESTIONS

Now that you have the basic tools to crack the multiple-choice section, use what you have learned on the following set of 10 questions. Use a watch to time how long it takes you to answer the questions accurately. The answers follow the quiz.

At the end of the answer key, we will show you what your time and score means and how you should adjust your pacing and strategy.

1. A port where goods are imported from other parts of the world, then re-exported for profit to foreign locations is known as a(n)

   (A) exclusive economic zone
   (B) break-in-bulk point
   (C) resource node
   (D) entrepôt
   (E) commodity chain

2. What type of economic production contributes to the majority of the GDP in the United States and Great Britain?

   (A) Agriculture
   (B) Real estate
   (C) Manufacturing
   (D) Services
   (E) Construction

3. The concept where all things in geographic space are related, but closer things are more related than others, is the basis of

   (A) environmental determinism
   (B) spatial analysis
   (C) spatial statistics
   (D) contagious diffusion
   (E) Tobler's law

4. Which of following would be a negative social effect of gentrification in cities?

   (A) Old homes would be converted with updated materials and fixtures.
   (B) Older residents would receive new homes in suburban areas.
   (C) Increased real estate prices and rents would force out poor residents.
   (D) Construction companies would have projects in areas of existing housing.
   (E) Older architecture would be preserved instead of building new structures.

5. In von Thünen's model of the Isolated State, the main factor in the cost-to-distance relationship of agricultural patterns and land rent is

   (A) the degree to which land use is labor-intensive
   (B) cost of energy, particularly fuel wood
   (C) cost of livestock and feed
   (D) volume of sales in the market center
   (E) the distance from transport lines, mainly rivers and roads

6. Communities of Russians who today live in Eastern Ukraine would be an example of

   (A) colonies
   (B) exclaves
   (C) enclaves
   (D) culture hearths
   (E) special economic zones

7. What is the major limitation of solar panel electricity production, in comparison to other "renewables"?

(A) They can be used only during the summer.
(B) The process requires large amounts of water.
(C) Solar panels have to be imported from foreign manufacturers.
(D) On average, electricity can be produced for only half of the day.
(E) The panel reflectance contributes to the greenhouse effect.

8. The origin of San Francisco, California, as a human settlement is based upon the site characteristic of its

(A) relative position halfway between New York and Hawaii
(B) location as a transport node at the intersection of the Pacific Ocean and the inland waterways of San Francisco Bay
(C) relative position halfway between Europe and Asia
(D) relative position halfway up the coast of California
(E) location as a resource node within the California gold mining region

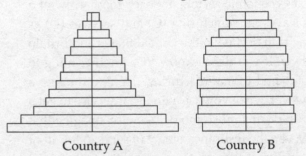

Country A   Country B

9. From the two population pyramids above, what can we deduce about these countries?

(A) Country A is slow-growing and Country B is growing quickly.
(B) Country A is likely in the Third World and Country B is in the First World.
(C) Country A has a low percentage dependent population and Country B has almost no dependants.
(D) Country A is a First World country and Country B is likely in the Third World.
(E) Country A is a shrinking population and Country B has stable population growth.

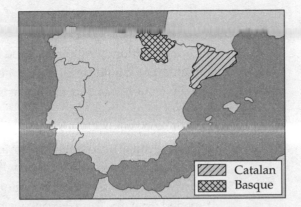

Catalan
Basque

10. These two areas within Spain have the following in common EXCEPT

(A) both nations have primary languages other than Spanish
(B) both areas have status as autonomous regions with limited self-government
(C) both nations have a strong French cultural influence
(D) both are areas of irredentism
(E) both are distinct culture regions separate from the main Spanish culture

ANSWERS TO PRACTICE QUESTIONS

1. **D** This is a definition question from the economic geography section of the course. An example of an entrepôt would be Singapore, a major port where manufactured goods are shipped in from the rest of Asia and then redistributed in global retail networks to consumers around the world.

   The other answers are all concepts from the economic geography section of the course. Exclusive economic zones, known as EEZs, are political boundaries which lie 200 nautical miles off the coast of a country. Within that boundary, countries control the economic resources of that sea or ocean territory. Break-in-bulk points are locations where goods are off-loaded from one form of transportation onto another form of transportation, thus breaking up goods into smaller units to be distributed. Resource nodes are where natural resources connect to lines of transportation. Commodity chains are the production linkages from resources to suppliers and then assemblage networks.

2. **D** The United States and Great Britain are First World economies where the majority of the GDP is derived from services. Although both the United States and United Kingdom are often referred to as "industrialized" countries, the percent of GDP gained from manufacturing has been in decline since the 1960s. Services such as finance, insurance, and real estate along with health care and entertainment create much of the wealth and employment for these countries. Remember that GDP is the total volume of economic production.

   Use POE to eliminate (A), agriculture, right away on this question. Real estate and construction, choices (B) and (E) respectively, as economic sectors are each too narrow of a category to be a "majority" of the GDP. This leaves manufacturing (C) and services (D) as your two choices. Knowing that manufacturing is in decline in the United States and Britain would give you the perfect guess-and-go answer. If you didn't know this, another thing to think about is the dollar value of services compared to manufacturing. Think of buying a new car. The sticker price may be $15,000. However, when you use a financial service to get a loan to pay for it, with interest you will wind up paying much more. Likewise, imagine that you just paid $100,000 for a dump truck. However, the insurance policy (a service) for all of a company's dump trucks combined with the value of the construction contracts (services) where these trucks will be used will be in the millions of dollars.

3. **E** Waldo Tobler was a geographer who specialized in spatial analysis. His idea about relationships in geographic space is one of the few "laws" in geographic science.

   Choice (A), environmental determinism, is the scientific ideology that the physical world shapes culture and society. As major subfields in geography, (B) and (C) are concepts that are too broad to be the answer for what is a specific definition question. Contagious diffusion, choice (D), is a process where an idea or technology moves across physical space, from location to location, in a contiguous pattern, where the idea or technology moves between locations that touch each other on the map.

4. **C**   In this theory question, similar to the "EXCEPT" questions, four out of five answers are likely to be things that may sound like positive social effects of gentrification. Your job is to pick out the negative one. Increased real estate prices as a result of gentrification often create a real estate market in which poor residents cannot afford increased rents or the ability to buy a home in their neighborhood.

Choice (A) is the answer for a definition question on gentrification. Choice (B) is not always true, but can be a possibility for those who still own older homes and use the proceeds to buy elsewhere. In (D), the term "construction" exists to distract you. Is construction bad? Many people complain about dust, equipment, or road construction. Or is it good? It doesn't matter. Choice (E) is often seen as a positive to those people who are concerned about historical preservation.

5. **A**   This is a theoretical model question that does not tell you the model. It is asking you about the principles behind the geography of the model. Von Thünen was not designing an agricultural landscape. He was observing common patterns in the landscape and asking why these patterns existed. At the center of this model were the most labor-intensive activities: dairying, vegetable farming, woodcutting for lumber and energy. At the outer edge of the model were activities such as animal grazing and grain crops, which required little tending. Land rents that farmers would pay were scaled upon the type of agriculture and intensity of the labor performed. Know your models!

6. **C**   An enclave is where a minority ethnic group is concentrated within a country. Russia and the Ukraine share a long political border, which overlaps the cultural "fuzzy" border between the two nations. Choice (A) can be eliminated, as the concept of the "colony" in political terms went out of use in the 1970s when the last European colonies in Africa gained independence. Choice (B) is where part of the political state is separated by land from the main body of the state. Russia, Armenia, Azerbaijan, and Oman all have exclaves. Even Alaska can be considered an exclave of the United States. Culture hearths, choice (D), can be eliminated, as they refer to areas where ancient civilizations began. Likewise, (E) can be eliminated as these refer to export processing zones in China.

7. **D**   Here is a difficult comparison question from the resources category.

Solar electricity has a number of technical development issues, as well as production costs. But there is one practical issue that may escape analytical comparison with other forms of renewable energy such as geothermal or hydropower; that is, the sun always shines for half a day, on average. In fact, none of the other answers are true. Here the distraction is caused by making you contemplate these wide-ranging possibilities.

8. **B**   San Francisco, although it is associated with the gold rush of 1849, was inhabited before Europeans arrived and was utilized as a transportation intersection between two major bodies of water. This is a definition-example question, where the term "transport node" is buried in one of the answers. And you must extract the "San Francisco" example from the question. The trick here is not to be distracted by the concept of relative position. Choices (A), (C), and (D) are all relatively true, but none are meaningful in determining the origins of human settlement in this place.

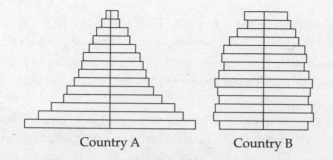

Country A   Country B

9. **B** Here's your graph question. You need to be able to interpret the shape of the population pyramids. Notice the question does not give you age cohorts or population sizes. Country A with its broad base and narrow top shows the typical equilateral pyramid shape of Third World countries. Here there are many children being born (a large youth dependent population), but very few old people. This large number of children indicates high fertility rates, typical of the Third World. Country B has the columnar shape typical of First World countries, where the narrow bottom shows a limited number of children in the total population, and thus low fertility rates and high survival rates.

Use POE to eliminate (A), (D), and (E) as a result. The issue of dependent populations in (C) is indeterminate. In each country, if you added up the young people and the old people, the total of the urban population could turn out to be about the same. The thing to watch out for here is the second part of (C), where it says that country B has almost no dependents. This cannot be true for any country.

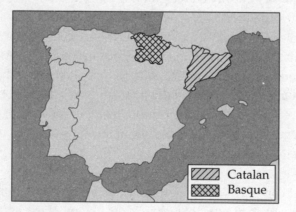

10. **C** Here is an example of both a map question and an "EXCEPT" question. Despite both of these areas being on Spain's northern border with France, neither the Basques nor the Catalan derived much, if any, of their culture from the French. Remember that four out of the five answers are correct. Catalan and Basque are both minority groups in Spain, which have their own language; in recent decades have gained limited autonomy, yet some in their community still yearn for political independence; and have well-defined culture regions surrounding the centers of Barcelona and Bilbao.

HOW DID I DO? HOW CAN I DO BETTER?

Remember: Our goal on Section I of the exam is to answer at least 50 of the 75 questions correctly. Therefore, we need to get two out of every three right. With just ten questions, that means that we need to get seven out of ten correct to support the score that we hope to receive after completing the essay section.

If you got six or fewer questions correct, see if you can identify what problems you are having and how you might use the rest of the book to solve them.

If you said,

I didn't know what the question was asking!

skip it and move on. This strategy saves you the critical time that you need to answer the other questions *correctly*.

If several of these questions were mysterious to you, then you need to review the material from those sections of the course. First, determine what kind of geography the question is drawn from (general foundations, population, agriculture and rural areas, land-use and natural resources, economic geography, political geography, cultural geography, or urbanization). Then determine what kind of question it was (definitions, definition-example, comparison, theory, models, maps, graphs, or tables). Once you have figured out that, for instance, you did not know the definition of an enclave or what examples existed, then you need to revisit that section on political geography and make sure that you know all the key terms and examples of them.

At the end of each of the review chapters in Part IV of this book, there will be a list of key terms. Make sure that you know these and other terms that your teacher or textbook has highlighted.

If you said,

There's so much different stuff to know; I can't keep a grip on this many different things!

don't despair. All of the material in the course is somehow interrelated. The key to knowing the material well is understanding the links between the subjects. Part IV of this book will focus on linkages to help you remember the material better.

If you looked at your watch at the end and said,

That took forever!

then you need to think about the four-step process and what we said about time at the beginning of this chapter. Remember: Once you've eliminated the incorrect answers, you'll need to quickly guess from your remaining choices and move on.

TIME AND THE 10 QUESTIONS

The optimal time for 10 questions is 7 minutes, 15 seconds. Arrive at this number by the ratio of 75 questions in 60 minutes. Then subtract a little additional time so that you have a few minutes at the end of the exam to go back and answer the questions you circled as "uncertain."

Using this 7:15 pace for 10 questions would leave you just over 5 minutes at the end of the 75-question exam period to handle any "unfinished" business, such as questions you wanted to revisit.

Of course, you probably didn't meet that goal time for this practice set and that is fine! Go through the four-step process and learn your strategies well, and you'll get quicker with more practice. And you'll get plenty of practice in the chapters to come.

LET'S REVIEW

Here are your essential four steps to answer any multiple choice question:

1. Read and Rephrase the Question
2. When? Who and Where? What?
3. Process of Elimination
4. Guess and Go

If you can't eliminate even one of the possibilities, or if you just don't know the subject matter of the question, *don't spend too much time contemplating*. There's no penalty for skipping. If you're deciding between the last two or three answers, you've already done your job by eliminating some bad answers. You HAVE to guess here, but don't take too long deciding. Relax. If you're down to two, your odds are pretty good. When you're down to two answers, always guess! Make sure to leave a few minutes before the end of the 60-minute period to go back and re-check the questions that you circled to come back to. Keep an eye on your watch.

In addition to the four-step process, we have also learned that there are different types of questions in the multiple-choice section of the test. The question types are as follows:

- Definition
- Definition-example
- Theory questions, including models
- Comparisons
- Map questions
- Graph and table questions

Be familiar with all of these types and be able to identify the type of question when you see it. Remember: Some questions can be more than one type. Knowing the question type as you answer will help you reformulate the question when going through step 1 and will make you feel more comfortable and confident as you go through the exam.

Now let's move on to essays!

2

How to Approach
Free-Response Questions

WHAT YOU NEED TO KNOW ABOUT
THE AP HUMAN GEOGRAPHY ESSAYS

After you finish the multiple-choice section, you will have a five-minute break before you begin Section II: Free-Response Questions, otherwise known as the essay section. In this part of the exam, you will be given a separate test booklet that contains the essay questions and lined paper to write your three essays. Let's review the basic facts of the essay section.

Number of Questions:	3
Time Allowed:	75 minutes
Writing Instrument:	Pen (preferable), but pencil is allowed
Goal:	60% of the available points in the essay section

Just like on the multiple-choice section, to do well on the essays you need to know your human geography *and* how to answer the AP Human Geography Exam essay questions. You may know the material from class and may consider yourself a decent writer, but if you don't know how to write *this* kind of essay then you won't get the credit you deserve.

Even if you aren't totally comfortable with the material in the course and even if you don't consider yourself the best writer, you can learn to write an effective point-winning AP Human Geography essay. Data from previous years shows that the average AP Human Geography student earns only 35 percent of the available points on the essay section. We'll show you how to get all those points that most students aren't earning.

How can you do this? You need strategies to earn the maximum number of points. In this section, we will give you the tools to score essay points and get a 4 or 5 on the exam—even if your English teacher tells you that you don't write well. We'll go through the scoring system, the writing style, and the rules.

THE SCORING SYSTEM

Each essay is scored by an individual reader—a real human being, who is either an AP Human Geography teacher or a geography professor. This person is part of a team of readers who are trained to read the same essay question and assign it a standard number of points.

Before the reading begins, each team establishes a scoring rubric. The rubric is a set of guidelines that tells the reader what they can give points for in each part of the essay answer. Each year in June after school is out, the readers are retrained and the rubric is recalculated to maintain accurate scores.

No Grading, Just Points

When readers begin to look at your essay, they begin with a blank slate of zero points. As they go through your essay, they will issue points when your writing matches the material on the scoring rubric. There is a set number of points available for each essay. This can range anywhere from 6 to 12 points per essay question. No half points are awarded.

Readers are not allowed to say, "That seemed like a nice essay. I'll give it 9 out of 10 points." They also may not think to themselves, "That essay would fail in my class. I'll give them only 2 points."

Instead they must use the rubric to score every essay. Readers' scoring is constantly checked for accuracy. Occasionally, they must explain how and why they gave points on a particular essay.

How a Rubric Works

The rubric divides the points available for each part of the essay. For instance, if you have an eight-point essay with three parts, there may be two points available on the first part and three points available on each of the second and third parts. These are the maximum number of points available for each part. The reader cannot give you extra credit just because you wrote very well in Part B. The reader also can't transfer points within an essay if you did better on one part than another. It's important to know that *there are no negative or penalty points in the essay section*. A reader cannot take points away that you've already earned just because you wrote something else incorrectly.

Unfortunately, you will not be able to tell how many points are available on each question. However, you can estimate the number of points available by examining the structure of the question. Generally, the first part of the question has the least amount of points available—between 1 and 3, usually. The later parts of the question generally carry the bulk of the points, anywhere from 3 to 6, depending on the structure. Later in this chapter, we will show you several practice essay questions, and explain how to estimate the number of points available.

To get the maximum number of points, make sure that you cover all parts of the question in your essay. *Most students lose points because they forget to answer part of the question.* We'll also show you in this chapter how to write a shorthand essay to prevent missing out on large chunks of available points. Likewise, students lose points because they don't use the vocabulary from the course to explain what they know. Using keywords is another critical tool, which we will discuss. Before we do that, let's find out about the kinds of questions you will see.

TYPES OF QUESTIONS

As we said in chapter 1, there is not a strict rule about the types of essay questions presented in the AP Human Geography Exam, nor are there requirements that any particular subject area be covered. However, there will not be two or more questions from the same subject area. For example, one question might be on political geography, the next one on agriculture, and a third on urbanization. The following year, there might be a political geography essay question again, but the next questions might be drawn from economic geography and energy resources.

There is no way of knowing what will show up as an essay question. However, we can tell you what questions have been asked in the past. These past questions won't be asked again any time in the near future. In fact, the reuse of past questions is wholly unlikely, given the large number of potential questions from the course.

Past AP Human Geography Essay Question Subjects:

2007
- Prediction of land use using von Thünen's model
- Revival of ethnic languages in the face of cultural globalization by English
- Global economic restructuring and the new international division of labor

2008
- Comparison of principles behind von Thünen and the Concentric Zone Model
- Recent patterns of internal migration in the United States
- Trends of increasing female school enrollments in the Third World

2009
- Patterns of church affiliation in the United States
- Characteristics of, factors that contribute to, and consequences of squatter settlements
- Factors that contribute to the decline in dairy farms and increase of organic farms

2010
- Ethanol manufacturing plants and Weber's industrial location theory
- Factors that contribute to the development of national identity
- Demographic transition and economic development

2011
- Mexico's urban geography and economic development
- Malthusian theory and prediction of future population issues
- The geography of automobile factory construction

2012
- Physical barriers used to establish international borders
- Shifting cultivation and subsistence agriculture
- Increasing Muslim populations in European countries

2013
- Development of the Silicon Valley in California and the Research Triangle in North Carolina
- Aging populations in developed countries
- The impact of rail and road systems on population distribution

What to Expect When You're Expecting (Essays)

It's not that Educational Testing Service will never again include an essay question on a particular topic. In fact, von Thünen's model was the focus of a question in 2007 and was half of a comparison question in 2008. Therefore, keep in mind that authors may use one of the topics again, but approach it from a different angle. For example, it's likely immigration to Europe will one day show up in a question asking about the relationship between low fertility rates and the need for guest workers (e.g., Turkish *gastarbeiter* in Germany). Don't count out previous topics; just be prepared to approach them from a few different angles.

There are some general expectations about AP Human Geography essay questions that you should keep in mind as you prepare. Repeating what we covered in the first chapter, here is a list of the things you can expect in the free-response section:

- At least one question will have a *map, table, diagram, or model* that you must analyze to answer part of the question or the entire question. It is wholly possible all three questions have some sort of visual element that you will have to analyze to some degree.
- Another essay question will likely require you to make a *critical argument* regarding a theory, principle, or issue in human geography. Basically, you will have to explain what is right and wrong about the theory or principle.
- Another common essay type are *process* questions, where you have to describe the details of a geographic theory, principle, or issue. In other words, how does something work in a particular order—factor A affects person X and causes them to migrate to place Z.
- Be aware that there are *hybrid questions* which may ask you to do two or more of these things in a single essay.

Be familiar with these question types and understand that how the question is written will give you an idea of what you are expected to present in your answer.

What You Are NOT Expecting

As you read through the list of past questions, you probably had at least one moment where you thought something like, "Poultry? You can't be serious! Neither my teacher nor the textbook ever mentioned chickens or turkeys!" Think of how the students in 2004 must have felt when they saw a question about the American poultry industry. Shock and panic must have struck many a student. To some degree, the exam is testing how well you deal with the unexpected and how well you can use what you know about people, places, and time periods to fill in information about other subjects.

The point is that you should expect one question on the exam to come from completely unexpected subject matter. *The key is to not panic*. Approach the question like you would the other essays. Here, you must read behind the question and get into the writer's head.

Generally, these unexpected topics ask you to apply the theories and principles that you have learned and apply them to places or situations that you have not. For example, in 2006 students were shown a photograph of a small industrial park and asked about the factors behind the change in land use from manufacturing to a telephone call center in a small southern town in the United States. Think of the picture and reference to the American South as *distractors* to some degree. The distractors should help guide your answer to the question, not make you freak out because you don't know the details.

The question really asked about the shift from manufacturing to service industries in the American economy, often referred to in textbooks as "deindustrialization" of First World economic restructuring. Regardless of where it is or what it looks like, the same principles apply: In today's economy, companies seek cheaper land, cheaper labor, and fewer regulations. The English language is necessary for call centers. That's why they are located in the less expensive and non-unionized southern states. Low-cost manufacturing, on the other hand, has moved to Third World and newly industrialized locations, where language is not an issue.

Answer these unexpected questions the best you can. Remember the rules and don't leave any question or part of a question blank. Make an outline and attempt each part of the question. You never know where you will pick up a point or two, or four.

AP HUMAN GEOGRAPHY EXAM ESSAY STRATEGY

In this section, we will explain the writing style for the essays, give you the rules for effective essay writing, show you the directions, and discuss time management. Combined, these strategies will improve your AP Human Geography Exam essay writing skills.

WRITING STYLE FOR THE AP HUMAN GEOGRAPHY EXAM

Here's something most people don't expect: *There is no required writing style* on the AP Human Geography Exam. This differs significantly from the AP history tests, where students are required to use a specific style that includes things such as thesis statements. On the AP Human Geography Exam, unless the question specifically requires an introduction, *you should **not** write an introductory paragraph, and you should **not** write a thesis statement for your essay*. This fact may drive your AP U.S. History and English teachers nuts, but it is the truth. The rubric doesn't give points for it, so you don't need it.

The author of this book has read thousands of AP Human Geography essays and has never given a student points because he or she wrote an introductory paragraph.

Unless you have some additional information to write about, the same policy goes for concluding paragraphs. Do not just write a concluding paragraph to restate the exact same things that you wrote in the body of your essay. As we will show you later in this chapter, use a concluding paragraph only to add points that you may have forgotten to cover earlier in your writing.

Just the Facts, Ma'am

You've probably always been told to put introductory and concluding paragraphs in your essays at school, but the simple cold fact is that the readers don't care since they *just want to see your straightforward answer to the question*. You should not write anything that is not going to earn you points. Just as in the multiple-choice section, *you cannot waste time*. To focus on all of the essay questions within the 75-minute time period, you need all the extra time you can get. Sure, it's better to say more than to say less to pick up additional points. However, you have only 75 minutes in which to finish.

Now, you should feel somewhat relieved. Not having to write so formally on the essays is one of the "easier" aspects of the AP Human Geography Exam. Nonetheless, you still need to approach the essay section with a plan for all contingencies. Before we get to the "what to do" parts of strategy, we are going give you the "what **not** to do" rules first.

The Rules for Effective Essay Writing

Here are a few rules to follow on the essay section. Violating these rules can eliminate your possibility of earning a 4 or 5 on the exam. Included are instructions for what you can do to get out of these situations:

Rule #1: Don't Leave Anything Blank

If you write two of the essays and leave a third one blank, it will be almost statistically impossible to score a 4 or 5 on the exam. If you are stumped on a question, you need to write at least a paragraph on what you know about the material or anything you think might be related. What's the difference between a blank sheet and a few sentences? It has to do with the type of score you'll be issued. A blank essay receives a "–" score, which will take you out of the running for that 4 or 5 score. A couple of lines of writing on the subject of the question will at least give you a "0" score, and if you use the right vocabulary might even earn you a point or two. This approach will significantly increase the possibility of earning at least a score of 4. Think of the 0 as a low score and the – as a disqualification.

Likewise, if there is a part of the question that you don't know the answer to, you should still write something using the technical vocabulary from the course. Do this just in case you can pick up a point or two for identifying significant issues. Another approach to get last-ditch points is to give a real-world example of something that you're not sure how to technically explain.

Rule #2: No Bullet Points

Although you may pick up a point or two for identifying important vocabulary, just writing a few bullet points won't get you enough points for a high score. Even if you don't think you know the full answer to the essay question, the parts that you do know should be written out to earn the maximum points possible. Why? Some scoring rubrics distribute points for each question part on a sliding scale. For example, you might get one point for identifying an issue or using vocabulary properly, a second point for a basic discussion, and a third point for a complex discussion of the issue.

Rule #3: No Artwork, Please

Even if the question refers to a particular geographic model or place, do not draw your answer as a diagram or map. The reader will not be able to give you any points, even if what you're writing is basically correct. Answers must be in essay format, plain and simple. If you're visualizing a model or a map, write down what you see in your mind. Don't just describe the structure or places; discuss processes and explain why things are in a particular place or how they got to be there. Don't forget to use the technical vocabulary from that part of the course.

Rule #4: Editt Yoru Worrk!

As much as you think it might be fun to spend what time you have left over to draw pictures or write poems about population pyramids in the back of the test booklet, this is not a good idea. Use this time to edit. See page 65 for tips on editing.

WHAT THE DIRECTIONS SAY

The essay instructions are straightforward, and they mean what they say. There's nothing hidden here:

Directions: You have 75 minutes to answer all three of the following questions. It is recommended that you spend approximately one-third of your time (25 minutes) on each question. It is suggested that you take up to 5 minutes of this time to plan and outline each answer. While a formal essay is not required, it is not enough to answer a question by merely listing facts. Illustrate your answers with substantive geographic examples where appropriate. Be sure that you number each of your answers, including individual parts, in the answer booklet as the questions are numbered below.

TIME MANAGEMENT

The most important thing in the directions is the advice on how to spend your time. What may sound confusing is the bit about "5 minutes." On average, here's how you would plan your time:

> Essay 1: 5 minutes to outline and 20 minutes to write
> Essay 2: 5 minutes to outline and 20 minutes to write
> Essay 3: 5 minutes to outline and 20 minutes to write for a total of 75 minutes.

However, after the exam you might find out that this would have been *a better schedule*:

Essay 2:   4 minutes to outline, 14 minutes to write and 2 minutes to edit

Essay 3:   6 minutes to outline, 19 minutes to write and 3 minutes to edit

Essay 1:   5 minutes to outline, 21 minutes to write and 1 minute to edit

Why? You are going answer the question that you know best first. Moreover, you are likely to spend less time doing it because the answer flows easily. And you won't need as much time to edit, so you'll just do the *quick editing* that we'll show you in a few pages. The second essay is one in which you also know the material, but it's trickier and you'll need more time to formulate and write your answer. The third essay is the tough one, possibly even a "stumper" that you are just not ready to answer. You are just going to answer this one to pick up as many points as possible.

The point is to be flexible with your time within the 75-minute time frame. Try to target 20 total minutes for the first essay you choose to write, 25 total minutes for the second essay, and 30 total minutes for the last essay. Within those totals, keep in mind that you need to outline, write, and edit your work.

A Few Other AP Essay-Writing Facts and Guidelines

- You may write the essays in any order in the answer booklet. For example, you can start with Essay 3, then Essay 1, and finish with Essay 2. Don't forget to write the number of the essay you are writing in the box at the top of each page.
- When you begin the next essay, start on a fresh page.
- With average-sized handwriting, most high-scoring essays use two to three pages of the answer booklet.
- There's no need to give your essay a title. Focus on getting points.
- You may double-space your essays.
- Very small and poor handwriting will harm your score. If a reader can't decipher your writing, then he or she can't give you points. Write carefully and legibly.
- Readers do not grade for spelling or grammar. You don't get extra points for spelling Zimbabwe correctly, nor can a reader deduct points for your attempt to spell "the palace of Verseye" when you meant Versailles. They still have to give you credit. Yes, they understand you are under pressure.

Also Keep in Mind...

It's important to recognize if the question specifies a certain place. If the question refers to, for instance, "European border policies' effect on free trade," then you must talk about Europe. If the question is more general, such as "Describe an example of a fuzzy border between two culture regions," then you can pick any example, such as the American "Dixie" border with the Northern United States.

Make sure to recognize any historical time frame. If the question says "since 1950," then make sure your descriptions and examples are not from a previous time period. Likewise, if the question specifies "geopolitics during the Cold War," then you should to refer to events between 1946 and 1991.

HOW TO CRACK THE AP HUMAN GEOGRAPHY ESSAY QUESTIONS

In this section, we will discuss outlining, keyword vocabulary, writing tools, and editing strategies. Keep in mind that you are not just writing; *you are constructing an answer.* Think about it: You could unknowingly write an answer that reads well but falls apart under the rubric. Or, using the following strategies you can construct an answer that "reads to the rubric" and considerably raises your essay section score.

Data show that the average student earns only one-third of the available points on the essay section. Why? In addition to the problems covered in the "rules" section above, students tend to have problems organizing their answers and using the intended vocabulary.

HOW TO MAKE A SHORTHAND OUTLINE

The key to writing an effective and organized essay is to understand that the questions are written with a particular structure in mind. This question structure is how you will want to *construct* your written answer. *The basic way to outline your essay is to outline the question.* One of the best things about the shorthand outline is that you answer each part of the question in the order asked. This is not required but it makes the essay more readable, decreasing the chance a reader will miss potential points. Moreover, by checking off each part of the essay that you complete, you will make sure that you answer all parts of the question, thus avoiding the trap that causes most students to lose points.

Where to Write Your Outline

The answer booklet for the AP Human Geography essays contains many blank sheets of lined paper. In fact there's far more paper than you actually need to write the three essays. You can write your outline in the booklet. Just label it as "outline" and the reader will go on to your essay. And no, you are not allowed to take scrap paper into the exam room.

There are two approaches you can take on where in the booklet to write your outline:

1. Before the Essay

Do this if you decide to approach and outline the questions one at a time. Open the booklet to the first two side-by-side blank pages. On the left-hand page, write the outline for the essay you have decided to answer first. On the right-hand page, begin writing the essay. When you finish the first essay, flip to the next two empty side-by-side pages and repeat for the second. Likewise for the third question. As we will show you later in this section, make sure to leave space next to the outline to insert keywords.

The advantage of this approach is that you have your outline right next to the essay as you write it. This will allow you not only to remember the order in which you are writing, but also to check off each section as you complete it.

2. In the Front or Back of the Book

If you read all three questions and have ideas coming out of your head for all of them, it might be better to do all of your outlines first. In this case, turn to either the first or last sheet of lined paper in the booklet. Write all three outlines on this sheet, or use the first three or last three pages if you need more space. Do this so that when you are mid-essay, you can easily flip back to the outline. Again, make sure to leave space for your keyword list.

The advantage here is that you won't have to estimate the size of each essay and possibly make a mistake by writing an outline on a page you'll need for an essay.

Double-Check Your Work

No matter which method you use, you should check off each part of the outline as you complete that part of the essay. Then move to the next part of the outline to consider the next point in your essay. At the end each essay, go over the outline one last time to make sure you didn't forget to address a part of the question. Something else might pop into your head at this point and you can add it in a follow-up paragraph.

HOW TO CRACK AN ESSAY

Let's take a sample question and show how it's done:

---

1. Many economic factors have advanced suburbanization in the United States.
    A. Describe **two** effects that service industries have had on the expansion of suburbs since the 1960s.
    B. Discuss the negative aspects of suburban sprawl for the following service sectors:
        Education
        Transportation
        Environmental Protection

A shorthand outline is just that—short. To save time outlining, use abbreviations for long terms that you know. Label each section to make sure you cover all parts of the question. Here's an example of what a shorthand outline would look like for this question.

Q1 Outline:

A. Define:
A1. Service jobs available in sub. CBDs
A2. Serv. consumers living in sub. areas.

B. Discuss:
B1a. Schools are expensive. Taxes are high.
B1b. More school blds. and land needed
B2a. Highways are expensive.
B2b. More roads, more problems
B2c. Cost of transportation
B3a. Change from nature to living space
B3b. New homes eat up land

LABELING EACH PART

Notice how we have numbered the outline Q1 as this is for the question numbered in the test booklet as "1" (not the first question you choose to answer). A1 and A2 refer to the parts of section A, which specifies "two" descriptions (often these requirements are in **bold** type). B1a through B3b refers to section B, which has three required example areas, and asks for aspects (plural), meaning you must discuss more than one aspect per example.

ABBREVIATE EVEN MORE

If you can, abbreviate terms in your outline even further than what we have done here. As long as you understand what you are writing, the more shorthand abbreviations you use, the more time you will save.

WHAT TO DO? OPERATOR TERMS

We need to consider what the question is asking you to do. Each question will direct you with an operator term that specifies what you are expected to do with the topic material.

To help guide your writing, put the operator term at the top of each section, as we have done in the outline above. These verbs include *describe, discuss, analyze, define, give an example, explain, compare, contrast,* or *assess.* In addition, a question may inquire *to what extent (or degree)* or ask *the limitations of* a particular principle or factor. What do these operators ask you to do?

Describe: Write out the details or component parts of the concept or issue that the question addresses. Emphasize the most important elements and say why these are significant. The author wants you to illustrate in your writing (but don't draw a picture).

Discuss: Write about both sides of an issue or concept. State the positive and negative aspects. Explain who benefits and who loses in the process or situation. Or, explain the impacts of the issue or concept.

Analyze: Write about the relationship between factors and their impacts. Look for cause and effect relationships. State why the process you describe is a problem or a benefit in the real world.

Define: Write out the definition of a term or process. Say why the concept is significant to geographic thinking or why it matters in the real world. Some definitions are simple (like "place") and other can be complex (like "environmental determinism").

Example: Write about a real-world place, process, or situation that captures the essence of the concept that the question addresses. Make sure that the example you give is the most topical. Don't just use one that you like. Some questions will give you the example and you will have to describe how and why that place fits the concept.

Explain: Write about a process that is implied in the question. In conceptual terms: A happens, resulting in B, which then leads to C. Say why these things occur. State why the process you describe is a problem or a benefit in the real world.

Compare: Take two or more concepts or examples and state their similarities (give more than one). If there are differences, list these as well. State why the similarities or differences are significant and say what impact they have.

Contrast: Specifically describe the differences between two or more concepts or examples. Make sure to find at least two differences (unless the question says to give only one or the primary difference).

Assess: Write about the importance, impact, or effectiveness of a concept or issue. You will need to determine the positives and negatives of the conceptual or real-world situation. It's okay if you state that positives and negatives balance out, or if the good outweighs the bad (or vice versa).

Some operators can ask you *to criticize a topic or issue,* such as

To what extent (or degree): Not all concepts or examples have the impact or effect they were supposed to. Sometimes intervening factors limit these impacts or effects. Your job is to illustrate these processes in your writing.

The limitations of: In addition to intervening factors, conflicts and controversies can emerge that dampen the expected result of a concept or process.

In either case, the important thing to keep in mind is that you are expected to be critical. Say why there is a problem with the concept. Think of it this way: Someone had a good idea, but other things made it impossible or only partly useful; or some idea was good in theory but not in practice, and here is why. When applicable, identify who the winners and losers are, like you would in a "discuss" question.

DIRECTIONS IN THE QUESTION

Read questions carefully so that you know what and how much is being asked of you in each question, and so that you construct your outline correctly. The question format matters a lot. This is why you use your outline of the question as your outline for the answer. If a question asks for one example, that's all you have to give. If it says two or if it ask for plural "examples," "descriptions," "countries," or "places," you must provide more than one in order to get points from the rubric.

Should you give more than what is asked in the question? Or what if you are not sure of the answer but have several ideas? The value of providing several answer possibilities in excess of what is asked is debatable and, depending on the question, the rubric may not give you more points for this. In addition, including many ideas in an essay may add little to your score and will waste valuable time that could be used earning points on the other essays.

GIVING EXAMPLES

Should You Make a Laundry List?

Giving several more examples than what's requested is known as "laundry listing," and most readers will treat it as a futile attempt to see what sticks to the rubric. In this situation, a reader is likely to give you points only for the first examples you give. For instance, let's say a question asks for two countries as examples and you list six. The reader will look at only the first two, see if they score on the rubric, and move on with the essay. This will be the case even if the first four are wrong and the fifth and sixth are correct—no points.

What If You're Not Sure which Examples to Give?

If you are unsure of your answer(s) and have more ideas than the number requested in mind, *add only one additional example* to the essay. A forgiving reader will see this as you being thorough, and will be less likely to see you as a laundry lister. Remember to put what you think are your best answers first, just in case the rubric or a reader rejects extra answers.

Should You Give Examples, Even If They Don't Ask?

Giving examples, even when they are not required, is a good strategy. This can help especially if you are not sure whether you have fully discussed or defined a topic. If you think your answer sounds weak, it probably is. Use an example to further illustrate your answer. Why? Some rubrics give points based upon the quality or depth of your answer. The rubric may look like this:

> 0 points: little to no discussion or no use of keywords
> 1 point: basic discussion or use of keywords
> 2 points: complex discussion

Using an example can be a sign of your mastery of the topic and can move you from a 1-point basic discussion to a 2-point complex discussion.

RUBRIC SCORING

Be the Rubric

In the end you want the reader to say (covering his mouth to make the Darth Vader voice), "The rubric is strong in this one." Well, not all the AP Human Geography readers are *Star Wars* fans, but you do want the reader to have that feeling that you have nailed down the rubric in your essay, or as a Zen Buddhist might proclaim, "Be at one with the rubric." Your goal is to estimate what the rubric might look like as you are writing your essay. This is not a requirement, but it can help you better conceptualize the question and your essay.

How Many Points?

The total number of points possible for a question varies. A question is usually divided up into anywhere from 6 to 12 available points. This does not mean that one essay is more valuable than another based upon the number of points available. In fact, the "weighted" value of each essay has more to do with the statistics of the overall student performance—you'll have no way of knowing.

However, you can attempt to estimate the point value of each question as you write the shorthand outline. In a two-part question, each section is worth at least 3 points, maybe more. If the question is divided into two or more sections, the first section will be worth equal to or less than the later parts. The later sections tend to have more points available, as they often ask for more complex descriptions. If a section is subdivided further, then the parts are likely of equal value (1 or 2 points each).

It's a 10

We are going to suppose the example question is a 10-point question. During the exam you'll never be sure. Estimate the number of points, but don't stress over whether you are correct. Remember: This is just a tool to help you better construct your answer. If you really want to know, you can find out the scoring guidelines from the ETS web site after the exam, in late July.

LET'S OUTLINE IT AGAIN

Now that we have given you these additional tips about examples and rubric scoring, let's look at the question again and see a more advanced outline. Here we will add our point estimate totals for each section. In addition, we're going to add an example. In this case, imagine that you may not be sure about the negative aspects of suburban transportation services:

---

1. Many economic factors have advanced suburbanization in the United States.
   A. Describe **two** effects that service industries have had on the expansion of suburbs since the 1960s.
   B. Discuss the negative aspects of suburban sprawl for the following service sectors:
   Education
   Transportation
   Environmental Protection

Q1 Outline: (10)

A. Describe (4):
A1. Service jobs available in sub. CBDs (2)
A2. Serv. consumers living in sub. areas. (2)

B. Discuss (6):
B1a. Schools are expensive. Taxes are high (1)
B1b. More school blds. and land needed (1)
B2a. Highways are expensive. (1?)
B2b. More roads, more problems (1?)
B2c. Cars favored over public transport (1?)

B3a. Change from nature to living space (1)
B3b. New homes eat up land (1)

In reality it could be a 12-point question if section A was 6 instead of 4 points. Again, this will depend on the intent of the question's author. These are things we will not know.

Just remember to give complete descriptions for TWO aspects of service industry impacts on suburbanization and use examples if need be.

We're not quite done preparing to write the essay. Let's see how applying keywords can enrich our outline and make for a more complete essay.

How to Crack It: Keyword Lists

There is an extensive vocabulary in the AP Human Geography course. A problem that many students have with the essay section is that they don't use the technical vocabulary and terms they learned in class. Doing so will earn additional points. Don't study vocabulary just in case you're asked a definition question on the multiple-choice section. *Study vocabulary so that you know what to say* in the essay section.

But It Sounds SO Geeky!

If you feel uncomfortable talking in terms of "core-periphery relationships" and "diffusion processes" or if it feels stupid to liken something to "economic restructuring," *get over it now!*

When you walk out of the exam, you can go back to using "Dude!" and "Whatever!?!" in daily conversation. During the essay section, the geeky-sounding terms earn points. Not only will you raise your AP score, but you will also start getting used to the fact that, in real life, people use technical terms in their work all the time.

Keyword Lists

Now that we have that out of the way, how do you know where to insert the vocabulary in your essay? What if you forget?

Using a keyword list is a good way to make sure that you use technical vocabulary at the right point in the essay. When you write your shorthand outline, leave room to the right of the outline to make a keyword list. Write down terms that you know are part of the material on the essay's topic. Try to write them alongside the part of the outline where they should fall in the essay. For example, using your outline for the example question, add appropriate words for each point.

---

1. Many economic factors have advanced suburbanization in the United States.
    A. Describe **two** effects that service industries have had on the expansion of suburbs since the 1960s.
    B. Discuss the negative aspects of suburban sprawl for the following service sectors:
        Education
        Transportation
        Environmental Protection

Q1 Outline: (10)

A. Describe (4):
A1. Service jobs available in sub. CBDs (2) R&D, office parks, white-collar,
A2. Serv. consumers living in sub. areas. (2) retail, professional services proximity

B. Discuss (6):
B1a. Schools are expensive. Taxes are high (1) local tax revenue
B1b. More school blds. and land needed (1) facilities
B2a. Highways are expensive. (1) infrastructure
B2b. More roads, more problems (1) congestion, commuter
B2c. Cars favored over public transport (?) sustainability
B3a. Change from nature to living space (1) population pressure
B3b. New homes eat up land (1) farmland preservation

THERE IT IS

Now you have a complete shorthand outline and are ready to write the essay answer.

As you write your essay, cross off the keywords so that you don't forget to use them. Although we have not done it here, you should abbreviate keywords as well.

HOW MUCH TIME TO OUTLINE?

Recall the time breakdowns from earlier in the chapter. Keep in mind that you need to complete the outline in *a target time of 5 minutes or less*. There's a lot to keep in mind just for the outline, but this will improve your score, so don't skip it. Don't spend a huge amount of time writing an elaborate outline or thinking about the rubric. Remember: The more shorthand you use, the better. To practice, use the essay questions at the end of this chapter. Make sure to time yourself on both the outline and the essay writing, separately.

EXAMPLE ESSAY

Using our completed shorthand outline, we've written an example of an essay in response to the question that would get all 10 points:

---

1. Many economic factors have advanced suburbanization in the United States.
   A. Describe **two** effects that service industries have had on the expansion of suburbs since the 1960s.
   B. Discuss the negative aspects of suburban sprawl for the following service sectors:
   Education
   Transportation
   Environmental Protection

Q1 Outline (10):

A. Describe (4):
A1. Service jobs available in sub. CBDs (2) R&D, office parks, white-collar,
A2. Serv. consumers living in sub. areas. (2) retail, professional services proximity

B. Discuss (6):
B1a. Schools are expensive. Taxes are high (1) local tax revenue
B1b. More school blds. and land needed (1) facilities
B2a. Highways are expensive. (1) infrastructure
B2b. More roads, more problems (1) congestion, commuter
B2c. Cars favored over public transport (?) sustainable
B3a. Change from nature to living space (1) population pressure
B3b. New homes eat up land (1) farmland preservation

1. In the 1960s many Americans continued the existing pattern of migration and settlement in suburban areas. Of the many factors that led to suburban expansion, the rise of service industries and decline of manufacturing has been important since that time. One effect has been the growth of service sector jobs that have emerged in suburban CBDs and edge cities. Many companies decided to locate in suburbs because affordable land space was available to build office parks and research and development facilities, like the Research Triangle Park in North Carolina. Thus, professionals and, later, Baby Boomers continued to settle in these areas due to job availability.

A second and related factor leading to the expansion of suburbs is that the wealthier consumers of services, like retailing, and professional services such as doctors and dentists, live in the suburbs. Instead of following the tradition of locating these services in old downtown CBDs, business people decided to select locations in close proximity to their consumers. Malls, medical and office buildings have thus been a part of the expansion of suburban land space.

The negative aspects of suburban sprawl have caused problems for public services like education, transportation and environmental protection. Education has suffered from the need to continuously expand school capacity. School construction and increasing teacher salaries have required increased local taxes, which homeowners complain about. In addition, schools can take up a lot of land and limited space in suburbs may make it difficult to find room for facilities.

Highways and public transportation are another increasing infrastructure expense for public services. Building new roads has become more costly as land prices have soared in suburban areas, plus there may be limited space to put in large highways. Some have also argued that building more roads will just lead to more commuter cars and congestion. Thus, governments must spend more money on sustainable public transportation solutions like rail and buses.

Another problem related sustainability problem is that when new suburbs are built, they consume existing natural areas and farmland. Protecting natural and historic environments has became an important political issue in the late 1960s. And suburban population pressure on the environment has been a problem. For example, some suburbs in California have encroached on the habitats of endangered species like giant redwoods and mountain lions. Problems like these led to legislation like the Endangered Species Act. Similarly, in Ohio laws have been passed to protect historic farmland from housing development.

(400 words)

ANOTHER WAY TO DO IT

Guide the reader by inserting numeric headings, like this:

Question 1.

A1.

In the 1960s many Americans continued the existing pattern of migration and settlement in suburban areas. Of the many factors that led to suburban expansion, the rise of service industries and decline of manufacturing has been important since that time. One effect has been the growth of service sector jobs that have emerged in suburban CBDs and edge cities. Many companies decided to locate in suburbs because affordable land space was available to build office parks and research and development facilities, like the Research Triangle Park in North Carolina. Thus, professionals and, later, Baby Boomers continued to settle in these areas due to job availability.

A2.

A second and related factor leading to the expansion of suburbs is that the wealthier consumers of services, like retailing, and professional services such as doctors and dentists, live in the suburbs. Instead of following the tradition of locating these services in old downtown CBDs, business people decided to select locations in close proximity to their consumers. Malls, medical and office buildings have thus been a part of the expansion of suburban land space.

B1.

The negative aspects of suburban sprawl have caused problems for public services like education, transportation, and environmental protection. Education has suffered from the need to continuously expand school capacity. School construction and increasing teacher salaries have required increased local taxes, which homeowners complain about. In addition, schools can take up a lot of land and limited space in suburbs may make it difficult to find room for facilities.

B2.

Highways and public transportation are another increasing infrastructure expense for public services. Building new roads has become more costly as land prices have soared in suburban areas, plus there may be limited space to put in large highways. Some have also argued that building more roads will just lead to more commuter cars and congestion. Thus, governments must spend more money on sustainable public transportation solutions like rail and buses.

B3.

Another related sustainability problem is that when new suburbs are built, they consume existing natural areas and farmland. Protecting natural and historic environments became an important political issue since the late 1960s. And suburban population pressure on the environment has been a problem. For example, some suburbs in California have encroached on the habitats of endangered species like giant redwoods and mountain lions. Problems like these led to legislation like the Endangered Species Act. Similarly, in Ohio laws have been passed to protect historic farmland from housing development.

The Labels

The labels help the reader figure out what part of the question you are answering. This is especially useful in questions with similar descriptions between two sections. If you accidentally include the correct information but under the wrong heading, don't worry. In this situation, readers are instructed to give you the point(s) anyway. Although it will help your writing and possibly your score to follow the structure of the question, you are not required to present the essay material in a particular order.

The Box

Note the box in the corner above the essay. You are instructed on the test to enter the number of the essay you are writing in this box. Make sure you do it for every page on which you have written. As you do practice essays, get into the habit of writing the question number in a box on the corner of every page. On the exam these boxes are meant to keep a reader from accidentally missing all or part of your essay.

THE RUBRIC

As we mentioned before, this is a 10-point question where the first part has 4 possible points and the second part has 6 possible points. What we don't know are the different possibilities for scoring. Depending on the subject matter you describe or discuss, you can earn 0, 1, or 2 points per item. Note that if you discuss something not on the rubric, then you get no points. Exceptions to the rubric are extremely rare, and you'd have to come up with a valid answer that the question's author, an expert in his or her field, may not have thought of when writing the rubric.

Example Question Rubric

Total Points: 10

Part A: 4 points (2 + 2)

For two (2) of the following categories, apply the following point structure:

Category
Education and Growth of Professional Suburban Population
Financial Services and Increased Mortgage Availability
Commercial Real Estate and Expanding Suburban Service Centers
Expanding Transport Services to Suburban Areas
Construction Services and Efficient Home Construction

0 points: little to no description

1 point: basic description or simple example

2 points: complex description with cause and effects

Part B: 6 points (2 + 2 + 2)

For the three (3) following categories, apply the following point structure.

> 0 points: little to no discussion
> 1 point: basic discussion item or use of keyword or example
> 2 points: complex discussion with key words or examples

Category	Possible Topics
Education	Tax burden on local property owners, expanded need for school buildings and concern for increased class sizes, increasing teacher salaries, increasing demand for teachers, expanded bus service.
Transportation	Increased congestion, cost of new highways, complaints about toll road fees, need for land to expand highways, use of eminent domain to take private land, need for more public transit, unpopularity of public transit in the United States.
Environmental Protection	New housing and office developments consuming habitat, wetlands, or open space in general. Farmland and parklands under threat from housing pressure. Air and solid waste pollution problems.

EDITING: DO IT AND EARN EXTRA POINTS!

Plan to take any leftover time to reread your essays and edit them. Try to leave at least 3 minutes in each essay for editing. When editing, you won't need to erase anything you've written. This is because readers cannot subtract points from the score that you've earned. If you think you have written something incorrectly, cross it out and write in the margin of the page next to where it should be. Or, in a concluding paragraph you can add the correct information, parenthetically noting that you're correcting a statement from before. If you see a place where you forgot to include an important vocabulary word, insert it with an arrow connecting it to where the term should fall within the text.

A smart tactic that the author has seen is to double-space your essays—skipping a blank line in the answer booklet while writing your essay. This will give you extra space to add edits during a reread of the essay. This also makes the essay easier to read (a good thing). Don't worry; there is plenty of space in the answer booklet.

WHAT IF YOU FORGOT SOMETHING AND NEED TO GO BACK?

Instead of a concluding paragraph that sums up and earns no extra points, consider a "follow-up paragraph" to add any extra details or examples. To do this, begin your follow-up statements with something like the following:

In addition to my previous description of _____, I would like to add...

or

To further illustrate my discussion on _____, I can offer the example of...

Regardless of how you begin this type of follow-up statement, it is important to direct the reader back to where the added text should have been included.

USE THE TIME WISELY

If you have time left at the end of the exam, spend the extra time editing or writing follow-ups. We know you just want to give your cramped hand a break, or you may have the desire to run out of the room to finally relax. Remember: In general it's better to say more than to say less if you have the time.

BUT DON'T SECOND-GUESS YOURSELF

Unless you are absolutely sure that you've written something incorrectly, don't erase or scratch out anything you've written. Readers cannot deduct points for incorrect information.

PRACTICE ESSAYS

Here are three practice essay questions. Check your watch or set a timer to see how you do on pacing. Make sure you have no distractions and are in a place where no one will distract you. Afterward, relax for a few minutes and then turn to page 68 to look at the scoring rubrics to see how you've done. Remember your goal of capturing 60 percent of the possible points.

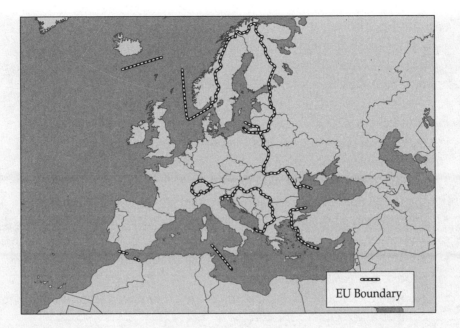

1.
   A. Use the map to define the concept of "Fortress Europe" in relation to the external boundary of the European Union.
   B. Explain the economic benefits of the European Union's open-border policy.
   C. Explain the challenges or difficulties involving the European Union's open-border policy.

2. Compare the concept of cultural identity between the following regions:

   Anglo North America

   Latin America

   Sub-Saharan Africa

   Explain how these concepts differ from the European identification with nationality as a means of determining ethnicity.

3. Describe the free-market reforms of the People's Republic of China since the 1980s.

   Give **two** examples of how China's engagement with the global economy has changed the country's landscape and economic geography.

PRACTICE ESSAY SCORING RUBRICS

Here are the rubrics and point distributions for the three practice questions. Turn to page 70 to total up your points and see how you've done.

1. (2 + 4 + 4 = 10 total points)

   Part A—2 points
   1 point for map identification or map example of border control.
   1 point for "Fortress Europe" as the concept of border controls on the outer political boundary but not the internal boundaries.

   Part B—4 points (2 + 2)
   Per example of economic benefits (a maximum of 2 examples):
   1 point for minor explanation or vocabulary keyword
   2 points for complex explanation using keywords
   For the following issues (maximum of 2 points for each bullet point):
   - Free movement of labor across internal EU borders/reduces labor shortages
   - Free movement of consumers across internal EU Borders/variety of markets
   - Free movement of commerce or shipping (trains, canals, trucks moving goods)/decreases transit costs
   - Knowledge or skill-sharing among the total European labor force/more competitive regional workforce
   - Accentuates free-trade policies of zero tariffs and/or common currency usage

   Part C—4 points (2 + 2)
   Per example of challenge or difficulty (a maximum of 2 examples):
   1 point for minor explanation or vocabulary keyword
   2 points for complex explanation using keywords
   For the following issues (maximum of 2 points for each bullet point):
   - No internal border controls in use to limit movement of criminals or terrorists
   - Once immigrants enter EU boundary there is no control over settlement locations
   - Labor force must be multilingual to participate in other EU member states
   - EU citizens have loss of local, regional, or national identity in favor of the general "European" ethnicity
   - EU member state governments complain about loss of sovereignty over their territory or borders

2. (3 + 3 + 3 = 9 total points)
   For each of the regions, the following point structure (a maximum of 3 points per region):
   1 point for minor discussion or vocabulary keyword
   2 points for complex discussion using keywords
   1 point for comparison to European nation identity

Anglo North America:
- Identity based on race and ethnicity, possibly combined with notion of an American or Canadian nation-state that reduces racial and ethnic differences

Latin America:
- Mixed identity based on varying degrees of Native American, European, and African heritage, possibly combined with post-colonial national identity

Sub-Saharan Africa:
- Identity based on tribal (and/or clan) identity, possibly combined with post-colonial national identity
- Must explain that European identity is traditionally built upon the nation or nation-state concept. Do not accept "European" as an identity.

3. (4 + 4 = 8 total points)

Free-Market Reforms—4 points (2 + 2)
Per example of reform (a maximum of 2 examples):
1 point for simple description or vocabulary keyword
2 points for complex description using keywords
Only 2 points maximum per bullet point
- Local agricultural markets allowed/farmers may sell excess produce beyond government production quotas
- Entrepreneurs allowed to open businesses/provide private services
- Foreign firms allowed to open factories in special economic zones (SEZs)
- Workers allowed free movement to relocate in different places
- Increased tourism

Changes in Chinese Geography—4 points (2 + 2)
Per example of geographic changes (a maximum of 2 examples):
1 point for simple description or vocabulary keyword
2 points for complex description using keywords
Only 2 points maximum per bullet point
- Significant economic growth of coastal cities/provinces/SEZs
- Significant population/labor force migration to coastal cities/provinces/SEZs
- Loss of young workers from inland agricultural counties/provinces/regions
- Wealth accumulated by those engaged in free-market economic activity compared to communist (Marxist) tradition of equal earnings. Emerging middle and upper classes.
- Damage to environment/pollution/increased resource demand

TOTAL UP YOUR POINTS

Now that you've had a chance to see the rubrics, reread each of your essays with the rubric right next to the page—this is how AP readers do it. You can tally up the points for each section as you read through. If you are not sure if your writing constitutes a minor or complex discussion or comparison, ask your teacher to review your work. Be fair to yourself. If you don't think your statements were thorough, give yourself only 1 instead of 2 points. If what you wrote was not on the rubric, then you don't earn points, no matter how thorough or well-written it was.

Question 1—10 points
A. 0–2 possible B. 0–4 possible C. 0–4 possible Total points

_____ + _____ + _____ = _____

6 total points or better for 60 percent goal

Question 2—9 points
A. 0–3 possible B. 0–3 possible C. 0–3 possible Total Points

_____ + _____ + _____ + _____

6 total points or better for 60 percent goal.

Question 3—8 points
A. 0–4 possible B. 0–4 possible Total Points

_____ + _____ = _____

5 total points or better for 60 percent goal.

WHAT IF YOU DIDN'T MEET THE 60 PERCENT GOALS?

If you thought you knew the answers but scored below 60 percent, go back through this chapter and see how you missed points. Did you violate any of the "rules"? Did you understand the question directions? Or were you not thorough enough in your answers?

Another thing to examine is how well your outlines mimic the rubric. Were you at least close on the point distributions? Did you understand the requirements for plural descriptions or examples?

Repeat what you have learned in this chapter when you take the full practice exams in the back of this book. Practice might not make perfect, but at least we can meet the 60 percent goals and earn a 4 or 5 on the exam.

PART ◆ IV

AP HUMAN GEOGRAPHY REVIEW

INTRODUCTION TO PART IV

The following chapters are a review of the basic content of the AP Human Geography course. The material in these sections was selected based on the commonly asked questions in the multiple-choice and essay portions of the exam. Of course there is no way of knowing precisely what material will appear on the exam, nor how it will be asked. However, due to the broad nature of the test material, you can expect that much of what you read in this book will appear on the exam in some form or another.

Pay especially close attention to spatial models and theories in the review, as these are valued highly among question authors. Learn the shape and parts of each model. However, it's equally important to understand why the models are shaped in different ways and how they have changed over time.

Keep note of keywords and technical vocabulary to know for multiple-choice questions and to use in your essay section answers. In the following text, important keywords appear in **bold**; note their definitions and use them in your essays to earn valuable points.

Finally, be aware that the subject matter in the following chapters has been written in the same style, length, and format in which you will want to write your essay responses during the AP Human Geography Exam. It's important to train your mind to write with straightforward descriptions, keywords, and definitions and to present detailed examples. The author has thrown in a few interesting stories along the way to keep you going as you prepare for the exam.

GEOGRAPHY:
ITS NATURE AND PERSPECTIVES

CHAPTER OUTLINE

In this chapter we will review the central concepts and tools in human geography that may show up on the AP exam. The first part focuses on the general concepts that encompass all of the six areas (covered in chapters 4–9) that you must know for the test. Then we'll review the necessary information regarding maps, map types, and map scale, as well as geographic technologies. There is also a list of several models that you are required to know for the exam, with information on where to find detailed explanations of them in this book. Finally, we will provide a list of the names of important geographers along with their contributions, and then the key terms for the chapter.

THE CENTRAL CONCEPTS

SPACE AND PLACE

Of the general concepts in geography, *space* and *place* are the two terms that human geographers consider most important. Most other scientific fields do not consider the importance of space and place, or do so only slightly, as opposed to geographers, who consider them central concepts in research and theory.

Space

When geographers talk about **space**, they're not talking about "the final frontier" or anything outside of Earth's atmosphere. Instead, geographers are referring to the geometric surface of the earth. It's best to think about geographic space as an abstract concept. Close your eyes and think of the global surface of the earth as an empty slate. Imagine placing objects on the earth's **spatial** surface that are defined by their location and are separated by some degree of distance from other things. These objects could be people, trees, buildings, or even whole cities—whatever you choose to visualize. Thinking spatially means understanding the pattern and distribution of objects and analyzing their relationships, connectedness, movement, growth, and change across space and over time.

Place

Well, that was deep! The concept of **place** is less abstract, but still important theoretically. It's important have an open and broad concept of place. Think of place as an area of bounded space of some human importance. People don't have to live there for it to be a place. Instead, you can have a sense of place about somewhere, even in the midst of a desert or an ocean. When human importance is recognized, it is common to assign a place name, or more technically a **toponym,** to that location. Place names often reveal the historical interrelatedness of location places. An area of bounded space could be somewhere small, such as a room, or as large as a continent. **Regions** are a type of place, and there are other categories of places, such as urban places, places of work, resource locations, and transportation nodes. When considering the importance of a location, region, town, or city, it is necessary to consider, why does this place matter?

The attributes of a place change over time. Over the long term, we can consider the concept of **sequent occupancy**, in other words, the succession of groups and cultural influences throughout a place's history. In many places we find that there are several different historical layers that contribute to a **place-specific** culture, society, local politics, and economy. For example, the place specificity of Santa Fe, New Mexico, is a complex mix of multiple Native American, Spanish colonial, and modern American influences based upon the sequence of past and current societal influences.

SCALE

Scale is the relationship of an object or place to the earth as a whole. Scale can be thought about two ways in geography. There is **map scale**, which describes the ratio of distance on a map and distance in the real world in absolute terms (more on map scale later in the chapter). And there is **relative scale**, or what can also be referred to as the **scale of analysis**. This describes the **level of aggregation**, or in other words, the level at which you group things together for examination. Scales can range from the individual or the local, from city to county and state, from regional to national to continental, or to the international and global scales.

Scale modifiers are good to use in the essay section of the exam. Specify whether a company is a transnational corporation or a local business or if you are discussing a local government, a federal regulation, or an international organization. Specifying the scale of the items you're being asked about may earn you points for detail or example material.

Relative scale is important to understand because it is false to compare different scales of analysis or places at different scales. For example, it would be wrong to visit just Atlanta and assume the rest of Georgia had the same characteristics. Likewise, if you examined economic data from Alabama and assumed the rest of the United States had the same median income, types of businesses, or unemployment rates, you would be incorrect.

REGIONS

Let's go over the three categories of regions: **formal, functional,** and **vernacular**. Keep in mind that there are many different types of regions, and a single place can exist in several regions simultaneously. For example, the Everglades in Florida exist within the Southern U.S. region and are also considered a wetland region. Regions exist at many different scales and can overlap. Have an open mind about what can be considered a region.

Formal Regions

As a type of place, the spatial definition of the formal region is an area of bounded space that possesses some **homogeneous characteristic** or **uniformity**. This means that across the region there is at least one thing that is the same everywhere within the regional boundary.

The defining homogeneous character can be as simple as a common language. In a **linguistic region**, everyone speaks the same language, but groups in that region can be very different culturally. For example, the United States and Australia are in the same linguistic region, but the two countries share little else in culture, economy, or landscape. Regional concepts can also be very complex. The

American South or "Dixie" is one such region; a multitude of factors define the region, such as dialect, vocabulary, food, architecture, climate, ethnicity, and religion. Reasonable people disagree over whether states like Virginia, West Virginia, and/or Maryland are parts of Dixie.

Regional boundaries differ based upon the type of region. **Culture regions** tend to have fuzzy borders. It's hard to tell where one region ends and the other begins, such as the border between Dixie and "the North" in the United States. Boundaries between **political regions** are finite and well-defined. Some political boundaries are porous, such as those between Canada and the United States, and other boundaries are protected, such as that between the United States and Mexico. **Environmental region** boundaries are transitional and measurable. The environmental transition zone between two **bioregions**, or **biomes**, is known as an **ecotone**. For example, the space between the Sahara Desert and the tropical savanna of Africa is a dry grassland region known as the Sahel.

Functional Regions

Functional regions or **nodal regions** are areas that have a **central place** or **node** that is a focus or point of origin that expresses some practical purpose. The influence of this point is strongest in the areas close to the center, and the strength of influence diminishes as distance increases from that point.

Market areas are a type of functional region. A professional sports team will have the strongest fan base and intensive media network coverage in areas close to the team's home city. There are fans and media viewing in the larger region around that city, but they diminish as you get farther and farther away. Eventually you reach a point where the fans transition to another team's functional region and the media networks are oriented in that direction.

Make the link: See the concept of **distance decay** on page 79.

An outlet mall can have a similar market area affect on consumers. Shoppers will come mostly from the local area and neighboring cities. Because outlets are often placed far apart, there will also be a larger **area of influence** for the mall that will have shoppers travelling from longer distances but making a fewer number of trips. Many outlet shoppers are "just passing through" on the interstate, who see a very brief **intervening opportunity** to do some discount shopping. An intervening opportunity is an attraction at a shorter distance that takes precedence over an attraction that is further away.

Vernacular Regions

The **vernacular region** is based upon the perception or collective **mental map** of the region's residents. The overall concept can vary within the region due to personal or group variations. Looking again at the American South, or "Dixie," some residents define it by the location of country music bands or fans, where others recognize the numbers of Southern Baptist church congregations or NASCAR races as the defining statistic. There are those who consider Dixieland only as the states of the Civil War–era Confederacy or the part of the country where it never (or almost never) snows. The author thinks it's defined by the areas where people have southern accents. He had one growing up in West

Virginia, a union state during the war. No matter what is used to spatially define the regional concept, the reason tends to be a point of pride for residents.

Be careful in your vernacular definitions. There are country music radio stations in all fifty U.S. states and throughout Canada (remember Shania Twain). Some of NASCAR's events with the largest attendance are in decidedly un-Southern states like Wisconsin, California, and New Hampshire.

LOCATION

The concept of location is similar to scale, and we can consider location in both relative and absolute terms. **Absolute location** defines a point or place on the map using coordinates such as latitude and longitude. **Relative location**, by contrast, refers to the location of a place compared to a known place or geographic feature.

Absolute Location

The most common way to fix a point on the earth's surface is using **latitude** and **longitude** coordinates (there are other more technical coordinates systems used in geography, such as Universal Transverse Mercator or UTM). Many students get confused and mix up the definitions of latitude and longitude. Here's an easy way to think about it:

> Lines of latitude measure distance, in degrees, north or south of the equator (latitude = ladder). Lines of longitude measure distance, in degrees, east or west of the Prime Meridian (longitude = how long the ladder is).

Some people remember the difference between the two as the lines of longitude being the longest lines on the globe, going all the way from pole to pole.

Notation is also important to keep in mind. Absolute location is given with latitude first and then longitude with a cardinal direction, separated by a comma. Degrees can be divided up into smaller minutes, and minutes can be divided up into seconds. For instance, the absolute location of the United States' Capitol building is

$$38°\ 53\ 23\ N, 77°\ 0\ 32\ W$$

meaning it lies at the point 38.889722 degrees north of the Equator and 77.008889 degrees west of the Prime Meridian. When decimals are used to divide partial degrees instead of minutes and seconds, the coordinate system used is known as **decimal degrees.**

The **equator** is 0° latitude. The **North and South Poles** are 90° latitude.

The **Prime Meridian** is 0° longitude. On the opposite side of the earth is the 180° line of longitude. Parts of this line compose the **International Date Line** that also meanders around a number of international boundaries.

What's Up with the Prime Meridian?

The Prime Meridian (0° longitude) runs through Great Britain because the means to accurately calculate longitude at sea was developed by the British Royal Navy. With the development of the chronometer, a gear-driven clock, by London jeweler John Harrison in 1785, British ships at sea could accurately determine their longitude. For practical purposes, 0° was fixed on the **Royal Naval Observatory** at Greenwich in London. This allowed ship captains to know how far they were east or west of their home country. The French, who were the other great naval power at the time, didn't mind so much because the line also runs directly through the center of France. Other nations soon accepted the standardized international system of longitude. The Prime Meridian was officially adopted as 0 degrees longitude at the 1884 International Meridian Conference.

Time Zones

Time zones are divided up in 15-degree-wide longitudinal zones around the world with some exceptions. This is because 360° divided by 24 hours a day equals 15°. One exception to this rule comes from China, where leaders established one time zone for the entire country. For practical purposes, dividing lines between time zones often follow political boundaries, sometimes even along local area divisions. Time zones were created relatively recently, in the era of transcontinental railways, to standardize time across long east-west train lines.

Relative Location

As was said before, relative location is based upon a place's relationship to other known geographic features or places. For instance, when someone from a metropolitan-area suburb is asked where they are from, the response is often relative and will refer to the larger city. A person from Arlington, Virginia, might say they are from Washington, D.C., and someone from Santa Monica, California, might say they are from Los Angeles, or simply L.A. (dude).

You might also put significant value on a place due to its relative location. In the early 1990s, Dublin, Ireland, became an important international business location due to its low-cost economy, English language skills, and close relative location to Great Britain, where the cost of doing business was extremely high (especially in London).

SITE AND SITUATION

Two locational concepts that work together are **site** and **situation.** Site refers to the physical characteristics of a place, such as the fact that New York City is located on a large, deep water harbor, next to the Atlantic Ocean. Situation refers to the place's interrelatedness with other places. How is a place related to other places?

In this case, New York City became the most prominent trade and finance center in the United States during the 1800s, due to its position as a terminal for trade goods on the ship-navigable Hudson River to and from the rest of New England, and as a major port-of-call on the Atlantic Circular Trade Route. As a result, New York City had much greater market potential than Boston, Philadelphia, or Charleston, South Carolina, all of which did not have the benefit of the large inland waterway above the main port location.

DISTANCE

Like scale and location, you should consider **distance** in both absolute and relative terms. Distance is measured absolutely, or it can be measured relatively in terms of the degree of interaction between places or in units of time traveled. Linear **absolute distance** is the distance between two places as measured in linear units such as miles or kilometers.

The effect of distance on relationships is important to understand, and geographers often utilize the concept of **distance decay** to explain **relative distance**. Distance decay means that the farther away different places are from a place of origin, the less likely interaction will be with the original place.

Relative distance is also expressed by the principle of **Tobler's law**, which states that all places are interrelated, but closer places are more related than farther ones. This law was developed by American-Swiss geographer and cartographer Waldo Tobler around 1970 and his exact phrasing was, "Everything is related to everything else, but near things are more related to each other." When the length of distance becomes a factor that inhibits the interaction between two points, this is known as the **friction of distance**. This can be seen when the combined time and cost of moving a product prevents it from being sold in far-off locations.

SPACE-TIME COMPRESSION

Decreased time and relative distance between places is referred to as **space-time compression**. Technology can reduce the relative distance between places. Modes of transportation such as airplanes reduce travel time between two distant points, and as a result, increase interaction. Even the Internet can be used as an example of how a whole network of physically distant places can be brought virtually together and increase interaction significantly. So significantly, in fact, that the author is currently ignoring email from at least two continents.

SPATIAL INTERACTIONS

Central Places

Central places can be thought of as any node of human activity. However, they are most often the centers of economic exchange. Markets are often located at transportation nodes, which provide accessibility to and from these points; market centers tend to be centrally located within the larger economic region.

Using this notion of centrality, the school of thought known as **central place theory** was developed in the 1930s by the German geographer Walter Christaller. He saw the economic world as an abstract spatial model. In the model, city location and the level of urban economic exchange could be analyzed using central places within hexagonal market areas, which overlapped each other at different scales. There's much more to this, as you have probably learned. To review, see Chapter 9 for more detail on central place theory, market areas, and the range and threshold of the service.

Core and Periphery

One thing that emerges from central place–type thinking is the idea of **core and periphery**. Many different regional, cultural, economic, political, and environmental phenomena and human activities display some sort of core and periphery relationship. Just as the **CBD** (central business district) is the core of the urban landscape, a country's capital is the core of its political landscape. Note that the core does not have to be exactly in the center of the peripheral region.

For example, in the Western United States, the core of the Mormon culture region is in the Salt Lake City-Provo-Ogden metropolitan area, also referred to as the Wasatch Front. This is where the highest concentration of members of the Church of Jesus Christ of Latter-Day Saints is located. However, there is a significant LDS population throughout most of the rest of Utah, eastern Nevada, southwestern Wyoming, northern Arizona, southern Idaho, and eastern Oregon. These areas compose the combined peripheral Mormon culture region.

When you analyze a map or a model for an essay question on the exam, explain the core-periphery relationships that you see as part of the larger question. This type of attention to technical detail can earn you additional points.

Pattern

Geographers also use special terms to describe different types of spatial patterns. When things are grouped together on the earth's surface, it is referred to as a **cluster**. When clustering occurs purposefully around a central point or an economic **growth pole**, it is referred to as **agglomeration**. When there is no rhyme or reason to the distribution of a spatial phenomenon, it is referred to as a **random pattern**. Objects that are normally ordered but appear dispersed can be referred to as **scattered**. If a pattern is in a straight line, it is **linear**, and if it's wavy, the pattern is **sinuous**—like the pattern of heartbeats on an EKG.

Land survey patterns have an effect on the property lines and political boundaries of states and provinces. East of central Ohio and Ontario, land surveys until the 1830s used natural landscape features to divide land on a system of **metes and bounds** (see below), which had been developed in Europe centuries earlier. After the 1830s, when new techniques to accurately determine longitude were transferred from sea navigation to land survey, surveyors in the United States and Canada used a rectilinear **township and range** survey system based upon lines of latitude and longitude. This produced the block-shaped property lines and more geometric shape to many western states and provinces. Former French colonial areas such as Québec and Louisiana have **long-lot patterns**. These have a narrow frontage along a road or waterway with a very long lot shape behind.

Land Survey Patterns in North America

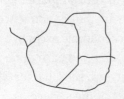 

Metes and Bounds   Township and Range   Long lots

Density

The concept of density is most often calculated by the number of things per square unit of distance. This is called **arithmetic density.** For instance, in the United States there are three Starbucks coffee shops per square mile—okay, not really, but it sometimes seems that way.

Agricultural density refers to the number of people per square unit of land actively used for farming. By comparison, **physiologic density** measures the number of people per square unit of arable land, meaning both the land that is farmed and the land that has the potential to be farmed but is not active.

Diffusion Patterns

There are a number of different ways and patterns in which human phenomena diffuse spatially or spread across the earth's surface. Most often we examine how culture, ideas, or technology spread from a point of origin to other parts of the world. Sometimes that point of origin or place of innovation is called a **hearth**. Here's a quick rundown of the different types of diffusion. For more details and examples, see Chapter 5. Hierarchical Diffusion, Contagious Diffusion, and Stimulus Diffusion are types of Expansion Diffusion.

Hierarchical Diffusion

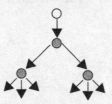

The pattern originates in a first-order location then moves down to second-order locations and from each of these to subordinate locations at increasingly local scales.

Contagious Diffusion

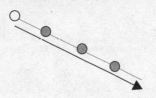

The pattern begins at a point of origin and then moves outward to nearby locations, especially those on adjoining transportation lines. This could be used to describe a disease but can also describe the movement of other things, such as the news in rural regions.

Stimulus Diffusion

Here a general or underlying principle diffuses and then stimulates the creation of new products or ideas. For example, stimulus diffusion occurs when vegetarian eating habits (principle) influence restaurants to offer more vegetarian dishes (new products).

Expansion Diffusion:

The pattern originates in a central place and then expands outward in all directions to other locations. Note that the distance does not have to be equal in all directions.

Relocation Diffusion

The pattern begins at a point of origin and then crosses a significant physical barrier, such as an ocean, mountain range, or desert, then relocates on the other side. Often the journey can influence and modify the items being diffused.

GEOGRAPHIC TOOLS

MAPS AND MAPPING CONCEPTS

For geographers, maps are important because they are what separate us from other social scientists, like sociologists or political scientists. Maps are not just a graphic art form; they are a science. Many scientific maps are the results of spatial analysis—the mathematical analysis of one or more quantitative geographic patterns.

Map Types

There are many map types, and there are a few specific ones that you should know for the AP Human Geography Exam:

Topographic maps: Show the contour lines of elevation, as well as the urban and vegetation surface with road, building, river, and other natural landscape features. These maps are highly accurate in terms of location and topography. They are used for engineering surveys and land navigation, especially in wilderness regions.

Thematic maps: A number of different map types can be grouped under this heading. Remember that each one expresses a particular subject and does not show land forms for other features. The theme could be something like a dot-density map showing the distribution of population within a country. It could also be very complex, showing multiple related subjects, such as a weather map that shows temperature contour lines (**isotherms**), wind patterns, pressure zones, and areas of precipitation. Here are a few common types of thematic maps:

- **Chloropleth maps** express the geographic variability of a particular theme using color variations. These variations can be expressed using colorized symbols, contour areas filled with different colors, or polygons denoting country boundaries filled with different colors to express the variability in the map data.

- **Isoline maps** calculate data values between points across a variable surface. Between point A (with a value of 5) and point B (with a value of 10), a series of contour lines can be drawn to show the change in data between the two points. If the value of each contour line is 1, then we would see four contour lines between point A and point B labeled 5, 6, 7, 8, 9, and 10. Point A would sit inside of the contour line labeled 5, and point B would fall within the area for contour line labeled 10. Each point is then interpolated with the other nearby or neighboring points to create a continuous surface of isoline contours. Weather maps showing temperature contours (isotherms) are the most common isoline maps.

- **Dot density maps** use dots to express the volume and density of a particular geographic feature. The dots can represent the number of people in an area, or can express the number of events or phenomena that occurred in an area. An example would be dots representing the number of people who suffer heart attacks on a state-by-state basis. Each state would have a number of dots inside of its boundary polygon representing the number of heart attacks. Oftentimes, each dot represents a certain number of events; in our example, the map might read, "one dot equals 1,000 heart attacks."

- **Flow-line maps** use lines of varying thickness to show the direction and volume of a particular geographic movement pattern. An example would be a map of flow lines showing the total number of foreign immigrants in the United States. Each line would begin in the immigrants' country of origin and point to the United States, with a thickness based upon the total number of immigrants. In this example, a thin line would be drawn from Portugal to the United States and a much thicker line would be drawn from Ireland to the United States.
- **Cartograms** use simplified geometries to represent real-world places. Political boundaries become polygons, and linear features such as roads become lines with basic angles often at 90° and 135°. Cartograms are more about the data being expressed than they are about landscape. Linear cartograms are often used in subway systems and other transportation maps where the exact geography of the route is less important than the items along the way.

What is a Mental Map?

Everyone has a mental map. It's the cognitive image of landscape in the human mind. What is common about each person's mental map is that we have very accurate geographies of the area around our home, school, and workplace. We also have very good knowledge of the landscape along the transportation corridors that we commonly travel. Elsewhere, our mental maps tends to be pretty much blank. By understanding the science behind location, distance, scale, and different map types, you can improve your mental map from the data that you read on both paper and computerized maps.

Map Scale

As we said earlier in the chapter, there are two different types of geographic scale: map scale and relative scale. Map scale is the "absolute" form of the scale concept. Map scales can be expressed in a couple of ways. Linear map scale expresses distance on the map surface. It can either be found in the legend or in a corner of the map, like so:

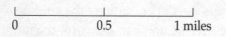

The ratio scale of the math will also be expressed on the map legend. This shows the mathematical relationship between the distance on the map compared to the real distance on the earth's surface. It will appear as a 1 separated by a colon from a much larger number, like so:

$$1:24,000$$

In this case, 1 inch on the map equals 24,000 inches on the earth's surface, or about two-thirds of a mile. This is the map scale used on topographic maps produced by the United States Geological Survey (USGS). This map scale can also be expressed as the mathematical ratio $\frac{1}{24,000}$.

A large-scale map is one with a ratio that is a comparatively large real number. A small-scale map is one with a ratio that is a comparatively very small real number. Consider the amount of area and level of detail expressed depending upon the type of map scale. Compare the following two map scales and ratios in terms of their size in real numbers to understand which one is the large-scale map and which one is the small-scale map, as well as what purpose each would serve:

Map Scale:	1:50,000	1:1,000,000
Ratio:	$\frac{1}{50,000}$	$\frac{1}{1,000,000}$
Scale Type:	Large Scale	Small Scale
Area Covered:	Small Area	Large Area
Level of Detail:	High Detail	Low Detail
Purpose:	City	State or Province

Although there is no agreed-upon convention as to a dividing line between large- and small-scale maps, think of 1:250,000 as the break point.

Projections

There probably won't be a question that asks you to differentiate between the projections on the AP Human Geography Exam, but they could ask you about the practical issues behind certain projections. Each given projection creates different levels of accuracy in terms of size and shape distortion for different parts of the earth. A map projection's level of accuracy is based upon two concepts: area preservation and shape preservation.

Equal-area projections attempt to maintain the relative spatial science and the areas on the map. However, these can distort the actual shape of polygons, such as the **Lambert projection** bending and squishing the northern Canadian islands to keep them at the same map scale as southern Canada on a flat sheet of paper.

Conformal projections attempt to maintain the shape of polygons on the map. The downside is that conformal projections can distort the relative area from one part of the map to the other. For instance, in the commonly used **Mercator projection**, the shape of Greenland is preserved, but it appears to be much larger than South America, when in reality it is much smaller.

Some map projections try to balance area and form, sacrificing a bit of both to create a more visually practical representation of the earth's surface. Examples would be the **Robinson projection** or the **Goode's homolosine projection**.

MODELS

WHAT ARE MODELS?

Unlike a map, a **model** is an abstract generalization of real-world geographies that share a common pattern. **Spatial models** attempt to show the commonalities in pattern among similar landscapes. For instance, **urban models** try to show how different cities have similar spatial relationships and economic or social structures. There are also some **non-spatial models**. The **demographic transition model**, for instance, uses population data to construct a general model of the dynamic growth in national scale populations without reference to space.

WHY DO WE USE THEM?

Despite being abstract generalizations, models give us a way to picture geographical patterns that are not normally visible to the human eye. These patterns are rarely evident on topographic or road maps. Models also allow us to address certain theoretical questions. For instance, the **concentric zone model** can be modified to create a graph showing the cost to distance relationship in urban real estate prices. The resulting **bid-rent curve** explains why land prices are relatively low in suburban areas, but exponentially higher in the central business district (CBD). See Chapter 9 for a detailed explanation of the bid-rent curve.

MODELS TO KNOW

Models are one part of the AP Human Geography Exam that students have significant difficulty with. There are several that you have to be prepared to explain in detail. Here is a list of where to find each of the major models and theories on the exam in this book:

Population Models: Chapter 4
Demographic transition model
Malthusian theory
Population pyramids

Agriculture Models: Chapter 7
Von Thünen's model of the Isolated State

Urban Models: Chapter 9
Central place theory
Concentric zone model
Sector model
Multiple-nuclei model
Galactic city model
Latin American city model

These are all detailed in the corresponding chapter's Know The Models section. Make sure to note the name of who developed the model and what historical context the model, or part of the model, represents.

THE GRAVITY MODEL: A CENTRAL MODEL IN GEOGRAPHY

The **gravity model** is a mathematical model that is used in a number of different types of spatial analysis. Gravity models are used to calculate transportation flow between two points, determine the area of influence of a city's businesses, and estimate the flow of migrants to a particular place. To do this, a gravity model multiplies the quantitative size of two places and divides that by the distance between them, squared. Here's a brief Know the Math moment to show you the formulaic definition:

$$\frac{\text{Location}_1 \text{ Population} \times \text{Location}_2 \text{ Population}}{\text{Distance}^2}$$

The result gives you a relative score that rates the gravity, or in other words, the pull or strength of the relationship between two places. In the following basic example we compare the potential business relationship of New York City (NYC) between London and Tokyo, which would estimate the comparative likelihood of business interactions:

NYC Population:	19,598,491 (metropolitan areas)
London Population:	13,614,409
Tokyo Population:	35,676,000

NYC to London Distance:	3,470 miles	Squared: 12,040,900
NYC to Tokyo Distance:	6,760 miles	Squared: 45,697,600

Gravity of NYC and London	$\dfrac{19,598,491 \times 13,614,409}{12,040,900}$	= 22,159,629
Gravity of NYC and Tokyo	$\dfrac{19,598,491 \times 35,676,000}{45,697,600}$	= 15,300,492

Despite the vastly greater distance from NYC to Tokyo, the gravity model score of that relationship is not much smaller than NYC and London's. This can help explain, for example, why there are very close relationships between financial investors in NYC and Tokyo, just as there are from NYC with London, Frankfurt, and Zurich. Or this can help explain the higher than expected amount of air travel between Tokyo and NYC compared to NYC to London.

GEOGRAPHIC TECHNOLOGY

GEOGRAPHIC INFORMATION SYSTEMS (GIS)

Geographic Information Systems (GIS) became practical with the onset of the desktop computer in the 1970s. GIS incorporate one or more **data layers** in a computer program capable of spatial analysis and mapping. Data layers are numerical, coded, or textual data that is attributed to specific geographic coordinates or areas. As all data is geographically fixed to specific locations, data between layers can be analyzed spatially. Each layer can show a different type of geographic feature.

Examples of GIS Usage

The **spatial analysis** capabilities of GIS are shown in the following example. Utah Valley University students used GIS for a 2005 analysis of the relationship between personal wealth and earthquake danger in Provo, Utah. One data layer quantified housing values, while other layers were coded for variable degrees of earthquake hazards based upon ground shaking potential, landslide potential, and soil liquefaction potential. In these layers each part of the city was coded for low, moderate, or severe damage.

The analysis showed that the largest category of homes in the city were at risk for the most severe damage (soil liquefaction is when sandy or sedimentary soils liquefy during a large earthquake). These neighborhoods were almost all middle-class housing zones. Thus, the analysis showed that the city's average-wealth homeowners, as a group, were at greatest risk during a large earthquake.

Another important example of GIS's benefit to society is 911 emergency phone systems. When you call 911 from a land line, your phone number is checked in a GIS database to automatically bring up your address. If you call from a cell phone, your phone location can be triangulated using three or more cell towers.

Data about your home are also stored in the 911 database. If you call to report a house fire, data regarding the type of heating (gas, propane, heating oil, or electric) used in your home are available to first responders. Some cities keep data on the number of elderly, disabled, or persons requiring oxygen in a residence in the case of rescue emergencies. This GIS data can save the lives of firefighters and residents alike.

Mapping using GIS has made the art and science of hand-drawn cartography an endangered species of sorts. GIS is used in a multitude of paper, computerized, and online mapping systems. In-car navigation systems are one of the most popular uses of GIS combined with Global Positioning System (GPS) data.

Global Positioning System (GPS)

"Turn right 500 feet" is a common phrase heard in American automobiles today. This is not coming from a person. Instead, this is a vocal cue from the in-car GPS system regarding the next turn toward your destination. In-car GPS systems are demonstrably popular around the world; more than half of all smart phones have the Google Maps app.

The **Global Positioning System (GPS)** utilizes a worldwide network of satellites, which emit a measurable radio signal. When this signal is available from three or more **Navstar satellites**, a GPS receiver is able to triangulate a coordinate location and display map data for the user. In addition, there are handheld GPS units for outdoor sporting use, GPS units on delivery trucks and emergency vehicles that notify supervisors of their location, and units that land surveyors use to locate property lines, find buried utility lines, and accurately lay out new construction sites.

Remote Sensing

Aerial photography and **satellite-based remote sensing** make up a large amount of the geographic and GIS data used today. Aerial photographs had been used for mapping since the mid-1800s. Like GIS, space-borne remote-sensing satellites became available in the 1970s. The difference between aerial photographs and remotely sensed imagery is in the recording media. Aerial photographs are just that; images of the earth from an aircraft, printed on film, but digital camera usage is on the increase. Instead of a camera, remote-sensing satellites use a computerized scanner to record data from the earth's surface. These data include not only visual light wavelengths, but also infrared and radar information.

Examples of Remote Sensing

Large-scale aerial photographs are commonly used by local governments to record property data and set tax assessments. Aerial photographs can also be used to revise topographic map data without having to send out a survey team to update old maps.

Remote sensing is currently used to monitor the loss of wetlands and barrier islands on the Gulf Coast of Louisiana. Each year, satellite data are collected and compared with GIS to show the areas and patterns of wetland and beach loss. This analysis is used by engineers and environmental planners to develop wetland and beach restoration projects.

Infrared satellite imagery is commonly used to determine the health of vegetation on the earth's surface. These data can be analyzed in a GIS to create crop yield predictions of agricultural harvests. The results are then used by commodity traders to set prices for staple food crops such as corn, wheat, and soybeans. These predictions keep food prices relatively stable over the long-term. Without satellite data, basic foodstuffs such as milk, bread, and cereal could be subject to wild price swings due to uncertainty in the national supply of cattle feed.

GEOGRAPHERS TO KNOW

In the remaining chapters of this book we will mention a number of geographers and allied scientists who have contributed significant research over the last 230 years. There have been examples of questions on the AP Human Geography Exam where you must be able to associate a geographer with a particular concept, theory, or model. Here's a short list.

Name:	Known For:	Page:
Ernest Burgess	Concentric zone model	270
Walter Christaller	Central place theory	266
William Denevan	Native American depopulation	168
Larry Ford and Ernst Griffin	Latin American city model	277
Homer Hoyt	Sector model	273
Thomas Malthus	Malthusian theory	114
Friedrich Ratzel	*Anthropogeographie*, father of human geography	163
Walt Rostow	Stages of growth	249
Carl Sauer	Possiblism, cultural landscape	163
Johann von Thünen	Isolated State model	230
Alfred Weber	Industrial location theory	253

KEY TERMS

space
spatial
place
toponym
regions
sequent occupancy
place-specific
scale
map scale
relative scale (scale of analysis)
level of aggregation
formal region
functional region
vernacular region
homogeneous characteristic
uniformity

linguistic region
regional boundaries
culture regions
political regions
environmental region
bioregions (biomes)
ecotone
nodal regions
central place (node)
market area
distance decay
area of influence
intervening opportunity
vernacular region
mental map
absolute location

relative location
latitude
longitude
notation
decimal degrees
equator
North Pole
South Pole
Prime Meridian
International Date Line
Royal Naval Observatory
site
situation
distance
absolute distance
distance decay
relative distance
Tobler's law
friction of distance
space-time compression
central places
central place theory
core and periphery
central business district (CBD)
cluster
growth pole
agglomeration
random pattern
scattered pattern
linear pattern
sinuous pattern
land survey patterns
metes and bounds
township and range
long-shot patterns
arithmetic density
agricultural density

physiologic density
Malthusian theory
diffusion patterns
expansion diffusion
hierarchical diffusion
relocation diffusion
contagious diffusion
stimulus diffusion
topographic maps
thematic maps
isotherms
chloropleth maps
isoline maps
dot density maps
flow-line maps
cartograms
equal-area projections
Lambert projection
conformal projections
Mercator projection
Robinson projection
Goode's homolosine projection
model
spatial model
urban model
non-spatial model
demographic transition model
concentric zone model
bid-rent curve
gravity model
Geographic Information Systems (GIS)
data layers
spatial analysis
Global Positioning System (GPS)
Navstar satellites
aerial photography
satellite-based remote sensing

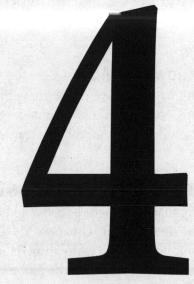

POPULATION AND MIGRATION

CHAPTER OUTLINE

This chapter is intended to help you better understand the dynamics, growth, and change of populations. First, we'll go over some basic math tools to help you recall many of the complicated statistics and numerical indicators. After that, we'll apply these concepts to the significant models in population geography. Then we'll review several related concepts that show up frequently on the exam, and we'll finish up with key terms.

KNOW THE MATH

In this section we're not going to drop a ton of math on you; instead, we'll give you a few helpful tips you need to know to understand how population changes occur. The concepts presented here use the math you probably learned in fourth grade. You can handle it.

BASIC POPULATION STATISTICS

Population growth is understood through the concepts of the **rate of natural increase (RNI)** and the **demographic equation**. The demographic equation uses **birth rates** and **death rates** along with **immigration** and **emigration** statistics to show **population growth** or change. Over the next few pages we walk you through the process of how population growth is calculated.

THE BIRTH RATE

The **crude birth rate (CBR)** or just the birth rate, as we will call it here, is an **annual statistic**. The total number of infants born living is counted for one calendar year and then calculated. This figure is then divided by the population divided by one thousand, or "every thousand members of the population," as it is often presented. Why? By standardizing the denominator (the lower number in the ratio), the resulting quotient will be a small integer number, such as 32 or 14. This makes the data much easier to work with.

The Birth Rate Formula

$$\frac{\text{Number of Live Births}}{\text{Total Population}} \times 1{,}000$$

Estimate and Simplify

So if you have a country with 100,000 live births in a year and a population of 5,000,000, the birth rate is 20; more precisely 20 live births for every 1,000 members of the population. To make this easier, 5,000,000 divided by 1,000 is 5,000. Knock the 3 zeros off the end of 1,000 and the end of 5,000,000 and you have a simplified ration of 5,000/1 or just 5,000. Do the same with 100,000 over the 5,000. Knock off the three zeros of each and you have 100/5 or 20.

What Does the Birth Rate Tell You?

Birth rate is just one piece of the larger demographic picture. When you examine the section on demographic transition later in this chapter you'll find that high birth rates (18 to 50) are found in mostly rural agricultural Third World countries and that low birth rates (8 to 17) are more likely to be found in urbanized industrial and service-based economies. However, without knowing what's going on with mortality in that country (death rate), it's hard to know whether the population is growing and how quickly if it is.

THE DEATH RATE

Okay, it sounds scary. Death is an emotional issue. What you need to do here is to think scientifically about these statistics. The crude death rate or CDR, or what we'll simply call the **death rate** is an annual statistic calculated in the same way. The number of deaths are counted for the calendar year in a country and divided by every thousand members of the population (or population/1,000).

The Death Rate Formula

$$\frac{\text{Number of Deaths}}{\text{Total Population}} \times 1,000$$

What Does the Death Rate Tell You?

Well, not much in today's world. High death rates usually indicate a country that is experiencing war, disease, or famine. Historically, higher death rates (20 to 50) were recorded in the poorest of Third World countries where the combination of poverty, poor nutrition, epidemic disease, and a lack of medical care resulted in low **life expectancy**. However, as conditions have improved in the Third World through the **Green Revolution** (increased food and nutrition) and access to sanitation, education and health care have increased, life expectancies have gone up, and the death rate has gone down. See more on mortality in the section on stage one, starting on page 103.

THE RATE OF NATURAL INCREASE

By comparing the birth rate and death rate for a country, we can calculate the rate of natural increase (RNI), sometimes referred to as the **natural increase rate (NIR).** We'll call it the RNI from here on. Simply put, if you subtract the death rate from the birth rate, the difference is the amount of population change per thousand members of the population for that year. But you are not done yet. Divide the result by 10 and then you will have the RNI. The RNI is also the annual percentage of population growth of that country for that one-year period. Make sure to put a % sign after you get the answer to the equation.

Formula for The Rate of Natural Increase (RNI)

$$\frac{\text{Birth Rate} - \text{Death Rate}}{10}$$

The Simple Math

Let's take an example. If a country has a birth rate of 27 and a death rate of 12, then the RNI equals 1.5 percent. If that country had 10,000,000 people the previous year, then the population this year would total 10,150,000. The added 150,000 people are 1.5 percent of the previous 10,000,000. We can check our work to see if the birth rate and death rate concur with the math. In this country the birth rate would be calculated as such: 270,000 infants born divided by $\frac{10,000,000}{1,000}$ or $\frac{270,000}{10,000} =$ 27; the death rate would be 120,000 deaths divided by $\frac{10,000,000}{1,000}$ or $\frac{120,000}{10,000} = 12$. Think about it: 270,000 − 120,000 = 150,000 new people added to the country's population.

The Negative RNI: Is It Possible?

In a couple of situations, it is possible to have a negative RNI. Mathematically, the death rate can be larger than the birth rate, resulting in a negative number that is divided by 10 to get the negative RNI. When the RNI is negative, it means the population has shrunk during the year the data was collected.

Shrinkage!?!

One explanation for a negative RNI are First World countries that are highly urbanized and where the roles of women in the country have become such that the traditional positions of mother and homemaker have deteriorated significantly. In these places, the status of women in society has become *increasingly* equal to that of men (not quite there, yet). When the majority of women are heavily engaged in business, political activity, and urban social networks, they are far less likely to have children (reduced **fecundity**), and phenomena such as **double-income no-kid (DINK)** households and single parent–single child homes are far more common. Higher rates of divorce are another sign.

Germany is a prime example where the already low birth rates have dipped below death rates and as a result the RNI has ranged between –0.1 percent and –0.2 percent, annually. For more examples, look at the stage one and stage four parts of the Demographic Transition model in this chapter.

Why "Natural" Increase?

An important thing to keep in mind regarding the rate of natural increase is that it does not account for immigration or emigration. A country with a high rate of natural increase can have an unexpectedly low long-term population prediction if there is a large amount of emigration. Conversely, a country with a low rate of natural increase can still grow significantly over time if the amount of immigrants is high. Data shows that migrant populations also have much higher fertility rates than the general population in the country. Therefore, in places such as the United States, population growth is not necessarily from the immigrants themselves crossing the border, but the fact that they will have large numbers of children once they have settled.

DOUBLING TIME

We can try to quickly estimate how long it would take for a country to double in size by this formula:

$$\text{Formula for Doubling Time}$$

$$\frac{70}{\text{Rate of Natural Increase}}$$

Using Bolivia as an example, an RNI of 1.9 percent would result in a doubling time of 36.8 years. That's fast, but unless something changes significantly in Bolivian society, we expect the 10 million people of today to grow to 20 million by 2050. But it won't. Why not? There is negative net migration in Bolivia. Out-migration to other countries reduces the long-term prediction to around 17 million by 2050. This is why we call the RNI an estimate.

The more accurate way would be to estimate the RNI for each year in the future by examining a country's position on the Demographic Transition Model. Then you would multiply each year's population by the RNI and add that to the next year's growth, and so on, and so on:

$$(\text{Pop.} \times \text{RNI}_1) \times \text{RNI}_2 \times \text{RNI}_3 \dots \times \text{RNI}_n = \text{Future Population.}$$

This is the same method used to estimate the value of a currency multiplied by annual inflation rates to find the real dollar value over time.

ADD MIGRATION AND VOILÀ! THE DEMOGRAPHIC EQUATION

The last part of the demographic equation to calculate population growth is factoring in migration. Using annual birth rates and death rates to calculate the natural increase in overall population (note that we're not talking about the "rate" of natural increase here, just the total number of people) we can add the balance to the **net migration rate**. This is the number of immigrants minus the number of emigrants for every thousand members of the population. Here is the formulaic way to calculate the net migration rate:

The Net Migration Rate Formula

$$\frac{\text{Number of Immigrants}}{\text{Population} \div 1{,}000} - \frac{\text{Number of Emigrants}}{\text{Population} \div 1{,}000}$$

Take this and add it to the birth rate minus the death rate and you will have total population growth per thousand members of the population. And, you have your demographic equation, like so:

The Demographic Equation

$$\frac{(\text{Birth Rate} - \text{Death Rate}) + \text{Net Migration Rate}}{10} = \text{Percentage Rate}$$

Take the United States as an example. The United States has a birth rate of 13 and a death rate of 8. Add the product to a net migration rate of 2.45 and we find that the United States adds about 7.5 people for every thousand in the population, annually. Divide by 10 to find that the population growth rate (including immigration) is 0.75 percent annually.

Shrinkage, Again!?!

Net migration rates can be negative. Guyana in South America has net emigration to such a degree that population is expected to fall over the long-term. Currently, Guyana's birth rate is 16 and the death rate is 7. Adding to the net migration rate of –13 (that is, by subtracting 13), we find that the population growth is negative 1 per thousand or 0.1 percent.

THE TOTAL FERTILITY RATE

By definition the **total fertility rate (TFR)** is the estimated average number of children born to each female of birthing age (15 to 45).

We can still use a basic formulaic definition to help remember TFR:

> ### Total Fertility Rate Formula
>
> $$\frac{\text{Number of Children Born}}{\text{Women Aged 15 to 45}}$$

However, the TFR *is not an annual statistic* like the RNI. It is more of an estimate, taken as a snapshot of fertility for birth over the prior 30 years. Thus, TFR and RNI are not comparable. They are two different things—apples and oranges. You cannot have a negative TFR, for one thing. TFR highlights the importance of replacement in the population.

THE REPLACEMENT RATE

By definition the replacement rate is a TFR of 2.1. Think about this in basic biological terms. If a mating pair has two offspring, they have replaced themselves. What about the remaining 0.1, you ask? This is what would be referred to as an error factor. We have to estimate that some small portion of the population will die before they reach adulthood—diseases and accidents do happen.

Thus, to truly replace itself, a large population must have 2.1 children per female of birthing age.

HOW TO REMEMBER RNI

When a country hits a TFR of 2.1 (the replacement rate) you've hit the brakes on the car and the speed of population growth slows down. It's not until the RNI hits 0 that the car comes to a complete halt and population stops growing altogether. The RNI can go negative and the car rolls backward, shrinking population as you fumble to find the emergency brake.

KNOW THE MODELS

THE DEMOGRAPHIC TRANSITION MODEL

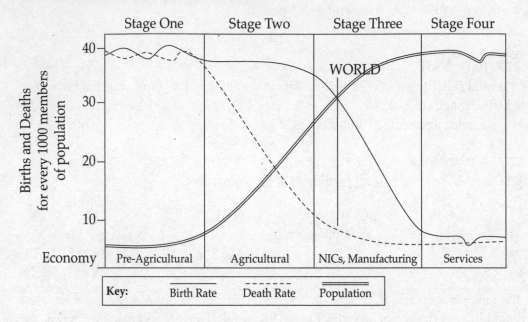

The **Demographic Transition Model** has a number of uses. You should think of it as a central unifying concept in your understanding of the AP Human Geography course. Not only is it a theory of how population changes over time, but it also provides important insights into issues of migration, fertility, economic development, industrialization, urbanization, labor, politics, and the roles of women.

By placing a country on the model, you are defining the **population dynamics** and **economic context** of that country. Knowing where a country falls on the model lets you know what kind of economy the country has, whether or not there is significant migration going on, and, like economic indicators, this "picture" of a country's population can tell you much about its quality of life. These are theoretical estimates and averages, and not all countries fit the model perfectly. The lines shown are approximate and not always representative of every country's birth and death statistics.

The Crystal Ball

The model also has a **predictive capability**. If a country currently falls within stage two of the transition, we can use this model to predict how its population will change over time and speculate as to how much it can grow in size. Likewise, you can also look at the whole world, which falls into early stage three. Knowing this, we can estimate a **population projection** that the planet's population has reached only about two-thirds of its potential. If the planet is currently at about 7.2 billion people, then we can expect that once global populations level off in stage four, global population will be somewhere around 10 billion people. This may happen sometime around 2060—in your lifetime.

And a Look into the Past

The model also provides insight into economic history. If we look at the United States, Canada, or Western Europe, we can apply dates to the bottom of the model to show how stage four countries have progressed through the system. Looking at the model below, we can see in Western Europe the beginning of the Renaissance; in Western Europe and in the United States and Canada, the **Industrial Revolution**; and likewise the recent **deindustrialization** or shift to **service-based economies**.

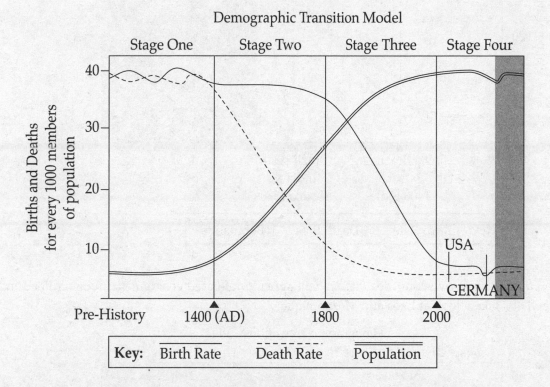

Demographic Transition Model

Pre-history goes all the way back to human beginnings. Fourteen hundred represents the time when there was both a cultural and economic renaissance in Europe. Eighteen hundred represents the industrial revolution, when countries like the United States and Great Britain were **newly industrialized countries (NICs)**. And 2000 represents a turning point of the rise of service-based economies of **more developed countries (MDCs)**. The typical MDC has a birth rate of 11 and a death rate of 10, or very little growth.

The NICs

Countries that are not as demographically or economically advanced can also be placed on the model, but you have to change the dates as to when they reach the significant turning point in their history. If we look at newly industrialized countries (NICs) such as Brazil, Mexico, and India, we can see a much more recent turning point from the **agricultural economy** of stage two to the **manufacturing-based economy** of stage three. Remember: This is a theoretical model and not all countries fit the trend. For example, China, due to its one-child policy, appears far more advanced than it should be, compared economically to other NICs. On the following page the NICs are shown in the model.

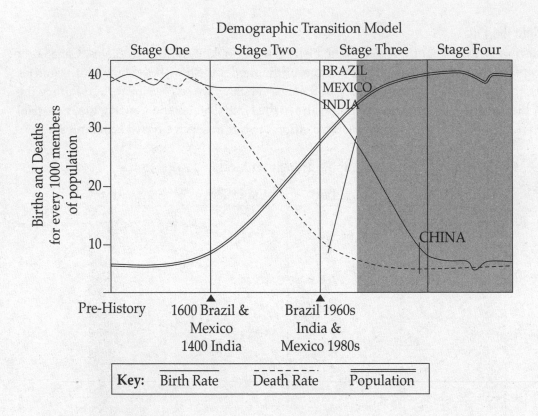

Demographic Transition Model

Even non-NIC stage two countries that are still agricultural-based economies can be outlined in the model. Let's take a look at Laos and Mozambique:

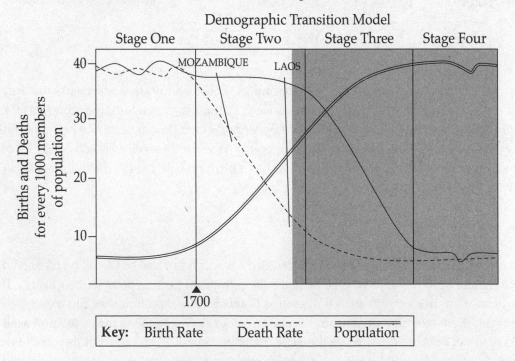

Demographic Transition Model

These stage two agricultural economies still have a lot of population growth ahead. Expect these countries to also have more rural to urban migration in the long-term.

The S-Curve of Population

You've probably noticed that the population line in the model has a distinct shape to it until stage four. This is what demographers (population scientists) and population biologists call the S-curve. Humans are not the only ones whose population follows such a pattern. In fact, give any animal population a vast amount of food or remove predators from their habitat and you will see rapid population growth followed by a plateau or decline due to a population reaching or exceeding the area's **carrying capacity.** Globally, humans may be doing the same thing and, as we mentioned before, the human population may reach **equilibrium** in the global habitat. Find out more when we talk about carrying capacity in the Know the Concepts part of this chapter.

STAGE BY STAGE

The best way to learn the model is not to memorize it, but to know *why* the birth rate and death rate and, as a result, population change over time. In this next part we examine the factors that affect population in each stage of the transition.

STAGE ONE

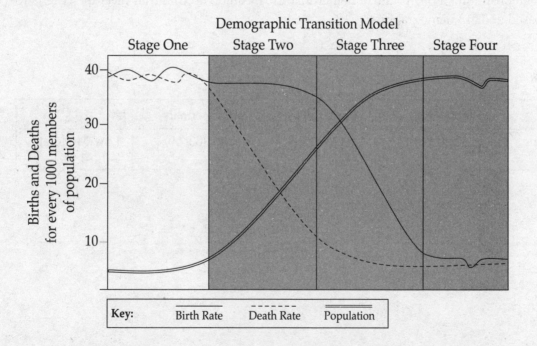

Historically, stage one was characterized by pre-agricultural societies engaged in **subsistence farming** and **transhumance**, that is, the seasonal migration for food and resources or owning livestock. Birth rates and death rates fluctuate as the result of factors such as climate, warfare, disease, and ecological factors, but overall both rates are high. The result is that there is little population growth until the later part of stage one when death rates begin to decline. Thus, the RNI is generally low (and can be negative in some cases), especially during disease epidemics.

Lots of Babies; Lots of Dead Folks, Too

Birth rates are high for a number of reasons. Children were an expression of a family's productivity and status. The more kids a family had, the more work that could be done raising crops, hunting, gathering, herding, or laboring in the **feudal political economy** as domestic servants or soldiers. **Child mortality** and **infant mortality** were also very high, which motivated parents to have a few extra children with the expectation that one or two would not live to adulthood.

Likewise, death rates are high for a multitude of reasons. In stage one the overall population has a very low **life expectancy.** The lack of modern medicine and health care, limited sanitation, low nutritional standards, and the effects of hazards such as famine and war all contribute to high death rates and low life expectancy. Hard physical labor and long migrations also had the effect of physically wearing down the body and thus decreasing lifespan.

Stage One Today?

Are there any stage one countries in existence today? Occasionally, yes. Typically we see that Third World countries engaged in long periods of warfare have late stage one characteristics. When they are peaceful, Third World agricultural countries generally have stage two birth rates and death rates. The AIDS epidemic in Southern African countries has historically created stage one demographic conditions and likewise harmed the economic development of the region. As of this printing, however, no country is demonstrating a death rate of higher than 20, meaning no countries meet the criteria for stage one based on 2013 demographics.

Let's Review

	Birth Rates	Death Rates	Life Expectancy	RNI
Stage One	High (25–50)	High (25–40)	Low (33–50)	Low-Moderate (–0.1–1.9%)

STAGE TWO

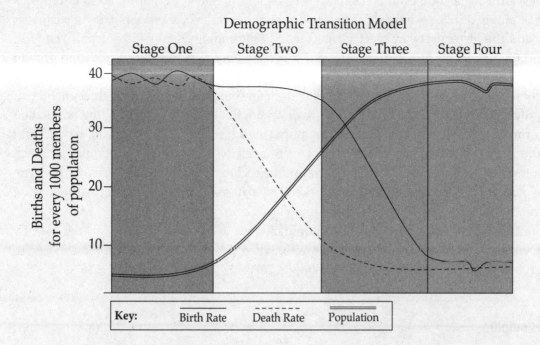

Demographic Transition Model

Stage One   Stage Two   Stage Three   Stage Four

Births and Deaths for every 1000 members of population

40

30

20

10

Key: Birth Rate — — — Death Rate ══ Population

Stage two countries are typically agricultural-based economies. In this economic context, where agriculture for trade (as opposed to subsistence) is the focus of the economy, birth rates remain high while death rates decline over time. As a result, the rate of natural increase (RNI) goes up significantly as birth rates and death rates diverge. Therefore, as a country advances, population growth explodes. This is why rapid population growth has been a concern when examining the quality of life in Third World countries. Life expectancy increases as the death rate declines, but is still low compared to the First World.

Babies Are Us

Birth rates remain high as stage two countries develop in a more organized fashion around a formalized agricultural economy. Compared to stage one, children are even more important as a source of labor on farms. Infant and child mortality is still an issue due to a lack of medical care and poor nutrition for expectant mothers and infants. The vast majority of populations in stage two countries live in rural regions as a result of agriculture's economic prominence. Most cities in these countries are far from reaching their population growth potential.

Not Dead Yet!

Death rates decrease due to a number of factors. Populations engaging in the expanded agricultural economy tend to permanently settle in farming areas, and seasonal migrations become far less common. This, along with improved farming methods and the domestication of draft animals, reduces the incidence of death from excessive labor and travel by foot. Likewise, the expanded trade in agricultural goods means there is a larger and more varied food supply available to the general population. This relative increase in food volume, year-round availability, and nutrient quality means that people live longer.

The Stage Twos

Ghana in West Africa is a good example. It has a very high birth rate at 32, but in recent decades its death rate has plunged to 8. As a result, the rate of natural increase is 2.4 percent growth each year (very high), and the life expectancy has increased to 65. An example from Asia is Nepal. The birth rate is 22 and the death rate is 7, with an RNI of 1.5 percent annual percentage population growth and a life expectancy of 67.

Both of these countries focus on agriculture as their main source of economic production. Statistically, this is revealed by examining the rates of urbanization. In Ghana 48 percent of the population still lives in rural areas. Historically, much of the population has been focused on the coastal port region around the capital, Accra, a primate city. (A primate city is a city with a population much larger than others in the same country or the surrounding region. More information about them can be found in Chapter 9: Urban Geography.) Landlocked Nepal has an even starker lack of urbanization with 83 percent of the population living in rural regions of the country.

These countries are expected to experience a population explosion over the next few decades. By 2050 Ghana, currently at 24 million, is expected to more than double in size to 48 million. Likewise, Nepal, which has 27 million, should reach 49 million in 2050.

Review and Compare

	Birth Rates	Death Rates	Life Expectancy	RNI
Stage One	High (25–50)	High (25–40)	Low (33–50)	Low-Moderate (–0.1–1.9%)
Stage Two	High (25–50)	Decreasing (8–25)	Increasing (<70)	Highest (1.5–3.5%)

HEY! MY TEXTBOOK USES DIFFERENT NAMES

Different human geography textbooks use different terms to describe the stages of the model. Some call the stages "phases." Don't be concerned; they're the same thing. Also, some might refer to stage one as pre-agrarian instead of pre-agricultural, or to stages two and three as "transitional." The names we use here relate the model to economic factors far better than general terms like "transitional."

STAGE TWO AND A HALF-ISH: NEWLY INDUSTRIALIZED COUNTRIES

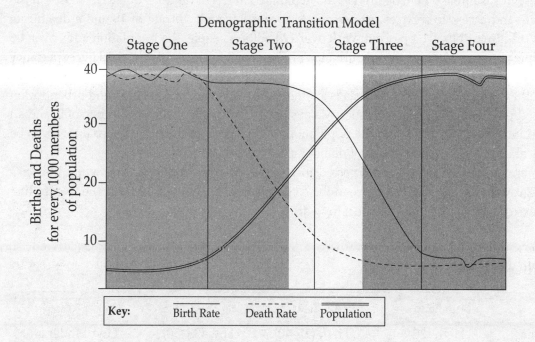

Demographic Transition Model

The NIC countries are characterized by economies that are transitioning their focus away from agriculture to manufacturing as the primary form of economic production and employment. This has two distinct effects on the population. One is that there is rapid population growth in NIC countries. Looking at the model, you can see that it's in this range between stages two and three where birth and death rates are furthest apart, resulting in high RNIs.

The second effect, which is not shown on the model, is the rapidly increasing rate of urbanization. As these countries shift to manufacturing, more factories are being built in urban areas. Migrants responding to the **pull factor** of employment opportunity rapidly fill the cities to take new and better-paying jobs than those available in rural regions.

Who Has the Time Anymore?

Birth rates begin to decline with urbanization. As families move to cities they find (in comparison to the rural agricultural lifestyle) that they have less time, less need, and moreover, less space for children. Most countries forbid child labor (it still happens, even in countries where it's illegal) and thus children in cities are less likely to be seen as a source of labor.

Getting Better All the Time

Death rates continue to decline as more urban societies have greater access to food markets, increased (but limited) access to health care and sanitation, reduced physical labor (factories compared to farming and mining), and increased education.

Around the Planet

Mexico is an NIC example where death rates have plunged in recent decades due to increases in the quality of life and access to services. At present, Mexicans have a birth rate of 19 and a death rate of 5, with a resulting RNI of 1.4 percent. With over 120 million people, the population adds over 1.6 million people per year. Mexico is mostly urban, with 78 percent in cities, and the total life expectancy has risen to 75 years old.

On the other side of the world, Malaysia is another NIC where industrialization and urbanization have changed the population characteristics. Malays have a birth rate of 20, a death rate of 5, and an RNI of 1.5. Life expectancy is 75, and the population is 73 percent urbanized. Mexico appears to be just slightly ahead of Malaysia in terms of demographic development.

In long-term growth, Malaysia is expected to increase sharply in population, while Mexico's population growth will slow and stabilize in the coming decades. By the middle of the twenty-first century, Mexico's population may even begin to drop.

Here's the NIC Review

	Birth Rates	Death Rates	Life Expectancy	RNI
Stage One	High (25–50)	High (25–40)	Low (33–50)	Low-Moderate (–0.1–1.9%)
Stage Two	High (25–50)	Decreasing (8–25)	Increasing (<70)	Highest (1.5–3.5%)
NICs	Decreasing (12–30)	Lowering (5–18)	Increasing (<75)	Higher (1.1–2.7%)

STAGE THREE

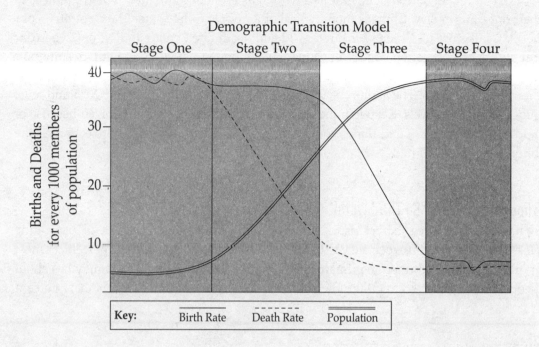

Demographic Transition Model

| Stage One | Stage Two | Stage Three | Stage Four |

Key: ——— Birth Rate   - - - - - Death Rate   ═══ Population

Stage three was historically where most "industrialized" or manufacturing-based countries were found in the transition. However, most of these First World (and many former European Communist Second World) countries have shifted their economies to a more service-based focus. During this time these same countries have completed the transition; that is, completing the S-curve and moving into stage four. Stage three is what we should expect many NICs to look like as they continue to industrialize.

Baby, Please Don't Go

Birth rates continue to decrease as the effects of urbanization (less space, time, and need factors) along with increases in health care, education, and female employment have negative effects on fertility. Access to health care has an important influence on the availability of contraceptives in more urbanized and developed economies. Women's education and employment also result in fewer children due to time constraints and the empowerment that women gain from their school and job experiences.

Pushing Up the Daisies

In stage three, access to health care, nutrition, sanitation, and education continue to increase life expectancy and decrease death rates. However, death rates eventually bottom out. Why? (Here's your existential moment, folks!) We're all worm bait. Everyone is going to die eventually and there is a statistical floor to the death rate—or a statistical base to the death rate. At some point, you just can't stop people from dying. Life expectancies can go up even further in stage four, but the death rate stays about the same.

One Child, No Waiting

China, as an NIC, is more advanced demographically than its economic situation would predict. As a result of their one-child policy, China is more typical of a middle-to-late stage three country, compared to other NICs like Brazil. China's birth rate is 12 and death rate 7, with an RNI of 0.5 percent. The long-term effects of population control in China will continue to slow its growth, despite policies being enforced less often. In fact, China, currently at 1.37 billion people, will likely complete the S-curve in the coming decades. The country is projected to reach 1.45 billion around 2025 and level off, maintaining population levels. Keep in mind that China is only 50 percent urbanized because of Mao's "Back to the Land" policy, and things could change in terms of population projections if the one-child policy is completely lifted.

Long Ago I Thought You Were "So Third World"

Uruguay also has late stage three characteristics with a birth rate of 13 and a death rate of 9, resulting in an RNI of 0.4. The country's life expectancy is 77, and it is extremely urbanized at 92 percent, as most of the country resides in and around the **primate city** of Montevideo. At present, Uruguay has about 3.3 million people and is expected to grow slowly to 3.7 million people by 2050, or about 11 percent.

The Comparisons

	Birth Rates	Death Rates	Life Expectancy	RNI
Stage One	High (25–50)	High (25–40)	Low (33–50)	Low-Moderate (−0.1–1.9%)
Stage Two	High (25–50)	Decreasing (8–25)	Increasing (<70)	Highest (1.5–3.5%)
NICs	Decreasing (12–30)	Lowering (5–18)	Increasing (<75)	Higher (1.1–2.7%)
Stage Three	Lowering (12–20)	Low (5–12)	Higher (<78)	Lowering (0.5–1.2%)

STAGE FOUR

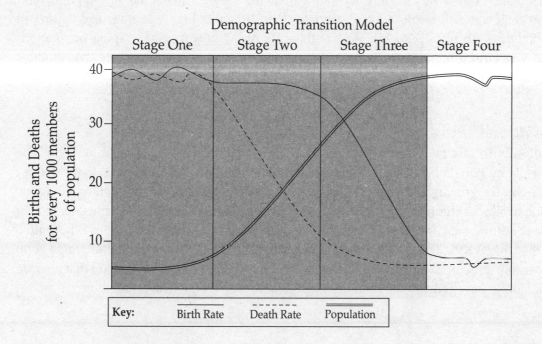

Demographic Transition Model

In stage four, birth and death rates converge to result in limited population growth and even population decline. Here we expect to find First World countries with service-based economies. As we discuss elsewhere, it's okay to think of them as "industrialized" countries, but keep in mind that these are service industries like finance, insurance, real estate, health care, and communications that drive the economy. Manufacturing is a dying breed in these countries. For example, in the United States, services are 80 percent of the **gross domestic product (GDP)** and manufacturing is only 20 percent. These are highly urbanized countries (over 70 percent) possessing the longest life expectancies, with some populations averaging over 80 years.

Gone, Baby, Gone

Birth rates bottom out into the lower teens. Not only is there a high degree of access to medical care, but the roles of women in society are such that most adult women are engaged in the labor force and are empowered politically and socially within the communities. The result is that fecundity is greatly reduced. When birth rates reach the same level of death rates, this is when you have a **zero population growth (ZPG)** and an RNI of 0.0 percent. Birth rates can decline to a point where they're actually lower than death rates. This results in a negative RNI and a shrinking population. Remember shrinkage?

Don't Fear the Reaper

Death rates remain low and vary slightly depending upon the age structure of the overall population. A younger average age will result in low death rates (5 to 10) and a higher average age will result in slightly higher death rates (7 to 14). Most of these countries, however, have aging populations, especially in Western Europe and in Anglo–North America. In these situations, there tends to be a large, over-65, dependent population.

Hockey Fans Wanted!

Canada, with a birth rate of 10 and death rate of 8, grows only around 0.2 percent per year. The population is 34 million, but by 2050 it should be around 42 million. Wait a minute, that's doesn't seem quite right. It's growing slowly, and population growth might hit zero, but you're telling me that it's going to add 8 million people to the population in the next few decades? We must remember that the rate of natural increase does not include migration into the country. Canada, like the United States and the United Kingdom, has positive net migration, and many international migrants go to Canada, especially those from other British Commonwealth countries. Also keep in mind that migrant populations tend to have much higher fertility rates compared to the general population.

Ciao, Baby? Or Just Ciao!

Italy, like Germany, is another example of a Western European country that has experienced negative population growth in recent years. The birth rate in Italy is 9, its death rate 10, and its RNI is –0.1 percent. By 2050 Italy, which currently has 60 million people, will reach about 62 million people due to labor immigration. A number of countries that are near or below zero population growth levels offer incentives to citizens to have more children. One of the reasons for this is that with so few children being born, fewer people enter the workforce over time. Many of these countries have become dependent upon foreign **guest workers**, like the *gastarbeiter* in Germany, many of whom have come from Turkey, North Africa, the Middle East, and more recently, the former Soviet Union.

It's also important to recognize that many former Communist countries of Eastern Europe have stage four demographic characteristics. The factors behind this have recently emerged. It appears that many young workers in Eastern Europe and Russia have emigrated for better paying work opportunities in the West. Despite their recent admission to the European Union, countries like Latvia (RNI –0.4 percent), Lithuania (RNI –0.2 percent), and Hungary (RNI –0.4 percent) have shrinking populations. Some have also pointed to the lingering social effects of Communism on the population in these countries. **Economic restructuring** has brought economic, political, and social hardship to many communities. During the Communist era, people received incentives from the state to have children. With government subsidies gone, many couples don't see any motivation to have a larger family.

Got it? Good!

Well, that was hopefully not too painful. The point here is to understand *why* the model works, as opposed to just memorizing the lines on a graph. Here is a review of the numbers and the complete model one more time, just to give you a last look:

	Birth Rates	Death Rates	Life Expectancy	RNI
Stage One	High (25–50)	High (25–40)	Low (33–50)	Low-Moderate (–0.1–1.9%)
Stage Two	High (25–50)	Decreasing (8–25)	Increasing (<70)	Highest (1.5–3.5%)
NICs	Decreasing (12–30)	Lowering (5–18)	Increasing (<75)	Higher (1.1–2.7%)
Stage Three	Lowering (12–20)	Low (5–12)	Higher (<78)	Lowering (0.5–1.2%)
Stage Four	Low (8–16)	Low (5–12)	Highest (<82)	Low to Negative (0.8 to –0.6%)

AND, THE MODEL ONE LAST TIME

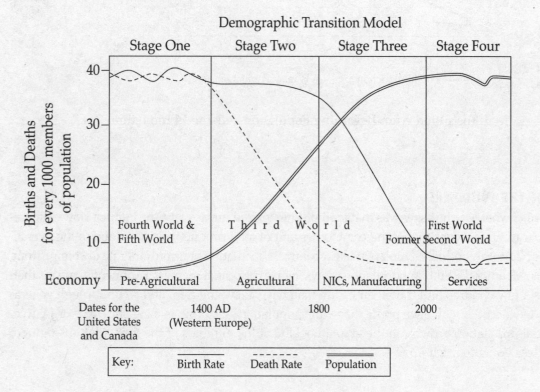

MALTHUSIAN THEORY

Englishman Thomas Malthus published *An Essay on the Principle of Population* in 1798. His main idea was that the global population would one day expand to the point where it could not produce enough food to feed everyone. He predicted this would happen before 1900. The Malthusian catastrophe did not happen by 1900 or even by today, but some more recent thinkers (neo-Malthusians) think it still could in the future.

Why did he have this idea? At the time the math made sense, as the United Kingdom was engaged in the industrial revolution and people were being born at a high rate. If we look at the Demographic Transition Model timeline, Britain was moving from stage two to stage three. Like we see in NICs of today, Malthus saw rapid migration to the cities and a population explosion.

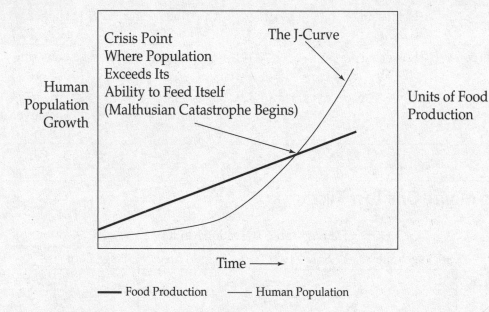

Malthus's Prediction Regarding Population and Food Production

IT WAS IN THE NUMBERS

Mathematically, what Malthus saw was that food production did grow over time but in a slow arithmetic manner. Arithmetic means that each year another unit of food production was added to the overall volume of agricultural products. Think of it like a volume + 1 situation or a constant rate of change from Algebra class. Meanwhile, human population grows in an exponential manner. Exponential means that a couple has a few children and then their children all have a few children, and so on through generations. Every few decades, you have population + the population^2, resulting in a logistic curve or **J-curve** of exponential population growth on the graph. Looking at the numbers of the time, Malthus figured population was going to catch up fast.

WHAT HAPPENED, INSTEAD?

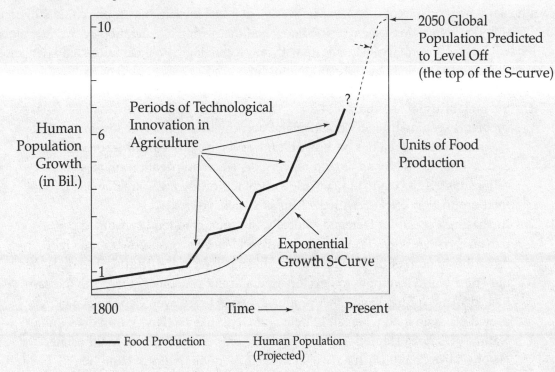

It wasn't that Malthus was wrong, but what he didn't know was that agricultural technology was soon going to boost food production several times over in the coming century. By 1900, massively important inventions such as the internal combustion engine, artificial fertilizers, pesticides, irrigation pumps, advanced plant and animal hybridization techniques, the tin can, and refrigeration were developed. As each of these new products and methods were adopted, another large volume of food would be added to global production and supply. Mathematically, this meant that food production has continued to stay ahead of population growth. For how long this will occur, we don't know. Let's hope that by 2050 or so, when the global population is predicted to level off around 10 billion (completing the top of the S-curve), that the world has food production in good working order.

WHAT ABOUT GENETICS? AVOID THE TRAP!

In the early 1800s, Gregor Mendel was the first to research and write about genes and plant reproduction. However, the science of genetics did not make any impact on global food production until the 1950s and genetically modified foods did not enter markets until the 1980s. If you are asked about why Malthus was wrong, talk about new technologies including plant and animal hybrids, but not genetics, since that affects agriculture only in much more recent years.

NEO-MALTHUSIANS: BE AFRAID, BE VERY AFRAID!

Neo-Malthusians are more recent theorists who warn that a Malthusian catastrophe could still occur. You might think that things don't seem too bad now and that within a generation or two, the global population will level off. Won't we just come up with new technologies to meet future food demands? Three important points are made by the neo-Malthusians:

1. **Sustainability.** When the world does reach 10 billion people, there may be problems keeping up with food demand over the long-term. Already, many major agricultural regions have significant ecological problems like soil erosion and soil nutrient loss and, in arid regions, depletion of irrigation sources and soil salinization. If too many of the world's current growing areas are damaged, can food production keep up with the increased demand?

2. **Increasing *Per Capita* Demand.** Globally, the amount of food consumed per person is rising. Why? The average First World citizen consumes around eight times the amount of food and resources that a person in the Third World does. As the Third World continues to develop economically, consumers there will increase their demand for food and other products several times over. Can the planet provide enough food when all 10 billion of us eat like the First World does today?

3. **Natural Resource Depletion.** Food is not the only concern of neo-Malthusians. Theorists like Paul Ehrlich have also warned about our over-consumption of other resources such as timber, minerals, energy, and other nonrenewables. Can a world with 10 billion people have enough material to house everyone, enough fuel to heat all the houses, and enough food to feed everyone? If not, we need to continue to conserve and look for alternatives so that we can stretch out supplies over time—until we have *Star Trek*–esque replicators to make food for us and fusion reactors to make energy.

THE POPULATION PYRAMID

Sounds like a game show, or a seriously geeky board game. Population pyramids are a graphical way to visualize the **population structure** of a country or place. More specifically, population pyramids reveal the **gender** and **age distribution** of the population. Like a country's position on the Demographic Transition Model, the shape of the pyramid can tell you a lot about that country's level of economic development.

GENERAL PRINCIPLES

Males are always on the left of the pyramid and females are on the right. Each bar is an age **cohort,** generally made up of five-year sets: 0–4, 5–9, 10–14, and so on. The origin (0-value) of each bar graph is the center and increases in value as you move left or right outward from the center. The single colored bar right or left of the origin is an **age-sex cohort,** with just one gender of that age group. (Note that age-sex cohorts may not always be colored on the exam.) Gaps, where there is an unexpectedly small bar, are important to recognize. A gap in a male cohort but not in females of the same age group is most commonly a sign of a past war that was fought outside the country. A gap in data for both males and females is likely a sign of past war inside that country, epidemic disease, or famine.

ONE PYRAMID TO ANOTHER

Not all population pyramids look the same. Depending upon who drew them, there may or may not be a column down the middle. Seeing the overall shape of the pyramid is what's important. We'll use both methods here so that you are used seeing it both ways. You never know what they going to put on the exam.

CHECK THE TYPE OF DATA

Be aware of whether the bars on the graph show the *percent* of the total population or the total *number* of people in the age-sex cohort.

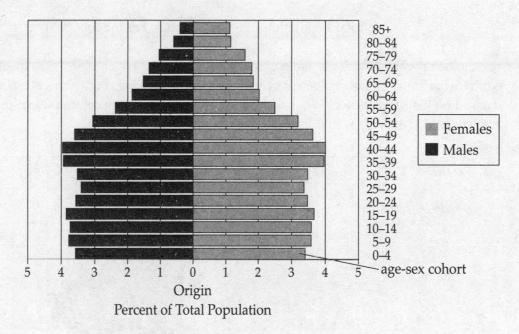

Percent Age-Sex Structure of Indiana in 2000

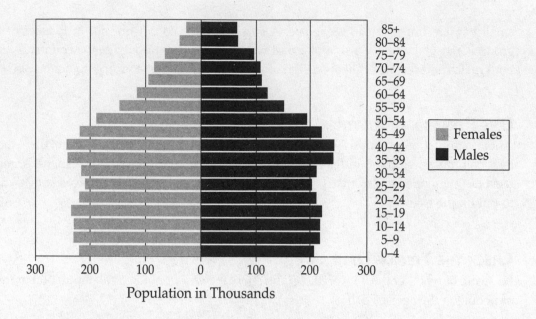

Total Population Age-Sex Structure For Indiana 2000

Yes, the two pyramids look the same, but we need to be sure when referring to the data that we recognize what kind of numbers (percent versus total) we are talking about—this is especially important if asked on the essay section. What about those pyramids with the column down the middle? Here is what the percent data would look like:

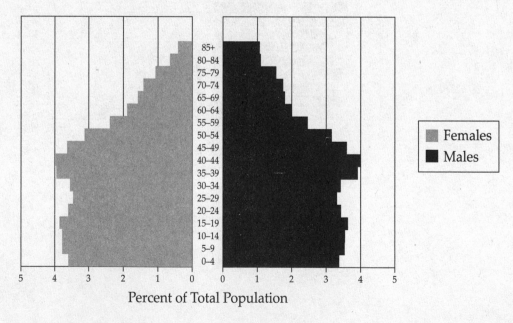

U.S. Census Bureau data

Percent Age-Sex Structure of Indiana in 2000 With Central Column

SHAPE MATTERS, BIG TIME

The general shape of the pyramid is what tells you about the character of the country, state, province, or city that is being diagrammed. In the case of countries, pyramid shapes are indicators of growth rates and of the level of economic development. Look at the diagram below to see the generalized differences:

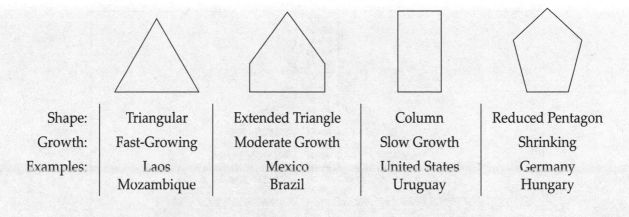

Shape:	Triangular	Extended Triangle	Column	Reduced Pentagon
Growth:	Fast-Growing	Moderate Growth	Slow Growth	Shrinking
Examples:	Laos Mozambique	Mexico Brazil	United States Uruguay	Germany Hungary

THE GAPS AND THE BUSTS!

What does a gap look like and what does it mean? Take a look at this generalized example. See the possible explanations for these gaps:

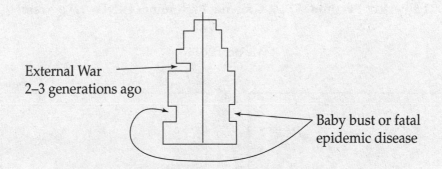

External War
2–3 generations ago

Baby bust or fatal
epidemic disease

What's the difference? The war is a given event in that it affected only one age cohort significantly and only men. Had the war happened in this country, you'd see some decline in the women, as well. That's why we refer to it as external. The baby bust followed a likely post-war baby boom. At some point, booming fertility will recede after the war generation exceeds child-bearing age.

WHO'S ON TOP?

Old folks, that's who. Of course, increased mortality from disease and old age causes significant declines in the **elder population**. That's why the top shrinks so quickly. You will notice that the male side of the pyramid decline in number far more quickly that the female side. Why? Fair or not, women live 4 to 5 years longer than men on average.

Countries, States, and Cities, Oh My!

You can have population pyramids for many different scales of population. Most commonly countries are shown, but states and cities may also show up on the exam. Let's first look at some country examples:

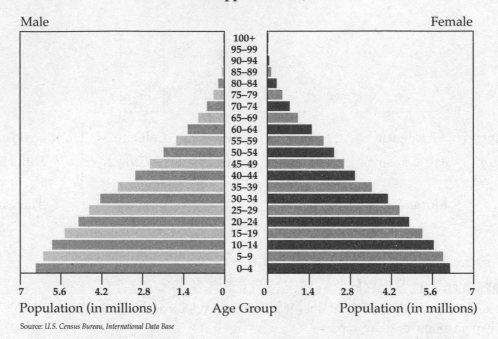

Philippines: 2014

The Perfect Pyramid, a Fast-Growing Philippines (RNI = 1.9 percent)

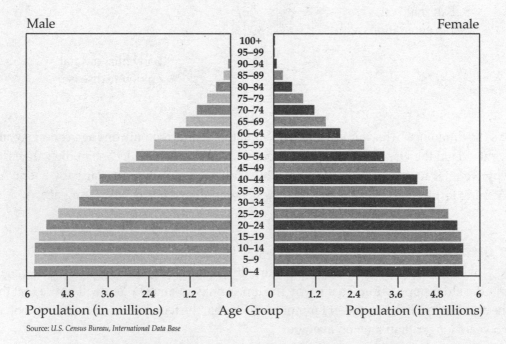

Mexico: 2014

Starting to Slow, an NIC Mexico (RNI = 1.4 percent)

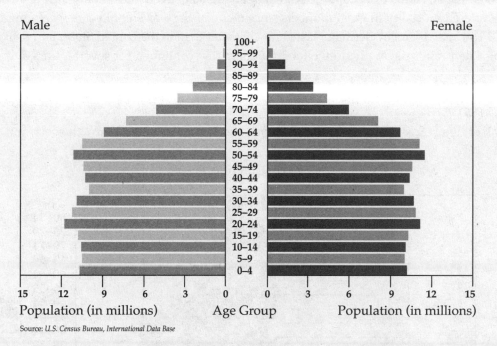

The Column-Shape of the United States (RNI = 0.5 percent).

Note the "baby boom" peak for the 50 to 54 cohort. Then the "baby bust" low point for the 35 to 39 cohort. And then the "mini-boom" 20 to 24s.

Germany: 2014

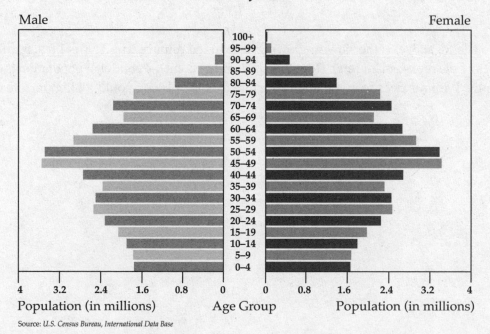

The Reducing Pentagon of Germany (RNI = –0.3 percent)

See those gaps? The 65 to 69 cohorts (both male and female) lived in Germany during World War II. Women suffered mortality in great numbers since many of the war's final years were fought on German soil. The baby boom in Germany lasted much longer than in the United States and peaked much later. This late peak is likely due to the food rationing that continued for several years after the war.

THE STATES

Let's look at two U.S. states from 2000 to see each end of the population growth spectrum:

Age Distribution, 2000

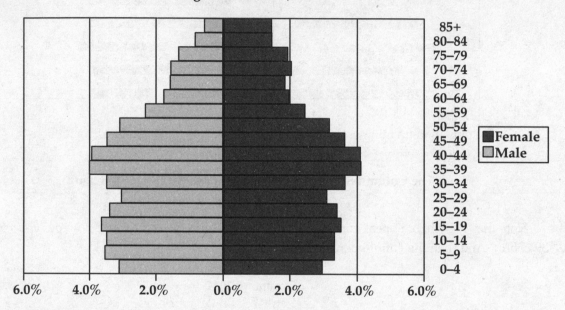

Rhode Island, above, is the slowest-growing state in the country. The TFR is 1.6 (0.5 children per female below the replacement rate). Despite a small mini-boom, the child-age population is declining significantly. Within a decade, population structure in Rhode Island could look more like Germany or Italy.

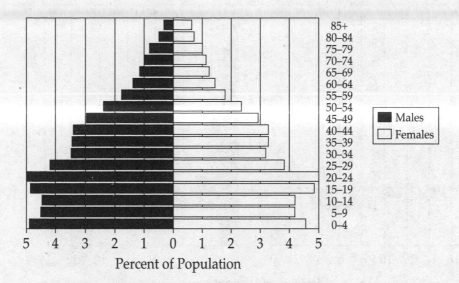

Utah, above, is one of the fastest-growing states due to immigration and a high fertility rate (TFR of 2.4). Here, the boom and bust cycles are at different times than those in Rhode Island.

Cities also have some interesting patterns. Here are three cities from around the United States:

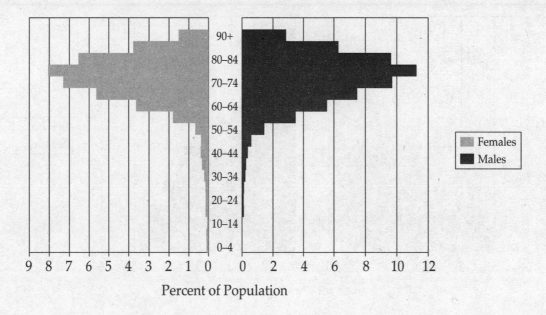

Sun City, Arizona, is a suburb of Phoenix that has long been a retirement destination for older Americans. Notice how there are almost no children.

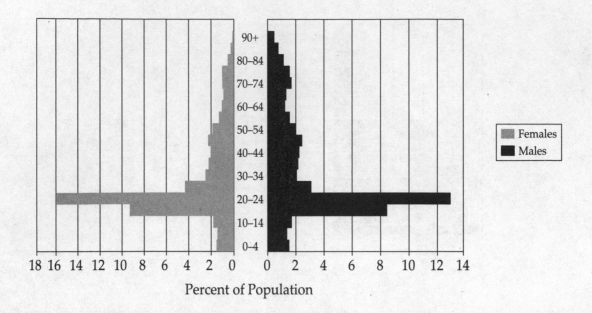

Morgantown, West Virginia, is a university town. Home to WVU, the city's structure is cross-shaped because of the large college-age cohorts.

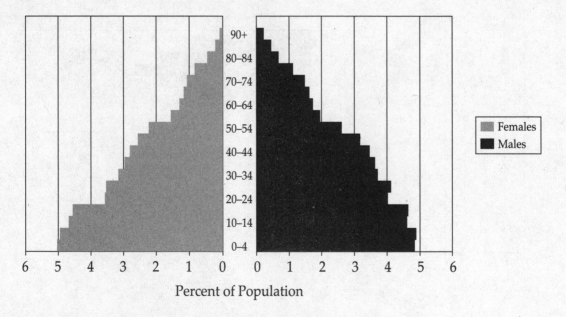

Brownsville, Texas, has an age structure similar to that of Mexico (which lies just across the Rio Grande). Immigrant communities in border towns can have a great effect on population growth.

KNOW THE CONCEPTS

POPULATION DENSITY

There are two main ways to calculate population density. The number of people per square unit of land is known as **arithmetic density**. Most island nations and microstates have extremely high arithmetic densities. Consider also the high arithmetic densities of countries such as India, Bangladesh, Japan, and South Korea.

The number of people per square unit of *farm* land is known as the **physiologic density**. Physiologic density can be seen as a more practical tool in understanding the sustainability of a population of a certain region or country. Physiologic density is especially important in understanding the geography of countries where the amount of **arable land**, land usable for farming, is limited.

Limits to physiologic density can include overcrowding on farms or a lack of abundant farming regions due to geography. For example, Iraq, Egypt, Uzbekistan, and Pakistan are all arid countries that have narrow farming regions around river systems and deltas.

In countries like the United States and China, arable land sits in the eastern third of the country and the west is dominated by mountain and desert regions. There, high physiologic densities in farming regions have led to populations being squeezed into cities or westward into grassland and arid regions to expand agriculture to new areas.

THE CENTER OF POPULATION

We can find the population center of a country by averaging the spatial weight of population across the country. This is different from the **geographic center** of the country, or **centroid**, which is simply the geometric center of the country's irregular polygon. To better understand the concept of "the spatial weight of population," imagine the country as a flat surface with the population standing on top in their home locations. The population center, or **population-weighted centroid**, would be the point where you could balance that weighted surface without tipping over.

In the United States, the population center has continuously moved west each decade since the first census in 1790. Originally, land in the Eastern United States was already owned and farm populations were high. Those wanting to have their own farms along with immigrants arriving in the country found no land available east of the Appalachian Mountains. Most migrated westward into the Midwest and Great Plains regions to settle and start their own farms. For this physiologic reason, the arithmetic density and population center moved westward through World War II.

After World War II, population shifted south and west due to the Sunbelt migration. See more on the Frostbelt to Sunbelt shift in a few pages.

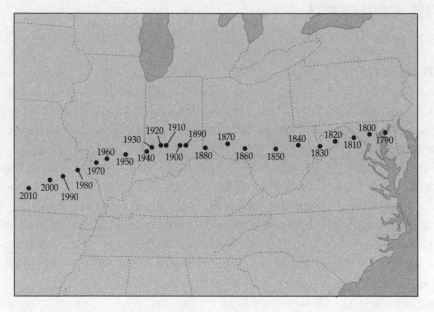

Source: US Census Bureau, International Data Base

Historic Population Centers from Each Decennial Census

Note the southwestern shift from 1950 onward, toward the Sunbelt.

POPULATION AND SUSTAINABILITY

The most important concept to understand about the **sustainability** of the global population is **carrying capacity**. At the global scale, we can ask this question: How many people can the earth sustain without triggering a **Malthusian catastrophe**? Similarly, at the regional scale we can examine the sustainability of certain **population densities**.

Across the **ecumene**, the living space of humans on the earth's surface, there are certain limits to how many people an environment can support in terms of the availability of food, water, and natural resources. Some regions support **human settlement** better than others. For instance, temperate grasslands support far more people than deserts do. That seems obvious, but why then are so many people, in this day and age, moving in greater number into **arid regions**? Secondly, how long before dry regions are pushed to their limits, especially in terms of fresh water?

Overpopulation is a major concern both in resource-poor regions and across the globe. Several Neo-Malthusian warnings have been issued regarding the excessive consumption of natural resources worldwide. The message is that certain resources such as clean water, endangered plant and animal habitats, and nonrenewable energy sources like oil will be depleted if **conservation** efforts and **population control** methods are not mandated by governments. Some theorists have expressed a need for the goal of zero population growth worldwide to stem the tide of resource depletion. To do this, some have proposed large-scale family-planning and contraceptive programs. However, many have rejected these ideas based primarily on religious or political beliefs.

Another benefit arising from population control would be alleviating concerns over decreasing amounts of **personal space** as population densities increase. Some worry that too many people crammed into densely packed urban areas will lead to social unrest and, potentially, armed conflicts.

Other population theorists have examined the role of conservation in global population sustainability. To achieve sustainable resource use in coming decades, with an expected 10 billion person global population, massive and systematic global programs enforcing recycling, energy conservation, sustainable farming practices, and a wholesale reduction of **personal consumption** are believed to be necessary. Without conservation, many resources could be depleted before we have the chance to save them.

MIGRATION

Migration is common and can take several different forms. **Inter-regional** or **internal migrants** move from one region of the country to another. This is the case with rural-to-urban migrants, who move from farmland to cities within the same country. There are intraregional migrants who move from one area to another within the same region, but they're not very interesting. There are also variations within international migration. **Transnational migration** occurs when migrants move from one country to another.

Migrants can take many forms, from slave to job-seeker to refugee. Humans move for many reasons and there are several theories to explain the practice of migration, both between countries and internally. On the international side, the human capital theory of migration contends that humans take their education, job skills, training, and language skills (also called human capital) to a country where they can make more money and reap a higher net return. Higher levels of human capital (education, training, language skills) increase the expected net gain from migration. This flow of human capital from one country to another causes wages to fall in the destination country while pushing wages up in the sending country. Migration between the two countries stops only when the individual expected net earnings and costs of migration are the same.

WHO IS WHO?

Migrants are generally those who voluntarily move from location to location. However, there are forms of **forced migration**. Governments can order their citizens to move to another place. Other people forced to move by war, disasters, or fear of government repression are known as **refugees**. Certain countries have official programs to receive refugees from other countries and grant them **asylum**, either temporarily (until danger at home subsides) or permanently. For example, many countries had asylum programs in the 1990s for people escaping **ethnic cleansing** in the former Yugoslavia, Rwanda, and Burundi. The host country often faces enormous economic burdens in providing a new home for refugees. Basic food, water, sanitation, and safety needs are often barely met in the host country if it is a developing nation already struggling to provide for its own people.

In most countries, people who come seeking refuge or employment opportunities but do not have government authorization (like a work visa or official refugee status) are considered illegal immigrants. Some countries have **amnesty programs** allowing illegal immigrants the opportunity to apply for official status or citizenship without facing arrest or deportation.

STEPS TO A BETTER LIFE

There are a few particular patterns of migration and specific ways that people migrate. **Step migration** is when people move up in a hierarchy of locations, with each move to a more advantageous or economically prosperous place. For example, a family might move from a farm to a neighboring town; then from that town to a regional city; then to the outskirts of a larger metropolitan area; and from there closer to the center of the city, each time to take advantage of better work opportunities. They might then move again closer to the center of the city once they achieve economic stability and want to have full access to the central business district. Along the way, **intervening opportunities** for work and economic improvement will increase the further migrants travel.

BUILDING THE CHAIN

Chain migration occurs when a pioneering individual or group settles in a new place, establishing a new migrant foothold. These people send information back to friends, family and business contacts. The pioneer provides information on employment opportunities, access to markets or social networks, and encourages others to migrate to the location. Over time, more and more people move in and a growing immigrant community is established.

CYCLIC MOVEMENT AND REMITTANCES

Some who migrate purely for employment purposes have a pattern of **cyclic movement**. In the case of transnational labor migrants, foreign employees work for a limited period of time before returning to their home countries. Sometimes this is also called **periodic movement** if it is on an annual or seasonal basis; for instance, agricultural workers coming from Mexico to the United States for different harvest periods, then returning home to help out during harvest on their family farms. Cyclic movement can last several years and even span the career of an individual. In some cases, a foreign worker comes to a country to find a job that they work through to retirement, and then they return to their home country when they reach old age.

The receiving countries benefit from the flow of cheap labor into their economies. The socio-economic cost of receiving this flow of immigrants includes crime, unemployment, the social welfare burden of providing the basics of life, and national security concerns. As for the sending countries, the loss of highly skilled workers poses a big challenge to those countries losing the migrants. The largest positive economic effect of migration is the sending of remittances. Remittances are monetary and other cash transfers sent from **transnational migrants** to their families and communities back home. Often, more money flows back home in the form of remittances than the sending country receives in official development assistance. Remittances create a strong positive impact in the migrant's home country. In rural Mexico, hundreds of communities are supported purely by the remittances of transnational labor migrants of their communities working in the United States

FROSTBELT TO SUNBELT SHIFT

Keep in mind that someone does not have to cross international borders to be considered a migrant. Many countries experience internal migrations that significantly change the country's population distribution. A common example is the Frostbelt to Sunbelt migration in the United States that has taken place over the past few decades. With declines in manufacturing employment, especially in the northeastern United States, many people left the colder, more populated regions of the northeastern upper Midwest for new service employment opportunities and better climates in the South and Southwestern United States.

If you examine the map of the United States population centroid on page 126, you'll notice that the average center of U.S. population has moved to the south and the west over the past 50 to 60 years. This is due to the growth of large Sunbelt cities such as Atlanta, Orlando, Dallas, Houston, San Antonio, Albuquerque, Phoenix, San Diego, Los Angeles, and Las Vegas. We can even include places you wouldn't normally consider the Sunbelt, such as Denver, San Francisco, Salt Lake City, Portland, and Seattle.

Look back at the Map of U.S. Population Centroids to see how this has affected population distribution.

Life-Course Changes

When people move because of major changes in the course of their life, these are referred to as **life-course changes**. Internal migration within a country is often explained by looking at life-course changes, such as going to college, moving for a better job, or retiring. Life-course changes can occur in many ways. Older people sometimes move when they retire. Almost 10% of Americans ages 60 and older migrated between counties in the five-year period 1995–2000. But don't be misled. Young people are more likely to pick up and move than senior citizens. From the time they leave home for college, young people begin a series of migrations that are based as much on life-course changes as on the amenities of place and quality of life.

PUSH AND PULL FACTORS

Newly industrialized countries (NICs) experience rapid internal rural-to-urban migration. Employment at urban manufacturing locations appears to be the main intervening opportunity for these internal immigrants. However, research has shown that a number of both push and pull factors cause people to leave a rural agricultural lifestyle and move to a city. **Push factors** are specific things about the rural agricultural landscape and livelihood that force people off the farm. **Pull factors** are specific things about cities that draw people to the urban landscape. It is important to remember that the opposite of a pull factor is not a push factor. For example, a pull factor cannot be the lack of employment opportunities in rural regions.

Push Factor: Armed Conflicts

Push factors include a number of issues related to the hardships faced in rural areas. One significant push factor is armed conflict. When rebel movements initiate military campaigns against governments, it is often in rural regions. When conflicts emerge in rural regions, many people flee and become refugees to the safety of cities. Terrorism and drug trafficking activity can have a similar effect and can frighten people off the land.

Push Factor: Environmental Hazards

Environmental pollution is another push factor. Excessive use of agricultural chemicals can poison soils and water supplies. In addition, improper usage of pesticides could lead to birth defects in children, forcing parents to move to cities to seek constant medical care for their children. Natural disasters can also work as push factors. A flood or drought can destroy a whole year's income and cause people to leave farming as their primary source of income.

Push Factor: The High Cost of Land

Increased land costs can also force people off the land. In newly industrialized countries, prices inflate, especially in markets for land. Farmers who own land may suddenly have the opportunity to sell their land and make far more money than they could in several years of farming. This money can then be used for migration to urban areas and pay for new city housing. In the cases where farmers are renting land, rents can increase significantly. Sometimes the farmers can no longer afford to pay rent or make enough money to support their families. Often these migrants arrive in cities homeless and are forced into squatter settlements (see Chapter 9). Even though land and other commodity prices may increase over time, basic food crop prices tend to change very little over the long-term, making farming far less profitable for small family farms.

The Pull Factors

The pull factors that draw people to cities are mainly employment-related. The higher number of job opportunities, higher pay rates, or the regularity of pay can be influential factors that motivate migrants to move to the city. Keep in mind that farmers generally make money only at the end of the growing season, when crops are sold. Having regular paychecks creates better financial security for migrants.

The Pull of Services

Other factors that pull workers into the city include access to services such as medical care or education, and service access to utilities such as electricity. Entertainment is often cited by migrants as a reason for moving from rural regions. Television, movies, festivals, and sporting events are all attractors to urban areas.

CLEAN WATER: DON'T GET CAUGHT IN THE TRAP!

The unfortunate reality for many Third World rural-to-urban migrants is that the water quality in rural regions may actually be better than the water quality found in cities. Even when there are municipal water systems in the Third World, water systems are often contaminated. The lesson here: If you are asked about access to service in Third World cities, clean water is not a valid answer, especially when talking about rural-to-urban migration factors.

MAKE THE LINK

Make sure to read where and how people in Latin America live as new urban migrants in Chapter 9.

OTHER RESOURCES

- World Population Data Sheet from the Population Reference Bureau at www.prb.org.
- The U.S. Census Bureau at www.census.gov.

KEY TERMS

rate of natural increase (RNI)

demographic equation

birth rates

death rates

immigration statistics

emigration statistics

population growth

crude birth rate (CBR)

annual statistic

life expectancy

Green Revolution

natural increase rate (NIR)

fecundity

double-income no-kid (DINK)

net migration rate

total fertility rate (TFR)

Demographic Transition Model

population dynamics

economic context

predictive capability

population projection

Industrial Revolution

deindustrialization

service-based economies

newly industrialized countries (NICs)

more developed countries (MDCs)

agricultural economy

manufacturing-based economy

carrying capacity

equilibrium

subsistence farming

transhumance

feudal political economy

child mortality

infant mortality

life expectancy

pull factor

primate city

gross domestic product (GDP)

zero population growth (ZPG)

guest workers

economic restructuring

J-curve

population structure

gender distribution

age distribution

cohort

age-sex cohort

elder population

arithmetic density

physiologic density

arable land

geographic center (centroid)

population-weighted centroid

sustainability

carrying capacity

Malthusian catastrophe

population densities

ecumene

human settlement

arid regions

overpopulation

conservation

population control

personal space

personal consumption

inter-retional (internal) migrants

transnational migration

forced migration

refugees

asylum

ethnic cleansing

amnesty programs

step migration

intervening opportunities

chain migration

cyclic movement

periodic movement

transnational migrants

life-course changes

push factors

pull factors

CULTURAL GEOGRAPHY

CHAPTER OUTLINE

This chapter is intended to help you better understand the diversity of cultures across the globe. First, the chapter presents the various components of culture. Then each component is described in terms of its relevance to the AP Human Geography Exam. Each component is detailed with examples both domestic and international. This is followed by discussions on the spatial aspects of cultural identity, cultural change, adaptation, globalization, and conflicts based on cultural differences.

WHAT IS CULTURE?

Let's be honest. Despite studying cultural geography for several years, the author personally doesn't have a stock answer to this question. However, you've paid good money for this book, so you deserve something better than waffling. The human geography textbooks all give a definition that says something like this:

Culture is the shared experience, traits, and activities of a group of people who have a common heritage.

Okay, so what does that mean? So, instead of trying to tell you what culture is, we'll give you the many components of the cultural landscape. To prepare for the AP exam, it is more effective to examine the categories of cultural expression than to try to define culture in a couple of sentences.

THE CULTURAL LANDSCAPE

Almost everything we see and hear in the human landscape expresses some form of culture. Culture is complex, and trying to take it all in and make sense of it can be confusing. To get a better grip on culture, we first have to understand how it is found on the **cultural landscape**. We can see the cultural landscape in the form of **signs** and **symbols** in the world around us—which is a general way of saying that there are different ways customs are imprinted on the several **components of culture**. Here is a list of the components of culture to give you a simpler way of understanding culture in general and how it is expressed:

Art	Clothing
Architecture	Social Interaction
Language	Religion
Music	Folklore
Film and Television	Land Use
Food	

Each component of culture is expressed in a multitude of ways that signify and symbolize cultural influences. These historical influences can be as simple as the language used on a street sign or as complex as the cooking methods and spice mix in Louisiana Cajun food. To prepare you, this chapter will detail each relevant component of culture and provide examples that will help you answer cultural geography questions on the exam.

READING THE CULTURAL LANDSCAPE

In some ways, we can think about the cultural landscape as a form of **text** that can be read. We can read the signs and symbols that we see within the different components of culture and understand that place's cultural background and heritage. This takes a keen eye to see, and it helps to know some history of the place to translate what you are seeing.

What we find is that some things are original to a single culture, but most things in the cultural landscape are the product of **cultural synthesis** or **syncretism**—the blending together of two or more cultural influences.

Hey, Y'all

An example of cultural synthesis is country music in the United States and Canada. It is often thought of as a product of American culture and is strongly tied to folk music traditions such as bluegrass. However, when we research the origins of country music, we find a culmination of influences from the Scots-Irish, the German, and African immigrants and slaves in the American interior south and Appalachia following the American Revolution. The mixture of musical sounds, vocabulary, rhythms, and instruments from these four culture groups came together to form a new style of music, as well as later developing into other American musical styles like jazz, the blues, and rock and roll.

THE COMPONENTS OF CULTURE EXPLAINED

Whether something is original to a single culture or is the product of cultural synthesis, it is important to understand the underpinnings of the things we see in the cultural landscape. Combined, the many components come together to identify and define a single **culture group** or **nation**.

Not all of these components are going to be questions on the AP exam. For each relevant component, we will give you detailed geographical examples from Anglo-America and internationally to help broaden your perspective on the subject.

Art

Different artistic forms are important signs of a cultural imprint on the landscape. However, art is not a subject that the AP Human Geography Exam tests. Be able to express art's importance as an identifier of groups and source of local pride if asked a general question on cultural landscape.

Architecture

Unlike art, architecture questions have appeared on the exam, so you need to be aware of a number of architectural styles. Housing types and religious buildings are especially relevant. These questions are most likely going to fall in the multiple-choice section of the exam and will have a picture or diagram to examine or decipher.

Concepts
Within the **built environment** of the human landscape, we find a multitude of **architectural forms** that are the product of cultural influence. When new buildings are constructed, much news is made over innovative designs in **modern** and **contemporary architecture**. This is in contrast to the existing forms of **traditional architecture,** some of which has been used for centuries.

Modern versus Contemporary Architecture
As in the art world, architects have a distinct modern period of architecture which differs from new, or shall we say contemporary, forms. Be specific when describing a home or building type. *Modern* means architecture developed during the twentieth century that expresses geometric, ordered forms such as the 1950s homes of Frank Lloyd Wright (seen below) or the rectangular steel and glass sky-scrapers built in the 1970s and 1980s.

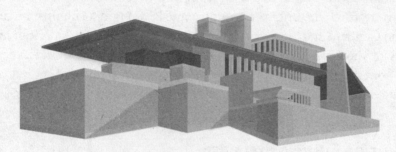

In contrast, the *contemporary* architecture of the present is more organic, with the use of curvature. **Postmodern** is a category within contemporary that means that the design abandons use of blocky rectilinear shapes in favor of wavy, crystalline, or bending shapes in the form of the home or building. Contemporary architecture can also incorporate **green energy** technologies, **recycled materials**, or non-traditional materials like metal sheeting on the exterior. This is exemplified in the Frank Gehry design of the Guggenheim Museum in Bilbao, Spain, or the Walt Disney Theater in Los Angeles (seen below).

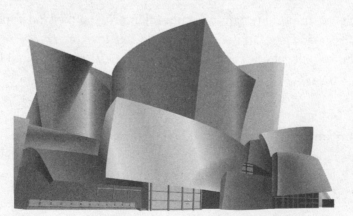

Traditional Architecture

Traditional architecture can express one of two patterns in building type. One form of traditional architecture seen in new **commercial buildings** incorporates the efficiency and simplicity of modern architecture into a standard building design with squared walls and utilizes traditional materials stone, brick, steel and glass. The other expression of traditional architecture seen in **housing** based upon **folk house** designs from different regions of the country. New homes built today often incorporate more than one element of folk house design like a hybrid Swiss chalet–Williamsburg-style home covered in stucco, with a clay tile roof. Let's go over the basic **traditional housing style** forms that could appear on the exam.

Housing Types

New England: Small one-story pitched roof "**Cape Cod**" style or the irregular roof "**Salt Box**" with one long pitched roof in front and a sort of low-angle roof in back (seen below).

Federalist or Georgian: Refers to the housing styles of the late 1700s and early 1800s in Anglo-America. These are often two- or three-story urban townhomes connected to one another. Architectural elements around windows and rooflines feature classical Greek and Roman designs and stone carvings. As stand-alone buildings, these are symmetrical homes with central doorways and equal numbers of windows on each side of the house (seen below).

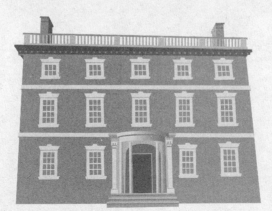

The I-house: A loose form of Federalist and Georgian influence on the average family home in the United States and Canada. Simple rectangular I-houses have a central door with one window on each side of the home's front and three symmetrical windows on the second floor (seen below). However, as the I-house style diffused westward, the rectangle shape and symmetry was lost. Later I-houses have the door moved to the side and have additions onto the back or side of the house. The I-house giveaways are the fireplaces on each end of the house and an even-pitched roof. The loss of form as the I-house moved across the Appalachian Mountains to the Midwest and across the Great Lakes to the Prairie Provinces is an example of **relocation diffusion**.

Religious Buildings and Places

Another area of architecture the AP Human Geography Exam tests is religious architecture. Here are the major world religious groups and their representative architectural forms for places of worship.

Christian: Traditional houses of worship tend to have a central steeple or two high bell towers in the front of the building. The steeple is typical of smaller churches, and bell towers are found in larger churches and cathedrals. Basilicas, like St. Peters in the Vatican or St. Paul's Cathedral in London, have central domes similar to the U.S. Capitol building. Symbolically, older churches, cathedrals, and basilicas feature a cross-shaped floor plan.

Chapel, Cathedral, Eastern Orthodox

National Cathedral, Washington, D.C.

Holy Virgin Orthodox Cathedral, San Francisco, California

Hindu: Temple and shrines tend to have a rectangular-shaped main body and feature one or more short towers of carved stone. The towers often feature stepped sides and display carvings of the heads and faces of deities. The most famous example of this design is the temple complex of Angkor Wat in Cambodia. The Kashi Vishwanath Temple in Varanasi, India, is shown below.

Hindu temple at Varanasi, India

Buddhist: Temples and shrines vary depending on which Buddhist tradition is followed in the region. In Nepal and Tibet, a temple can be a **stupa**, with a dome or tower featuring a pair of eyes. In East Asia, the tower-style **pagoda** with several levels that each feature winged roofs extending outward is common. Temples and shrines in China and in Shinto Japan (a Buddhist offshoot) feature one- or two-story buildings with large, curved, winged roofs (seen below). Temples are often guarded by large lion statues, such as those at the Temple of the Sun and Moon in the Forbidden City of Beijing. Temples in Southeast Asia tend to have several towers with thin pointed spires that point outward at an angle (seen below).

Mahayana Buddhist Temple (China, Japan)

Theravada Buddhist Temple (Thailand)

Stupa, a Type of Vajrayana
(Tibet, Nepal, Bhutan)

Islamic: Mosques can take a variety of forms, though many have central domes. The giveaway feature of a mosque is one or more **minarets**, narrow towers that are pointed on top. Famous mosques include the Al-Kaaba Mosque in Mecca, the most holy place in Islam, an open-air mosque with a large black cube at its center (seen below).

The third most holy place in Islam is the Al-Aqsa mosque in Jerusalem that sits alongside the Dome of the Rock, an eight-sided mosque with a high central dome and thin spire on top featuring a crescent moon. Another large mosque is the Hagia Sofia in Istanbul. A former Eastern Orthodox cathedral, it has a broad central dome and fours spires, one in each corner of the square-shaped building. Almost all mosques are built on an angle that places the main prayer area toward Mecca.

Dome of the Rock (Temple Mount in Jerusalem)

Judaic: There is not a common architectural design style to synagogues. The most holy place in Judaism is the Western Wall of the former Temple of Solomon, next to the Dome of the Rock. Known as the **Wailing Wall**, the old foundation walls feature large rectangular stone blocks where Jews pray and place written prayers in the cracks between the blocks.

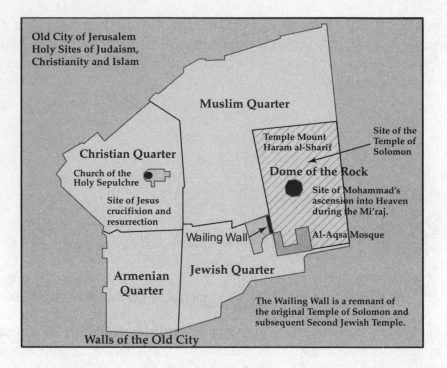

Old City of Jerusalem
Holy Sites of Judaism,
Christianity and Islam

Muslim Quarter

Christian Quarter

Church of the
Holy Sepulchre

Site of Jesus
crucifixion and
resurrection

Temple Mount
Haram al-Sharif

Site of the
Temple of
Solomon

Dome of the Rock

Site of Mohammad's
ascension into Heaven
during the Mi'raj.

Wailing Wall

Al-Aqsa Mosque

Armenian
Quarter

Jewish Quarter

The Wailing Wall is a remnant of
the original Temple of Solomon and
subsequent Second Jewish Temple.

Walls of the Old City

Language

When we think about language, we most often think about the common tongue of the country that we live in. In terms of **official languages**, the United States federal government has not designated one. Some states have English-only laws and provisions. These affect education standards and state government publications such as driver's licensing exams, since much of the United States tends to be **monolingual** (knowing one language—English—only). Other states such as California accept that they have a large **multilingual** immigrant population and made provisions (especially for public safety) to provide some services in multiple languages including Spanish, Chinese, and Vietnamese.

In Canada, there are two official languages: English and French. Therefore, Canada is **bilingual**. Another example of a multilingual society is the Netherlands. In school, students not only learn their native Dutch, but are required to also learn English, French, and some German. Likewise, it's common in South Africa for citizens to be able to speak varying levels of English, Afrikaans (a Dutch derivative), and one or more African languages such as Xhosa, Sotho, or Zulu.

Aussie, Aussie, Aussie! Oy! Oy! Oy!

Depending upon where you are in a larger **linguistic region**, the way a common language is spoken can sound different, depending upon who is speaking it. In the global English linguistic region, **dialect** changes from nation to nation. Although the English spoken by English people and Australian people sounds similar, there is a distinct "strain" of English spoken in Australia with a variety of different **word sounds** and **vocabulary**. Even between the United States and Canada there are subtle differences, such as the strong Canadian "O" in the word *about*, pronounced "a-boat." Within countries, dialect can change from region to region, such as the changes heard when traveling in the United States from New England to the American South.

Cheerlo! Or not!?

Even within Great Britain, varieties of dialect are shaped in part by national heritage. English spoken in England proper is quite different from English in the other nations or culture areas of Scotland, Wales, Ireland, Cornwall, or the Isle of Man. These variations are due in part to the degree of Celtic influence and the degree to which Anglo-Saxon invaders, who brought their Germanic language with them, settled in the region during the first millennium C.E. What some refer to as the King's English or "posh" English is linguistically known as **received pronunciation**. Conversely, **Cockney** English is the language of the working-class areas of the East London docklands and surrounding neighborhoods, which sounds distinctly not posh. Cockney is also thought to be very influential in the formation of Australian English.

It's the Dog's Bollocks

Cockney rhyming slang is an odd but humorous use of code phrases to describe everyday situations. In slang, "going up the apples" means going up the stairs; stairs rhymes with pears, heard in the fruit markets as "apples and pears," and thus, stairs is replaced with apples. This can be seen in the 2001 movie *Ocean's Eleven* with the character Basher, played by Don Cheadle, who when confronted with a major problem cryptically tells the gang that "We're in Barney!" And then has to explain, "Barney Rubble!?! Trouble!"

Pidgin, Creole, and Patois

Slang is similar to other heavily modified dialects of pidgin English. **Pidgin** languages are simplified forms of the language that use key vocabulary words and limited grammar. This is often heard in the spoken English of Hindustani Indian immigrants to Britain, Canada, and the United States.

Pidgin language forms can evolve into their own individual language groups over time. In Haiti, **French Creole** is spoken, which incorporates continental French with African dialectal sounds and vocabulary. In fact, many of the French overseas territories (*departments outré mer* or *DOM*) have their own forms of **patois**, like the one spoken in the islands of Martinique or Reunion, formed by local or immigrant linguistic syntheses. Pidgin, Creole, and patois can all be thought of as syncretic language forms that integrate both colonial and indigenous language forms.

Eet Iz zee Lingua Franca, Monsieur

French itself has long been a language used to bridge the linguistic gap between people of different national heritage. So much so that the term *lingua franca* was coined to describe its utility as a bridge language. Why *franca*? France has long been a center for learning, literature, and diplomacy. There were also a number of French colonies around the world, and Great Britain has long had territorial claims in France, necessitating French literacy among British aristocrats, diplomats, and merchants.

Today **English** is accepted as the **global lingua franca** as different forms of popular culture media, the Internet, and the business world are dominated by the English language. A notable use is that English is the required language of all airline pilots and air traffic controllers around the world. This is done mainly for safety reasons, but is evidence of the United States and Britain's international business dominance in the post–World War II era.

Major Language Families

Around the world, there are a small number of major **language families** represented by the early or prehistoric language roots. The largest members of these language families are as follows:

> Indo-European (2.5 billion people)
> Sino-Tibetan (1.4 billion people)
> Afro-Asiatic (284 million people)
> Austronesian (244 million people, from Southeastern Asia, Oceania, and Hawaii)
> Dravidian (203 million people, from on and around the Indian subcontinent)
> Niger-Congo (172 million people)
> Altaic (128 million people, from Eastern Europe through Central and Eastern Asia)
> Japanese (122 million people)
> Korean (67 million people)

Each language family can be broken into **language groups**. Some larger language families such as the Indo-European and Sino-Tibetan can be broken down into **language subfamilies** and then into smaller language groups. For example, the English language draws from the Indo-European family, Germanic subfamily, and Western Germanic group, along with German Dutch and Afrikaans. Hindi is also from the Indo-European family, but from the Indo-Iranian subfamily and Indian group along with Bengali and Nepali. The Indo-European concept is derived from linguistic analysis and genetic evidence of **prehistoric migrations** from the Indian subcontinent into Europe. These early immigrants brought their Indo-European root language with them, which then divided locally and evolved into the contemporary European languages of today.

Anatolian or Kurgan Theories

There are two competing theories regarding the origins of European language, each with their own **hearth**, or launching point. The **Anatolian theory** holds that this group of migrants from the Indian subcontinent and their language were for some time concentrated in the peninsula that makes up most of present-day Turkey, known historically as Asia Minor or Anatolia. From there, a large migration crossed the **Hellespont** into continental Europe and spread outward into what was possibly a relatively unpopulated region.

The **Kurgan theory** holds that the same group of migrants from the Indian subcontinent instead made their way into Central Asia, and then migrated across the **Eurasian steppe** into central and Western Europe, taking their language with them. Without significant archaeological discovery or possibly extensive genetic research, it will be difficult to prove whether either theory holds true. (See the map on the following page.)

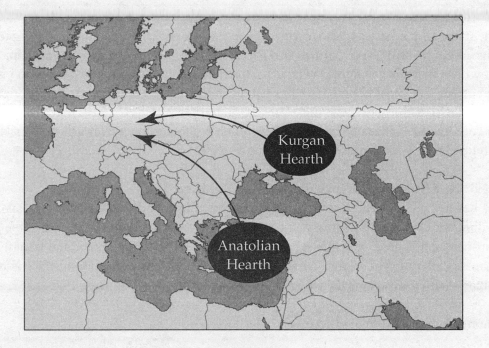

Europeans from India?

Genetic research shows that almost all Europeans are derived genetically from populations that in prehistoric times inhabited the Indian subcontinent. There are a number of hypotheses as to why this light-skinned population, similar to many light-skinned Aryan Indians, pulled up their roots and moved west. But we can tell that they did take their language and genes with them. Unusual genetic markers such as the Celtic trait for red hair are drawn from the Himalayan foothills of what is today northern India and Pakistan, where people with red hair can still be found. It's some weird stuff!

Music

Like language, music is a form of non-material culture that has geographic roots and regional variation. You should know a few things about the geography of musical culture since it can show up on the AP exam.

Folkies and Pop Stars

Music that is original to a specific culture is categorized as **folk music**. Folk music traditions often incorporate instruments unique to that region or have orchestrations that are specific to that culture. **Folk song** lyrics often incorporate cultural stories and religious tradition, which can be described as **folklore**. It tends to be "unplugged" as well, without electronic instruments.

By contrast, **popular culture** generates a global flow of **pop music** that often has the effect of drowning out local folk music traditions from radio and other media. In the cases where you do hear electronic instrumentation in folk music, this indicates a form of acculturation in which folk traditions are accepting the influence of popular music.

Fiddlin' and Pickin'

As was mentioned earlier in this chapter, American folk music and contemporary popularized country music have origins in Scots-Irish, German, and African culture. Folk traditions in **Appalachia** are often realized by the playing of the fiddle, a variant of the European violin, and the banjo—an instrument of African origin. The most popular folk music type in the region is **bluegrass**, which originated in Kentucky (known as the "Bluegrass State" after both the plant and the music). In bluegrass, fiddle and banjo are the lead instruments. There are a number of other folk styles across Appalachia; the region stretches from Mississippi to the Maritime provinces.

"We Got Both Kinds of Music: Country and Western!"

Bluegrass has heavily influenced contemporary country music, and more recently, so has rock and roll. The difference between bluegrass and country is that country music tends toward the guitar as the lead instrument. The guitar is linked back from country to "Western" music and from there, back to the Spanish Americans of colonial Mexico and the American Southwest. Besides Kentucky, there are the other hearths, or historic development cores of country music.

Folk Music Forms and World Music

Hearths of American Country Music Styles

Many of the recordings sold today in the United States and Canada as World Music are actually folk musicians from other culture groups. Of these, one of the most popular groups is the top-selling Gypsy Kings. The band is from France, but their families had left Spain decades earlier due to persecution by the Franco-led fascist government of **Gypsies**, who are also known as **Roma** or Romani in Europe.

The Gypsy Kings play from a variety of folk traditions and languages, including their native Roma to Spanish flamenco, as well as Basque and Catalan folk songs, which they have popularized.

Celtic folk music traditions are played anywhere Celtics, Irish, Welsh, Scots, Manx (from the Isle of Man), (Spanish) Galicians, or (French) Bretons or their migrant descendents are found. Irish Celtic music has a particularly large following. The traditional music features a multitude of instruments including the fiddle, flutes, the tin whistle, harp, concertina accordion, the bodhrán drum and "Uilleann" or Irish pipes—the smaller cousin of the Scottish bagpipes. Today, it is common to hear Pan-Celtic music that draws from more than one Celtic region and utilizes other non-Celtic instruments like guitar, banjo, and bouzouki (a Greek mandolin).

Next time you listen to country or bluegrass, see if you can pick out the Celtic Scots-Irish folk musical influence.

Film and Television

Different forms of film and television are important signs of a cultural imprint on the land. However, film and TV, like art, are not subjects that the AP Human Geography Exam tests. You should be able to express film and television's importance if asked a general question on cultural landscape. Also, understand that these media forms are major conduits for cultural globalization, which is discussed on page 169.

Food

Food is a material form of culture that varies regionally and is rooted in a number geographic ways. **Continental cuisine** refers to the formal food traditions that emerged from mainland Europe in the 1800s. It is embodied in **haute cuisine**, French for "high cooking," where traditionally a main meat course is served with a flour, cream, or wine-based sauce and side dishes of vegetables and potato. Some haute cuisine dishes favored in North America are duck à l'orange, filet mignon, and chocolate mousse as a dessert. This style of cooking can also include regional influences from folk traditions in France such as *escargots* (snails in garlic butter) from Provence in Southern France and *coq au vin* (rooster in red wine sauce) found in a number of *regions*—these are foods of the French farmer raised to a higher form.

And You Thought Arnold Schwarzenegger was the Only Austrian in Malibu...

Nouvelle cuisine is the contemporary form of the continental styles mainly from France, Spain, and Italy. Although there is a strong nouvelle style in France, the lighter, fresh fare of California-style cuisine has become very popular worldwide. Gone are the heavy sauces in favor of healthier sauce applications with citrus juices, olive oil, or white wine atop a lighter variety of meats including salmon, chicken breast, or mahi mahi. These have been popularized by celebrity chefs such as the Austrian-born Californian Wolfgang Puck, who utilizes a number of **Mediterranean** agriculture products such as avocado, artichoke, olives, and citrus fruits in his dishes.

Mmm, Roy's

Wolfgang Puck is also seen as a proponent of **fusion cuisine**, where more than one global tradition is incorporated in dishes. Japanese-American celebrity chef Roy Yamaguchi in Honolulu is one of the leaders of the fusion movement that integrates dishes and flavors from Japan, China, Southeast Asia, Polynesia, and Europe. Hawaii's location makes it a place of heavy immigration from these parts of the world, where cultural synthesis in food and other cultural components such as music takes place.

Folk Dishes From Around The World: Japanese Sushi

Of course, all of these forms are based on original forms of **folk food** dishes. **Sushi** is a simple but artistic form of folk food from Japan. The simplest sushi is *sashimi*, raw fish cut in a special manner to sever potentially harmful parasitic worms—did we just ruin the *maguro* for you? Sashimi on a small pat of rice is another simple folk form called *nigiri*. Sushi has also become stylized in the contemporary form with special rolls, *makizushi* or just *maki*: Inside seaweed wraps (*nori*) are sticky rice and a variety of ingredients like raw, smoked, or fried seafood and fresh vegetables. The condiment *wasabi* is also part of this folk food tradition; it's pickled horseradish root, and it's spicy!

I Thought Hummus Was Soil?

The **Moroccan** folk food tradition utilizes a number of regional ingredients from the Mediterranean and North Africa. Main dishes incorporate familiar meats such as chicken and lamb, since cattle are rare in North Africa and pork consumption is *haraam*, or banned by Islam. Permitted meats must be slaughtered under religious rules to be *halal*, or fit for consumption by Muslims. Meat is often served with couscous, a very small-grained pasta, chick peas (garbanzo beans), and root vegetables grown in the high Atlas Mountains. Food is flavored with a variety of spices including cinnamon, turmeric, and saffron and is often cooked in a traditional clay pot known as a *tajine*. Chick peas can also be ground and mixed with a sesame seed paste called *tahini*, along with olive oil, salt, and lemon to make *hummus*, which is increasingly popular in Europe and Anglo-America as a dip served traditionally with toasted pita bread. (Don't get it confused with humus, the organic material in soil.)

Clothing

Different clothing styles are other signs of a cultural imprint on the landscape. However, clothing, like art, is not a subject that the AP Human Geography Exam tests students. Do be able to express clothing's importance, if asked a general question on cultural landscape, since the way people dress is an important sign of their ethnicity. Note also that clothing, like film and TV, is a conduit for cultural globalization, discussed on page 169.

Social Interaction

Different types of **social interaction** are **culturally constructed**, meaning they were traditions devised by a specific culture group. Physical **greetings** are a basic example of culturally different social interaction. In the West a **handshake** is a common physical greeting, whereas in Japan, the **bow** still holds as the primary formal greeting. The traditional New Zealand Maori physical greeting is the pressing together of the forehead and noses.

Smoochy, Smoochy!

Formal, non-touching **cheek kissing** is another example. Kiss four times in Paris, France, upon greeting, twice on each side; in Serbia and the Netherlands, three times, right side first; twice in Spain, Austria, and Scandinavia; no kisses in Germany and the United Kingdom; and a variable number of kisses in Italy and Greece, where if you don't know the local rules, it's better to just extend a handshake.

Personal Space Violation?

Personal space also varies from country to country. If you like a large personal space bubble, you'll feel uncomfortable in Peru, where it's considered rude not to sit in an empty seat next to someone, even if they're a stranger. Think about this the next time you select a seat at the movie theatre or on a bus.

Religion

Religions, also referred to as **belief systems** by some social scientists, are as numerous as languages. Like languages, specific religions are drawn from a number of larger global groups. Categorically, religions can be characterized by their expanse: **Universalizing religions** accept followers from all ethnicities worldwide; as opposed to **ethnic religions,** which are confined to members of a specific culture group. All organized religions have one or more books of **scripture**, said to be written of **divine origin**. They also have formal **doctrine** that governs religious practice, worship, and ethical behavior in society.

Religions and their component **denominations** can also be understood by their ability to compromise and change ideologically. **Compromising religions** are often cited for the ability to reform or integrate other beliefs into their doctrinal practices. **Fundamentalists**, on the other hand, are known to have little interest in compromising their beliefs or doctrine and strictly adhere to scriptural dictates. Know that fundamentalists tend to focus on particular relevant parts of scripture but can ignore the dictates in scriptures that may not be relevant or legal in contemporary life.

Know Your World Religions

There tend to be a significant number of questions on the exam that rely upon your knowledge of religious geography. At the most basic level, there are three major traditions of belief systems, from oldest to most recent:

> **Animist Tradition:** Various ethnic, tribal, and forms of nature worship
> * Though geographically unrelated, these groups have common themes, worship practices, and morality tales, which define a right and ethical way to live.
> * *Animus* means spirit in Latin. Animists share the common belief that items in nature can have spiritual being, including landforms, animals, and trees.

> **Hindu-Buddhist Tradition:** Hinduism, Buddhism, Jainism
> * The oldest universalizing religions began with Hinduism 5,000 years ago. These **polytheistic** (believing in more than one supreme god) denominations spread throughout Asia by the 1200s C.E.
> * The commonalities are that there are many levels of existence, the highest being **nirvana**, where someone achieves total consciousness or enlightenment.

- One's soul is reincarnated over and over into different forms. Karma, the balance between good and evil deeds in life, determines the outcome of reincarnation into a lower, similar, or higher form of existence in the next life.

Abrahamic Tradition: Judaism, Christianity, and Islam
- Each of these religions has similar scriptural descriptions of the earth's genesis and the story of Abraham as a morality tale of respect for the will of God or Allah.
- Each is a **monotheistic** belief system with a singular supreme being. There can also be sub-deities such as saints, angels, and archangels.
- Significance is placed upon prophecy that predicts the coming or return of a messianic figure that defeats the forces of a satanic evil for souls of followers.

These traditions can be further broken down into major religious groups. Here is a quick and basic comparative guide to the world's major religious groups, with diagrams of their diffusion patterns.

Animist Religions

There are hundreds of animist belief systems. Here are two that are commonly described in human geography:

Native American

Who? The pre-Columbian civilizations in the Americas and some descendants

When? From the last period of glaciation (18,000 years before present)

Where? Alaska to the Tierra del Fuego

Scripture: None. System based upon belief in a supreme or Great Spirit that oversees the universe. Instead, spiritual interpretation is provided by **shamans,** sometimes referred to as "medicine men" who are practitioners that lead worship and religious rites.

Doctrine: Depends upon tribal following. Prayers or appeals to sun, moon, animal spirits, and climatic features (wind and rain) are significant in most practices.

Denominations: Hundreds of different tribal interpretations

Historical Diffusion: By **migration diffusion** north to south through the Americas

Voodoun (Voodoo)

Who? West African; Afro-Brazilian and Afro-Caribbean descendents

When? From prehistory to present

Where? Nigeria, Benin, Ghana, and other states in the region; Haiti, Cuba, Dominican Republic, Brazil, and other small communities in the region

Scripture: None. System based upon multiple deities that control different parts of the lived world. Like other animist groups, **shamanism** is part of the system of worship.

Doctrine: Depending upon the community. Common practices often attempt to bring worshippers in contact with deities and family ancestors in the spiritual world though different ceremonies, dance and sacrificial practices.

Denominations: Distinct difference depending upon region and the degree of influence from parallel Christian worship by Voodoun followers.

Historical Diffusion: From West Africa **relocation diffusion** by forced migration under European-directed slavery to the Caribbean and coastal American mainland areas such as northern Brazil, Belize, and Louisiana.

Hindu-Buddhist Religions
Hinduism

Who? South Asians and some Southeast Asians

When? Earliest forms 7,500 years before present

Where? Mainly India; also today Bali in Indonesia, London, Manchester, and other parts of the former British Empire, with significant populations in Guyana, Trinidad, Fiji, Malaysia, and South Africa

Scripture: Vedas, Upanishads, Bhagavad Gita, and other early Sanskrit religious texts

Doctrine: The main personal practice is to work continuously toward multiple reincarnations and eventually nirvana. Practice of temple based worship and festivals to praise particular supreme gods, including humanistic forms Vishnu, Shiva, Krishna, and animal forms Ganesha (elephant god) and Naga (serpent gods). Several doctrinal writings depict the historical moral traditions and practices.

Denominations: Different denominations are often based upon cults to deities. And based upon a hierarchical **caste system**, which is based upon the reincarnation principle, in which people are born into a particular social level where they remain for the rest of their lives.

Historical Diffusion: Expansion diffusion from the Hindu hearth in Northern India. Later relocation diffusion across the Bay of Bengal to Southeast Asia (consider the historical Hindu temple complex at Angkor Wat in Cambodia) and to Indonesia where a remnant population is found today on the island of Bali.

Jainism

Who? A fundamentalist interpretation of Hinduism

When? Around 2,900 years before present

Where? Western India

Scripture: Several texts collectively known as **Agamas**. The most commonly cited is the Tattvartha Sutra.

Doctrine: At the core of religious practice is the complete respect for all other animal life, in that every living soul is potentially a divine god. Followers are strict vegetarians and often wear face masks to prevent the inhalation of insects.

Denominations: Three main groups exist that differ in practice and worship.

Historical Diffusion: Some Jain communities relocated to places such as Great Britain during the colonial period, 1830s to 1940s. Mohandas Gandhi's mother was a devout Jain and her compassion for all life influenced her son's civil rights and peace activism.

Buddhism

Who? An ideological following that rejected the caste system and other Hindu practices

When? About 2,500 years before present

Where? Hearth in the Gangetic Plain (Ganges river basin) of North Central India and spread throughout Asia (see map on following page)

Scripture: Early Hindu texts combined with the Tipitaka (aka "Pali Canon"), part of which contains the life and teachings of Siddhartha Gautama, the founder of Buddhism

Doctrine: Different doctrinal texts including the *Tao Te Ching*. A main doctrinal difference with Hinduism is the belief that nirvana can be achieved in a single lifetime, with intensive study, meditation, and moral thought. This is through an understanding of the effects of suffering on human life and the following of a "Middle Way" or non-extremist pathway toward enlightenment. Buddhism also rejected the Hindu caste system as oppressive and not in line with Buddhists' view of human suffering.

Denominations: Three distinct traditions: Tibetan (Vajrayana); Southeast Asian (Theravada); and East Asian (Mahayana), each broken into smaller regional and philosophical denominations. Tibetan Buddhists tend to be universalizing, accepting westerners into their community but uncompromising in their beliefs. Theravada tends to be far less universalizing and does not compromise their traditions; Mahayana Buddhism is both universalizing and compromising. This Eastern tradition incorporates a number of different philosophical forms such as Zen, Confucianism, Shinto, and Taoism.

Historical Diffusion: Several examples of Buddhism **relocating** across physical barriers: Tibetan Buddhism across the Himalayas and Tarim Basin desert to Siberia and Mongolia; Theravada from Sri Lanka across the Bay of Bengal to Southeast Asia; and Mahayana across the Himalayas to Eastern China.

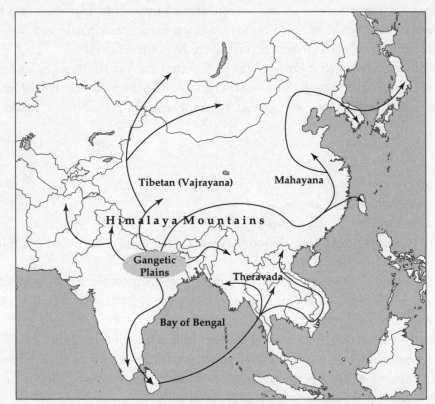

Arrows show the diffusion of Buddhism across the
Himalayas and the Bay of Bengal

Caste System in India

The Hindu scriptures describe a **cosmology** (a belief in the structure of universe) in which there are several levels of existence, from the lowest animal forms to human forms and then higher animal forms, which are considered sacred, such as cattle, elephants and snakes. The levels are known as *chakras*. As a soul is reincarnated it can be elevated to a higher *chakra*, if the soul has a positive karmic balance. **Karma** is the balance between the good and evil deeds in one's life.

Once someone is born into a caste, he remains there for the rest of his life, no matter how rich or poor he becomes. The lowest human forms, *dalits*, are considered less holy due to their distance from nirvana on the *chakras*, whereas the Brahmans, the highest human form, are considered the priesthood of Hindus due to their relatively close position to the enlightened. Here are the five levels, or *varna*, within the human *chakra* that define the caste system in Hinduism (from highest to lowest):

1. Brahmans
   - The priestly caste. Brahmans are responsible for temples and leading religious worship.
   - Some can be selected as high government officials. Others may eschew all material possessions to live as monks, who might live as hermits meditating or as ascetics who sit on sidewalks and perform prayers for those who provide their food donations.
2. Kshatriyas
   - The aristocratic and warrior caste. Despite their political power, hereditary princes and kings still bow to the Brahmans.
   - Many are landowners, government leaders, and wealthy businesspeople.
3. Vaisyas
   - The merchant and professional caste.
   - These tend to be the doctors, lawyers, accountants, and middle-ranking officials in the government.
   - Mohandas Gandhi was born into the vaisya caste and trained as a lawyer prior to his life as a human rights leader.
4. Sudras
   - The caste of tradespeople and farmers.
   - The caste is broken up into several hundred sub-castes, or jati, including potters, glassworkers, and jewelers.
5. Dalits
   - The "untouchables," a name derived for their low position in the system and considered unholy by higher castes. Dalits were often segregated from other Hindu housing areas and social networks.
   - Dalit sub-castes were divided among trades and duties in the community such as leather work (cattle are sacred, and only the lowest-caste humans could handle their flesh), cleaners of train stations, and sewers.
   - Elected in 1997, Indian President K. R. Narayanan was born into the dalit caste, and he has been a symbol of affirmative action for the untouchables.

Since India gained independence in 1948, its government has initiated a number of efforts to eliminate the caste structure in Indian society. There have been several programs to elevate the social and political standing of the lower castes, including compulsory elementary education, and opening public trade schools, high schools and universities to large numbers of lower-caste members who had been discriminated against in the past.

Caste difference in Indian cities have become minimal, while it is still recognizable in rural India. Among many Indian families, marriage is still one area in which there is an emphasis on caste, as most traditional parents desire their children to marry within their caste.

Abrahamic Religions
Judaism
Who? Larger groups including European Ashkenazi Jews, Sephardic Jews from North Africa, and the Middle East and Native Israelis known as *Sabra*

When? Over 5,700 years before present. January 1, 2015, will be during the year 5775 on the Hebrew calendar.

Where? Hearth in Israel, peripheral communities in Europe, United States, and Canada, particularly the metropolitan area around New York City and other urban areas worldwide, such as London, Antwerp, Paris, Los Angeles, Toronto, and Cleveland

Scripture: Torah (includes several books also used in the Christian old Testament) and Talmud

Doctrine: Varies between groups. Shared between all are the atonement for sins annually during Yom Kippur and Rosh Hashanah

Denominations: Orthodox, Conservative, Reform, and Reconstructionism

Historical Diffusion: The Jewish Diaspora begins in 70 C.E. with the Roman destruction of the Temple in Jerusalem, where Jews were forced out to other parts of the Empire. The post–WWII era following the Nazi Holocaust marks the beginning of the Jews' movement to Israel from Europe. Conflicts in the 1950s and 1960s caused migrations from North Africa and the Middle East to Israel.

Christianity
Who? Originates in the Roman Empire but not recognized officially until the fourth century C.E.

When? Following begins around 30 C.E.; begins expansion outside the Mediterranean in the sixth century.

Where? Europe, the Americas, Sub-Saharan Africa, Philippines, Austronesia

Scripture: Bible, divided into an Old Testament, a modification of the Torah and sharing major dictates such as the Ten Commandments; and a New Testament, which depicts the messianic life of Jesus of Nazareth and includes the writings of his disciples and early followers

Doctrine: Varies depending on the denomination. Typically involve communion practices and baptisms.

Denominations: Eastern Orthodox, Armenian, Antiochian, Greek Orthodox, Coptic, Roman Catholic, Protestant; each can be subdivided into further denominations

Historical Diffusion: From the Mediterranean hearth, Christianity diffused hierarchically to large cities such as Rome, Constantinople, Alexandria, and Marseilles. From there missionaries spread the religion to other towns and cities where it diffused to smaller communities. These patterns of diffusion become recognizable through the hierarchy of holy sees, archbishoprics, bishoprics, and local parishes.

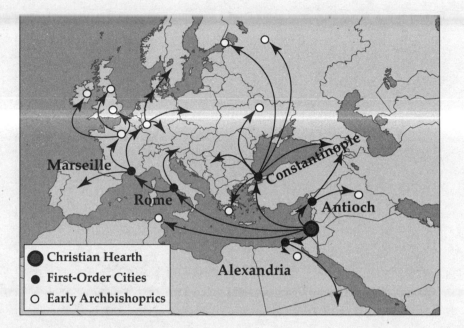

Islam

Who? Originates with the peoples of the Arabian Peninsula along the Red Sea, particularly Mecca, Medina, and Jeddah

When? Early 600s C.E.

Where? Today the Islamic realm spans from Mauritania in West Africa, east to Indonesia and the Philippine Island of Mindanao; north to Chechnya, Kazakhstan, and Xinjiang in Western China; and south to Tanzania

Scripture: Koran (Quran), the scriptures received by Muhammad

Doctrine: Haddith, the recorded sayings of Muhammad. All sects emphasize at least five pillars of Islam, if not more.

Denominations: Sunni (85 percent) and Shia (15 percent) sects with a number of denominations within, such as the Ismaili Shiite and Wahabi Sunni. Differences between the two major sects are based upon the emphasis by Shiites on the necessity for **Imams** (religious leaders) to have a direct blood line back to Muhammad.

Historical Diffusion: From Mecca, Islam diffused in an expansion pattern in all directions very quickly. By 700 C.E., all of the Middle East and much of North Africa was adherent to Islam. Further expansion into Europe and Asia occurred through to the 1600s. Some relocation diffusion was seen, such as that to Indonesia in the 1200s (seen on the following page).

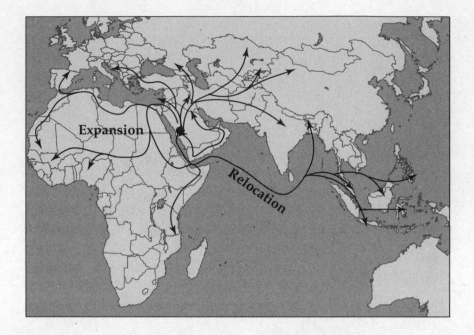

Islamic States: Theocracy, *Sharia,* and Secular Governance

You may have learned that a few countries in the Middle East are **theocracies**, where religious leaders hold the senior positions of governance. In fact, only Iran has a supreme religious council that serves as the **head of state** and can overrule the elected parliament and president. Some but not all Middle-Eastern states are **republics** or **monarchies** that abide by *Sharia,* or Islamic law, based on the Koran and Haddith. A few absolute monarchies (that unlike constitutional monarchies have no elected parliament) have all-powerful kings and large aristocracies, who in turn enforce religious standards on the populace.

Other states in the region are more **secular**, meaning the state is not directly governed in a religious manner and instead often utilize French or British legal tradition and government structure. Even in these states, the influence of religion on government policy remains, and tension between the secular government and religious activists can cause difficulty or violent conflict.

Here are a few Middle-Eastern examples of each case:

Theocracy:	Iran, formerly Afghanistan under the Taliban
Sharia States:	Saudi Arabia, Kuwait, Yemen
Secular States:	Jordan, Turkey

Syncretic Religions

There are some religions, known as syncretic religions, that synthesize the core beliefs from two or more other religions. Examples of these include the **Druze,** who incorporate both Christian and Islamic principles, and the **Sikhs,** who incorporate principles from both Islam and Hinduism. Like Buddhists, Sikhs reject the concept of a caste-based social hierarchy.

Moral Principles in the Abrahamic Traditions: The Five Pillars of Islam

The Judeo-Christian system has its Ten Commandments from the Book of Exodus, which serves as a basic moral code for all followers. Likewise, the Koran emphasizes five pillars that guide followers with a moral system. The **five pillars of Islam** are as follows:

1. Five Daily Prayers
   - The call to prayer is heard on loudspeakers in cities throughout the Muslim world at designated hours.
   - For the devout, all work stops and prayer mats are unrolled.
   - Prayer is done facing Mecca. Islamic astronomers and geographers have for centuries worked to determine the azimuth, the angle of direction, from Mecca to other parts of the Earth.

2. Islamic Creed
   - "There is only one god, Allah, and Muhammad is his prophet."
   - The creed is a statement of monotheism. Prior to Muhammad's religious conversion of the Arabian peninsula, many of the peoples in the region believed in polytheistic Animist or tribal religions.
   - Muslims believe in a number of prophets shared with the Judeo-Christian traditions, such as Moses, Isaac, Ishmael, and Jesus, but Muhammad is the supreme prophet, as he is the author who received the Koran from Allah.

3. Alms to the Poor
   - It is the duty of all Muslims to care for and donate to the poor and sick within their communities.
   - Large charitable foundations in the Islamic world help alleviate poverty, extend health care and educate children.
   - Many of these international charities have come under increased scrutiny by the U.S. government following September 11, 2001, due to accusations that charities were being used to funnel money to terrorist groups.

4. Observance of Ramadan
   - Ramadan is a period of spiritual cleansing and repentance for past sins.
   - During Ramadan, there is fasting during daylight hours, with plain evening meals of sparing quantity.
   - Ramadan, like the Christian Easter and Lenten period, the Jewish holidays, and Buddhist New Years, is set on a lunar calendar. The lunar month of Ramadan can fall during a wide range of months in our Gregorian calendar.

5. The Hajj
   - Each Muslim who is able must make at least one pilgrimage to Mecca during his lifetime. "Haji" is an honorific name for those who make the journey.
   - The most popular time for the Hajj is during Ramadan, when Mecca can swell with several hundred thousand visitors.
   - Even prior to the twentieth century, Hajis made multi-month-long voyages across desert and oceans to complete the pilgrimage.

More on Religious Geography

The geography of religion can be further broken down by denomination and region. There are important sections later in this chapter and in Chapter 6 regarding religious-based conflict. There is also some discussion on religion and ethnicity in urban American neighborhoods in the Know the Models discussion of the sector model in Chapter 9.

Folklore

Folklore are the collected stories, spoken-word histories (such as Norse sagas), and writings that are specific to a culture and tell the societal histories and morality tales that define a culture's ethical foundations. The morality tales serve a purpose similar to religious scriptures, dictating culturally constructed rules of behavior. **Aesop's fables** are an example of folklore from the classical Greeks. Each fable had a moral to the story, a lesson to be learned regarding proper behavior. Many American forms of folklore, such as Paul Bunyan, John Henry, and Mike Fink, mix a bit of the unreal to tell tales of a strong work ethic, a product of Puritan Protestantism.

When a culture's history and its folklore intersect, it can often lead to distortions of reality in the lives of historical figures, like the myth of George Washington chopping down his father's cherry tree. Also see the stylized tales of American frontiersmen like Daniel Boone or Davy Crockett, whose Hollywood movie depictions have furthered fictions and half-truths about the long-dead historical persons.

Cristóbal Colón, American Hero? The Historical Geography of Folklore

In many parts of the Americas, a folklore has been built around the life and travels of Christopher Columbus. The myths and facts are intertwined and the folklore varies from country to country. Here's a comparison of the folklore and truths regarding Columbus from the United States' point of view:

"Columbus Discovered America."
- Archaeological evidence shows that Norsemen (Scandinavian Vikings) established settlements on the northeastern tip of Newfoundland at L'Anse aux Meadows around 1000 C.E. These were likely abandoned 100 years later when a significant global climate cooling event resulted in crop failures. Settlers likely evacuated to other settlements in Greenland or Iceland.
- Columbus never saw or set foot on the mainland United States. He did explore Puerto Rico and also landed on the mainland of South and Central America.

"Columbus sailed the ocean blue with his ships the *Nina, Pinta,* and *Santa Maria.*"
- Well, sort of. These are the ships he departed with in 1492 from Seville in Spain on his first voyage. What you might not know is that the *Santa Maria* struck a reef off the northern coast of what is today Haiti, the island Columbus named *Hispañola.*
- The shipwreck forced Columbus to leave behind 40 men at a colony named for the Spanish Queen, *Isabella.* This was in part to establish trade with the Indians.

Upon Columbus's return 366 days later on his second voyage, not a single sign of the 40 men was found at the village. This caused severe grief for Columbus and the other crew that had returned to rescue their comrades.

"Columbus was a famous Spaniard who gained the title 'Admiral of the Seas.'"

- First, Columbus was Genoese (from Genoa—a coastal city in what is today northern Italy).
- Columbus sought funding for his expedition to the Indies (today's India, Indonesia, and China), but was turned down by a number of potential donors when he proposed sailing westward across the Atlantic instead of around Africa, as was already done by the Portuguese.
- The Spanish Royal Court of Ferdinand and Isabella was receptive to Columbus's plan for two reasons:
  - Spain was nearly bankrupt from years of war trying to remove the Muslim Moors from the southern Iberian Peninsula and needed the new trade route to raise money for their treasury. The western sailing route to land had been long rumored. Basque fisherman had likely sailed off the coast of Brazil and Canada following cod fish and Columbus was aware of their land sightings—assuming they were India.
  - The Portuguese were keen on protecting their African trade route and would likely fight to protect it. They also possessed sailing charts of the route, maps to which the Spanish did not have access.
- Columbus did receive the title of Admiral of the Seas but did not receive the promised 10 percent of treasure from the New World that the position was entitled to. Only after his death were his sons able to extract money from the Spanish government. Columbus was not a folk hero in Spain; he died blind in Spain in 1506 at the age of 54.

This may seem like a "historical" example. However, the Columbus myth and the settlement of Latin America is an area of extensive research in cultural geography. This kind of thing is fair game on the exam, and you need to be prepared for it. Read Carl Sauer's *Northern Mists* about the Nordic voyagers and *The Early Spanish Main* for an accurate description of the Columbus voyages and the first Spanish settlement in the New World.

Land Use

Land survey techniques can also reveal something about the cultural landscape. How property is utilized, shared, or divided can say something about culture through its imprint on the landscape.

Farming Practices

Cultural differences in agriculture are not limited to the types of foods produced. How farming is done can also be culturally specific and is heavily influenced by technology. It is, after all, agri-*culture*. Cultural farming practices range from swidden, or a "slash and burn" style of agriculture seen in forest regions, to the highly technological large-scale farming seen in the First World. Keep in mind, traditional farming practices seen in the Third World are quickly disappearing in favor of modern, mechanized farming.

Blue Sheep's Milk?

Also, don't forget that in the First World there are still some significant culturally specific and low-tech farming practices. Examples of this can be found in Vermont with the production of maple syrup from trees. Or look to Europe for the production of regionally specific cheeses, such as Roquefort (a blue sheep's milk cheese) in France or Parmagianno Reggiano (a hard cow's milk cheese) in Italy. These are high-value **appellations** that designate a culturally specific farm product that brings high value. These appellations, including Champagne and Vermont Maple Syrup, have their name usage protected by international trade laws.

Find out more about appellations and specialized agriculture in Chapter 7.

Residential Patterns

How living space is distributed is also an important indicator of culture, especially in rural and tribal areas. Often, cultural traditions impose rules on living space that depend on singular clan relations, extended family units with more than one clan, or whole tribal communities with multiple clans living in one shared residential area.

For the distribution of urban land use, see Chapter 9.

Land Ownership

As was mentioned in Chapter 3, in Europe, much of Latin America, and Anglo-America east of Central Ohio and Ontario, land surveys used natural landscape features to divide up land on a system of **metes and bounds** that had been developed in Europe centuries earlier. Metes and bounds are also evidence of the European feudalist political economy (See Chapter 6 for more details). In its early form, the irregular property boundaries were the territorial claims of large aristocratic landholdings.

Over time, these became subdivided via partial land sales or by nationwide land reform efforts. Land reform often divided properties into smaller polygons. France and French colonial areas such as Québec and Louisiana have **long-lot** patterns. These have a narrow frontage along a road or waterway with a very long lot shape behind.

In the 1830s, new techniques to accurately determine longitude were transferred from sea navigation to land survey; land survey in the United States and Canada used a rectilinear **township and range** survey system based on lines of latitude and longitude. This produced the block-shaped property lines and the geometric shape of many western U.S. states and Canadian provinces. It is also evidence of the impact of **technology** on the cultural landscape.

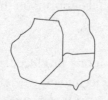
Metes and Bounds

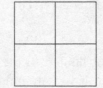
Township and Range

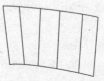
Long lots

CULTURAL IDENTITY

How people are identified and how they identify themselves is another important aspect of cultural geography. This section examines the several dimensions of identity that may appear on the exam.

NATION AND ETHNICITY

The term *nation* is used loosely in normal conversation. However, cultural geographers and political geographers have a specific definition for the term. Nation, in its most basic definition, is a population represented by a singular culture. Another term for nation would be a *culture group*. What defines a nation is a common identity, which is a complex of genetic heritage and political allegiance embodied in the term *ethnicity*. Ethnic groups often claim a single identifiable lineage or heritage, which all members tend to identify with as a common social bond. Keep in mind, as with our prior example of the English language, several ethnicities can exist within the same linguistic region. Likewise, within a single ethnicity more than one language can be used, such as the French Canadians, South Asian Indians, or Belgians.

Not all nations have a representative state, as a state in its most simple form is a population represented by a single government. This is the case with our previous music example of the Gypsies, Roma or Romani peoples of Europe. Likewise, the Kurds of northern Iraq, southeastern Turkey, northeastern Syria, and western Iran are similar in that they are defined groups with no official government. The Kurds are attempting to establish a Kurdistan in what is today northern Iraq and northeastern Syria. However, the geopolitical relationship between the United States and Turkey prevents the Kurds from being recognized as a sovereign independent state.

Ethnicity can be modified in the process of migration. In the United States and Canada, there are many migrant groups, including Italian-Americans and Irish-Canadians. This modified ethnicity is more than symbolic, and can be evidence of acculturation by immigrants to culture in their new home country.

See the section on acculturation later in this chapter.

RACE

Ethnicity and race are two commonly confused cultural identifiers. Whereas **ethnicity** represents the national heritage of an individual, *race* refers to the physical characteristics of a common genetic heritage. The concept of race was developed by physical anthropologists in the 1800s. Researchers categorized racial groups based on a number of variables including skin color, bone structure, and the shape of the hair shafts (straight, wavy, or curly). Keep in mind that over time these formerly scientific ideas were used crudely as the basis for **racism** within society and have lead to oppression, suffering, and war throughout the world.

Racial Group Physiology

Three large, distinct racial groups emerged from this research: the Mongoloid or Asiatic, with a tan or yellowish skin tone, small body structure, and straight hair shaft; the Caucasian or Indo-European, with a light to dark skin tone, medium body type, and wavy hair shaft; and the Negroid or African, with a dark skin tone, medium body shape, and a curly hair shaft.

The Names Explained

Mongolians appeared to have physical features common to all Asians. Native Americans, who were at the time hypothesized to be from Asia, shared many Asiatic features with Mongolians. Archeological and genetic research has since added to a body of theory connecting Native Americans to origins in Asia. The Caucasus Mountains region, which separates Europe from Asia, is believed to be a major migration route from the Indian subcontinent to Europe during the prehistoric era. The term *negro* is the Latin and French term for the color black.

The Pacific Islands

In addition, four small populations of physical anthropological groups were identified within the Pacific Islands. **Melanesians**, found in New Guinea, New Caledonia, and Fiji, so named because of their dark skin coloration, have comparatively thin bodies and angular facial features, with a curly hair shaft. **Polynesians**, living in Tonga, Samoa, New Zealand, Tahiti, and Hawaii, have a lighter brown skin color, heavyset body shape, and curly hair shaft. **Micronesians**, the name coming from the small island atolls of the Marshalls and Caroline Islands, have a light brown skin color, medium body shape, and curly hair shaft. And **Aboriginals** in Australia have light brown skin, a medium body type, and a wavy hair shaft.

Race and Identity

In the contemporary era, race has become less of an identifier. Oppression and discrimination based on race was popularly opposed and systematically deregulated in many countries during the latter part of the twentieth century. Racism still exists today; however, the 2008 election of Barack Obama as president of the United States signifies progress.

Mixed-Race Cultures

For many parts the world, identity is based on a single race being the **indigenous population**—the people who originally settled an area. In other parts of the world, identities are defined by multiple mixed races. In Latin America and the Caribbean, for example, identity based on mixed races is the norm. Across the region, several thousand terms are used to describe varying degrees of mixed heritage.

For the purposes of the exam, we focus on the larger representative groups. **Mestizos** are people who have cultural and genetic heritage from European and Native American backgrounds. **Mulattos** are people who have mixed African and European heritage. (This term has fallen out of favor and use because of its history as a derogatory term.) There is one significant group of mixed Native American and African peoples, known as the **Garifuna**. The Garifuna live in the Caribbean islands of St. Vincent, Dominica, and Trinidad, as well as the coast of Honduras, including Roatan Island.

Creole is a term used to describe people or culture that is derived from all three racial groups—European, Native American, and African. Originally, the term in Spanish meant someone who was born in the New World, regardless of heritage, and could refer to colonists with two European parents. Creole heritage and culture is mainly found in the Greater Antilles (Cuba, Haiti, the Dominican Republic, Puerto Rico, and Jamaica), as well as coastal Louisiana, Texas, and Mississippi, Belize, Colombia, and Brazil. An example of the Creole food culture would be gumbo. It's a French Mediterranean soup like bouillabaisse with *file*, a spice used in Native American cooking made of sassafras. The rice first used in American cooking of gumbo in the 1600s was West African red rice.

Environmental Determinism and Racism

In the 1800s, at the same time anthropologists were establishing the physical characteristic of race, human geographers developed the concept of environmental determinism to explain cultural differences around the world. By definition environmental determinism is the former scientific ideology that states that a culture's traits are defined by the physical geography of its native hearth or culture region. Contemporary human geography as a science was originally based on deterministic philosophies. The *Anthropogeographie* of the German geographer **Friedrich Ratzel**, considered the father of modern human geography, and his students such as American Ellen Churchill Semple, built a large body of research claiming that all aspects of culture were defined by physical geographic factors such as climate, landforms, mineral resources, timber, food, and water supplies.

The problem with environmental determinism was that science was being used to reinforce the racist ideologies of the 1800s and early 1900s. An example of this racist logic would be that people from extremely hot tropical regions are considered lazy, as they would not want to work during the midday heat. Conversely, people from colder regions had to be physically and mentally hardier to survive the cold winters. Although these ideas may seem plausible, they are scientifically incorrect and based on flimsy evidence. In truth, different races and culture groups are essentially the same physiologically, and each can survive in a multitude of climates and environments.

The Determinism Debate and Possibilism

Despite the global elimination of slavery by the late 1800s, racism and environmental determinism were widely accepted both socially and scientifically. To change the scientific perspective, human geographers including **Carl Sauer** debated and opposed the environmental determinists. **Possibilism** was the revised concept proposed by Sauer and other like-minded geographers. This ideology stated that cultures were to a *partial* degree shaped by their environment and the material resources available to them. However, culture groups have the ability to adjust and modify the environment. The research of Sauer and others from the 1920s onward showed that in many cases, cultures made massive modifications to the landscape to meet their food and resource needs, often destroying the natural environment in the process.

Nazism and Determinism: Be Careful What Science Creates!

Despite Sauer's contribution of possibilism to the science of human geography in the 1920s, the deterministic ideas first proposed by Ratzel had become ingrained in the European society and psychology. The concepts of Nazism proposed by Hitler in the 1920s and put into practice in the 1930s were in part based on Ratzel's concept of *lebensraum*, in which the living space for each distinct nation was based upon the optimal physical geography of the culture group. Hitler's idea was to expand the living space of the Germanic or Aryan race across the European landscape. Of course, this was at the expense of other European ethnic groups, who by the way were also Caucasians.

Despite Germany's defeat during World War II, Nazi ideologies still persist among some extremist groups in the United States and Europe. This neo-Nazism is not based on *lebensraum* or ethnicity, but is instead violent racism against non-whites and immigrants. This is also a violent expression of **xenophobia,** the fear of outsiders.

INTERNAL VERSUS EXTERNAL IDENTITY

How people express their identity is dependent on the audience with which they are communicating. **Internal identity** is used by individuals to express their cultural heritage, ethnicity, or place of origin to people who share their heritage or place of origin. **External identity** is used by individuals to express their cultural heritage, ethnicity, or place of origin to people who do not share a common cultural or geographic background.

Egyptian or Arab?

For example, imagine an Egyptian in London being introduced to another person of Egyptian descent. Immediately the conversation includes geographic specifics such as local place-names, family names, and culturally specific language. Compare this to that same Egyptian an hour later, meeting someone from Canada. In this conversation, there is little geographic specificity; just basic identifiers such as Egypt or terms like "near Cairo."

On the other side of the conversation, the Canadian may have her own misconceptions, which can further distance the cultural goals between the two people. For instance, by referring to Egyptians as Arabs, the Canadian may lose face, as many Egyptians consider themselves a single culture group as opposed to those who live in the Arabian Peninsula, a few hundred miles away, despite their common language. From the Egyptian's point of view, she might as well refer to the Canadian as an American. It is quite possible that we use external identity to compensate for the lack of cultural knowledge from one group to another.

SPATIAL CONCEPTS IN CULTURAL GEOGRAPHY

CULTURAL REGION

The world is covered with several overlapping culture regions that create multiple layers on the local to global scale. As was stated in Chapter 3, a region is an area of bounded space with a homogeneous characteristic. In the case of **culture regions**, the homogeneous characteristic can be one or more components of culture, such as language. Likewise, the cultural concept of a **nation** or **ethnicity** can also represent the culture region. In these cases where ethnicity defines the culture region, look for a multitude of cultural components with which to define a number of homogeneous characteristics as a complex of defining factors.

The Fuzzy Borders of Cultural Regions

One of the things that sets apart cultural regions from other types of regions is its border characteristics. Cultural regions tend to have what are called **"fuzzy"** borders. They are referred to as fuzzy because it's hard to tell where one cultural region ends and another begins. In addition, the transition from one culture region to another is not easily measured, as compared to the way you can measure the transition between one bioregion to another. The fact is that cultural regions overlap in an irregular manner.

An example of a fuzzy border would be where **Dixie** ends and the American Northeast or Midwest begins. Some try to apply a political boundary to it, like the Mason-Dixon Line, but this is a very poor definition. The Mason-Dixon Line actually runs south and west of Delaware and north of Maryland. These are **border states** where one part of the state is decidedly Southern and another part seems more Northeastern. There's no one place where you could put a road sign saying, "Welcome to Dixie!"

Others have attempted to quantify certain cultural symbols in the hope of determining Dixie's regional boundary. If you were to estimate the concentration of NASCAR fans or the market areas of country music radio listeners, you might be able to see the extent of the Dixie culture region. However, you would find much inconsistency along its edges, and you would find that the phenomena of NASCAR and country music extends far beyond the South proper.

CULTURE HEARTHS

Our Ties to Ancient Culture Hearths

The **culture hearth** is based on the idea that every culture has a localized area where it originated or has its main population center. **Contemporary culture hearths** exist in today's world. Human geographers also discuss the concept of **ancient culture hearths**, which developed ideas with technology that exist today. The most common of these technologies is the domestication of **staple food crops**.

In the ancient world, staple food crops were very important, as they fed the conquering armies of empires, provided sustenance for the labor force, and were the primary commodity for commercial trade networks. Most large ancient civilizations had a single staple food, which they either domesticated or utilized heavily. The following table provides some examples of ancient culture hearths and their staple food crops:

Culture Hearth	Staple Food	Civilizations
Nile River	Wheat	Ancient Egyptian
Mesopotamia	Wheat*	Sumerian, Assyria, Babylon
The Indus Valley	Wheat	Harappan
Mesoamerica	Corn	Olmec, Maya, Aztec
The Andean Highlands	Potato*	Inca
Northeast China	Rice	Ancient Chinese
West Africa	Yams*	Malian, Songhai
*Indicates place of original domestication.		

The classical civilizations of Rome and Greece were also major consumers of wheat. However, wheat had been domesticated long before, in Mesopotamia. Archaeologists believed this occurred in what is present-day northern Iraq and southeastern Turkey. The cultural hearth of ancient Greece and Rome drew much of the culture traditions, such as their shared mythology, from the earlier Minoan culture of Crete. Likewise, Western societies today draw upon much from Greek and Roman politics, such as the concepts of democracy and the republic.

Culture Hearths of Today: Core and Periphery of Mormonism

Hearths can represent the core of a **contemporary culture region**. An example of a region with a distinct core and a wider periphery is the Mormon culture region of the American West. The **Latter-Day Saints** (LDS) religion, of course, is the homogeneous characteristic shared by the region. However, a distinct Mormon culture has emerged, evidenced by cultural products like the LDS film industry. LDS filmmakers have produced notable expressions of the region's culture, such as the hit comedy *Napoleon Dynamite*.

The population and cultural core of the region is the Salt Lake City-Ogden-Provo metropolitan area, a long, continuous north-south urban corridor also known as the Wasatch Front. The area has around 1.5 million people, the majority of whom are practicing church members. At its cultural heart is Temple Square in downtown Salt Lake City, where the church has its main offices, a large convention center, and historic temple and tabernacle.

Outside of the Wasatch Front, the region is predominantly rural and agricultural. The peripheral Mormon culture region spreads across the irrigated farms and dry ranchlands of Utah and the border region of the surrounding states of Idaho, Wyoming, Colorado, Arizona, and Nevada, and extends with significant populations in rural eastern Oregon and suburban Southern California. As you head farther away from the Wasatch Front, the cultural signs (the ward church house) and symbols (the beehive of industry) become fewer, especially when you leave Utah's borders. But even in this peripheral region, Mormonism is still detectable and existent in the population. Las Vegas, Idaho Falls, Boise, Denver, Phoenix, and Los Angeles all have large active Mormon communities.

Formal or Functional Culture Region?

As we discussed in Chapter 3, there are both formal regions, with homogeneity across the region, and functional or nodal regions, with a distinct central place. Functional regions can be defined as organized networks with a distinct node at the center and connections radiating throughout the region.

In the previous example, we could argue the Mormon culture region as both functional and formal to some degree. As a formal region, Mormon culture is evident through the population of followers who are concentrated in the Intermountain West. Even though not everyone who lives there is LDS, Mormons in the region are a large and distinguishable populace. Conversely, the Salt Lake City–based Church of Jesus Christ of Latter-Day Saints, the largest denomination in the LDS faith (there are a few much smaller LDS faiths), is a very well organized and hierarchical network of neighborhood ward, local, state, and regional church administration that is coordinated from the SLC headquarters. As such, the Mormon culture region is also a functional or nodal region.

The Global Islamic Culture Region: Culture Hearth versus Population Center

The culture hearth of Islam is the region along the Red Sea coast of Saudi Arabia. Inland from the sea, at its heart is the most holy city of Islam, Mecca, where Muhammad was born. But don't forget Islam's second-most holy city of Medina, where Muhammad wrote the Koran. As centers of Islamic learning and traditional philosophy, these are the spiritual centers of the faith.

However, the Middle East is not a very well-populated area compared to other parts of the Islamic world. In fact, the majority of the world's Muslims are not in the Middle East. If you combine the

Islamic populations of Pakistan (160 million), India (120 million), Bangladesh (140 million), Malaysia (25 million), and the world's largest Muslim state, Indonesia (210 million), you will find 66 percent, or two-thirds, of the world's 1 billion Muslims.

CULTURAL CHANGE

SEQUENT OCCUPANCE

Long-term cultural changes can be seen in all of the world's populated regions. One way this is observed is through the concept of **sequent occupance**. That is, for a single place or region, different dominant cultures replace each other over time. To visualize this, think of layers of culture building up on top of each other, much like layers of sediment building up a geologic stratigraphy. When we examine the cultural landscape of a place, we often see remnants of previous cultural influences.

An example would be European architecture found in former colonial cities of Africa like Lagos, Nigeria. Deposited upon this is a postcolonial Nigerian landscape with modern buildings, a product of globalized architecture, and place names and street names with Nigerian references that replaced the British colonial names after independence in 1960.

New York City was at one point under British colonial rule (think of neighborhood place-names such as Greenwich Village, Williamsburg, and the borough of Queens). But prior to this, the city was controlled by the Dutch (place-names like Harlem, Van Cortlandt, and Stuyvesant). And before that, several Native American groups populated the shores of New York Harbor, which were rich in oysters and other seafood. Strata can be seen in construction site excavations along the waterfront where shell middens, large garbage dumps of mainly oyster shells and other artifacts of Native American life, are uncovered. Atop all these layers are signs and symbols of the postcolonial and modern American cultural occupants.

CULTURAL ADAPTATION

The cultural landscape also retains the imprint of minority and immigrant groups. The ethnic neighborhood is the best example of how these groups make their way into the layers of sequent occupance at a much smaller scale. In the case of New York, Little Italy or Chinatown immediately come to mind. You can also cite the example of Spanish Harlem, where Puerto Rican and Dominican immigrants settled from the 1950s onward.

ACCULTURATE OR ASSIMILATE—WHICH IS IT?

When the European immigrants came to America in the early part of the twentieth century they adopted many new beliefs and behaviors in their new home. They still kept much of their original culture, but they learned the American norms as they adjusted to life in America. This is an example of **acculturation**—the process of adapting to a new culture while still keeping some of one's original culture. Usually acculturation is a two-way street, with both the original and the incoming culture group swapping cultural traits.

Assimilation is more of an "all-or-nothing" process. Assimilation is a complete change in the identity of a minority culture group as it becomes part of the majority culture group. A great example of assimilation occurred when the U.S. government adopted a policy of "forced assimilation" of the Native American population. The government forced the Native Americans to move to reservations where they were taught in government-run schools. The people were made to learn English and give up their native tongue. The government insisted they adopt the dress, manners, language, and ways of the dominant American culture. The "old ways" were forbidden. This total absorption into the dominant culture is one-way and usually "encouraged" by government policy when the new residents are forced to learn the new languages and embrace the new ways.

CULTURAL SURVIVAL

In other parts of the world, national cultures have historically been threatened by outside influences, such as military invasions, mass migrations or the decline of the indigenous culture. The term **indigenous** means the people who were the original occupants of place or region. The **indigenous culture** is, therefore, the original culture of that same region. The loss of indigenous culture has become a significant concern among citizens and a major policy issue among governments. In some cases, the indigenous culture is merely threatened by external cultural influences. Yet in many other cases around the world, cultures are in danger of extinction if something is not done to help protect and promote the **preservation of cultural heritage**.

William Denevan and the Depopulation of Native Americans

One of the most important bodies of research on the destruction of indigenous culture groups is the work of geographer **William Denevan** on the depopulation of Native Americans in the early colonial era after 1492. By collecting years of archaeological research on the extent and productivity of agriculture by Native Americans, Denevan and allied researchers have established that the **pre-Columbian** population of North and South America combined was approximately 54 million people. By comparison, their research into colonial census data, collected journals, and colonial government reports revealed that the total native population had declined to around 5 million people by 1635.

Understanding what caused the massive indigenous population decline was the next part of Denevan's research. By examining Spanish colonial era documents such as the journals of Jesuit priests, the logs of ship captains, and the personal diaries of other individuals, Denevan found that diseases of European origin were the main culprit behind the decline, which in some cases wiped out whole native culture groups. Diseases such as influenza, measles, and cholera were unknown to the Americas prior to the arrival of European colonists. Native Americans had no immune system defense against these pathogens to which they had not been previously exposed. As a result, diseases like the flu, which normally has very low mortality, resulted in deadly **epidemics** with very high rates of mortality among indigenous groups. Research has shown that deaths from European diseases vastly outnumbered all other causes of death including warfare, forced labor, and relocation combined.

From a cultural perspective, disease epidemics had a devastating effect on the survival of many unique and advanced civilizations in the Americas. In addition to the large Aztec and Inca empires that the Spanish systematically eliminated through military conquest, there is a growing body of theory that a large agrarian civilization existed in the Amazon basin that may have been completely wiped out by European disease. The difference here is that Amazonian peoples did not utilize stone-work construction. Over time, the rapid physical deterioration of wooden houses and buildings in the tropical environment left little evidence of what is believed to be a large and extensive agricultural society.

To learn more about ancient Amazonian civilization, look for research into *terra preta* soil formations, which are the focus of archaeological and geographic research.

CONTEMPORARY CULTURAL CONFLICTS

Today, a number of indigenous cultures from around the world are under threat from a variety of forces that have the potential to eventually wipe them out. The concept of **cultural survival** is used to describe the efforts to research, understand, and promote the protection of indigenous cultures. In addition to protecting the identity and promoting the livelihood of indigenous peoples, indigenous cultures are seen as invaluable to the social, anthropological, and geographical composition and diversity of humankind. Thus, indigenous cultures are important to their people and representative governments, as well as to researchers.

An example would be the current research of geographer Kendra McSweeney. She investigates the cultural and economic livelihood of the Miskito Indians along the Caribbean coastal region of Honduras (the bugs are named after them). The Miskito live in an environmentally sensitive tropical forest region that is under threat from a number of development interests, including plantation agriculture for crops such as bananas and sugar, and land development for new towns, mining, and ranching. McSweeney's research from both environmental data and field interviews shows that there is continuous encroachment, both physically and economically, on the traditional territory of these indigenous people. Without official protections instituted by the Honduran government, the Miskito will continue to suffer from the shrinkage of their indigenous territory and their culture and way of life will be threatened.

CULTURAL GLOBALIZATION

Another set of factors that can harm indigenous cultures and threaten the constitution of national cultures is **cultural globalization**. A number of influences such as literature, music, motion pictures, the Internet, and satellite and cable television, mainly from English-language sources, combine to diminish and potentially eliminate the media and culture of other linguistic groups. Other globalizing factors such as architecture, transportation infrastructure, food retailing, clothing styles, and the missionary efforts of **proselytic religions** also threaten many unique cultures around the world.

The problem with cultural globalization is that when people are fully immersed in globalized popular culture, they are denying the importance of their own ethnic culture. Over time, unique and socially important traditions can be forgotten and lost. People who lose their connection to their heritage are also losing part of their personal **connection to nature**. This can leave people feeling disconnected from the natural world and humanity, causing social and psychological problems—things we geographers will leave to psychologists to better understand and explain.

Economically, culture has value. By protecting national cultures from the negative effects of globalization, a nation can promote its own cultural economy and products from creative arts and media. At a basic level, these artistic products can be a significant draw for cultural tourism. At its most valuable level, whole media industries can generate large amounts of employment and value. An example would be the Bollywood movie industry based in Mumbai, India (formerly Bombay, hence the name *Bollywood*). In 2008, the release of the film *Slumdog Millionaire* generated its own global economic presence with theater receipts over $50 million by early 2009, and the Academy Award for Best Picture.

National Regulations and Laws

To combat the negative effects of cultural globalization, a number of national governments around the world have instituted laws and regulations that lessen the impact of foreign influence on their home cultures. These laws and regulations in many cases restrict certain types or limit the volume of foreign media and other external cultural influences. In some cases, there are attempts to completely ban external cultural influence.

As a First World example, the French government has taken a number of steps to significantly limit the volume of English-language films and television released or broadcast within France. Furthermore, the French government, through its Culture Ministry, provides funding to develop and promote French-language media for internal release and export. These media exports are intended for both Francophone countries and non-French-speaking countries, in an effort to push back against the English-dominated global media. Similar programs exist in Québec, where the Canadian and Québécois governments provide special funding for French-Canadian media.

Perhaps the most extreme case is the country of Bhutan, which places a number of limits on the importation of foreign media. Set in the Himalayan foothills and surrounded by northeastern India with China to its north, Bhutan severely limits the number of entrance visas for foreigners. Tourist visas are restricted to less than 10,000 each year. This is an effort by the royal government to preserve the ancient Buddhist culture and protect its people from the undue influence of popularized global media brought in and demanded by foreign visitors.

ETHNIC AND RELIGIOUS CONFLICTS

Cultural conflicts have existed throughout human history and unfortunately are still with us today. Some cultural conflicts are continuously negotiated between groups that do not result in violence or armed conflict. However, in a number of cases, bloodshed has resulted merely from the cultural differences of people occupying the same region.

Places such as the former Yugoslavia, the Caucasus Mountains, East Timor, Rwanda, Burundi, the Darfur region of Sudan, and Syria have been in the international eye for the bloody armed conflicts of their inhabitants. Yet, what can lead to war is something as simple as differences in language or as complex as differences in religion.

Yugoslavia

The former Yugoslavia was created as a state during the post–World War I **Treaty of Versailles** in 1919. Prior to that time, there was no such thing as a Yugoslav either politically or culturally. This part of the Balkan Peninsula contained a multitude of different overlapping ethnic regions, including groups such as Serbs, Croats, Bosnian Muslims, Slovenians, Montenegrins, Kosovars, and Macedonians. The victors in World War I (Britain, France, and the United States) thought the best plan of action was to put them all together as one state. In historical terms, the idea was short-lived.

Following the 1980 death of the country's longtime Communist leader, Josip Tito, there was a power vacuum that left no particular individual or group in control. Tito was born a Croat, but fought alongside Serbians against the Germans during World War II. In this way, he was a representative of an artificial Yugoslav identity, which did not exist before the twentieth century. After his death, with no Yugoslav heir apparent, people and politicians began to revitalize their centuries-long ethnic and religious arguments.

Croats, as an ethnic group, are predominantly Roman Catholic. Serbians are Eastern Orthodox Christians. Despite their shared Christianity and Serbo-Croatian language, these are two separate ethnic groups from two very different religious traditions. In 1989, localized fighting broke out in northern Yugoslavia between these groups. Croats forced Serbs out of Serbian **enclaves** in Croatia and Serbs did the same, forcing Croats to leave northern Serbia. Here we see the first mention of the term **ethnic cleansing,** where people of one ethnic group are eliminated by another, often under threat of violence or death.

Despite this conflict being quickly resolved by international diplomacy, by 1990 fighting and ethnic cleansing had flared up in Bosnia between ethnic Croats, Serbs, and Bosnian Muslims who fought to control various parts of the mountainous country. Several thousand men and older boys were executed in Bosnia just for being potential combatants in war. The war was curtailed in 1994 by the **Dayton Peace Accords**. Today, roughly 20,000 foreign peacekeeping troops are on duty in Bosnia and neighboring Kosovo (southern Serbia).

Since then, several political and military leaders have been charged with **crimes against humanity** for their war crimes in Bosnia. In late 2008, Radovan Karadzic, a Bosnian Serb leader, was arrested after living several years in bearded disguise as an herbal medicine practitioner in Belgrade. He has been charged with ordering the genocide of Bosnian Muslim males in Srebrenica, where several mass graves have since been uncovered.

Never Again?

Genocide, a large-scale systematic killing of people of one ethnic group, has been seen in a number of ethnic conflicts. Most famous is the **Holocaust** of Jews at the hand of the Nazis in World War II where 6 million were killed. More recent cases involve the deaths of several hundred thousand Tutsis by Hutus in Rwanda during 1994. And today the genocide label has been applied to the situation in the west Sudanese province of Darfur, where Christians and Animist people have been killed by Muslim militia groups known as *Janjaweed*.

See more on culture as a source of conflict in Chapter 6.

OTHER RESOURCES

- For more cultural geography material see *The Human Mosaic,* by Terry G. Jordan-Bychkov, Mona Domosh, Roderick P. Neumann, and Patricia L. Price.
- Also see *Cultural Geography in Practice* by Alison Blunt, Pyrs Gruffudd, Jon May, and Miles Ogborn.

KEY TERMS

cultural landscape
signs
symbols
components of culture
cultural synthesis (syncretism)
culture group (nation)
built environment
architectural forms
modern architecture
contemporary architecture
traditional architecture
postmodern
green energy
recycled materials
commercial buildings
housing
folk house
traditional housing style
New England style
Cape Cod
Salt Box
Federalist (Georgian) style
I-house
relocation diffusion
Christian buildings
Hindu buildings
Buddhist buildings
stupa
pagoda
Islamic buildings
minarets
Judaic buildings
Wailing Wall

official languages
monolingual
multilingual
linguistic region
dialect
word sounds
vocabulary
received pronunciation
Cockney
Cockney rhyming slang
pidgin
French Creole
patois
lingua franca
English
global lingua franca
language families
language groups
language subfamilies
prehistoric migrations
hearth
Anatolian theory
Hellespont
Kurgan theory
Eurasian steppe
folk music
folk song
folklore
popular culture
pop music
Appalachia
bluegrass
Gypsies (Roma)

continental cuisine

haute cuisine

nouvelle cuisine

Mediterranean

fusion cuisine

folk food

sushi

Moroccan

social interaction

culturally constructed

handshake

bow

cheek kissing

personal space

religions (belief system)

universalizing religions

ethnic religions

scripture

divine origin

doctrine

denominations

compromising religions

fundamentalists

animist tradition

Hindu-Buddhist tradition

polytheistic

nirvana

Abrahamic tradition

monotheistic

shamans

shamanism

migration diffusion

relocation diffusion

caste system

Agamas

relocating

cosmology

karma

Imams

theocracies

head of state

republics

monarchies

Sharia

secular

Druze

Sikhs

five pillars of Islam

Aesop's fables

appellations

metes and bounds

long-log patterns

township and range

technology

ethnicity

racism

Melanesians

Polynesians

Micronesians

Aboriginals

indigenous population

mestizos

mulattos

Garifuna

Creole

Friedrich Ratzel

Carl Sauer

possibilism

lebensraum

xenophobia

internal identity

external identity

culture regions

nation (ethnicity)

"fuzzy" borders

Dixie

border states

culture hearths

contemporary culture hearths

ancient culture hearths

staple food crops

contemporary culture region

Latter-Day Saints (LDS)

sequent occupance

acculturation

assimilation

indigenous
indigenous culture
preservation of cultural heritage
William Denevan
pre-Columbian
epidemics
cultural survival
cultural globalization
proselytic religions
connection to nature
Treaty of Versailles
enclaves
ethnic cleansing
Dayton Peace Accords
crimes against humanity
genocide
Holocaust

POLITICAL GEOGRAPHY

CHAPTER OUTLINE

This chapter is divided into two major parts: Know the Concepts and Know the Models. The concepts section contains examples of political state units and nationalism, the organization of states, spatial concepts and borders, electoral representation, political-economic systems, and finally, geopolitics. The models section details Mackinder's Heartland-Rimland model, Cohen's Shatterbelts, and Cold War containment theory.

KNOW THE CONCEPTS

UNITS OF POLITICAL ORGANIZATION

There are a number of political geography terms such as nation and state that we use in everyday speech as synonyms. However, the technical definitions of these terms have specific and important meaning in the geography of politics. Here's how to keep them straight:

> **Country:** an identifiable land area
> **Nation:** a population with a single culture
> **State:** a population under a single government
> **Nation-state:** a single culture under a single government

A nation is the same as a **culture group**. "State" implies that there is a **sovereign territory**. Sovereignty generally means that a state is fully independent from outside control, holds territory, and that it has **international recognition** from other states or the United Nations. Use these examples to keep the differences in your mind:

Nations	State Name	Country
England, Scotland, Wales, Northern Ireland, Isle of Man, and the Channel Islands	United Kingdom of Great Britain and Northern Ireland	Great Britain or the British Isles
Han, Manchu, Zhuang, Miao, Uygur, Tibetan, and others	People's Republic of China	China
Anglo-Canadian, Québécois, and First Nations	Canada (former name Dominion of Canada)	Canada
French, German, Italian, and Romansch	*Confoederatio Helvetica* (in Latin)	Switzerland (French: *Suisse*) (German: *Schweiz*)

These examples, the United States, and most other sovereign states are **multinational states** made up of a number of different nations represented by the multitude of culture groups who have migrated and intermixed around the world. Multinational, sometimes called **multi-ethnic states,** are most common in the Americas, where there are no nation-states.

NATION-STATES

There are a number of nation-states in which one culture group is represented by a singular government. Many are smaller states or island countries. Although no nation-state is truly made up of only one cultural group, places such as Japan, Iceland, Tonga, Ireland, Portugal, and Lesotho (pronounced Lesu-too) are places that have not seen permanent invasion or mass immigration from other culture groups in their histories.

The term *nation-state* is also applied, theoretically, to multinational states where the state has come to represent a singular and contemporary culture, as opposed to the ancient cultures from which the population originates. One could argue that there is an identifiable American culture in the United States, or a unique Brazilian culture in Brazil. In both of these cases, the new political nation is the result of the blending of several culture groups together along with the idea of political nationalism.

NATIONALISM

Nationalism can derive from an existing culture group that desires political representation or independence, or from a political state that bonds and unifies culture groups. Politicians use nationalism as motivation to support the state and oppose foreign or other political influences. Individuals tend to take pride in their nationalist identities, even though they or their neighbors may be from a mix of different ethnic backgrounds.

STATELESS NATIONS

Although many culture groups are politically represented or are part of larger political entities, there are some **stateless nations,** where a culture group is not included or allowed share in the state political cal process. Here are a few examples:

> **Kurds** are an ethnic group spread across northern Iraq, western Iran, eastern Syria and southeastern Turkey. A semi-autonomous Kurdistan has existed in Iraq since the U.S.-led invasion in 2003. However, full independence is limited geopolitically due to Turkish government resistance to their sovereignty, based upon Kurdish Marxist rebels, the PKK, who have been fighting in Turkey for several decades. Since the start of the Syrian Civil War, Kurds have taken territory and started a semi-autonomous government.
>
> **Basques** are an ethnic group in northern Spain and southwestern France who do not have Celtic or Latin cultural or language roots. In fact, their people's origin is poorly understood by historians. Spain has granted limited autonomy to the Basque region around the city of Bilbao, but many Basque nationalists seek full independence and statehood. A militant group, ETA, has used terror tactics to

fight against Spanish rule.

Hmong are mountain peoples who have existed in rural highlands isolated from others in Laos, Vietnam, Thailand, and southern China. However, their alliance with the United States against the Communists during the Vietnam War caused many families to leave their traditional homeland. Today many Hmong (pronounced "mung") have resettled in the upper Midwestern states of Wisconsin and Minnesota. Hmong immigrants are featured in the 2008 film *Gran Torino*.

Other stateless nations include Karen, Gypsies (Roma or Romani), Karelians, Tartars, Tuvans, Chechens, Sami, Uygurs (pronounced Vigers), Tibetans, and Tamils. Some groups have been granted limited autonomy, while others have active nationalist and independence movements. See the section on **irredentism** in this chapter for more on independence and sovereignty in the post-Soviet era.

ORGANIZATIONS OF STATES

THE BIG FELLAS

Federal states and **confederations** are a common approach to government. The United States, Australia, Canada, Germany, Brazil, Russia, and Mexico are all confederations of several smaller states or provinces under a federal government. Like an umbrella, the federal state provides military protection, administers foreign diplomacy, and regulates trade as well as a number of internal administrative (executive branch), legislative, and judicial services across the country. The states each have their own governments, legislatures, regulations and services. The overlapping roles in the administration may seem redundant, but each has their own division of responsibilities. For instance, the federal government regulates interstate trade, whereas states can make rules about the sale of goods within each state.

THE WEE FELLAS

At the other end of the international scale, **microstates** are sovereign states that despite their very small size still hold the same position of much larger states like the United States or Canada. Many are island states, ports, or city-states, or they sit landlocked with no access to the sea. The following table provides a list of microstates that are full members of the United Nations (UN):

State	Geography
Andorra	Landlocked
Antigua and Barbuda	Islands
Bahrain	Islands
Barbados	Island
Comoros	Islands
Djibouti	Port
Dominica	Island
Grenada	Islands
Liechtenstein	Landlocked
Luxembourg	Landlocked
Malta	Islands
Monaco	Port and City-state
Nauru	Island
Palau	Islands
St. Kitts and Nevis	Islands
St. Lucia	Island
Samoa (Western Samoa)	Islands
San Marino	Landlocked
Singapore	Port, Islands, and City-state

The Vatican City is also a sovereign microstate but is not a member of the UN. It is not a nation-state despite the common religion of its residents, who are mostly clergy drawn from around the world and a small Ethiopian boy's school.

MULTI-STATE ORGANIZATIONS

Supranationalism is the concept of two or more sovereign states aligned together for a common purpose. A number of **supranational organizations** have been formed for the purposes of trade alliances, military cooperation, and diplomacy. The largest of these is the **United Nations** (193 member states) whose purpose is primarily diplomatic. The UN also provides a number of services internationally through its World Health Organization (WHO), Food and Agriculture Organization (FAO), Development Program (UNDP), International Children's Education Fund (UNICEF), peacekeeping forces, and other smaller directorates such as the UN High Commissariat for Refugees (UNHCR). Each of these units is an important supranational organization in its own right.

Detailed Example: The EU

Another important supranational organization with several purposes is the **European Union** (EU). In 2013, the EU grew to 28 member states with a small number of applicant states awaiting membership. The EU was named in 1991 under the Treaty of Maastricht, which expanded the organization's role beyond trade relations. Prior to that, the European Coal and Steel Community (created in 1957) helped strengthen steel production between Italy, France, Luxembourg, Belgium, and the Netherlands. The success of this limited free-trade network encouraged the development of the European Economic Community, "the Common Market" or EEC. By 1973, the EEC eliminated all tariffs on trade goods between its 12 Western European member states.

Today, the EU acts like a federal government for Europe but lacks some of the administrative aspects of other confederations like the United States. The modern EU serves five main purposes

- **Free-trade union:** No taxes or tariffs are charged on goods and services that cross the internal borders of the EU. By eliminating these fees, European businesses can save money and be more economically competitive with the United States and Japan.
- **Open-border policy**: Between EU member states there are no longer any border controls stations for immigration or customs inspections. People and commercial vehicles cross internal EU borders without stopping. This began with the **Schengen plan** in 1985 when West Germany, France, Belgium, Luxembourg, and the Netherlands opened their borders to one another. Workers can now take jobs in other EU states without applying for work permits (some professions may be protected from this).
- **Monetary union:** In 2000 the first EU members began converting to the Euro and phasing out their old forms of money. This eliminated the costs of currency exchange fees. Only 12 members retained their own currencies. The United Kingdon kept the British pound due to its high value—converting to the less valuable Euro would have cause significant financial problems in the United Kingdom. New member states have to meet strict EU economic regulations before they can join the monetary union. However, the world financial crisis of 2008 revealed some weaknesses of the Euro as indebted countries were unable to devalue the Euro as they'd been able to with national currencies. Countries like Greece, Ireland, and Portugal received bailouts as part of the Eurozone crisis. These events have forced countries to question the desirability of using the Euro currency.
- **Judicial union:** The European Court of Justice in Luxembourg provides a legal venue for cases between litigants in separate EU member states. With the increase in cross-border trade and labor, there were bound to be lawsuits and contract issues that would require the EU's decisions. In addition, a European Court of Human Rights has been established to preserve civil rights regardless of their member states' local laws.

- **Legislative and regulatory bodies:** The 785-seat EU Parliament was established to propose and approve laws within the union. The European Commission is a separate council with one seat for each member state. Each year the presidency shifts to one member state, allowing it to set the year's policy agenda. The European Commission also acts as the executive branch of the union to enact programs and enforce regulations set by the EU Parliament and Council. The EU Commission president is appointed by the European Council.

The EU as the World's Largest Economy

In sum, EU governance has been successful in creating a singular economy through free trade, open borders, free movement of labor, free exchange of currency, and a level playing field for business and labor in terms of laws and regulations. Instead of 28 small economies, the EU acts as one state economy that is highly competitive with the United States, Japan, and emerging economies like Russia, China, India, Brazil, or a proposed Free Trade Zone of the Americas. In terms of total gross domestic product (GDP), the 2012 *CIA World Factbook* reports the EU has an economy just over 17 trillion compared to a U.S. economy just under 17 trillion dollars.

Something Rotten in Denmark?

Despite the economic success of the EU, a number of problems have emerged from the perspective of its citizens and member states. Even though free trade, open borders, and the Euro reduced the cost of doing business and reduced the cost of goods and services, the EU government's main source of revenue is a 17.5 percent sales tax, known as the **value-added tax** or VAT. Many complain that the cost of EU governance has significantly increased the cost of many items in Europe. Member state governments have also complained that the European courts have threatened the sovereignty of national and local courts and laws.

Likewise, open borders have made it difficult to control crime and terrorism. Once someone gets inside the EU's borders, he can move around freely regardless of citizenship, making it difficult to stop and apprehend criminals. Externally, the EU has had to strengthen its borders against illegal immigration and the flow of contraband. The term **Fortress Europe** has been used to describe the concept of sealing EU borders. This is a rather difficult problem, since much of the eastern borders of the EU are undefended and only road and rail border crossings are inspected by immigration or customs officers.

No Constitution for You! Yet...

In terms of further expansion of the EU system of governance, a **European Union Constitution** was proposed for ratification in 2004. The complex 65,000 word document was poorly understood by the citizens and members of parliament who had to vote on the constitution. Concepts like a common EU foreign policy among all states were unclear. Many voters and politicians were concerned about the continued loss of sovereignty for member state governments. Political leftists saw the constitution as being too pro-business. And right-wing sentiment against Turkey in the EU also resulted in "No" votes against ratification. The constitution was voted down in the Netherlands and France in 2005, thus forcing the European Commission to go back to the drawing board.

Additional Supranational Organizations

Other examples of Supranational Organizations	Purpose
North Atlantic Treaty Organization (NATO)	Military
Organization of Petroleum Exporting Countries (OPEC)	Oil Pricing Cartel
North American Free Trade Agreement (NAFTA)	Free-Trade Zone
Organization of African Union (OAU)	Regional Diplomacy
World Bank and International Monetary Fund (IMF)	Government Loans

SPATIAL CONCEPTS OF POLITICAL GEOGRAPHY

Territoriality is the expression of political control over space. The concept of the state implies that the government controls land and the people who live there. **Citizenship** is the legal identity of a person based on the state where he was born or where he was naturalized as an immigrant. Keep in mind that when citizens go outside their state's political borders, they retain their citizen status and thus become an extension of their state (unless they apply for new citizenship as immigrants). This is why we strictly define the state as a population represented by a single government, without mentioning territory. However, don't forget that space matters; as it's not much of a state if it has no land, which can happen in the case of a government in exile, such as the Dutch or Polish governments during World War II.

POLITICAL BORDERS

The borders between political states and political sub-unit areas (counties, parishes, parliamentary districts, and city limits) are strictly **finite lines**. Political boundaries, as expressions of political control, must be definable and clear. Sometimes the **physical geography**, such as rivers or other water bodies, define boundaries, and sometimes border lines are measured surveys based on treaties or other agreements between states. Non-physical boundaries often reflect **cultural divisions,** but these are not always accurate. Such borders can be the result of aristocratic land holdings from Feudalistic eras, or be the front lines at the secession of armed conflict between states—however, treaties can change these lines.

Outside The Lines

Countries with large **expatriate** populations (citizens living outside of their borders) have to provide consular services in large foreign cities. Citizens living in foreign countries often have to visit their country's embassies or consulates to process legal documents, passports, and visa applications. When citizens get trapped in war zones or disasters in foreign countries, it's up to their government's diplomats and military to get them out.

Enclave and Exclave

Borderlines may be finite, but they can become quite irregular in pattern especially where the cultural borderlines become fuzzy. An **enclave** is a minority culture group concentrated inside a country that is dominated by a different, larger culture group. This could be as simple as an ethnic neighborhood or a large area such as Québec. As part of the 1994 Dayton Peace Accords, several enclaves were formally established within Bosnia to separate warring Serb, Croat, and Muslim communities.

An **exclave** is a fragmented piece of sovereign territory separated by land from the main part of the state's territory. Occasionally, neighboring states attempt to claim exclaves in the name of cultural nationalism. Often armed conflicts result, but sometimes diplomatic negotiations result in official permanent exclaves. Other times states purchase territory or receive fragments of territory under peace treaties. Islands are not considered exclaves. Here are a few examples of exclaves:

Exclave	Controlling State	Separated by
Alaska	United States	Canada
Port Roberts	United States	Canada
Kaliningrad (Koenigsberg)	Russia	Lithuania, Belarus
Nagorno-Karabakh	Armenia	Azerbaijan
Nakhchivan	Azerbaijan	Armenia
Cabinda	Angola	Dem. Rep. of Congo
Musandam	Oman	United Arab Emirates
Llívia	Spain	France
Ceuta and Melilla	Spain	Morocco

Water Borders at Sea

Historically, borders at sea were poorly defined, and each country had its own laws regarding where territorial claims began and ended. Often, more than one sovereign state claimed the same piece of water. This all changed in 1982 with the **United Nations Conference on the Law of the Seas** (UNCLOS), which proposed standard oceanic boundaries for all UN member states, and was fully ratified in 1994. The border system under UNCLOS is in the following two parts:

> **Territorial sea**: Sovereign territory includes the area of sea from shore out to the 12-nautical-mile limit. Within 12 nautical miles all the laws of a country apply.

Exclusive Economic Zone (EEZ): Exclusive economic rights from shore out to the 200-nautical-mile limit. Within 200 nautical miles of its shores, a state controls all aspects of natural resource exploration and extraction. This includes fisheries, oil and gas production, salvage operations, and permits for such activity. Two hundred nautical miles is beyond the shallow water **continental shelf** in almost all cases.

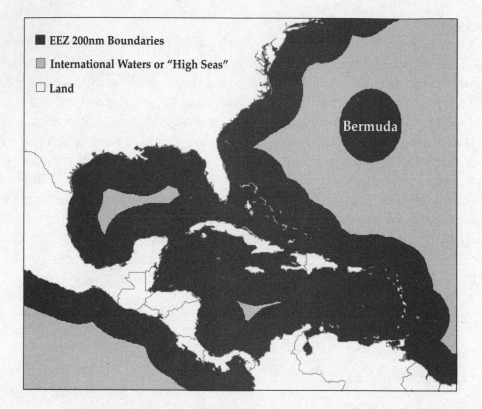

EEZ Boundaries and High Seas off the Eastern United States

The **high seas** are technically outside of the 12-mile limit. Past that line, cruise ships can open their casinos and ship captains gain the authority to marry couples or arrest thieves onboard their ships. These are provisions made under **admiralty law**, a part of international law that dictates legal procedures on the high seas. Beyond the 200-mile limit, international fishing fleets can hook or net whatever ocean life they choose and in unregulated amounts.

The only exceptions are when international treaties limit the capture of certain species. The 1986 **International Whaling Commission** moratorium on commercial whale hunts banned whaling after centuries of hunting dangerously depleted populations. Norway and Japan still hunt whales, claiming their hunts are for scientific research. This claim is heavily criticized by environmental organizations who state that whale meat still makes it way to market in these countries.

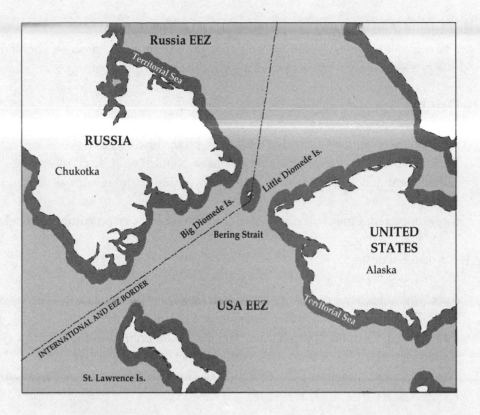

International Political Borders Compared to EEZs and Territorial Seas

Political Borders on the Map, Not EEZs

When you look at the map above you can see that normal political boundaries and the real EEZ boundaries are very different. The cartographic borders are often rectangular around islands. In reality, territorial seas and EEZs create circular boundaries, especially around islands—each of which extends a country's EEZ out another 200 nautical miles.

Overlapping Borders at Sea and Disputes

The UNCLOS makes provisions for a UN **arbitration board** to settle disputes regarding boundaries at sea. Often countries with overlapping sea claims generally agree to split the lines halfway. Where it becomes difficult is when uninhabited small islets, exposed reefs, and sandbars above water are claimed by more than one country. It can take years of negotiation to settle such disputes, and occasionally troops are deployed to precariously small pieces of land, just to claim rights to the surrounding EEZ. For example, two areas of the South China Sea, the **Spratly Islands** and the **Paracel Islands,** are claimed concurrently by China, Vietnam, Indonesia, the Philippines, Malaysia, and Brunei. Oil is believed to be under both island groups, and these are areas of potential future armed conflict if arbitration fails.

Boundary Origins and Border Types

This topic can be confusing due to the varied terminology used to describe processes behind boundary creation and the types of borders that exist. Let's see if we can simplify this:

Boundary Origins

Antecedent: Boundary lines that exist from prehistoric times
Relic: Former state boundaries that still have political or cultural meaning
Subsequent: Lines resulting from conflict or cultural changes, such as war and migration
Superimposed: Lines laid down for political reasons overtop cultural boundaries

Important Historical Examples:

Antecedent: French-Spanish border along the Pyrenees
Relic: Scotland-England border after The Act of Union in 1652
Subsequent: German-Polish border after 1945; Kaliningrad to the USSR in 1946
Superimposed: Sub-Saharan Africa after the Berlin Conference of 1884; Yugoslavia and Iraq after the 1919 Treaty of Versailles (Each of these resulted in recent conflicts.)

Boundary Process

Definition: When borders are claimed, negotiated, or captured
Delimitation: When borders are put on the map
Demarcation: When markers are placed on the ground to show where borders lay

Border Type

Physical: Natural boundaries—rivers, lakes, oceans, mountains, or deserts
Cultural: Estimated boundaries between nations, ethnic groups, or tribes
Geometric: Boundaries surveyed mostly along lines of latitude and longitude

Border Disputes

Definitional: When border treaties are interpreted two different ways by states
Locational: When the border moves, like a river changing course or lake drying up
Operational: When borders are agreed to, but passage across the border is a problem
Allocational: When a resource lies on two sides of a border. Who gets what?

Important Historical Examples:

Definitional: Russian-Japanese Kuril Islands under Soviet control in 1945
Locational: India-Bangladesh territory along the Ganges-Brahmaputra River Delta
Operational: New passport requirements for entry into the United States after September 11, 2001
Allocational: Mexico-United States river allocations for irrigation and drinking water on the Colorado River and Rio Grande (Rio Bravo)

Border Conflicts: Frontier War or Peace?

Historically, when land was either unexplored or unsurveyed, the term **frontier** was used to describe the open and undefined territory. There are a few disputed small frontier regions in the world today. The only remaining large land frontier is Antarctica, where the Antarctic Treaty (1959) has set aside the continent (actually several large islands covered by an ice cap) for scientific research and prohibits any military action and commercial mineral or energy extraction.

Peaceful Resolution to Border Conflicts

Prior to the 1846 Oregon Treaty that set the border at 49° North latitude, the western border between Canada and the United States was undefined. Much of the frontier region of what is today Montana, Idaho, Oregon, Washington, Alberta, and British Columbia was claimed concurrently by Great Britain and the United States. Diplomacy was the key to a peaceful settlement of the border dispute, but it nearly led to war as many in the United States were heard to say, "Fifty-Four Forty or Fight!"—the claim that the U.S. border should be 54°40′ North. Not all parts of the world have been so lucky to resolve their frontier claims peacefully. In fact, many border treaties have led to violence later on.

Post-Colonial Boundary Conflicts

An international example of a former frontier dispute that has led to conflict today is in Central Africa. The **Conference of Berlin** (1884) was a diplomatic meeting between the European colonial powers to set the internal political boundaries in Africa. Africa was one of the last areas of European colonial expansion. Most colonies were in coastal areas, but the interior of the continent had only recently been explored by Europeans. Diplomats at the conference went about carving up the continent's interior and settling disputed claims. The final agreed-upon map is very similar to the political boundaries in Africa today. However, there are many problems with the 1884 border design that did not emerge until after **decolonization** in the late twentieth century. Most African colonial states achieved **self-determination** as fully independent sovereign states between 1960 and the early 1990s.

The main problem with the European-set boundaries in Africa is that they do not match the cultural boundaries. This **superimposed boundary** situation is what Africans refer to as the **Tyranny of the Map.** Instead of the large artificial nation-states that the Europeans envisioned, the reality is that political allegiance in Sub-Saharan Africa is based upon tribal identity, and at a much smaller relative scale. The result has been that within post-colonial African states, a number of tribes have been grouped together in a confined area, some of whom have long precolonial histories of conflict.

Tyranny of the Map Example: Rwanda

An example of one such postcolonial conflict zone is Rwanda, where in 1994 ethnic Hutus and Tutsis fought to control the small landlocked and mountainous country. Tutsis had migrated to the region some 400 years earlier, but upon independence from Belgium in 1962, Hutus went about **ethnic cleansing,** forcing many Tutsi refugees into the former Zaire and to Uganda. In 1994, after a plane carrying the presidents of Rwanda and neighboring Burundi was shot down, large-scale reactionary violence erupted by Hutus against local Tutsis, who were blamed for the crash. In response, Tutsi refugees flooded back into the country to fight back. In the end, each ethnic group lost around 500,000 people to the violent **genocide**.

In the years following, Hutu versus Tutsi violence has spilled over to Burundi and eastern parts of the Democratic Republic of Congo, where ethnic-based violence and fighting continues today. The Eastern Congo is seen by many researchers to be the next area of widespread **armed conflict in Africa**. Due to ethnic fighting in and along the Democratic Republic of Congo and invasion by the armies of Uganda and Zambia, the region's 1884 borders are all but meaningless lines on the map.

Other postcolonial frontier border disputes:		
Frontier	**States in Dispute**	**Cause or Reason**
Kashmir	India, Pakistan, China	Mountainous region and British Partition in 1948 (Remains in conflict)
Empty Quarter	Saudi Arabia, U.A.E., Oman	Open sand dune desert (Rub al-Khali) (Saudis and Yemen settled in 2000)
Neutral Zones	Saudi Arabia, Iraq, Kuwait	Uqair Protocol of 1922 and open desert (Saudis and Kuwait settled in 1970) (Saudis and Iraq settled in 1991)

TERRITORIAL MORPHOLOGY

The shape of a country is often what helps you identify it on a map. To some degree, the shape of a country also impacts its society and external relations with other countries. Here is a list of the major types of state morphology (shape):

Type	Description	Examples
Compact:	Shape without irregularity	Nigeria, Colorado
Fragmented:	Broken into pieces; archipelagos	Philippines, Newfoundland
Elongated:	Appears stretched-out, long	Chile, Tennessee
Prorupt:	Has a panhandle or peninsula	Italy, Michigan
Perforated:	Has a hole(s) (country, large lake)	South Africa, Utah
Landlocked:	Has no sea or ocean borders	Switzerland, Wyoming

The Swiss Navy?

Although Switzerland can register and flag **merchant ships**, due to its landlocked morphology it has never had a navy. Humorously, the term "Swiss Navy" is either an oxymoron or pure idiocy. The latter appears to be the historical case. In the early 1990s, pilots from the Swiss Air Force were the first outside of the U.S. Navy and Marines to fly the F-18 Hornet aircraft. The United States gave permission for the Swiss Air Force to use all existing American F-18 training programs and facilities. For some this went as far as the ultimate in military flight training, carrier landing school. Upon completion of carrier training, some pilots were awarded certificates which had "Swiss Navy" printed on them.

Territorial Change

In addition to wars and other subsequent border changes, there are a few other ways in which state territory can change shape. Decolonization after World War II significantly reduced the area and number of territorial and colonial holdings of the European powers and the United States. Although most areas were granted independence, some colonial holdings were **incorporated** and residents integrated with full citizen status. Examples include Hawaii, Alaska, and the French *departments* of Guadeloupe, Martinique, Reunion, and French Guyana. Residents of these places have full voting rights, pay taxes, and receive benefits just like the other citizens of the United States and France.

Annexation is another term used to describe when territory is added as a result of a land **purchase** or when a territorial claim is extended through **incorporation**. The United States originally purchased Alaska from the Russian Empire in 1867 for $7,000,000 in gold—a bargain of Manhattan-esque proportion—and it became a full state in 1948. The U.S. Virgin Islands resulted from a cash sale of St. Thomas, St. John, and St. Croix by a financially strapped Danish government in 1917 (during World War I).

Capitals

We can't forget that each state has to have a capital city. Why? There will always need to be a **seat of government** where political power is centered. In a way, political power is a form of currency just like money. And just as market areas need financial centers of exchange, politicians need a place to have organized exchanges of power. Occasionally they make laws and have elections, as well. Federal states can have several scales of capitals, just as they have several scales of sub-state units.

Federal State Example	
Place, Description	**Relative Scale**
Akron, county seat of Summit County, Ohio	Local, County, or Parish
Columbus, state capital of Ohio	State, Provincial, or Regional Scale
Washington, D.C., capital of the United States	National (nation-state), Federal

Most countries have one national capital, but some have more than one. Often this is done to share power across different regions of the country. Here are a few examples of countries with more than one capital:

State	Capitals
South Africa	Pretoria, Bloemfontein, Cape Town
Bolivia	La Paz, Sucre
Netherlands	Amsterdam, The Hague
Ivory Coast	Abidjan, Yamoussoukro

Occasionally countries change the location of their capital. Sometimes this is due to a shift in political power or can be due to congestion in the old capital. Some new capitals are often **planned capital cities,** which are located in places where cities did not previously exist:

Planned Capital City Examples		
New Capital	**Old Capital**	**State**
Washington, D.C.	New York City	United States
Brasilia	Rio de Janeiro	Brazil
Canberra	Sydney	Australia
Abuja	Lagos	Nigeria

Other capitals were moved to existing cities for political reasons.

Other Historical Capital Changes			
New Capital	Old Capital	State	Reason
Berlin	Bonn, East Berlin	Germany	Reunification
New Delhi	Calcutta	India	Center of colony
Ankara	Istanbul	Turkey	Congestion, centrality
Moscow	St. Petersburg	Russia	Russian Revolution
Jerusalem*	Tel Aviv	Israel	Israeli annexation of West Bank

*Some countries do not officially recognize this—the U.S. Embassy is in Tel Aviv

ELECTORAL POLITICS AND INTERNAL BOUNDARIES

Who Can Vote?

Suffrage in terms of age, race, and gender has varied historically from state to state. The Nineteenth Amendment to the U.S. Constitution set the voting age at 18 in 1920. Women gained the right to vote in these selected examples:

State	Year Women's Suffrage Granted
New Zealand	1893
Canada	1917
United Kingdom	1918 (but only after age 30 until 1928)
United States	1920
Mexico	1947
Honduras	1955
Paraguay	1961

In addition to gender, race has historically been a barrier to voting rights. Apartheid in white, minority-ruled South Africa, which racially segregated almost all aspects of life and residential geography, also denied the voting rights of non-white citizens. In 1994, the first full and free elections in South Africa resulted in the presidency of former political prisoner and civil rights activist Nelson Mandela, who was from the African Xhosa tribe (pronounced Ho-sah). This was the world's last case of official government restriction, or *de jure* (by law) on voting due to race. However, in many countries there is still *de facto* (a matter of fact) racial and ethnic discrimination that restricts voting by minority citizens, via fear and intimidation tactics.

Voting for Local and Regional Representation

All democracies have some form of parliamentary system where at least one lawmaking body or house has **popular representation.** Each country has its own system regarding the number of seats and the size of **voting districts.** In the United States, division of the 435 seats of the House of Representatives is apportioned relative to each state's population. Every state is divided into a number of congressional districts, each district having one seat in the Congress; California has the most, at 53, and the least-populated state, Wyoming, has 1. In the United Kingdom and Canada, members of parliament (MPs) are selected from local constituencies based upon population, but unlike the United States, these are averaged from across the country. Due to its relatively dense population, Ontario holds 106 of the House of Commons' 308 MPs. Senators in Canada are appointed.

The Electoral College

In the United States, presidential elections are decided through voting by the **electoral college**. After the November presidential election, electoral votes are assigned state by state in December, based on the popular vote in each state. Most states are "winner take all," but a few, like Maine and Nebraska, split electoral votes proportional to the popular vote. The number of electoral votes is based on the total number of representative seats, plus the two senators' seats from each state—the District of Columbia also has 3 electoral votes. It follows that California has the most electoral votes, with 55, and Wyoming the least, at 3. It takes at least 270 (> 50 percent) electoral votes to win the presidential election. If the candidates tie or have fewer than 270 due to a third party, then Congress chooses the new president.

Every ten years following the census, the United States **reapportions** the 435 seats of the House of Representatives. In many states, this generally causes some changes to the number of congressional seats and, as a result, the number of electoral votes a state has. If the number goes up or down (and sometimes even when the number doesn't change), state governments draw new congressional district border lines to reapportion districts into equal-sized populations.

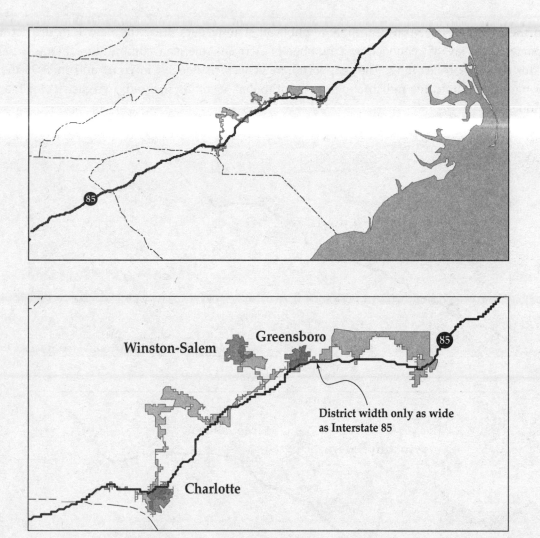

Map of the North Carolina 12th Congressional District

Gerrymandering

Sometimes reapportionment mapping is done in a straightforward manner with regional or compact districts. Other times the shapes of new or redrawn districts are very irregular. The irregularly shaped districts that are highly elongated and prorupt are often referred to as **gerrymandering**, named for Massachusetts Governor Elbridge Gerry who first attempted irregularly shaped districts in 1812.

In 1990 and 2000, a number of gerrymanders were attempted that tried to stack votes guaranteeing congressional support for one particular party within each district, making the outcomes of elections predictable and in the favor of the political majority in state government. Others were attempted that created "minority-majority districts" where lines were drawn to encompass only minority population centers.

In the 1992 case of North Carolina, Republican state leaders drew the new 12th district along Interstate Highway 85, connecting a number of African-American communities along a narrow corridor over 200 miles long. The reapportionment was challenged in court and in 1993 the U.S. Supreme Court found the redistricting unconstitutional, resulting in a redrawn district for the 1998 election cycle.

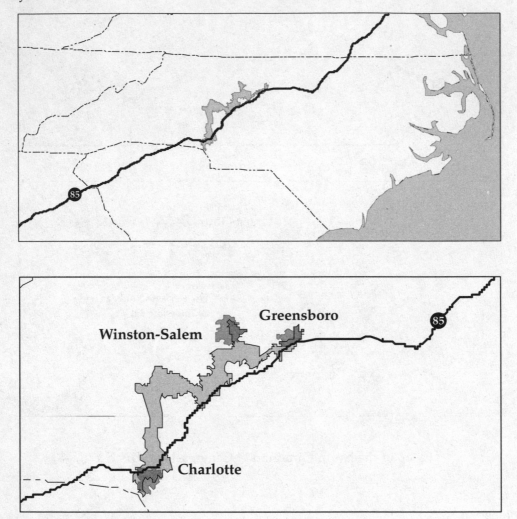

Redrawn Map Approved by the Supreme Court in 1997

POLITICAL ECONOMY

In terms of current and historical context, it is important to keep in mind the concept of political economy when you are discussing a country (especially on the essays). Why political economy? For one, it's often difficult to discuss the political situation in a state without explaining the economic aspects. In addition, these political-economic systems have important links to other parts of the AP Human Geography material. Here are the major categories to consider, with examples:

FEUDALISM AND ITS DECLINE

Feudal political economies operated with the vast majority of land and wealth being controlled by an **aristocracy**—a **peerage** of lords, earls, marquis, barons, dukes, princes, kings, and queens. Conversely, the vast majority of the population, as peasants, commoners, serfs, or slaves, were poor farmers and laborers who worked the land controlled by aristocrats. Peasants paid rents and had their harvests taxed for the right to live on and work the land. This system kept peasants in a cycle of debt, known as **debt peonage,** as they were never able to fully pay off rents and taxes.

Feudal states tended to have **absolute monarchy.** This is where the supreme aristocrat, a king, prince, or duke, is both **head of state** and **head of government,** and therefore does not share power with anyone. Like medieval-style feudalism, the concept of absolute monarchy has diminished over time and mostly exists in the Islamic world. A few absolute monarchies exist today:

Saudi Arabia
Brunei
Morocco (limited power-sharing)
Emirates within the United Arab Emirates

THE DECLINE OF FEUDALISM AND EMPIRES

Revolutions and wars from the late 1700s to the 1900s forced many feudal states to accept some form of democracy. Events such as the French Revolution of 1789 inspired many monarchs to accept power-sharing with commoners to avoid losing control of their states. Under **constitutional monarchy,** the supreme aristocrat remains head of state, but the leader of the elected parliament is the head of government, with integrated legislative and executive powers. In most cases this is a **prime minister** or **premier**, who appoints senior members of parliament to be ministers or secretaries of executive-branch departments.

In most constitutional monarchies, the monarch retains the power to dismiss parliament; appoints judges, ambassadors, and other officials; is commander and chief of the military; and retains significant land holdings and estates. However, the monarch's political power is mostly diminished to a symbolic role, and he or she holds a small but important position in dictating policy and proposing laws.

Here are some examples of constitutional monarchies:

> Great Britain
> Belgium
> The Netherlands
> Japan
> Norway
> Denmark
> Sweden
> Spain
> Thailand
> Luxembourg
> Kuwait
> Jordan
> Bahrain
> Monaco
> Cambodia

Example: The British Aristocracy and Government

The current form of constitutional monarchy in Great Britain has been in place since the Magna Carta was signed in 1215. Feudalism has reigned throughout, but in the Magna Carta there was some degree of power-sharing with the aristocracy and later with commoners voting in elections (1689).

Today, feudal rents to local aristocrats are still technically paid in a number of rural areas of the United Kingdom, although many are symbolic and small fees. A majority of Britons live in urban areas and are not subject to these fees. Many rural farms are now owned privately, though some may still be required to pay feudal rents.

The British aristocracy's structure and role has also been modified in recent years. Traditionally, aristocratic peers sat in the **House of Lords,** the upper house of parliament, which also serves as the supreme court. The House of Lords numbers more than 760 members. When the king or queen elevated someone to the peerage, a new seat was added. Eventually, they had too many members. Beginning in 1999, Queen Elizabeth II reformed the house with two types of members. Hereditary peers, who at death pass their title and seat to their firstborn son, were reduced in number, and life peers, mainly senior public servants who were rewarded with a title, kept their title and seat for their lifetime only.

Since the late 1600s, the power has steadily increased the **House of Commons**, the lower house of parliament. The Commons has 650 seats apportioned to local districts across the U.K.; Scotland, Wales, and Northern Ireland also have regional parliaments of their own. The Prime Minister (PM) is head of government, but is also a member of parliament (MP). Generally the PM is the political leader of the party with the most MPs. Other senior MPs from this **ruling party** serve as ministers of the executive branch of government. This is another example of how parliamentary democracy integrates the three branches of government.

Commonwealth Countries

Most but not all member states of the **Commonwealth of Nations** (independent former parts of the British Empire) retain the British monarch as their head of state. These commonwealth countries have their own parliaments and prime ministers as head of government. Each also has a royally appointed governor-general as the crown representative in the country. The governor-general's role, like the monarch's, is a mostly symbolic and ceremonial position. These countries are nonetheless considered independent sovereign states. Yet they do retain some minor political link to the U.K.—most provide military support to the U.K. in times of war. The following countries claim the British monarch as head of state:

Canada
Jamaica
Dominica
St. Vincent and the Grenadines
New Zealand
Australia
Fiji
Papua New Guinea
Belize
Guyana
Bahamas
Antigua and Barbuda
Grenada

India, Pakistan, Sri Lanka, Nigeria, and Kenya are a few of the commonwealth members that do *not* claim the British monarch as head of state. However, all commonwealth nations have parliamentary governments, which integrate executive, legislative, and judicial powers, like that of Great Britain. In addition, the Commonwealth of Nations is an important supranational organization that provides special trade, education services, government funding, and preferred immigration status between member governments and citizens.

Former colonies that are now dependent territories (not sovereign states) of the U.K. are not Commonwealth members, and are still controlled from London with limited local governance; these include Anguilla, Cayman Islands, Turks and Caicos, British Virgin Islands, Bermuda, Montserrat, the Falkland Islands, St. Helena, Ascension Island, and Gibraltar.

POLITICAL ECONOMY: FREE-MARKET DEMOCRACY

Generally, countries with elected representative parliamentary systems such as the United States, the United Kingdom, commonwealth countries, and other constitutional monarchies or republics are classified as **free-market democracies**. Internal to a state, this system generally relies upon balancing the relationship between the elected representative government, its citizens, and business interests. In most cases, there is a variable system of regulation and taxation by the state. As a result, the marketplace is not totally free, as it would be in a completely unregulated *laissez-faire* economic system, but it's close enough.

Government regulatory influence of the private lives of its citizens and practices of businesses is usually limited to areas concerning public safety and economic protections. The point of democracy is that people have a say in who makes the rules and thus have some influence over the rule-making process.

What's a Republic?

Without going in too deeply into your AP Government material, keep in mind that France, Germany, Italy, and many former colonial states are technically republics, under the broader category of free-market democracy. Some republics, like France, are centrally governed from a single capital. Others, like Germany or the United States, are confederations that apportion some government power of legislation and administration to their component states or provinces (*Lander* in Germany). The main thing to keep in mind is that **republics** are free of aristocracy or monarchal control. The governments are fully under the control of the "common" people, as opposed to hereditary monarchy.

Unlike parliamentary systems that assign legislative, executive, and judicial power to the same people, republics generally have a **separation of powers.** Here, the executive, legislative, and judicial branches of government are held by separate groups of people that keep each other in check. This may seem less efficient, but it reduces the potential for corruption of the whole government. If one branch's leadership fails or its practices are called into question, the other branches can act to correct problems or replace leadership if necessary.

Problems Within Republics

This is not to say that republics are perfect systems, as you might feel if you read too much Plato. The written **constitutions** of these governments need to be flexible enough to allow governments to deal with political and other crises when they occur. The United States has had two constitutions, the former being the Articles of Confederation, which did not work out. The French have had five different types of government since the revolution, and the current government system in France is known as the "Fifth Republic." There is no perfect constitution, but a constitution can be refined over time by the addition of amendments. Another problem is that wealthy businesspeople and corporations have replaced the aristocracy in terms of the control of money, land, and resources. Their personal and corporate **political influence** overshadows that of many thousands of private citizens. The purchase of political favoritism to influence the setting of regulations is a constant problem in republics, as it is in other democracies, especially within the legislative branch. This has created uneven power relations in free-market democracies.

Another type of separation is sometimes employed to blunt the **power of the executive branch** is to have separate presidents and prime ministers (or chancellors in Germany). In the United States, Mexico, and Argentina, the president is both head of state and head of government. In most other republics there is executive separation. Depending on the country, this can be done in a couple of ways. In France, the president is head of government and the prime minister is head of state, but it's the opposite in Italy. Aye! It's too many variables to keep straight, but make sure to know a couple of examples.

POLITICAL ECONOMY: MARXIST-SOCIALISM

Under **Communism**, Karl Marx's political-economic theories attempted to right the wrongs of feudalism and inequalities of capitalism in free-market democracies. One of the main goals of **Marxism** was to create a class-free society where there were no inequalities in terms or wealth or power. To do this, the state would own all land and industry, the government would direct economic productivity, and everyone regardless of labor position would earn the same amount of money.

The key to this working was the **planned economy**, which did not rely on supply and demand like capitalism. The central government would calculate the economic needs of the state, its industries, and people. Then the government would set **quotas** for each individual operational unit of agricultural or manufacturing production to meet these needs. Theoretically, the productivity of the economy would result in a collective wealth that would be shared equally across the population. It's a utopian ideal that the system should create a harmonious peaceful social existence, but Communism in practice failed to reproduce Marx's utopia.

What Happened with Communism?

You may have heard the statement, "A good idea in theory but not in practice." This is true for Communism. Marx died in 1883 and the first Communist country, the Union of Soviet Socialist Republics (USSR or Soviet Union), was established in 1917, with the fall of the czar's absolute monarchy in Russia. This time gap is significant. Had Marx seen how his ideas were put into practice, he'd have "blown a fuse," "had a cow," "had kittens"—pick your own analogy. On an essay you could describe him as upset or disapproving.

There were a number of unintended consequences to the Russian revolution, including a protracted and bloody civil war, human rights violations, murders on the part of the Communist government, and forced resettlement of over a million citizens. Despite all this, Soviet Communism emerged functioning under Marx's basic principles. Under Stalin, the USSR developed **Five-Year Plans**, which were comprehensive long-term economic plans that dictated all production in minute detail. In the 1930s, when the rest of the world was suffering through the poverty of the Great Depression, the Soviets were doing comparatively well.

However, fifty years later the USSR was falling apart. The **devolution** of the Soviet system was due in part to several political-economic problems in the USSR. One thing that would have caught Marx's eye was that, in reality, **three classes of Soviet citizens** emerged early in the Soviet Union. Most were workers, as Marx had envisioned his **proletariat**. However, to achieve an important position in Soviet society, like government officials, professors, or factory managers, you had to join the **Communist Party**. Party members made up of about 6 percent of the USSR population and enjoyed many perks such as special stores, nicer homes, and personal cars. Likewise, a **military officer class** emerged that had a similarly high quality of life in comparison to the regular working class.

Working-class people were resentful. But what could they do? Heavy-handed secret police and laws that made public protest punishable by hard labor in prison camps (known as *gulags*) kept open criticism to a minimum. Creative, inventive, and industrious people stagnated. Another reason for this was that there was a **lack of incentive** in the system that would motivate people to have better lives. It didn't matter if you were a brain surgeon or a garbage man; you got the same monthly pay. Sure, there are some perks to being a doctor, but were these enough to struggle through examinations and years of training with no financial reward? This was a problem.

The lack of incentive also affected economic productivity. Neither farms nor factories had any reason to produce more food or products than what was stipulated in government quotas. This resulted in a **lack of surplus**, leaving many stores with few items on the shelf and lines of people waiting to receive rations for food and clothing. More about the effects of the Cold War on the devolution of the USSR are ahead in this chapter.

These problems have also plagued other communist countries, and now only two cases of Soviet-style Communism remain: Cuba and North Korea. To see what has happened with economic reforms in Communist China and Vietnam, see Chapter 8.

What About the Socialism Part?

The positive things that came out of Communism were mainly in the realm of infrastructure and social welfare. Health care is a good example. Prior to Communism in the Soviet Union, China, and Cuba there had been almost no health care available to the common people. Socialism meant that everyone had a right to health care, and early on hospitals, clinics and rural travelling doctor programs were established. Similarly, infrastructure programs for public schools, free universities, drinking water, care for the elderly and public transit were built to improve the efficiency and quality of life in Communist society. It may not look glamorous today, but it successfully replaced the utter poverty that existed under the former feudal and corrupt capitalist societies in these countries.

These socialist successes impacted the non-Communist world as well during the latter twentieth century. Government leadership and control of health care, education, and pensions are Marxist-socialist ideals which have since been incorporated in Western free-market democracies like Canada and Great Britain.

GEOPOLITICS

The term **geopolitics** refers to the global-scale relationships between sovereign states. The theme of political-economic conflict between democracies and Communist countries during the Cold War (1945–1991) is a common area of geopolitical questions on the AP Human Geography Exam. This will be covered in more detail in the Know the Models section at the end of this chapter. Here are a number of other important geopolitical issues that you need to be prepared for on the exam.

CENTRIPETAL AND CENTRIFUGAL FORCES

These are two terms that students mix up all the time. Here are the definitions and a way to remember which one is which:

> **Centripetal forces** are factors that hold together the social and political fabric of the state. (Pedals make the bike go.)
> **Centrifugal forces** are factors that tear apart the social and political fabric of the state. (A centrifuge separates blood into its different parts.)

In every country there are a number of forces at work that both reinforce and destabilize the state. When the balance shifts too far in the category of centripetal forces, the survival of the state is at risk and indicates the likelihood of **armed conflict**—in the form of an **internal civil war**, or the possibility of conflict spilling over into **external cross-border war**.

Examples of centripetal forces:	Examples of centrifugal forces:
Political beliefs of nationalism A strong and well-liked national leader An effective and productive economy Effective government social welfare programs	Ethnic, racial, or religious difference or conflicts Political corruption Failing economic conditions Natural disasters or a wartime defeat

Example: Yugoslavia

As we mentioned in the Cultural Conflicts section of Chapter 5, Yugoslavia was an artificial state created after World War I that had several different ethnic and religious groups living within its borders. The post-World War II Communist leader of the country was the Croatian Josip Tito. As a Croat who fought alongside Serbians against the Nazis, Tito was a good choice as president. He became a centripetal force representing the two largest ethnic groups in the country. A strong nationalist belief in Communism among Yugoslavians helped Tito build an economically strong and socially harmonious multi-ethnic society. These were additional centripetal forces that held the state together.

When Tito died in 1980, the lack of an effective multi-ethnic leader to replace him created a political **power vacuum** that opened the way for different nationalist leaders representing different ethnicities to attempt to seize power for themselves and their constituents. These ethnic differences, combined with differences in religion between groups, had many histories of conflicts and warfare. These became powerful centrifugal forces that ripped apart the Yugoslav social and political fabric and, in combination with the fall of Communism in Europe, doomed the country to ethnic violence and dissolution. In a way, you can think of Tito's death as a centrifugal force in itself.

Balkanization and Irredentism

The case of the former Yugoslavia is also an important example of **balkanization**. This is due to the fact that Yugoslavia sits in the Balkan Peninsula, which has historically been divided among a large number of ethnic and religious groups—hence the term "balkanization." The definition of balkanization is when the political landscape goes from a larger state to several smaller states. In the last one hundred years of European history, the continent has geopolitically gone from being dominated by large **empire states** to being dominated by several small **nation-states**.

Sovereign states in Europe: 1909: 27 states   2014: 50 states

After World War I, much of the early cases of balkanization were due to a realignment of German borders and the dissolution of the Austro-Hungarian Empire into six sovereign states. After World War II, some borders changed but the number of states changed only slightly. It was after the fall of

Communism in Eastern Europe and in the Soviet Union in 1991 that the political landscape began to break apart.

Examples of Balkanization:		
Old State (end date)	New States	
Yugoslavia (1991–2008)	Slovenia Croatia Serbia Bosnia-Herzegovina	Montenegro Macedonia Kosovo (disputed)
Czechoslovakia (1993)	Czech Republic	Slovakia
Austro-Hungarian Empire (1918)	Poland (part) Czechoslovakia Hungary	Austria Yugoslavia (part) Liechtenstein
USSR (1991)	Russia Belarus Ukraine Estonia Latvia Lithuania Moldova Georgia	Armenia Azerbaijan Kazakhstan Uzbekistan Tajikistan Kyrgyzstan Turkmenistan

Irredentism as the Cause of Balkanization

Irredentism tends to follow one of two definitions: when a minority ethnic group desires to break away from a multi-ethnic state and form its own nation-state, or break away and align itself with a culturally similar state. Almost all of the cases of balkanization discussed in the previous section fall into these two categories. Cases of irredentism continue, and Russia is one of the most significant situations where a number of groups are seeking independence or **annexation** by a neighboring sovereign state that is culturally similar.

Chechnya is one such place. Chechens, like more than 25 other **autonomous republics** in Russia, were granted limited local self-governance by the Russian Federation. However, Chechens are ethnically Turkic peoples who are predominantly Muslim; very different from Slavic, Eastern Orthodox Christian Russians. It stands to reason that both religion and ethnicity are the centrifugal forces in this case.

Soon after the fall of Communism, Chechens began to declare independence from Russia. As a result the Russian government moved in troops and a regional armed conflict has ensued. Russia fears the loss of oil resources and pipelines in the region, but a larger geopolitical issue looms. If Russia were to allow Chechnya to become independent or be annexed by Azerbaijan, then many of the other autonomous republics would push for secession, leaving the Russian Federation without much of its current land and resources.

Recent Irredentist Conflicts:		
Location:	Island of **Timor**	**Ossetia**
Irredentists:	East Timorese (Catholic)	South Ossetia (Muslims)
Resistant State:	Indonesian (Muslim)	Rep of. Georgia (Christian)
Status:	Independence in 2002 after UN Intervention with Australian peace-keeping troops	Russian military as of 2008 protects the Ossetian autonomous region in Georgia

Reunification

In a few irredentism cases, nations or culture groups were torn apart into separate states as a result of war or other historical events. In the post–Cold War era there have been a few cases of **reunification** of note: (East and West) Germany, Yemen (North Yemen and Yemen Democratic Republic) and the return of the Canal Zone to Panama. There are also some places where, despite potential armed conflict, there is occasional talk of reunification between China and Taiwan, and North and South Korea.

KNOW THE MODELS

HEARTLAND-RIMLAND MODEL

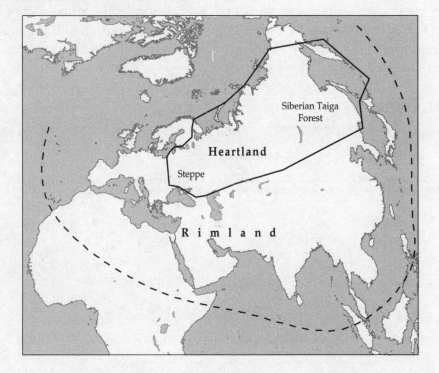

The Agricultural and Resource Heartland Is Surrounded by Rimland

The main geopolitical model in the AP Human Geography course encompasses the two world wars and the Cold War. In 1904, British geographer Halford Mackinder proposed what would become known as the **Heartland-Rimland model**. Mackinder's model was an effort to define the global geopolitical landscape and determine areas of potential future conflict. He identified agricultural land as the primary commodity that states were interested in. Several states with limited land area wanted to expand their territory—as they had done by expanding their colonial empires. However, they also eyed one another's European farming areas.

The largest of these was the **Eastern European steppe**, a very productive area of grain cultivation mostly controlled by the Russian Empire at the time. This, combined with the mineral and timber-rich region across the Urals into Siberia, was identified by Mackinder as the **Heartland.** It was this portion of the earth's surface that bordering **Rimland** states such as the German Empire, the Austro-Hungarian Empire, and Romania were potential invaders of. The Rimland also contained other **landwolves** eager to grab at neighboring territory such as France and Italy. Likewise, there were **seawolves,** such as Great Britain and Japan, who would use their navies to leverage geopolitical power.

Predictive Power of the Model

In effect, Mackinder accurately predicted the battle lines of the Eastern Front during World War I. In 1921, he revised the model, expanding the Heartland further into Central Europe. In essence, Mackinder stated that the same geopolitical situation remained, with land still being the primary **commodity of conflict**: the thing that countries were willing to fight over.

From 1904 onward, Mackinder points out that the areas of future conflict are the borderlines between the Heartland and Rimland. This prediction comes true again with the 1931 invasion of Manchuria by the Japanese, which some Asian scholars identify as the actual start of World War II. The European border conflict areas in the model are also realized with the 1939 German invasion of Poland, a country within the redrawn Heartland.

SHATTERBELT THEORY

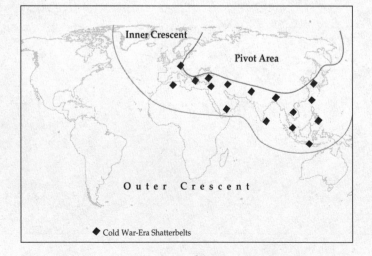

Conflicts Are Likely to Occur in the Inner Crescent

The Cold War: Shatterbelts and Containment Theory

Mackinder died in 1947, but his legacy lived on in Cold War–era geopolitical models and theory. In 1950, American geographer Saul Cohen proposed the **Shatterbelt theory**. He modified Mackinder's Heartland into the "Pivot Area" and Rimland into the "Inner Crescent." The rest of the world became the "Outer Crescent," including the United States. His land-based concept was that Cold War conflicts would likely occur within the Inner Crescent. He pointed out several Inner Crescent areas of geopolitical weakness that he called Shatterbelts. Like Mackinder's earlier predictions, Cohen's Shatterbelts accurately identified numerous areas where wars emerged between 1950 and the end of the Cold War in 1991.

CONTAINMENT THEORY

Some of these conflict areas were ones that the Soviet Union and the People's Republic of China would attempt to capture to create **buffer states,** lands that would protect them by creating a surrounding buffer of sympathetic countries. Influenced by Mackinder and Nicholas Spykman's theoretical work, U.S. diplomat George Kennan first proposed the strategic policy of **containment** to the American government in 1947. In this proposal, the United States and its allies would attempt to build a containment wall around the core Communist states. Anytime the USSR or China attempted to expand the realm of influence politically or militarily, the forces of NATO and other democratic state allies should be deployed to stop them.

This was a successful strategy at first, and Communist movements were thwarted in Greece, Iran, and Malaysia. At the same time, West Germany, Italy, and Japan were rebuilt as industrialized free-market democracies as part of the containment wall, under the Marshall and MacArthur Plans. However, Communists reached a military stalemate in Korea in 1953, and won military victories against the French (1958) and Americans (1975) in Vietnam. These combined with quick Communist takeovers of Hungary (1956), Czechoslovakia (1969), as well as Angola (1975), Cuba (1959) and Nicaragua (1979) were evidence of containment theory's limitations put into practice, as Communism spread even to parts of the Outer Crescent.

The United States and allied states had to contain these Soviet-supported **satellite states** to prevent Communism from spreading further. They feared a **domino effect** where one state would fall to Communism and then inspire and support Communist uprisings in neighboring states.

Containment's Long-Term Success

Despite the failings of the containment approach, Communism was limited to a large degree to the pivot area and a number of buffer states. The containment effort had a devastating effect on the economy of the Soviet Union and its allies. At certain points during the Cold War, it is estimated that upwards of 50 percent of the USSR's gross national product was focused on military production and other activities to support the expansion of Communism. This stressed the Soviet economy to the breaking point and created further shortages of food and consumer goods for its citizens, which in turn created further problems within Soviet society and the Communist government.

By the 1980s cracks began to appear in the social fabric of the USSR. Numerous dissidents publicly criticized the government's expansion efforts and costly nuclear arms arsenal. Similarly, the mothers of the Red Army soldiers killed in the **War in Afghanistan** (1979–1989) publicly protested in the streets of Moscow, despite the potential of arrest and deportation to Siberia. They learned that not even the most coldhearted Communist leaders could jail the mother of a soldier killed in action. Continuing the containment tradition, monies spent by the United States in the 1980s to arm Afghan Mujahideen rebels with arms, including Stinger shoulder-launched anti-aircraft missiles, paid off in the end with Soviet troops returning in defeat. This was a centrifugal force that reverberated throughout the USSR, and its government fell two years later in 1991.

TERRORISM

Which is harder to do, define "terrorism" or prevent it? Both are proving to be very challenging. The use of terrorism—planned violent attacks on people and places to provoke fear and cause a change in government policy—is as old as Time. **State terrorism** occurs when governments use violence and intimidation to control their own people. Roman armies attacked Carthage in 146 B.C. and totally destroyed the city and its inhabitants. They even threw salt on the fields so no food could be grown. Nazi Germany, the Stalinist Soviet Union, and Pol Pot's regime in Cambodia are all sad examples of state terrorism during the twentieth century.

KEY TERMS

country
nation
state
nation-state
culture group
sovereign territory
international recognition
multinational states
multi-ethnic states
nationalism
stateless nations
Kurds
Basques
Hmong
irredentism
federal states
confederations
microstates
supranational organizations
United Nations
European Union
free trade union
open-border policy

Schengen plan
monetary union
judicial union
legislative and regulatory bodies
value-added tax (VAT)
Fortress Europe
European Union Constitution
territoriality
citizenship
finite lines
physical geography
cultural divisions
expatriate
enclave
exclave
United Nations Conference on the
  Law of the Seas
territorial sea
Exclusive Economic Zone (EEZ)
continental shelf
high seas
admiralty law
International Whaling Commission

arbitration board

Spratly Island

Paracel Islands

antecedent boundaries

relic boundaries

subsequent boundaries

superimposed boundaries

definition

delimitation

demarcation

physical border

cultural border

geometric border

definitional border disputes

locational border disputes

operational border disputes

allocational border disputes

frontier

Conference of Berlin

decolonizaton

self-determination

superimposed boundary

Tyranny of the Map

ethnic cleansing

genocide

armed conflict in Africa

merchant ships

annexation

purchase

incorporation

seat of government

planned capital cities

suffrage

popular representation

voting districts

electoral college

reapportions

gerrymandering

aristocracy

peerage

debt peonage

absolute monarchy

head of state

head of government

constitutional monarchy

prime minister (premier)

House of Lords

House of Commons

ruling party

Commonwealth of Nations

free-market democracies

republics

separation of powers

constitutions

political influence

power of the executive branch

Communism

Marxism

planned economy

quotas

Five-Year Plans

devolution

three classes of Soviet citizens

proletariat

Communist Party

military officer class

lack of incentive

lack of surplus

geopolitics

centripetal

centrifugal

armed conflict

internal civil war

external cross-border war

power vacuum

balkanization

empire states

nation-states

irredentism

annexation

Chechnya

autonomous republics

reunification

Heartland-Rimland model

Eastern European steppe

Heartland

Rimland
landwolves
seawolves
commodity of conflict
Shatterbelt theory
buffer states
containment
satellite states
domino effect
War in Afghanistan
state terrorism

7

AGRICULTURE

CHAPTER OUTLINE

First we will go through the general concepts of the geography of agriculture. Then we'll discuss the several revolutions in global agriculture to give the necessary historical perspective on innovations in farming. This is followed by a section on contemporary issues within specialized agriculture. At the end of the chapter there is a detailed presentation on the sole model in agricultural geography, von Thünen's Model.

KNOW THE CONCEPTS

THE LINKS ACROSS HUMAN GEOGRAPHY

Agriculture is one of the activities that makes up the **primary economy**, which also includes timber, fisheries, and mineral and energy resources. These other areas are discussed in Chapter 8, "Economic Geography." Agriculture is connected to the **Demographic Transition Model** and **Third World countries**. In stage two of the model and in the Third World, agriculture is the primary mode of economic productivity in these situations. That means that in stage two and in the Third World, the majority of the population is engaged in agriculture for **employment** and the majority of the countries' **gross domestic product (GDP)** comes from the sale of agricultural products.

CONCEPTS: INTENSIVE VERSUS EXTENSIVE

Agricultural activity can be classified by how concentrated the labor and area of activity is for a particular type of farming. There are two main classifications:

> **Intensive agriculture:** Requires lots of labor inputs or is focused on a small plot of land, or both.
>
> **Extensive agriculture:** Requires limited labor inputs or is spread across large areas of land, or both.

PRE-AGRICULTURAL SOCIETY

The earliest forms of agriculture emerged from **hunting and gathering societies** in prehistoric times. These peoples travelled the land, making seasonal migrations to areas where food and water were periodically abundant. This is the concept of **transhumance,** where groups moved seasonally not only to avoid harsh climates, but to follow animal herds and walk to areas where native plants were in fruit. This activity is associated with stage one of the Demographic Transition Model.

ANIMAL DOMESTICATION

Hunting of animals eventually led to the live capture and eventual domestication of cattle, horse, pigs, donkey, sheep, goats, reindeer, llama, alpaca, and water buffalo. These herd animals could be raised for meat or milk, or used as draft animals to carry or pull loads and plow fields. Birds that were captured, domesticated, and kept for meat and eggs included chicken, turkey, guinea hen, duck, goose, and pigeon.

The domestication of herd animals led to **pastoralism**, or agriculture based on the seasonal movement of animals from winter to summer pastures and back again. Also known as **nomadic herding**, in this practice whole communities would drive their herds from one seasonal grazing area to another following an annual cycle that was repeated over centuries. Don't forget the domestication of dogs to help in driving and protecting livestock. Just a few border collies can replace the work of several human shepherds.

PLANT DOMESTICATION

Seasonal migrations to different plant habitats revealed fruits and grains that could be harvested from wild plants and trees. The seeds of these plants could be replanted along seasonal migration routes to provide food during transit. Eventually, people learned to domesticate and grow more abundant plants, which led to more permanent and organized farm settlements. Over time, other plant **cultivars** were added to these early farms so that there were a variety of crops. People used the plants for food, and used plant fibers to make clothing out of flax and cotton. Plant and animal domestication is discussed further in the section First Agricultural Revolution later in this chapter.

SUBSISTENCE FARMING

The multi-cropping approach was more secure than single-crop **monoculture**. If one crop failed or was damaged by pests, another crop would provide a backup food supply. However, monoculture became common in the era of early political civilization and empires, when farms produced a **staple crop** in large order to feed whole societies and armies with a basic carbohydrate. Grain staple crops, like wheat, also dried on the stalk and could be preserved. These along with tubers and root vegetables such as rice, potatoes, or yams could be kept in dry storage for many months before being cooked or ground into flour to make bread.

Early crop farmers added domesticated animals to their holdings, resulting in **mixed farming**. This is also referred to as **general farming**, where multiple crops and animals exist on a single farm to provide diverse nutritional intake and non-food items such as bone for tools and leather for different materials such as saddles, rope, or coats.

Intensive mixed farming that provides for all of the food and material needs of a household is commonly called **subsistence agriculture**. A single farm can produce staple grain crops, fruits, and vegetables along with meat, eggs, milk, wool, and leather, having animals pull plows during planting and loads during harvest. Essentially all the daily needs of the household could be provided for on the farm. This allows people to settle permanently and subsist without having to migrate seasonally. Even when most of the farm's production is focused on staple crops to pay taxes or fulfill government quotas, other plants and animals are grown to fulfill the subsistence needs of the farming family.

Extensive subsistence agriculture occurs when there are low amounts of labor inputs per unit of land. This is more likely to occur in less populated regions such as South America or in less habitable areas where pastoralism is common, such as Siberia or Sahelian Africa (the dry grassland areas just south of the Sahara Desert).

Today, most subsistence agriculture is usually very intensive and done on small plots of land. In much of the Third World, the **physiologic density** or number of people per unit of **arable land** (farmable land) is very high compared to the First World. This means that more people have to be fed off of much less land in the Third World. This makes many rural communities much more susceptible to famine from drought or armed conflicts.

Food Preservation

Subsistence practices require farmers to have innate knowledge of plants, animals, soils, and climate and the ability to preserve foods for long-term consumption and for times of need. **Food preservation** via drying, pickling, cooking, and storage jars has been a necessity for survival for thousands of years. It has also led to many cultural variations in food consumption.

As a result, many **specialized crops** were grown for both immediate consumption and preservation. For example, cabbages spiced with red pepper and soaked in vinegar were buried in clay storage jars to make *kimchi* in Korea starting eight thousand years ago. Likewise, cucumbers were grown in Eastern Europe and preserved in either lime or salt water to make pickles. Meats are preserved by drying, smoking, sugar-curing, or salting for long-term preservation. These storage and preservation techniques did not require refrigeration—don't forget that we have had refrigerators only for the last one hundred years.

Specialized and Nutritious (for Long Life)

Over time, people learned that certain foods lead to improved health. What they didn't know was the science of nutrition. For example, pickled cabbages such as sauerkraut and *kimchi* are an important source of vitamin C. People didn't know this, but they did know they didn't get scurvy when they ate it. Today we are dependent on citrus, such as orange juice, to provide vitamin C. Imagine what it was like in earlier times when nutrients were harder to come by. Link this to what you know from the Demographic Transition Model in stages one and two, where people have poor nutrition and, as a result, much lower life expectancies.

Non-subsistence Agriculture

The opposite of intensive subsistence farming is **cash-cropping** to sell farm goods at market. This is a form of extensive agriculture in which harvested crops are exchanged for currency, goods, or credit. The credit is then used to buy equipment or seed for the next planting season and in part to buy food, clothing, and other necessities for the farm family. The **commercial crops** are transported, sold at other markets, and finally preserved or processed into other goods for sale. That describes small-scale cash-cropping, but large scale corporate operations also engage in non-subsistence farming. In addition, farming under communism was also done on a non-subsistence basis, with much of the food grown being produced collectively in farm communities and distributed across the country.

Plantation Agriculture

In the tropical and sub-tropical climates of the world, it is common to find extensive **plantation agriculture**, specialized crops intended for both **domestic consumption** and for **export** to other parts of the world. These plantations tend to be large, extensive monoculture farms that are reliant upon low-wage labor and, historically in the United States until 1865, slave labor.

Today, tropical plantation export crops are still found the world over, mainly in Third World locations. They still serve much the same purpose they have historically: to export value from large-scale monoculture. Here are some examples and locations:

Plantation Crop:	Countries:
Banana	Brazil, Dominica, Costa Rica, Honduras
Cane Sugar	United States (Florida), Brazil, Cuba, China
Coffee	Ethiopia, Kenya, Colombia, Brazil, United States (Hawaii)
Tea	Sri Lanka, India, China, Thailand
Rubber	Brazil, Malaysia, Indonesia, Mexico
Cacao (chocolate)	Ghana, Brazil, Mexico, Indonesia
Palm Oil	Indonesia, Malaysia, Nigeria, Thailand

As exports, these crops can produce a significant amount of economic value for their countries. However, frequent fluctuations in the commodity prices for these goods can make them highly profitable one year and then unprofitable the next. As a form of monoculture, plantation production can prove to be a risky financial investment for many countries. This has led to attempts to diversify the types of crops grown for export and thus reduce the potential for national economic downturns due to losses from a single crop.

Plantation-Style Agriculture Declines in the United States

In the United States, cotton and tobacco were Southern plantation crops that sold domestically and for export. In the twentieth century, these were replaced by other crops such as soybeans, peanuts, and yellow pine trees for timber. Cotton production in the South was severely damaged by boll weevil infestations in the 1890s through the 1920s. Today, most of the cotton in the United States is grown in California. Tobacco production was cut back in the 1990s after tobacco industry litigation in which state attorneys general pointed out the costly health dangers of smoking. Like other family-owned farms in the United States, old plantations are a dying breed in the face of large corporate farms.

COMMUNISM AND AGRICULTURE

Throughout much of human history, wealthy landholders and aristocrats (in **feudal** political economies) owned most of the arable land. Yet, these people made up only a small part of the population, around 5 percent. This meant that upwards of 90 percent of the population were peasants, serfs, and sometimes slaves who farmed land that they never owned. Peasants were forced to pay rent to farm land that sustained their families and produced goods for the landowners. In the late 1700s, both the American and French revolutions rejected this system that had created a large **income disparity** between rich and poor.

In the late 1800s, armed with knowledge from Karl Marx and Friedrich Engels's *Communist Manifesto* (1848), peasants staged uprisings in Eastern Europe that called for not only a rejection of aristocracy and landlords, but of the whole capitalist system. The Russian Revolution in 1917 had a number of political and military causes combined with a crisis of poverty in many rural Russian farming communities. The prescribed solution under the Marxist-Socialist political economy was the collectivization of farms and elimination of privately owned land. The **communes** that resulted were large farms where several families were organized as labor units. The land was owned collectively by the whole state. Similar collectives and communes were established in Eastern Europe, China, and other Soviet satellites after World War II.

How the Communist System Worked

The collectivization of agricultural production often had the initial effect of leading to food shortages due to disorganized production networks. However, over time farming communes began to produce crop yields similar to those in capitalist economies. Communes were assigned **quotas** by the government that detailed exactly how much each farm should produce each year. Falling short of the quota meant government reprisals and penalties, but making the quota was met with celebrations and awards.

The main problem with this system, compared to the capitalist system, was that there were no **incentives** to produce over the quota or produce other crops or products outside the mandated crop, which usually encouraged monoculture. The result was a system that had no surplus food available and not much variety available to consumers. Stores and food shops tended to have very limited supplies of basic food products, and lines often formed in front of stores for items like bread and toilet paper. Fruits and summer vegetables were a rarity. The lack of surplus was exacerbated by the heavy food demands of the Soviet military. In times of regional drought, food had to be transferred from other areas, causing nationwide shortages.

These and other problems combined to cause the downfall of Soviet Communism in 1991. See Chapter 6 for more on this subject.

HUMAN ECOLOGY: FARMING TECHNIQUES

The term *human ecology* is used to describe human interactions with nature. Earlier geographic research in the 1940s and '50s focused primarily on the "man to land relationship" specific to farming. *Human ecology* as a term has since fallen out of favor, and now the broader term *human-environment interactions* is more commonly used to describe forestry techniques, fisheries, and environmental regulation in addition to farming practices.

Our ecological relationship to the land can be conceived of as a **food web** in which each type of crop and animal is dependent on a number of human inputs, soil and climate conditions, and other crops. The term **food chain** describes the order of predators in the animal world and is also used to describe several integrated human and mechanical inputs, from developing seeds to planting, fertilizing, harvesting, processing, packaging, and transporting food to market and finally to your dinner plate.

Much of what you need to know for the exam has to do with specific farming practices. The following section provides a number of key words in relation to farming practices.

Types of Cropping

Crop rotation occurs when one crop is planted on a plot of land and then switched to another plot in subsequent years. The rotation cycle will vary back and forth due to one or more factors. Soil nitrogen quality is a common factor in North American farming. Corn is a heavily nitrogen-dependent plant and often requires artificial fertilizers to maintain soil quality. However, soybeans "fix" nitrogen in the soil, meaning the roots of soy plants emit nitrogen back into the soil. Farmers can rotate between corn and soybeans, thus saving money since they won't have to buy as much fertilizer.

Multi-cropping involves the planting of more than one crop on the same plot of land. In contrast to monoculture, this is an intensive strategy where crops are either planted together simultaneously or when one crop is planted right after another in the same row. For instance, after summer vegetables are harvested, winter vegetables and cold-tolerant plants like kale and spinach can be planted and harvested before the freeze. **Double cropping** implies planting two crops one after another on a single plot in a year, and triple cropping means three crops in the same year. These practices often rely on fertilizers and irrigation, especially in dry-land growing areas such as Southern California's Imperial Valley.

Growing Seasons

Each crop has its own specific **growing season**, but the general rule of thumb is to plant in spring, grow in summer, and harvest in fall. However, some crops have variations, such as spring wheat and winter wheat. **Spring wheat** follows the normal growing season: It is planted in the spring and harvested in late summer. Spring wheat is grown in northern areas such as Minnesota, the Dakotas, Alberta, and Saskatchewan. By comparison, **winter wheat** is grown in more southern areas of the Great Plains, where ground freezing is less likely. Winter wheat is planted in the fall, lies dormant in the winter, and then grows in the spring to be harvested by the start of summer. Kansas, Oklahoma, and Colorado make up most of the winter wheat production in the United States.

Irrigation Agriculture

The practice of **irrigation** opens up more land to cultivation than would normally be possible in arid climates. Irrigation agriculture is responsible for close to three-quarters of world freshwater use and up to 90 percent of freshwater use in the most poverty-stricken countries of the world. Governments often heavily subsidize irrigation agriculture with the result that the crops produced are often worth less than the water. The Nile Valley in Egypt is an example of heavily subsidized irrigation agriculture. Unfortunately, the water for these irrigation farms comes from underground water tables called aquifers. These aquifers are being depleted at a rapid rate and large-scale grain producing countries such as India, China, and the United States are examples of those caught in this predicament.

Sustainable Farming

Farming practices can be criticized for their dependence on external inputs such as fuel, agricultural chemicals like pesticides and fertilizers, and the effects of farming on soil erosion and local water usage. As soils become depleted and water becomes the earth's most precious commodity, a new movement has grown and spread to conserve and protect these resources. **Conservation** is the practice of preserving and carefully managing the environment and its natural resources. A new method of farming, **conservation agriculture**, has become increasingly important as a way of providing a sustainable farming system without sacrificing crop production. One of the methods used involves not plowing the soil (called "no-tillage") so that soil erosion is greatly reduced and soil fertility is increased by retaining natural vegetation. Crop rotation and inter-planting are two other methods used to increase soil fertility and discourage pests. Inter-planting means planting fast-growing crops alongside slow-growing crops. Inter-planting allows a farmer to harvest the fast-growing crop before the slow-growing crop shades it out. **Sustainable yield** describes the amount of crops or animals that can be raised without endangering local resources such as soil, irrigation, or groundwater, or it describes what can be raised without too many expensive inputs that would make farming unprofitable. Thus, **sustainability** can be viewed in both environmental and economic terms. Either way, by reducing inputs and using ecologically sound methods, farmers can reduce the risk that their farming practices may lead to long-term environmental or economic problems.

Non-Food Crops

Not all agriculture is done to create human food; a number of crops are raised for industrial use, **textiles** (clothing), or **animal feed**. Cotton and flax have long been used to make cloth and linens. Soybeans have been used since the 1950s to make paints, ink, and synthetic polymers like nylon. Even the parts of animals that are not eaten are utilized to make products like leather (animal skins), soaps (from fats and bone meal), and organic fertilizers (fish parts).

Alternative energy crops have become important as oil prices have increased over time. Since the 1970s, corn has been used to make **ethanol**, an alcohol that can supplement gasoline and make it burn cleaner. In the last few years, demands for wholly alternative vehicle fuels have opened markets for corn-based E85 ethanol fuel to replace gasoline and be used in "flex-fuel" vehicles. In Brazil, a large percentage of cars run on sugar cane–derived alcohol fuels that have reduced the country's dependence on oil imports. Likewise, **biodiesel** from soybeans and vegetable oils (even waste oil from fryers) has become an alternative to petroleum-based diesel fuel for trucking in the United States, Canada, and Europe.

Shifting Cultivation

In many parts of the agricultural Third World, farming occurs in environmentally sensitive areas such as tropical rainforest or dry grasslands. Traditionally, **slash and burn agriculture** (also known as **swidden**) has occurred in tropical rainforest regions with farmers shifting from one plot of land to another every few years as soil nutrients become depleted. Land abandoned by farmers was allowed to **fallow**, and natural vegetation would return and increase the nutrient biomass of the area. This cycle of cutting and fallowing has occurred throughout human history and until the population explosion of the twentieth century was ecologically sustainable because of the small number of active areas. Today, slash and burn is considered unsustainable due to the large amount of forest land burned.

Clearing → farming → moving

The Problem of Tropical Deforestation

Contrary to popular belief, rainforest soils are very poor due to the water and nutrients in the environment being sapped up by the natural vegetation. When rainforest is cut today, large trees are sold to logging companies and the remaining vegetation is burned to create a nutrient layer of ash atop the soil. People who have moved to the forest to claim their own land and escape overcrowded cities in countries like Brazil or Indonesia often discover that they can farm for only a few seasons before soil nutrients are sapped or eroded by heavy tropical rains. The forest settlers often have to sell their farm to cattle ranchers and move to another plot of land to continue the cycle. The problem is that tens of thousands of farm families are now doing this, which puts dangerous pressure on a very sensitive and valuable natural resource. Rainforests are often considered the lungs of the earth because of the large amounts of oxygen produced and CO_2 consumed by trees.

Desertification

Extensive pastoralism, the shifting of animal herds between grazing pastures, has remained popular in several arid parts of the world, especially Africa, the Middle East, and Central Asia, where dry grassland is the common landcover. The contemporary problem is similar to that of rainforest destruction, since too many people and too many animals are placing **population pressure** on too little land. **Overgrazing** has led to significant amounts of dry grassland being denuded, eroded, and as a result, desertified. **Desertification** is any human process that turns a vegetated environment into a desert-like landscape. In addition to overgrazing, deforestation and **soil salinization** can also lead to desertification.

Soil Salinization

One of the risks of farming in dryland and desert regions is that the evaporation of water can trap **mineral salts** on the surface soil layer. High daytime temperatures cause water vapor to be drawn out of irrigated farmland. As evaporation continues over several growing seasons, the amount of mineral salt can build to toxic levels and poison crops. The land has to be either abandoned or flooded by about 18 inches of fresh water over a couple of months to draw out the salts. Fresh water, though, tends to be expensive and in short supply in these dry areas.

KNOW YOUR AGRICULTURAL HISTORY

THE AGRICULTURAL REVOLUTIONS

Think of these revolutions as significant innovations in farming. These new farming methods are important since they often reduced the amount of labor needed to produce goods and increased the amount of goods harvested per unit of land. Relate these practices and technological innovations to the Know the Models section on criticism of Malthusian theory in Chapter 4.

Note that these revolutions did not occur all at once. Instead, these changes occurred in different places at different times. The general historical pattern is that revolutions began in one place and diffused around the world over time—sometimes an innovation could take many decades before being adopted elsewhere. In fact, there are still a few hunting and gathering societies found today, such as the Bushmen of the Kalahari in Southern Africa and the highland tribes of Papua New Guinea, who are untouched by these changes.

First Agricultural Revolution

After thousands of years of humans hunting, gathering, or fishing for food, people transitioned to an organized form of farming. The prevailing theory of early farming is **vegetative planting,** where the shoots, stems, and roots of existing wild plants were collected and grown together. Later on, this became **seed agriculture**, where the fertilized seed grains and fruits of plants were collected and replanted together.

Over time, early farmers rejected the poorly growing crops, and took cuttings or seeds from the more productive, better-tasting plants to grow future generations. The **domestication of plants** took place in this way. Domestication led to early forms of **horticulture**, where plant varieties that thrived in different soil or climate conditions were cultivated. Specific varietals were selected for different sizes, colors, flavors, foliage, and fruit. As a result, regions of agriculture emerged where certain crops were grown under optimal conditions for the specific cultural tastes of the area's inhabitants.

Who's Your Husband?

Animal domestication also took place in different areas at different times in history. Just as with plants, wild breeds were first taken captive. The most productive of these were purposely interbred or hybridized to be reproduced through **animal husbandry.** The diffusion of animal hybrids was also specific to certain regions—those with specific climatic and natural vegetative conditions that allowed them to thrive.

Geographic Considerations

The **growing areas** of crops and livestock expanded as domesticated varieties were traded and diffused across the landscape. However, there were geographic limits to this diffusion. Keep in mind that most plants grow in particular habitats. These growing areas are usually defined by the amount of rainfall and temperature range. In temperate climates, the growing season of many vegetables and fruits are also limited by periods of freezing. And there were cultural limits to crops and animals that did not meet the tastes of certain societies.

Early farms produced at a very small scale and were mainly for the subsistence of the family or local community. Until the 1900s, the vast majority of the world's population lived in rural farming areas and was dependent upon local crop production to survive. This type of farming was a labor-intensive form of farming, especially compared to the commercial mechanized farming of today. Relate this to what you learned from the Demographic Transition Model in Chapter 4, in stages one and two when birth rates are very high because children are seen as additional farm labor. The more children you had, the more labor that could be done, and the larger the herd or area of land that could be farmed.

In Addition: The Columbian Exchange

There's another important historical event in the history of agriculture that you need to know for the AP Human Geography Exam. With the conquest of mainland Central and South America in the early 1500s, a number of domesticated New World crops made their way to the rest of the world through **relocation diffusion.** We call this the **Columbian exchange**, as it is historically symbolized by diffusion that occurred after the voyages of Christopher Columbus. Animals also diffused during this time, but mostly in the opposite direction of plants: Many Old World animals made their way to the New World. Explorers took animals to the New World and brought plants back with them. Here are a few agricultural examples of the Columbian exchange:

New World to the Old World:	Old World to the New World:
Maize (corn)	Wheat
Cayenne pepper	Rice (initially red rice from Africa; later Asian white rice)
Bell peppers	Coffee
Potato	Apples
Tomato	Citrus
Manioc (tuber also known as yuca or casava)	Horses
Tobacco	Cattle
Rubber	Hogs
Peanuts	Chickens
Cacao (chocolate)	Sheep
Turkeys	Goats

The Second Agricultural Revolution

From the beginning of the Industrial Revolution in the late 1700s, technological changes in agriculture were enabled by parallel innovations in manufacturing. Devices such as Whitney's cotton gin in 1793 or the McCormick reaper in the 1830s drastically reduced labor requirements and increased the scale of farm production.

However, bigger changes came in the mid-1800s to early 1900s with the development of specialized **hybrids**, artificial **chemical fertilizers**, early **chemical pesticides,** and **mechanization** in the form of trucks, tractors, and pumps. **Tractors** were originally driven by steam and then in the early 1900s by the internal combustion engine. They were used to plow, plant, fertilize, and harvest crops, and they radically eliminated the need for large numbers of farm laborers. Combine harvesters that remove cobs or grains from plant stalks, mechanical hay balers, and a number of mechanized food processing devices made vast improvements in crop yields for farmers through labor reduction and increases.

From the early 1900s to today, agricultural chemicals, hybridization and large-scale highly mechanized farms around the world have enabled the global population to expand from two billion to more than over six billion in just over one hundred years.

It's Soooo Wittle!

In addition to the development of mechanical devices, modern science has had a critical role to play in horticulture and chemistry. Scientific horticulture uses laboratory techniques to develop plant and animal hybrids that grow larger or under certain climatic conditions to meet the needs of farmers in different regions. **Dwarf varieties** were an important plant hybrid innovation. Shorter breeds of both wheat and rice were found to be hardier and more productive because the plant spent less time and energy growing a stalk, resulting in more and larger grains on each head.

Dead Bugs

Chemists in Germany were the first to synthesize both artificial fertilizers and chemical insecticides. Ammonium nitrate was first mass-produced as a fertilizer in 1909 to replace lost nitrogen in soils, mainly for corn and wheat farming. Pesticides were developed during the 1840s from natural sources and from synthetic chemicals in the early 1900s. They include insecticides, fungicides, herbicides, rodenticides (rat and mouse poisons; rodents cause huge amounts of crop damage, both in fields and in crop storage), and nematocides, which kill harmful worms either in soils or within foods.

Geographic and Historical Considerations

These technical innovations led to larger farms and fewer farmers. Link this to early stage three in the Demographic Transition Model in Europe and North America. During industrialization in the 1800s and early 1900s, there was rapid rural-to-urban migration. As work opportunities were eliminated in agriculture, manufacturing job opportunities increased. However, these innovations took decades to reach the Third World.

Green Revolution in the Third World

The technical innovations in farming that took place in Europe and North America in the 1800s and early 1900s did not diffuse to most of the Third World until after World War II. The **Green Revolution** occurred in the 1950s and '60s when tropical plant and animal hybrids and chemical fertilizers and pesticides began to be used in Third World agriculture. Mechanization has, by comparison, been much slower to diffuse, mainly due to the high cost of large-scale farm equipment as well as tractors or combines and the small-scale farm plots that are still maintained by hand labor. An exception to this would be **irrigation pumps** that can be purchased at low cost to move water to dryland farming regions.

The other thing to remember about the Green Revolution is that its impact on the Third World has made for far greater amounts of crop production on small plots of land. The technology transfer from First to Third World has also enabled the expansion of populations in Third World countries. Without **expanded food production**, the rapidly growing populations in the post–World War II developing world would have led to disastrous global food shortages, as opposed to the periodic regional famines that occur within some countries, often initiated by drought or civil war.

That's Some Bull

An example of a Third World innovation is the **Brahman cattle** (or Brahmas), which is a hybrid of European cattle and the Zebu cattle of India. This beef cow produces far more meat than other tropical cows. And the Zebu's heritage allows it to thrive in higher temperatures and humidity, conditions which lead to illness in European cattle breeds. As a result, Brahmans have diffused to many warmer regions of the world including Africa, South Asia, and even south Texas, where they compete economically with the prized Texas longhorns.

Modern Commercial Agriculture

The Third Agricultural Revolution marked the start of a more inclusive way of farming as well as the internationalization of industrialized farming. Modern commercial agriculture is now more than just growing one or more crops. Farmers now produce one or more crops (primary economic activity), process the crop (secondary economic activity) and advertise and market it through a farmer's coop or other market, as well (tertiary economic activity). This broader economic activity is the first important fact you should remember about the Third Agricultural Revolution.

The use of larger, more powerful agricultural machinery is the second hallmark of modern commercial agriculture. Use of more powerful equipment started to replace both man and beast in the early twentieth century in the United States and then spread to Europe after World War II. The third and last important fact you need to know about the Third Agricultural Revolution is that research in biotechnology and food processing has made agribusiness truly "big business."

The Green Revolution, starting in the 1940s with the arrival of agricultural scientists in Mexico to export wheat-growing technology, was only one part of the Third Agricultural Revolution—the widespread globalization of industrialized agriculture. Higher-yield hybrid seeds, used in conjunction with new, improved chemical pesticides, fertilizers, and herbicides, gave farmers in other regions of the world the ability to greatly increase crop yields. Regions depending on the staple grains of wheat and rice benefited the most from the Green Revolution technologies.

What Do You Get When You Cross a Bacterium with a Corn Plant?

In addition to the previously mentioned Green Revolution technologies, **genetic engineering** has further increased the possibilities and productivity of global agriculture. Veterinary science and **biotechnology** research have developed vaccines, antibiotics, and growth hormones that have reduced farm animal mortality and increased the yields of meat, eggs, and other materials. These factors have all combined to enable industrial agriculture, also known as **factory farming.**

There is more on consumer resistance to these types of farming later in this chapter.

A significant example of genetic engineering is **BT corn**. Genes from *Bacillus thuringiensis,* or BT, a bacterium that produces toxins deadly to certain insects and fungi, have been spliced into the genes of different varieties of corn to make them pest-resistant. This creates significant cost savings for farmers and has environmental benefits due to the reduced need for spraying chemical pesticides. The seeds to grow the corn do cost more than regular seeds, but the fact that farmers don't have to pay for pesticide spraying means there are potentially higher profits.

My Cow's on 'Roids, Dude!

Biotechnology has had a major impact on the productivity of meat and milk. **Recombinant Bovine Growth Hormone** or **rBGH** is used widely in both the production of beef and milk in the United States and some other countries. These are synthetic hormones that mimic the real growth-stimulating hormones produced by a cow's pituitary glands. The result is that cattle grow bigger and cows produce more milk. From the farmer's perspective, an investment in these drugs can significantly increase meat and milk yields and thus increase farm profitability.

The Egg Factory

The combination of genetically modified chicken breeds, avian (bird) growth hormones, and **antibiotics** to prevent bacterial diseases from spreading in large flocks have made large indoor egg farming operations possible. Some egg-production facilities have several hundred thousand hens. Egg producers claim that this is a safe and economical way to produce eggs at very low cost. Keep in mind eggs are not just for scrambling in the morning. Egg powders and proteins are found in everything from cake mix to baby formula to cosmetics. These large-scale farms are necessary to meet the globally increasing demand for egg products.

Recent Turning Points for Farming in the United States and Canada

In Anglo-America today, agriculture is moving toward **extensive monoculture of staple crops**, namely corn, soybeans, and wheat. Corporate ownership of farms is the norm, whereas the family owned farm is becoming a thing of the past. The high-cost technical developments of the Third Agricultural Revolution have combined with low **commodity prices** of crops and animals to push small-scale farms out of business. However, there has been significant consumer resistance to genetic engineering and biotechnology. This has opened the door for some highly specialized or organic small farms to survive the rise of agribusiness.

Agribusiness

Modern commercial agriculture has radically changed the organization of farming. The dominant form today is **corporate agriculture,** or **agribusiness,** where large-scale extensive farms of several thousand acres or several thousand animals are controlled by a single regional business.

Large multinational corporations, including seed and agricultural chemical companies, purchase hundreds of thousands of acres that are then leased to local contractors who use the company's seed or chemicals to produce crops. With crop prices at historical lows, one of the few ways to continue farming low-price staple crops like corn, soybeans, and wheat is to consolidate smaller farms under one company to spread costs and create profitability through volume.

The Politics of Agroindustry

Though agriculture produces only 3 percent of the United States and Canadian GDP (manufacturing is about 17 percent and services 80 percent), corporate agribusiness has significant political power, especially in Midwestern states and prairie provinces. Many of these companies receive the same tax breaks, low-cost loans, and direct government subsidies that family farmers are given to help keep them in business. Cargill, the largest privately owned company in the United States; the Archer Daniels Midland Corporation (ADM); Monsanto; and other firms lobby the government to keep programs running that subsidize their business.

Where the Factory Meets the Farm

To keep costs down, agribusinesses have become increasingly dependent on factory farms. Like the earlier egg farm example, beef cattle, pigs, and poultry are increasingly farmed in large, densely packed facilities where thousands of food animals are bred, grown, and (sometimes in the same location) slaughtered. Poultry are raised indoors in large houses with automated feeding and building-cleaning systems. Dairy cattle are kept outside but are milked two to three times daily in large, increasingly automated indoor facilities where cow health is monitored to prevent potential milk supply contamination. Hogs are also raised increasingly in indoor facilities but can wind up in large feedlots.

By contrast, most beef cattle are kept for all or part of their lives in large outdoor feedlots which, due to the density of cows, have no natural vegetation. Feed is either dumped from trucks or sent through pipes to feed troughs in a wet slurry. Once the cattle are fattened, they are shipped at night to slaughterhouses that process all their parts. To keep animals healthy enough for animal inspectors, feedlot operations are heavily dependent on antibiotics. **Downer cattle** are beef cows that appear ill or are lame and cannot be used for human consumption, but can wind up in pet food or animal feed instead.

Farm Crisis

Low crop prices and low profitability, increasing fuel costs, and competition from big agribusiness firms have made farming very difficult for the traditional small-scale family farm. Beginning in the 1970s, the United States and Canadian governments extended vast amounts of low-interest loans, price supports, and other subsidy programs to aid farmers who at the time had significant political influence in agricultural states and provinces. This was a necessary bailout of farms, which would have shut down without the public supply of credit to buy seed, chemicals, and equipment at the start of planting seasons. Most banks saw farms as risky creditors, and the government had to step in as a lender of last resort.

Death of the Family Farm in America

If the government hadn't bailed out farmers, a mass closure of farms would have led to wild price swings in food, and things were bad enough with fuel prices in the 1970s at then all-time highs. Many farms' mortgages were foreclosed due to the farmers' inability to make money as a result of low **commodity prices** for crops (the prices set by market traders at mercantile exchanges for volumes of crops like bushels of corn or pork bellies). Eventually agribusiness stepped in during the 1980s and '90s, buying up and consolidating many farms into larger holdings. As a result, some farm communities nearly disappeared as people left to find a new life in other parts of the country.

SPECIALIZED AGRICULTURE

FAMILY FARM SURVIVAL AND THE RISE OF SPECIALIZED AGRICULTURE

For those who wanted to survive the farm crisis in rural areas, there were a few options: Start farming as a contractor for agribusiness, buy out other farmers and go into agribusiness for yourself, or stick with your current farm and get into **specialized farm products**.

The increased industrialization of farming by agribusiness has created an important opportunity for farmers who are willing to give up the technological advancements of the Second and Third Agricultural Revolutions, or willing to switch to alternative and nontraditional crops. The public and consumers resistant to **genetically modified organisms (GMOs)**, skeptics of artificial hormones, and those concerned about **animal welfare** have rejected many of the farming practices used by agribusiness and other farmers. As a result, a large market for so-called **natural food products** has emerged, and many small family farms have restructured their operations to meet the rapidly increasing demand for such products.

Non-GMO Foods

By raising crops or animals that are not themselves GMO or the offspring of genetically engineered organisms, farmers can certify their products as non-GMO. In the United States and Canada this can bring a premium price from natural foods processors and consumers looking for the non-GMO label. By contrast, in the European Union, food from GMOs must carry a label warning consumers of the product's contents. All other products are assumed to be non-GMO and do not carry special labels. Many small American family farms market their non-GMO crops and meats to EU markets and food processors.

Note that there is no evidence that GMOs cause harm to humans, but many consumers have health concerns regarding GMOs. Many also worry that genetically modified plants and animals could interbreed and contaminate natural food supplies or the environment, thus doing potential long-term harm.

Organics

In most places, including the United States and Canada, to be labeled **organic,** crops and animals must not be grown using genetic engineering, must be free of pesticides, antibiotics, and synthetic hormones, must not use artificial fertilizers, and must feed on completely organic crops. The organic label brings even higher prices than the non-GMO label, since it is far more costly to grow crops and animals without artificial inputs. For instance, a gallon of regular milk costs roughly $2.75 to $3.40 in a grocery store, whereas a gallon of organic milk in the same store can cost anywhere from $5.80 to $7.50. Small family dairy farms can make far more money per cow compared to traditional dairies, thus increasing their profitability and making farming economically possible. Organics are also seen as a much more sustainable form of farming due to the lack of artificial chemicals, which have lingering downstream effects on natural ecology.

Antibiotic and Hormone-Free

When farmers cannot guarantee that milk or animals are not genetically modified or that fertilizers or feed are not organic-quality, they can still market their products as "antibiotic and hormone free." Poultry meat and cheeses designated as such are now widely demanded by U.S. consumers and often cost less than organics.

HEIRLOOM VARIETIES

Many crops have been so highly modified by hybridization that only a few commercial varieties are available to consumers, despite the fact that many older and less commercially known varieties exist. Russet apples, black Russian tomatoes, blue corn, and fingerling potatoes are often found for sale in farmers markets and at specialty food stores where consumers are often willing to pay four to five times more for heirlooms than the going price for standard commercial varieties. One former heirloom varietal, Silver Queen corn, has become so popular that it is widely sold in regular grocery stores during the summer months.

FREE RANGE

Concerns over animal welfare and loss of flavor in agribusiness-produced meats and eggs have led to increased consumer demand for free-range poultry, eggs, and beef. To attain this designation, farmers must have open pastures or large outdoor poultry pens where natural vegetation grows. Free-range labels attract consumers who have ethical positions against factory farming and inhumane treatment of animals. Free-range animals can still eat feeds from non-organic and genetically modified sources.

GRASS-FED BEEF

Grass-fed cattle have also brought significantly higher prices to gourmet consumers who seek the more natural-tasting beef, as corn- and soy-based cattle feed has been blamed for less flavorful beef. There are also concerns that even cattle feeds labeled as organic can have protein supplements made from other animals. Nerve and brain tissue from other animals has been blamed for outbreaks of Bovine Spongiform Encephalopathy (BSE), otherwise known as Mad Cow Disease. Grass-fed animals would not be at risk of BSE.

ALTERNATIVE LIVESTOCK

Although lamb, goose, and duck are consumed widely and aren't that "alternative," many small farms have expanded or switched to these meats since they also produce wool and feather down for clothing and housewares for added farm earnings. However, other "exotic" animal products and clothing fibers have emerged as economic options for small-scale specialty farmers. Examples include ostrich for meat and feathers; bison for low-fat meat and skins; llamas and alpaca as draft animals and for specialty wools; goats for meat, milk, and cheeses; and kangaroo for meat and leather to make athletic cleats.

VALUE-ADDED AGRICULTURE

Likewise, there is increased consumer demand for value-added agricultural products, where food is processed on the farm and significantly increases in value and more money goes to the farmer. Examples of value-added products are wine, specialty cheeses, olive oil and nut oils, fruit and tree syrups, and smoked and dried meats. Chocolate has also become a **cottage industry** in dairy farming areas. The quality of chocolate is highly dependent on the quality of the milk used. Chocolates using non-GMO or organic whole milk is of very high quality and can fetch high prices.

Many value added products are advertised by their **appellation**, the local or regional geographic name for the product. Napa or Sonoma wines from California are associated with a particular high quality that consumers are willing to pay for. These names are protected so that only products produced in the local area or region can have the appellation on the label.

WINE AND CHEESE PARTIES: BIG MONEY FOR EUROPEAN FARMERS

Champagne can be labeled as such only if the grapes are grown and bottled in the Champagne region of France. Imitators must bear the label "sparkling wine" or "*methode champagnoise*," but not "Champagne," otherwise they'll find themselves in court being sued by the French government for violating international trade agreements. Likewise, you can sell parmesan cheese made in Wisconsin, but don't dare label it Parmigiano-Reggiano or you'll face similar litigation. This type of cheese can carry the specific appellation only if it is made in the area surrounding the city of Parma in Italy.

The key with appellations are the higher price these place-names bring at market. A basic sparkling wine from Spain or California will cost $10 per bottle, while a true French Champagne will fetch anywhere from $35 to $180 in stores, and only the true wine snobs can tell the difference. Similarly, domestic parmesan costs about $8 per pound, whereas the Italian appellation will cost $18 per pound. These high prices keep French and Italian grape and dairy farmers in business and keep them competitive with big agribusiness.

AQUACULTURE

Fish farming may not seem like traditional agriculture, but it is a rapidly growing industry that small farmers can engage in and be profitable. Large catfish farms have been developed in Arkansas, and tilapia, a South American fish, is being farmed in California and Texas. These fish are popular because they don't cost much to raise but fetch a high price at the market. In the Pacific Northwest, New England, and the Maritime Provinces, aquaculture in bays and estuaries has resulted in very profitable small-scale oyster and salmon farms. Even geoducks (pronounced gooey-ducks), a large species of clam, are now farmed in tidal mudflats of Washington state and British Columbia. Why? The Japanese will pay $25 per pound to get geoducks for their sushi restaurants.

SPECIALIZED AGRICULTURE IN GENERAL

In contrast to staple grain farming of corn, rice, soybeans, and wheat, specialized crops play an important role in the diversity of foods in terms of both farm economy and the cultural specificity of consumers. Both small family farms and commercial farms grow specialized crops that bring much higher amounts of money per acre than basic grain staples. These farms tend to be smaller than grain farms, but specialized crops can still be produced in large-scale operations.

Truck farms in the eastern United States and Canada grow specialty crops during the summer growing season and are important sources of earnings, since much industrial dairy production has moved to the upper Midwest (Wisconsin). "Truck" comes from the old term for agricultural exchange of goods. Examples of these highly profitable crops are tomatoes, lettuce, strawberries, and tree crops like apples and peaches. These can be sold fresh in stores, canned, or frozen for later use. **Suitcase farmers** are those farm owners who have city jobs but still own land in rural areas. They also tend to engage in specialty crop farming for added personal earnings and to keep old family traditions and farms alive.

MEETING DEMAND THROUGHOUT THE YEAR

In Florida, south Texas, and Southern California, specialty crops can be grown year-round with two and sometimes three growing seasons depending on the crop. These, along with crops grown in areas of northern Mexico (lettuce, tomatoes, broccoli, green beans) and imports from Chile (grapes, berries) and even as far as New Zealand or Australia (lamb, apples, kiwifruit), keep American and Canadian stores stocked with fruits and vegetables. Even in the winter, salad bars have fresh produce, and if you so choose you can pay $4.00 for a half pint of fresh Chilean raspberries.

SPECIALIZED CROPS: MEDITERRANEAN AGRICULTURE

The areas of Africa, Asia, and Europe that surround the Mediterranean Sea have a warm, dry climate with short periods of rain in winter and spring. In this region, the domestication of plants has specialized certain varieties of crops that today bring significant value to farmers. Here is a short list of **Mediterranean agriculture** crops that have been domesticated and continuously grown in the region:

Crops	Details
Citrus	Oranges, lemons, limes, grapefruit, blood oranges
Nut trees	Pistachio, almonds
Palms	Different varieties produce dates, palm oil, hearts of palm
Olives	Many varieties for both eating and pressing for oil
Artichokes	Flowers sold fresh for cooking or hearts preserved in oil
Avocadoes	Dark-skinned Haas variety and larger green Florida type
Grapes*	Raisins and fresh fruit pressed for wine production
*Wine is often identified with the Mediterranean, but wine grapes also grow in cooler temperate regions such as northern France and Germany. Thus, grapes are not exclusively grown in Mediterranean climates.	

Other parts of the world with climates similar to the Mediterranean have also adopted these specialized crops. Some growing regions are small but produce these valuable crops in large order for domestic cash crops and export. Here is a list of areas outside of the Mediterranean that have a similar climate and produce Mediterranean crops:

Southern and Central California
Central Florida
South Texas
Southern and Central Brazil
Southern China and Southeast Asia
Hawaii

Northern Argentina
Uruguay
Central Chile
Black Sea Coastal Areas
South Africa
Southern Australia

SPECIALIZED CROPS: DAIRY

Dairying is done mainly with cows but can also be a specialized agricultural activity using goats and buffalo for cheese production. Dairying cow's milk is today a massive global operation that yields milk for drinking, cheeses, yogurt, butter, and cream. A major concern with milk is spoilage, hence the long history of producing cheeses and yogurt to preserve excess milk for long-term usage.

With the development of pasteurization in the 1860s by French scientist Louis Pasteur, milk that was briefly heated to kill potentially harmful bacteria had an increased shelf life from a couple of days to up to two weeks. This development expanded the amount of area that could be served by dairies. In terms of travel time and distance, the region around a city to which **fresh milk** is delivered without spoiling is known as the **milkshed**. Multiple large dairies are necessary to supply large cities.

Processed dairy like cheese and yogurt production has continually moved westward over the last 150 years. Formerly, New England dominated cheese production in the late 1800s and early 1900s. But the wider availability of cheap land and the need for larger dairy farms has driven large-scale cheese production westward over time to "America's Dairyland," Wisconsin, and other parts of the upper Midwest. Most of the milk produced in Wisconsin is processed, whereas most of the milk produced in New England today ends up in jugs and cartons to be sold at stores in nearby urban areas.

I'LL HAVE A SKINNY LATTE, NO FOAM

Milk is sold in a number of grades based on the amount of fat content. Whole milk has had the cream removed from the raw milk. This cream is sold separately. Reduced fat milk is healthier as it reduces the potential for heart disease from excess saturated fat and cholesterol consumption. Skim milk has all of the milk fat removed and is considered the most healthful for humans age four and older. Parts removed from the raw milk are highly valuable; milk fat is used to produce butter, and milk solids are used in making glue, cosmetics, and moisturizers. Milk is often enriched to increase the nutritional complement of the fat-soluble vitamins A and D to people's daily consumption. Milk is often homogenized—mixed in large batches—to create a consistent flavor.

In the 1980s a new milk preservation method called **ultra-high temperature (UHT) pasteurization** was devised. Here milk is flash-pasteurized at very high temperatures and under pressure to keep the water in it from turning to steam. This is then stored in a sterile box container that is sealed in plastic to prevent contamination. These UHT packages can keep milk fresh for up to a year. As a result, UHT milk has a global milkshed.

KNOW THE MODEL

VON THÜNEN'S MODEL

Johann Heinrich von Thünen wrote his book *The Isolated State* in 1826. In it, he described the pattern of agricultural land use surrounding a theoretical European town, village, or city. In terms of context, von Thünen was writing about the agrarian geography of Europe, despite publishing his work in the early industrial period.

The key to understanding von Thünen's model is that land use (the type of farming) is determined by how **labor intensive** the type of farming is. Crops or animals that require lots of attention are going to be closest to the town, and the ones that require the least attention will be farthest.

Von Thünen's Model

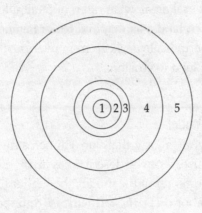

1: Town, village, or city as the central place.
2: Intensive farming: Vegetables, dairying, market gardens
3: Village forest or "wood"
4: Extensive farming: Grain crops, hay fields
5: Grazing lands, meadows

Each Ring Explained

1. **Village.** Even though this model predates Walter Christaller by a hundred years, today von Thünen's model is considered a type of **central place model** due to the organization of a central marketplace and place of consumption for the agricultural goods produced in the surrounding area.

2. **Labor-intensive crops** include fruits, garden vegetables, herbs, and anything that required constant tending or weeding or that needed to be picked for market at a particular time to ensure ripeness. **Labor-intensive animals** include dairy cows and poultry for eggs. Dairy cows require twice-daily milking and, being perishable, milk needed to be near markets to prevent spoilage. **Medicinal crops** such as herbs were grown along with vegetables in town **market gardens** for local sale.

3. A **managed forest** was needed to meet the energy and lumber needs of the community. Due to wood's weight and bulk, these trees were located close to town to minimize transportation costs. Managed cutting and replanting of trees was often done in a highly sustainable manner, allowing these town woods to be used continuously as a local **renewable resource**.

4. **Labor-extensive crops** require far less tending. Crops like wheat, barley, and rye (the grain crops commonly grown in von Thünen's Germany) require little tending other than planting and harvest. Why? These species, like corn, are members of the grass family (*Poaceae*), and grasses tend to dominate their growing environment, choking out most potential weed invaders. Large plots of land are required to grow these staple food crops that are needed in much larger volumes than vegetables. Thus, this ring covers a very wide area.

5. **Grazing** land is the least labor-intensive. A single shepherd could tend to well over a hundred head of beef cattle (as opposed to dairy cows) or sheep. Of course he was not alone, since domesticated herding dogs were used to drive herds from pasture to pasture and provide security from predators like wolves. **Highlands** in peripheral areas were often not suitable for crop farming but perfect for grazing. Like grain farming, lots of land was required for grazing. In this intensive form of pastoralism, animals have to be moved periodically to keep from overgrazing meadows and pastures, which could destroy native grasses and lead to erosion.

Land Economics of von Thünen's Model

From an economic perspective, you can say that von Thünen's model explains the **cost-to-distance relationship** in agricultural land use. It can be described as an inverse relationship between the value of labor and the distance from the center of the model; the higher the total labor costs, the closer it is to the center, and the lower the labor costs, the farther it is from the center.

Labor costs can be equated to the price of rent paid by peasants to farm a piece of land generally owned by aristocrats under the political economy of feudalism. The more labor inputs required, the higher the rents paid on land to produce a specific good will be. As a result, prices for goods in markets are a product of rent and labor inputs. Thus, fruits and vegetables are much more expensive by volume than wheat.

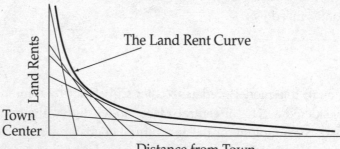

If you chart the price of rent for different locations on the model, you can draw a line to represent the cost-to-distance relationship for each of the rings. The combined lines create a cost surface upon which you can draw the **land-rent curve,** a mathematical function that shows the changes in rent prices across the model. Notice how rents for grazing and grain farming are relatively low, and that rent prices jump **exponentially** as you move toward the town's center.

KEY TERMS

primary economy
Demographic Transition Model
Third World countries
employment
gross domestic produce (GDP)
intensive agriculture
extensive agriculture
hunting and gathering societies
transhumance
pastoralism
nomadic herding
cultivars
monoculture
staple crop
mixed farming
general farming
subsistence agriculture
extensive subsistence agriculture
physiologic density
arable land
food preservation
specialized crops
cash cropping
commercial crops
plantation agriculture
domestic consumption
export
feudal
income disparity
Communist Manifesto
communes
incentives
human ecology
food web
food chain
crop rotation
multi-cropping
double cropping
triple cropping
growing season
spring wheat
winter wheat

irrigation
conservation
conservation agriculture
sustainable yield
sustainability
textiles
animal feed
alternative energy crops
ethanol
biodiesel
slash and burn agriculture (swidden)
fallow
extensive pastoralism
population pressure
overgrazing
desertification
soil salinization
mineral salts
vegetative planting
seed agriculture
domestication of plants
horticulture
animal domestication
animal husbandry
growing areas
relocation diffusion
Columbian exchange
hybrids
chemical fertilizers
chemical pesticides
mechanization
tractors
dwarf varieties
Green Revolution
irrigation pumps
expanded food production
Brahman cattle
genetic engineering
biotechnology
factory farming
BT corn
Recombinant Bovine Growth Hormone (rBGH)

antibiotics
extensive monoculture of staple crops
commodity prices
corporate agriculture (agribusiness)
downer cattle
specialized farm products
genetically modified organisms (GMOs)
animal welfare
natural food products
organic
cottage industry
appellation
truck farms
suitcase farmers
Mediterranean agriculture
fresh milk
milkshed
processed dairy
ultra-high temperature (UHT) pasteurization
Johann Heinrich von Thünen
labor intensive
central place model
labor-intensive crops
labor-intensive animals
medicinal crops
market gardens
managed forest
renewable resource
labor-extensive crops
grazing
highlands
cost-to-distance relationship
land-rent curve
exponentially

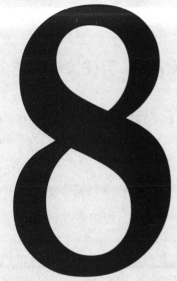

ECONOMIC GEOGRAPHY

CHAPTER OUTLINE

This chapter is broken into three parts: Know the Concepts, Know the Math, and Know the Theories. In the section on concepts we discuss sectors of the economy and country-scale levels of development. The math section discusses the development indicators used to measure economic volume and level of development for states. Finally, the theory section discusses development theory and location theories along with related theoretical concepts.

KNOW THE CONCEPTS

SECTORS OF PRODUCTION

The economy can be divided into different categories known as **sectors**. What composes a sector of the economy can vary depending upon what is being categorized. One common way to group economic activity and employment is by its stage in the production process, from primary production onward. This results in three to five categories. Another way is to categorize sectors by the types of products or services they create, such as mining or communications. This results in a much larger number of categories.

Sector Categories by Stage of Production

Primary production includes agriculture, mining, energy, forestry, and fisheries. These activities and jobs deal with the extraction of natural resources from the earth.

Secondary production includes the processing of the raw materials drawn from the primary sector. These activities and jobs also include the fabrication of components and the assembly of finished goods. In sum, secondary production reflects all forms of **manufacturing**. Keep in mind, manufacturing is a type of industry, but not all industries are manufacturing. Other industries can include fisheries or service industries.

Tertiary production includes the transportation, wholesaling, and retailing of finished goods to consumers. Commonly, tertiary production can include other types of services that could be categorized as quaternary, such as finance, or quinary, such as government. They are detailed here separately but are collectively categorized as **services** in the tertiary sector:

> **Optional Service Categories:**
> **Quaternary production** includes wholesaling, finance, banking, insurance, real estate, advertising, and marketing. These are collectively called "business services."
> **Quinary production** includes retailing, tourism, entertainment, and communications, government, or semi-public services such as health, education, and utilities. These are known as "consumer services."

All the world's countries include each of these stages. Depending on a country's level of development, one sector will be more prevalent than the others.

Sector Categories by Product or Service Type

Dividing economic sectors by product or service type creates a detailed system and a large number of categories. It is important to consider the cash value of what is produced in one sector compared to other sectors. This helps explain why certain products and services are emphasized in an economy and why others might decline or be abandoned.

Agriculture

Whether it's done by hand in the Third World or mechanized in the First World, it's still agriculture. Economically, what is measured is the combined cash value of what is produced, not the volume in bushels or weight in tons. Of the major product type categories, agriculture is the least valuable, despite the fact that a majority of the world's population still lives in rural agricultural regions.

People obviously need food, but how they get it differs geographically. In less developed parts of the world, subsistence farming is very common, with agriculture supporting the farm family and local people. Farmers in the Third World who farm plantations or work in cash-cropping generally send crops around in search of buyers. In the more developed countries, farming is most commonly done on a commercial basis, with processed products sold and distributed globally. Here company-owned farms have overtaken the family farm as the most common type of agricultural unit.

Commodity Chain

Ever wonder who grew the tiny little tea leaf that contributed itself to your tall, frosted glass of iced tea? Commodity chain analysis explains the links between producers and consumers in the production and distribution of a commodity. **Commodity chains** exist from the small-scale, family-based producers selling directly from the farm or through local farmers' markets to transnational supply networks selling to an international customer base. Let's look at the commodity chain of tea.

Tea production employs millions of people worldwide, most of them living in remote poverty-stricken rural communities. The tea supply chain is very intricate and involves many players. Tea leaves are grown either on large estates with their own processing factories or by thousands of small farmers, who send their tea leaves to a local factory. From there, the tea moves to a broker, who auctions it off to an international trader. The international trader sells the tea to various tea companies, who then sell the product to retailing and catering companies and the consumer finally gets the box of tea bags. In this long and detailed commodity chain, only a few powerful multinational companies control the buying and retailing of tea. Most of the profits are made at the retail end of tea's commodity chain and the oversupply of tea (combined with the poverty of the producers) is a matter of great concern to international aid groups.

Natural Resources

Natural resource production can be divided into two pairs of linked sectors based on their renewability and prices:

Mining and **energy extraction** can be valuable depending on the global commodity prices. Oil (petroleum), for instance, became highly valuable in 2008 and was traded for over $120 per barrel mid-summer, only to fall below $50 per barrel by the year's end. Oil export-based economies like Saudi Arabia and Venezuela can rise and crash with the radical price changes. Such price volatility is difficult for both producers and consumers.

Likewise, copper-mining countries like Zambia are doing well now that metal prices are riding high. However, this **resource-dependent country** was economically devastated in the early 1980s when one of the largest consumers of copper, the U.S. Mint, decided to switch to cheaper zinc cores for pennies—a move that caused a global crash in the price of copper.

Fisheries and **timber markets** are not as volatile, but have increased in price and value over the years due to reduced supply. However, in these heavily regulated and increasingly protected natural resources, companies must use more technology and larger processing facilities to remain profitable and meet growing consumer demand, especially from large and growing newly industrialized markets like China and India.

Renewability

We can also classify resources by their renewability. Minerals and fossil fuel energy are **nonrenewable products**. Once they are extracted, the earth cannot reproduce them. Some mineral products like metals and glass can be recycled. For some products like steel and aluminum, it's far cheaper to buy scrap metal to recycle than to mine new mineral ores. That's why you can sometimes get rebates for turning in your soda cans and bottles. Non–fossil fuel energy sources are generally **renewable** if managed properly. With the exception of hydroelectricity, **alternative energy** sources such as solar, wind, nuclear, tidal, and geothermal power tend to be more expensive to harness than fossil fuels and are thus less common. Despite this history, technological advances continue to bring down the cost of renewable energy to bring it closer to parity with nonrenewable energy.

Alternative forms of energy are being developed and used to shift energy usage away from non-renewable resources such as coal and oil. Wind power, solar energy, and nuclear power are alternate energy sources that work with differing degrees of utility to power industries and generate electricity. France relies heavily on nuclear power and certain coastal regions of Spain have enough constant, steady wind to power wind energy parks. California continues progress toward developing alternative energy sources; its Ivanpah Solar Electric Generating System is currently the largest solar power installation in the world.

Sustainability

Products drawn from living resources like fisheries and forestry are renewable. Here our ability to continuously rely on a resource depends on the **sustainable use** of the resource. This means that fish cannot be taken from the sea in amounts that they cannot replace themselves (with or without the help of hatcheries). Likewise, forest replanting is necessary for trees to be available perpetually.

How trees are cut and how fish are caught makes a difference in terms of overall **ecosystem** survival and sustainability. Using two-mile long microfilament gill nets to catch fish is considered an unsustainable practice that harms the ocean ecosystem. These massive nets can easily tear and then float free in the ocean, trapping and killing other sea life. Likewise, clear cutting of virgin forests destroys not only the trees, but also the delicate habitats of the many other species in the forest community. Tree farms with one species of tree are, by comparison, much less diverse and are not considered natural. Most animals and plants that are found in natural forests are rarely seen on tree farms.

Manufacturing

Manufacturing remains the hallmark of economic development, and factory-made products far out-value those of agricultural and natural resource–based economies. Why? Manufactured goods are farm products and natural resources that have been taken through **value-added processing.** The more complex and technology-driven the manufacturing is, the higher value applied to the finished product. The utility of a product and the demand for it can also influence its value.

Manufacturing can be divided into groups in a couple of different ways. One system, **durable goods** and **non-durable goods**, divides production based on the amount of time the product is going to be used. Goods that are intended for use of more than a year are classified as durable goods. Those intended for use of less than a year are classified as non-durable. Durable goods tend to have greater value and represent a more lucrative form of production.

Another categorization can be made by product type. Here is a list of manufacturing sectors based on product category:

Resource processing: oil refineries, metals, plastics, chemicals, lumber, paper, food and beverage, concrete and cement, glass

Textiles: clothing, shoes and leather products, artificial fibers and thread

Furniture: home, office, bedding

Appliances: home appliances, commercial equipment, power tools, lighting

Transport: automotive, rail, aerospace, shipbuilding, recreational vehicles

Health: pharmaceuticals, medical devices, personal care products

Technology: home computers, business computing and servers, industrial control devices, phones, television and audio entertainment

Services

Services are intangible products, as opposed to manufactured goods, which are physically tangible or touchable. As a group, services are the most valuable form of economic production. However, not all services are as valuable as others.

One way to classify them is by the level of pay and benefits they provide employees. **Low-benefit services** are sectors where the labor force tends to be hourly employees who receive few if any additional benefits, like paid vacation or health insurance (not an issue in Canada or Europe where there is free public health care). Examples of low-benefit service jobs include hotel and food services, retail, customer services, contract agricultural labor, and construction.

Conversely, **high-benefit services** are sectors in which pay tends to be salaried and includes considerable fringe benefits like health, dental, vision, vacation, sick days, and retirement reimbursements. Note that the benefits are provided by other high-benefit service industries such as insurance companies. High-benefit positions include the areas of business services, health care, government, and education.

The more common way to classify **service firms** is by the type of activity performed as part of the service:

Retailing
Labor and workforce services
Food, travel and tourism (hospitality services)
Government
Education
Transportation and delivery services
Environmental and waste management services
Construction and engineering
Energy utilities
Communications utilities

Media and entertainment
Advertising and marketing
Medical, health, and personal care
Finance and banking
Insurance
Real estate
Accounting and business consulting
Legal services
Software, data, and computer consulting
Research and development

Remember that these are all tertiary services and represent the most valuable areas of economic production worldwide.

Deindustrialization: Why America is Not a Manufacturing-Based Economy

When we analyze the overall economic productivity of First World countries like the United States and Canada, it soon becomes clear that services produce the majority of the countries' economic value and employment. In recent history the United States and Canada, like other service-based economies, have **deindustrialized**, shifting away from manufacturing as the main source of economic production. Roughly 80 percent of these economies' value is drawn from services, only 19 percent from manufacturing and resources, and a mere 1 percent from agriculture (despite the massive amount of land dedicated to farming and ranching). In employment figures, the labor force percentages are similar, with 83 percent in services, 16 percent in manufacturing, and 1 percent in agriculture.

The downside is that in the 1970s and 1980s when deindustrialization was widespread in Anglo-America and Western Europe, millions of factory workers lost jobs and many old industrial cities suffered from the economic downturn. The workforce had to adjust to new service sector employment that paid less and had fewer benefits compared to unionized factory jobs. Manufacturing businesses also had to focus on highly priced manufactured goods like vehicles, heavy equipment, and computing devices to keep profits and investment up amid **foreign competition** and keep the remaining First World manufacturing labor force paid and employed.

See the discussion on the Old Asian Tigers on page 243 for more on foreign competition, and see Chapter 9 for the effects of deindustrialization.

Understanding Why Services Are Important in America

Why are the United States and Canadian economies based on services instead of manufacturing? Sure, there are cheaper **off-shore locations** overseas to build factories. But deindustrialization really has to do with the **investment value** of each sector. Investors in new businesses are looking to maximize their **returns on investment,** and services are the most valuable investments out there.

To illustrate this, consider the following thought experiment: If you could fill your classroom with corn, that corn might be worth $1,000 or so depending on the size of the room. Fill the room with coal, and you might have $3,000. Now, imagine that there are three dump trucks filling most of the room, instead or corn or coal. The combined price of those trucks would be about $270,000. You can see that moving from natural resources to manufactured products adds a massive amount of value.

Now imagine the room empty, and you're standing there with a manila folder in hand. This folder represents a service product. Inside that folder is a corporate insurance policy, or maybe a stock portfolio. It could be a software license or a patent on a new drug therapy. Whatever it is, imagine that it is worth $5 million. Now fill the room with folders. The billions of dollars in this one room is why investors see services as the best potential investment in the United States and Canada, and it's why they are far less interested in manufacturing and agriculture.

The Importance of High Technology for Services

In addition to the fill-the-room analogy, another way to better understand services is to think historically about how technology has affected economies. When we look at agriculture's long history, the development of the **plow** is the technical advancement that revolutionized farming and radically increased the amount of land that could be cultivated. During the industrial era, the product that made all manufacturing possible was **steel**. Everything from railroad locomotives to skyscrapers and automobiles are made possible by steel alloys, as iron alone is too brittle and heavy.

In the service economy era, the **computer** makes all sectors of the service economy more efficient and capable of handling large numbers of consumers and data. Even more specific is the impact of the **microchip,** as these miniature processor circuits have made desktop computers possible as well as smaller handheld and wireless devices. Without computers and micro-devices, the services industries in the First World today would not exist without a much larger administrative labor force and the labor costs would make many of the services too expensive to afford.

LEVELS OF DEVELOPMENT

We can categorize countries in terms of their level of economic development. We use the following terms to compare development level verbally and to acknowledge the patterns of **uneven development** in the world economy. Some categories are better descriptors than others and some countries aren't categorized as easily as others. Make sure to use terms appropriately.

The First World and Third World categories are two of the most commonly used. However, there are related characterizations at second, fourth, and fifth levels:

First World: Industrialized and **service-based economies** that have free markets, a high level of productivity value per person and thus, a high quality of life. In addition to the United States and Canada, there are the European Union countries, Norway, Switzerland, Iceland, Israel, Australia, New Zealand, Japan, South Korea, Singapore, Taiwan, and Middle-Eastern oil states Saudi Arabia, Kuwait, United Arab Emirates, Oman, and Bahrain.

Borderline First World economies might include Argentina, Chile, South Africa, and some island nations like Trinidad and the Seychelles. These have productivity statistics that are higher than the Third World, but not quite at First World levels yet. You might be tempted to call them Second World, but that term has a very different meaning.

Second World: Describes the **Communist** countries of which only two "hard line" Communist states remain today: Cuba and North Korea. These states still have centrally planned economies. The term is occasionally used to designate "former Communist" states that are still **restructuring** their economy to free-market systems like the former Soviet Union and Eastern European states, although many have joined the EU. It can also describe China and Vietnam, which are newly industrialized countries still controlled by Communist parties but that have adapted **free-market reforms** to their economies.

Third World: Countries with mainly **agricultural** and **resource-based economies** that have low levels of per-person productivity and a low quality of life. These **underdeveloped states** are found across Latin America, the Caribbean, Africa, and the Asian countries not listed above. Some Third World states have made a distinct economic shift toward industrialization and urbanization (see newly industrialized countries or NICs, below), while others remain firmly in a rural, agricultural category. Examples of the poorest Third World states are Haiti, Niger, Malawi, Tanzania, Madagascar, Nepal, and the former USSR countries Kyrgyzstan and Tajikistan.

Fourth World: Third World states that have experienced some sort of **economic crisis** that has immobilized the national economy. Crises can include a crash of the country's banking system, devaluation of a country's currency, a failed government taxation system, or events that shut down the economy such as warfare and natural disasters.

Fifth World: Third World states that both lack a functioning economy (like Fourth World states) and have no formal national government.

Countries that are More Developed or Less Developed...

More developed countries (MDCs) and **less developed countries** (LDCs) are terms used to describe the relative economic differences between states. First and Second World countries generally tend to fit in the MDC category, while Third, Fourth, and Fifth World are LDCs—even if they are NICs (Newly Industrialized Countries--discussed below).

Where the dividing line is between the two categories is up to debate. If you are asked to assign MDC or LDC status to a country based on gross national product *per capita* or GNI PPP, use the following basic rule: $10,000 GNP per capita, above it are MDCs, below it, LDCs. You can argue against this dollar value on a number of technical points. It's just a simple dividing line to help you analyze data that you may be presented with on the exam.

Newly Industrialized Countries

Newly industrialized countries (NICs) are Third World states that have economies that have made a distinct shift away from agriculture and toward manufacturing as the focus of economic development and production. Industrialization is a long-term process that can last decades in larger countries. NICs are in a constant process of building **infrastructure** (roads, ports, power plants, water systems, railways), which facilitate the construction and operation of factories.

Two characteristics of NICs link back to your knowledge of population and migration. First, NICs have **rapid population growth** and are usually on the border of stage two and stage three of the demographic transition model. Several of the more advanced NICs like Brazil, Mexico, and India are well into early stage three. China, due to its one-child policy, appears to be the most advanced in terms of demographic transition, but in fact it should be economically categorized with the other NICs. Secondly, NICs experience **rapid rural-to-urban migration** as their economies industrialize and, as a result, urbanize.

Here is a List of NICs (with their important sectors):

Mexico (manufacturing, oil, tourism)*

Brazil (manufacturing, heavy industry, services)*

Dominican Republic (manufacturing, tourism)

Nigeria (oil, chemicals)

Gabon (oil)

Indonesia (manufacturing, oil, tourism)

Vietnam (manufacturing)

China (manufacturing, high tech, heavy industry, finance, transport)*

India (manufacturing, pharmaceuticals, high tech, computing services)*

Thailand (manufacturing, medical services)*

Malaysia (manufacturing, high tech)*

Philippines (manufacturing)

*These countries have had longer experience with industrialization and are thus further along in the manufacturing development process.

NIC Development Funding

Funds to develop infrastructure and factories can come from internal sources, **foreign aid,** or from **foreign direct investment (FDI). Development loans** are also sought by NICs to help pay for new large-scale infrastructure projects. Foreign development aid is money provided by **donor state** governments in the First World that is not expected to be given back.

Rarely does foreign aid go to building for-profit private businesses. Instead it often provides public funding for schools, nutrition, health programs, and other government spending. Military aid is one of the largest areas and plays the practical purpose of providing security for the state, which reassures foreign firms and investors doing business in the NIC. A less expensive but important source of foreign aid comes in the form of **technology transfer**, where technical knowledge, training and industrial equipment is provided to NIC governments to increase business efficiency and capacity.

How Foreign Direct Investment Works

FDI is money from international **private investors** or **investment firms** in other countries who are looking to earn a profit. These investors put up money to start a new business or build a new factory in an NIC. As the business grows or the factory operates over time, investors are paid back plus a portion of the profits. If the venture is unprofitable, then investors may get less back, or in the case of business failure, they could get nothing—the accepted risk of investing. When there is high demand for cheaply made products in the world, factory investment in NICs can have high returns on investment of 10 to 15 percent within a few years of factories opening.

Development Loans

To help develop the necessary infrastructure to attract FDI, some NICs seek international development loans from organizations like the **World Bank**. These loans are most often given to help build major infrastructure projects such as electric power systems, dams, water purification and waste treatment centers, pipelines, highways, and national rail systems. The expectation is that these new services can charge fees that will be used to pay back the loans to the donor agency.

In many cases worldwide, NICs and other Third World states have defaulted on loans due to the inability of LDC economic systems to pay the full principle and interest payments. Criticism has also been made that some development loans don't make the positive impact on the economy that was intended, or cause costly and significant environmental problems, but they still have to be paid back.

Even Better than the Real Thing

In recent years, U2 lead singer Bono has led an effort with help from former U.S. Treasury Secretary Paul Volcker to have several LDC development loans cancelled or have the loans forgiven. The reasoning behind Bono's campaign is that many LDC governments can't afford to repay loans without taking needed public money away from schools, health programs, nutrition, and other social services. Furthermore, if the First World truly wants to help these struggling countries, then maybe they shouldn't burden them with loans.

India's Jump to Services

Indian export development had been centered on manufacturing areas like cotton, textiles, and steel for many years until the 1990s, when an important change occurred in investment patterns. High-tech markets in software development and computing services began to open up in India due to certain **comparative advantages** it has over other NICs.

The English-language heritage of India's colonial past with Britain has two distinctly positive effects: access to the American technology markets via language and a large number of educated workers who speak the language. Not everyone in India speaks English, but it is common among highly educated workers. There are many English speakers due to the colonial legacy of British-style high schools and universities—many of which were begun during the colonial period that ended in 1948.

American tech firms like Dell Computer have opened several customer service and technical assistance phone centers in India. Likewise, Microsoft has partnered with a number of Indian sub-contracting firms to write software for existing products like word processing and spreadsheet programs that need upgrading. Both of these are examples of the **off-shoring** of computing services from the United States to NICs in recent years.

Comparative Advantage

The term **comparative advantage** means that a country has the ability or resources to produce a good or service at less cost and more efficiently than other states. As such these advantageous goods and services are selected for industrial production over other possible alternatives.

China's Demand for Energy

Industrial development in China and the newly earned wealth of the Chinese people have combined to create a large demand for energy in industry and transportation. Coal has been the primary source for electrical production and is plentiful in the country. Oil demand is also high, as industry and Chinese citizens have more use for truck and personal cars. China is not oil-rich and has invested heavily in oil exploration and production in the Third World, including in politically sensitive countries like Sudan and Myanmar. The other problems faced by the Chinese are pollution in the form of urban smog, acid rain, and an increasingly large portion of the world's greenhouse gas emissions.

During the 2008 Beijing Olympics, news commentators remarked that the skies over the city appeared clean during the games. Why? Factories in the region were closed for a week beforehand and thousands of cars were restricted from use until after the games ended.

Not Such a Good Idea

Sometimes terms are used to describe levels of development that don't work well. An example is the **North versus South analogy** that some economists use in describing the developed world (North) and less developed countries (South). It's problematic geographically in two ways. One, Australia and New Zealand are First World countries that lie in the southern hemisphere, south of many LDCs. Furthermore, most of the world's less developed economies sit at or north of the equator.

Another thing to avoid, especially when writing AP exam essays, is referring to less developed economies or countries as "backward" or to their people in negative or racial terms. This is a sign to the essay readers who score your test that you may not deserve additional points for discussion of examples. Don't risk it.

Asian Tigers: Old and New

The **Asian Tigers** is a term used to describe the industrial economies of Asia that have been aggressive in terms of economic growth rates and their ability to compete for consumers. There are two classes of Asian Tigers depending on the age of the manufacturing economy and a few other important factors:

Old Asian Tigers	Source of Development Funding	Manufacturing Redevelopment Period
Japan		
South Korea		
Taiwan	Foreign aid programs such as the Macarthur Plan	1950s–1970s
Hong Kong		
Singapore		

The building of a large manufacturing capacity in the Old Asian Tigers was the result of Cold War realities in the region. These states were seen as free-market bastions against the spread of Communism. The United States and Britain had no choice but to pour in foreign aid money to support development and democracy in the region. These funds were not loans and were not paid back. U.S. money was critical to the rebuilding of war-torn Japan and South Korea. Likewise, the fledgling refugee state of Taiwan, following the Chinese Civil War, was desperate for American funding to aid in development. The British rebuilt industry in their two colonial possessions as they had both suffered damage in World War II.

The irony of postwar development aid in the region is that by the 1970s these countries had become competitive with the United States and the United Kingdom for global markets in manufactured goods. By the 1980s, highly efficient factories and a focus on product quality in both Japan and Korea had created significant **market share** in the American automobile and electronics markets. This **foreign competition** along with the **oil shocks of the 1970s** triggered the deindustrialization in the United States, Canada, and Western Europe.

New Asian Tigers	Source of Development Funding	Manufacturing Development Period
China		
India		1980s–1990s (until the 1997 Asian Economic Crisis)
Indonesia	Foreign direct investment (FDI)	
Malaysia		
Thailand		
Vietnam		

Manufacturing development in the New Asian Tigers was mainly funded through FDI that came from firms in New York, London, and Tokyo, as well as from companies in South Korea and Taiwan that constructed and operated the factories in the New Tigers. These new locations proved to be profitable investments for all involved, including foreign investors and the newly industrialized countries.

Demand for Off-shoring Locations

Growth in these countries was made possible by the global demand for low-cost consumer products. The New Asian Tigers offered **cheap labor** and **low-cost land and resources**, as well as **few labor and environmental regulations** that had become costly for businesses in the First World. In some low-end product lines, like clothing and shoes, these countries proved to be the only profitable manufacturing locations. China had the lowest costs of all and had a large available labor force. Therefore, companies flocked to the special economic zones to open factories and, in turn, help fund China's free-market reform movement.

The Asian Economic Crisis

Growth in all of Asia came to an abrupt halt in 1997. A banking crash in South Korea rippled through the region and resulted in a **credit crisis**. This is sometimes referred to as a "credit crunch" and results from banks and investors holding back on industrial loans and investment. As a result, money to develop new factories and infrastructure projects in the New Asian Tigers dried up. After a short rebound, the 2008 credit crisis in the United States has similarly slowed investment and development in the region.

The 1997 Asian economic crisis also was the trigger for **deindustrialization** in the Old Asian Tigers. Many large firms, like Japan's Toyota and the Korean Hyundai conglomerate, had employed extra workers and their adult children under an old traditional benefits system of **guaranteed family employment**. Likewise, corporate cartels (*kiretsu* in Japan and *chaebol* in South Korea), headed by major automakers and electronics firms, propped up money-losing partner companies such as steel manufacturers.

The whole system had to change. Payrolls were cut and workers laid off by the hundreds of thousands. Several unprofitable companies shut down as they could no longer get loans from banks or their corporate cartels. Like Western First World economies in the 1970s and 1980s, the Old Asian Tigers now focus much of their new investment on service sectors and only in the most valuable and high-priced forms of manufacturing such as cars, electronics, and medical devices.

KNOW THE MATH

MEASURES OF DEVELOPMENT

We use **economic indicators** to help understand the variable levels of development and measure the degrees of **uneven development** between states. In these figures, we can see the country-level economic differences created by gaps in development, technology gaps, and the poor standards of living created by the effects of colonialism, war, and disasters.

Gross Domestic Product (GDP)

GDP is the dollar value of all goods and services produced in a country in one year. It measures the **total volume** of a country's economy. This is done without adjusting for international trade; therefore it measures only the domestic economy. Here is a formula-based way to remember the GDP definition:

GOODS + SERVICES

In addition, GDP is often reported in the news as "…quarterly GDP increasing by 3.5 percent…" This means that GDP for the most recent three-month quarter of the year grew by 3.5 percent over the previous three months (sometimes it's compared to the same quarter in the previous year).

Gross National Income (GNI)

GNI is the dollar value of all goods and services produced in a country, plus the dollar value of **exports minus imports** in the same year. It also measures economic volume. However, it adjusts for the "national" wealth lost when imported goods are purchased from abroad. And GNP includes wealth gained when money comes from other countries for exports. Here is a formula-based way to remember the GNI definition:

GOODS + SERVICES + (EXPORTS – IMPORTS)

Many economists argue that GNI is a much more accurate measure of economic volume compared to GDP. In most countries, there is a foreign trade imbalance represented by either a positive or negative impact on the volume of the economy. In countries where export value exceeds import value, there is a **trade surplus**, which adds value to the economy. Conversely, in countries where import value exceeds export value there is a **trade deficit**, which removes value from the economy. Mathematically, this is what can happen:

Trade Surplus: (EXPORTS > IMPORTS)
This is a positive number, and adds value to the economy.

Trade Deficit: (EXPORTS < IMPORTS)
This is a negative number, and removes value from the economy.

In the United States there is a large trade deficit of nearly $540 billion in 2012 caused by one significant imported good: oil. The large volume of petroleum needed to fuel the U.S. economy and car culture requires the import of such a large dollar amount of oil that it erases the value of American exports to other parts of the world.

Per Capita Calculations

To compare the level of development between countries, we have to use a *per capita* average. *Per capita* means in Latin literally "for every head," meaning for each person. Gross national income (GNI) *per capita* is the estimated income of a person converted to U.S. dollars at currency exchange rates. It is a modified form of GDP *per capita*. These **level of development comparisons** are done by dividing the volume of the economy by the population, like so:

GDP *per capita*:   (GOODS + SERVICES) ÷ POPULATION

GNI *per capita*:   [(GOODS + SERVICES) + (EXPORTS – IMPORTS)] ÷ POPULATION

These data are converted to U.S. dollars for comparison purposes. However, it's important to understand that these numbers are not indicators of personal income or the average salary of each worker. Instead, they are basically a measure of the country's collective wealth or productivity. It indicates a relative **standard of living** measured by the services that such productivity provides for the population.

Purchasing Power Estimates

Economists have refined these comparative indicators further as relative indicators of income and purchasing power between countries. These are complicated estimated indicators that do not have simple formulaic definitions.

Gross National Income Purchasing Power Parity

Gross national income purchasing power parity (GNI PPP) is an estimate that takes into account differences in prices between countries. By comparison, gross national income *per capita* can make a First World country appear more prosperous than other states and can make larger Third World countries appear less prosperous, but it doesn't factor in the cost of living in each country. The purchasing power parity correction theoretically makes a basic good, like a loaf of bread, the same price in all countries.

Here's an example to illustrate the difference between the two indicators: In the United States, a loaf of bread costs $2.20, but in China it costs the equivalent of $1.63. In China, the GNI *per capita* is about $5,740, but this does not represent that money's true value. China's GNI PPP is $9,210, which reflects the estimated actual value of an individual's purchasing power, using the same ratio as the bread example.

Alternative: Human Development Index

The Human Development Index (HDI) was designed by the United Nations to measure the level of development of states based on a number of social indicators in addition to economic production. An indexed score from 0.00 to 1.00 is calculated for countries by combining GDP *per capita*, the adult literacy rate, average level of education, and total life expectancy. The intent is to provide a more balanced measure of development and indicate some of the factors that illustrate the negative impact of poverty on economic potential in Third World countries.

Economic Indicator Data for Selected Countries

Here is a comparison of the different major indicators for nine countries. Know at least three countries' GNI PPP and HDI for the exam. At minimum, pick one MDC, one NIC, and one LDC.

State	GNI per capita	GNI PPP	HDI	Categories
United States	50,120	50,610	0.937	First World, MDC
Canada	50,970	42,690	0.911	First World, MDC
United Kingdom	38,250	35,800	0.875	First World, MDC
Russia	12,700	22,760	0.788	Second World, MDC
China	5,740	9,210	0.699	Second World, NIC
India	1,530	3,840	0.554	Third World, NIC
Kenya	840	1,760	0.519	Third World, LDC
Haiti	760	1,240	0.456	Third World, LDC
Nepal	700	1,500	0.463	Third World, LDC

Other Alternatives

Here's a brief summary of two other alternative development indicators:

The **Gini coefficient** measures the level of **income disparity** between the country's richest and poorest population groups on a scale of 0 to 100. Higher numbers indicate a wide gap between the rich and poor and suggest major issues with poverty and the distribution of wealth in the country. Lower numbers indicate the existence of a large middle-class population where the nation's wealth is more equitably distributed.

The **Gender-Related Development Index (GDI)** takes the same indicators used to calculate HDI but replaces GDP *per capita* with income. Then the data between men and women is mathematically compared by dividing the female score by the male score. The closer the score is to 1.00, the higher women's roles are in society. The closer the score is to 0.00, the more subjugated and fewer rights women have in the country. Comparing **gender equality** can be an effective indicator of social development.

KNOW THE THEORIES

DEVELOPMENT THEORIES

The Demographic Transition Link

To help remember the path of development that countries generally follow, you can relate development theory to the demographic transition model from Chapter 4. Remember that each of the stages represents a type of economic context, and that the economy directly impacts the patterns of birth rates, death rates, and population. Here is the composite model again.

The Demographic Transition Model

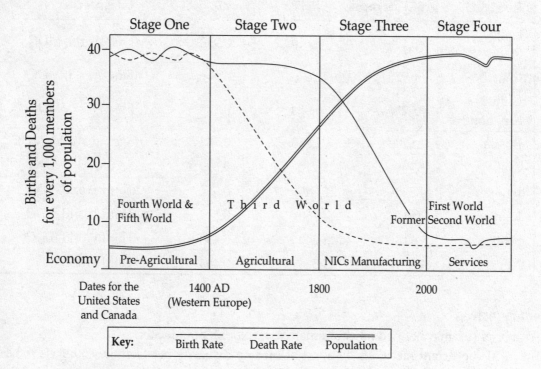

Rostow's Stages of Growth

Another approach to understanding the development process was developed in the 1950s by theorist Walt Rostow, who later became national security adviser to President Lyndon Johnson. Rostow proposed that countries went through five stages of growth between agricultural and service-based economies. One of Rostow's assumptions was that each country had at least some form of **comparative advantage** that could be utilized in international trade and thus fund the country's economic development over time. The five stages progressed in the following pattern of growth:

1. **Traditional society:** The economy is focused on primary production such as agriculture and fishing. The country's limited wealth is spent internally on things that do not promote economic development. Technical knowledge is low.
2. **Preconditions for takeoff:** The country's leadership begins to invest the country's wealth in infrastructure such as roads, ports, electrification, and school systems that promote economic development and trade relations with other nations. More technical knowledge is learned that stimulates the economy.
3. **Takeoff:** The economy begins to shift focus onto a limited number of industrial exports. Much of the country still participates in traditional agriculture, but the labor force begins to shift to factory work. Technical experience is gained in industrial production and business management.
4. **Drive to maturity:** Technical (or technology) advancements diffuse throughout the country. Advancements in industrial production are seen in many sectors of the economy, which grows rapidly. Workers become increasingly skilled and educated, and fewer people are engaged in traditional activities like agriculture.
5. **Age of mass consumption:** An industrial trade economy develops where highly specialized production such as vehicles, energy, and consumer products dominate the economy. Technical knowledge and education levels are high. Agriculture is mechanized (no longer traditional) and employs a small labor force.

Criticism of Rostow's Stages of Growth

Rostow's model is based on the historical development patterns of the United States and other industrialized countries. Although the model provides a framework for the economic development of nations, not all countries have had the capacity to utilize potential comparative advantages for international trade. For example, colonial powers extracted many of the valuable natural resources in the Third World. When these colonies gained independence, they had limited or zero access to the wealth that had been extracted from their countries during the colonial era. And many of the resources that existed within their borders were technically owned by multinational corporations.

The **colonial legacy** and other barriers to development such as **government corruption** or **capital flight** (see the dependency theory, below) are not accounted for in Rostow's theory. He assumed that all countries could progress smoothly through the stages if their investment focused on trade and technology development. Realistically, the world economy tends to leave many countries far behind, as the large sums of international investment needed to develop an industrial economy tend to be focused only on the most capable and stable newly industrialized countries (NICs).

Dependency Theory

Dependency theory holds that most LDCs (including all NICs) are highly dependent on foreign-owned factories, foreign direct investment, and technology from MDCs to provide employment opportunities and infrastructure. The main problem arises when Third World countries get stuck in a continuous **cycle of dependency** on First World loans to pay for additional economic development needs.

These concerns were first raised in Argentina in 1950 by economist Raul Prebisch. The **Prebisch thesis** detailed the dependency of Third World economies on First World loans and investments to pay for the building of new industries and infrastructure. Money made by LDCs from the sale of manufactured goods and natural resources is then used to pay off loans and investments and to buy manufactured products from the First World such as vehicles, heavy equipment, and consumer goods.

In the end, LDCs are left with little money to show for their productivity, while MDCs grow richer. Thus, Third World countries have few funds in their banking systems to invest in their own new business and investment opportunities. Their only choice is to again seek First World funding to keep people working and expand productivity, therefore continuing the cycle of dependency.

At the heart of Prebisch's theory stands a claim about the dominant role of First World–based **transnational corporations** (TNCs) and investors in a postcolonial exploitation of the Third World in which MDCs have economically and politically subordinated LDC populations. Some describe this as **economic imperialism** in a modern reference to the European empires of the colonial era.

Dependency creates additional **economic risks**, as Third World economies are also subject to the level of demand for LDC-made products and the overall global economic climate. If demand and investment decline, as it has in the recent economic crisis, then LDCs suffer job layoffs, and international loan payments are unable to be made. This risk is magnified if the LDCs trade economy is based solely on the export of one or two agricultural or mineral resources. **Market stagnation** in an LDC product can be catastrophic to its economy and harm the quality of life of its citizens.

Breaking the Cycle of Dependency

As dependency theory was expanded over the years, theorists and politicians have suggested approaches in which Third World governments incorporate policies to break the cycle of dependency. Many of these efforts were focused on keeping the money made from industrial production in the country, to be used later for **internal investment** in local development projects. Here are some LDC policies and programs that attempted to increase **capital accumulation** within Third World national economies:

- **Internalization of economic capital**: Requires companies to deposit profits from factories in LDC banks and reinvest locally. This is to prevent capital flight, which is when factory earnings are sent to banks back in the First World where they cannot be used to further local development in the LDC. Wealthier citizens can also be required to keep their money in national banks instead of hiding their money "off-shore."

- **Import substitution:** Instead of buying simple First World–made consumer products like laundry soap, this approach calls for building laundry soap factories and producing it within the LDC. The manufacturing profits can then be sent to LDC banks and reinvested locally.
- **Nationalization of natural resource-based industries:** Foreign corporate ownership of oil fields and mines robs the national government and local companies of potential earnings. If these resources are "nationalized," kicking out the foreign companies but keeping their infrastructure, the money made from the production of publicly owned resources can then be used for local economic development.
- **Profit-sharing agreements:** In China, Vietnam, and a few local cases elsewhere, foreign companies are given permission to build new factories on land leased to them by the government. In exchange, the foreign companies agree to share a portion of the factory's profits with the government, which are then used for further internal investment by government-owned companies.
- **Technology development programs:** Some countries have used their limited public funds to invest in high-technology equipment and worker training for locally owned manufacturers. These companies can then compete globally for contracts to produce goods as sub-contractors to First World corporations. The factory profits then stay with locally owned companies.

In sum, the point of these programs is to accumulate a pool of national wealth that is recycled into the country's economy to help local businesses and improve the overall quality of life through funding for public services and utility infrastructure. Doing this without financial help from the First World is a positive sign of development.

Additional Development Approaches

There are a number of other factors that can give a country a distinct advantage in trade or development. Here are three important areas to know for the exam:

Tourism

By attracting international tourists, countries can gain large inputs of cash from foreign countries without having to export manufactured goods. There are tradeoffs, though, because the countries must provide a large, low-benefit service workforce for the hospitality industry and must be perceived as safe from crime, warfare, and terrorism. To attract tourists, the country must have some degree of historical value, natural beauty, sport recreation locations, or combinations thereof. Beach resorts, golf, skiing, wine regions, historical districts, and cultural attractions like festivals and archaeological sites can all create **tourist draw**.

In the past 30 years, **ecotourism** has become very popular. Rainforest, marine reef, savannah grassland, and polar habitats have all become destinations for paying tourists. These were once the travel sites of hunters, fishermen, and adventurers, but today there are well-established and accessible ecotourism resorts or cruise ships. Countries that once had little international tourist draw such as Ecuador, Honduras, Belize, Costa Rica, Tanzania, Botswana, and Chile have become valuable ecotourism destinations.

Free-Trade Agreements

Regional free-trade agreements between states have become a common way to improve international trade. Supranational **free-trade zones** like the European Union (EU) and North American Free Trade Agreement (NAFTA) have made regional economies of multiple states much stronger and have opened the doors of development for less developed neighbors. In the case of the EU, new member states that were once part of the Soviet Union or former Communist states in Eastern Europe have been able to develop their free-market economies more quickly. See Chapter 6 for more on the EU.

Mexico has benefited significantly from its free-trade relationship with the United States and Canada. The NAFTA treaty, signed in 1991, went into full effect in 2001 with the full removal of all **tariffs** (taxes on goods that cross international borders) between the three members. Mexico had already become a location for some U.S. and Canadian firms seeking a low-cost manufacturing location. NAFTA, however, opened the flood gates and allowed several hundred firms to build facilities and contract with local firms in Mexico to produce goods.

This shift in production location moved the manufacturing of everything from boots to light pickup trucks to northern Mexican border communities. *Maquiladoras*, northern factory cities like Tijuana, Mexicali, Nogales, Ciudad Juarez, and Monterrey, have grown rapidly in terms of both population and manufacturing output as a result. Better-paying jobs and increased services in these cities have improved the quality of life for many residents. However, growth has been so rapid that many employed people still lack permanent housing and access to services such as clean water.

Free-Market Reforms

In the 1980s, Communist states like China and Vietnam began to reform the old soviet-style **command economy** in which all economic production was managed and planned by the central government. These reforms included allowing farmers to sell surplus agricultural goods in local and regional markets for profit. In cities, the reforms allowed people to open privately owned businesses like restaurants, repair services, and transportation companies. Other reforms such as the free movement of labor and the ability to purchase private real estate have also been introduced.

The most significant reform is allowing foreign companies to open factories and retail services in these countries. China established the first **special economic zones (SEZs)** in 1980, in which foreign firms were allowed to build facilities in coastal port cities. SEZs are a type of **export processing zone,** defined as port locations where foreign firms are given special tax privileges to incentivize trade.

China's SEZs were such a success that by the late 1990s, all of the coastal provinces in China and Vietnam had been opened to foreign manufacturing firms. Low-cost labor, land, and utilities provided by provincial governments were in large demand by transnational corporations seeking to maximize factory profits, which are shared with the Chinese and Vietnamese governments.

Economic productivity has more than tripled in China and Vietnam since the introduction of the reforms. Due to its large size, China has been able to integrate itself into the global economy through their state-owned corporations that have purchased Western brand-name product lines, like

Whirlpool. Chinese state-owned banking and finance firms also play a significant role in China's trade integration with export markets, especially in the United States, which sells many of its treasury bonds to China. Free-market reforms have enabled China to become an important player in the global economy; so important that the United States has become dependent on China for low-priced manufactured goods and to support the U.S. government's finances.

LOCATION THEORY

Industrial Location Theory

The location of factories has been the focus of much economic and geographic study. Going back to the work of **Alfred Weber**, whose 1909 *Theory of Industrial Location* is still influential, the selection of optimal factory locations has much to do with the minimization of land, labor, resource, and transportation costs. By their nature, manufactured goods have a variable-cost framework that affects the potential location of factory sites. Weber states that in terms of location, manufactured goods can be classified into two categories based on the amount of inputs in relation to product output:

Weight-losing or **bulk-reducing manufacturing** involves a large amount of inputs that are reduced to a final product that weighs less or has less volume or bulk than the inputs. These factories tend to be located near the inputs that lose the most bulk in the manufacturing process, like trees or metal ore.

Weight-gaining or **bulk-gaining manufacturing** involves a number of inputs that are combined to make a final product that gains bulk, volume, or weight in the production process. These factories tend to be located closer to consumers because the cost of transporting the finished product is more than the cost of transporting the inputs, like refrigerators.

Weight-Losing Industries

In weight-losing processing where there is only one major input, such as seafood packaging, lumber mills, and metal ore-processing or smelting, the industrial location is in very close proximity to the resource location. By comparison, where there are a number of major inputs to the production process, location must be balanced given the variable transportation costs of each input. The inputs that lose the most bulk in the production process are relatively more expensive to transport than those inputs that could represent a more significant portion of the finished product.

Example: Steel

The industrial location of steel factories is dependent on four major inputs: iron ore, coal, limestone, and water. Of these, iron ore has lowest loss of volume of the finished product. Limestone is used to refine the steel and give its comparative lightness and strength. However, limestone makes up only a small proportion of the final product, and much of its bulk is lost in the manufacturing process. Coal, refined into coke to burn hotter, is completely lost during production, as is water, which is required in large amounts to cool steel products so that they retain their form. Condensers often capture steam produced and recycle it into liquid.

Therefore, iron ore is most **distance elastic**, meaning it can be transported over short or long distances to the steel plant, whereas coal, limestone, and water need to be in **close proximity**, as shown in the following table and example locations:

Industrial Location and Steel Production		
Resources	**Production Loss**	**Location**
Iron Ore	Low Loss	Distance Elastic
Limestone	High Loss	Close Proximity
Coal	High Loss	Close Proximity
Water	High Loss	Close Proximity

Using Pittsburgh and the cities of Essen and Dortmund in the Ruhr valley of Germany as examples, you can describe weight-losing industrial locations in relation to multiple natural resources:

In Pittsburgh	From:
Iron Ore	Mesabi and Iron Ranges (Northern Michigan, Wisconsin, and Minnesota)
Limestone	Ohio Valley
Coal	Monongahela Valley
Water	The "Three Rivers" (Ohio, Monongahela, and Allegheny Rivers)
In the Ruhr Valley	**From:**
Iron Ore	Harz (Eastern Germany) and Jura (Alps) Mountains
Limestone	Ruhr Valley
Coal	Ruhr Valley
Water	Ruhr and Rhine Rivers

In the United States, steel production around Pittsburgh had consolidated in the 1870s using small local sources of iron. As production later expanded, the iron fields near Lake Superior became the main supplier of iron ore (taconite) to large firms like United States Steel. At this time, the steel industry expanded to port locations on the Great Lakes like Cleveland, Toledo, Detroit, and Gary, Indiana. In the case of U.S. Steel's plant in Gary, just outside Chicago, the company found that by not having to transport ore from Lake Erie to Pittsburgh by rail, they were able to cut **transportation costs**. Elbert Gary first made this proposal to Andrew Carnegie, president of U.S. Steel, who named the new city for his company's vice president in 1906.

Today, new steel plants tend to be much smaller operations that focus on specialized steel products. Steel **mini-mills** run by companies such as NUCOR or Arcelor Mittal have a number of building materials, vehicle parts, and high-tech steel alloys for medical and aerospace sectors. Some of these mills are located in old steel-producing cities, but others have been constructed in Southern states where land and labor are less expensive and there are fewer regulations.

Weight-Gaining Industries

Weight-gaining manufacturing generally involves the assembly of several inputs into a finished product. As this finished product is more bulky and thus more costly to transport, the factory location should be relatively close to consumers to minimize delivery costs.

A basic example is bread. Flour from wheat grown in regions like the Great Plains is combined with water, sugar, and yeast to make dough that rises from the yeast's CO_2 production. Once baking is complete, the loaf of bread has gained significant volume compared to its inputs. An added issue for food products like bread is the limited **shelf life** that also affects industrial location. Bread, milk, and other **perishable products** tend to be manufactured in many individual plants that serve the local regions. This **decentralized network** approach keeps fresh products in stores longer by reducing transportation time. Bread production is so decentralized that bakeries are found in all cities and are an example of **ubiquitous industries**.

Conversely, when shelf life is not an issue for weight-gaining manufacturing, production tends to be **centralized** within larger consumer market areas. Frozen foods, for example, are made in large centralized facilities, which then ship to stores and grocery warehouses across the country. When Luigino's Inc., maker of Michelina's brand frozen dinners, first selected a plant location, they chose the small town of Jackson, Ohio, a central location in the eastern half of the United States. From this low-cost rural location, delivery trucks could easily access a number of nearby interstate highways. Within twenty-four hours, trucks leaving Jackson could reach 60 percent of their consumers in the United States and Canada.

The Geography of Supply Chains

A **supply chain** is when parts are assembled into components that are then assembled together to create larger finished products. Automobiles are an example of heavy industry that requires a large supply chain network to support the assembly of a final product. As price and corporate profit requirements have increased over time, the size of supply chain regions have expanded. In 1903, when Henry Ford opened his River Rouge plant in Detroit, every part of the car was made in one large factory complex, with the exception of tires, which were a highly specialized product made for Ford by Firestone in Akron, Ohio. **Fordist production (Fordism)** relied on a single company owning all aspects of production, from steel manufacture to advertising.

In the **Post-Fordist era**, car companies changed and became dependent on large networks of regional supply chains that, in the case of Detroit-area assembly plants, stretch throughout the Midwestern United States, with some specialized electronic parts coming from overseas suppliers. **Outsourcing** is common in auto parts, and car companies rely on several other companies to provide vehicle components such as brakes, electronics, glass, and specialized plastics. Car companies must still oversee the quality of supplier products.

To minimize inventory costs and keep factories efficient, car companies today also utilize **just-in-time production** methods, where suppliers send parts to assembly plants on an as-needed basis. These practices minimize potential cost-overruns due to over-supply and save space and money by not requiring warehouse and handling facilities for parts. In addition, car models change design more frequently now, sometimes even annually. If you get too many parts for a model that goes out of style, they will go unused and would be a wasted production cost.

Retail Location Theory

The market area of a city is defined by two factors: **threshold** and **range.** As is described in the section on central place theory in Chapter 9, the threshold of a service is the minimum number of people required to support a business. The range is the maximum distance people are willing to travel to gain access to a service.

However, the precise location of **retail services** is spatially dependent on the relationship between variable cost and revenue surfaces based on local geography. Business owners look to find locations where they can maximize profits. In economic geography, we use the concept of the **spatial margin of profitability** to define these areas of maximization. The spatial margin of profitability is the area where local demand for a service creates revenue higher than the local costs of doing business, as shown in the diagram below:

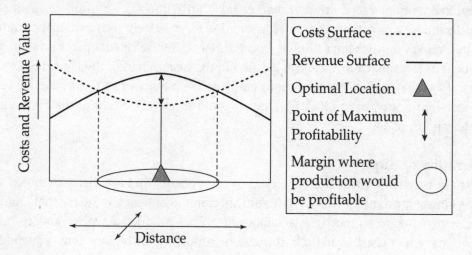

The diagram shows a theoretical location where revenues would exceed costs. The spot where revenues are furthest above costs is the point of maximum profit, or the optimal location for this theoretical retail location. Not all businesses will be able to locate exactly on this point due to the availability of commercial real estate. However, business owners will want to be as close to this point as possible to assure profitability. Other factors such as the consumer's ability to access the optimal location have to be considered before a location choice can be finalized. You could find the perfect spot to put your bakery, but if it's down a flood-prone dirt road, no one will be able to get to it.

Service Location Theory

The location of businesses in the service economy era (since the 1990s) has become a new area of research in economic geography. Compared to the older retail location theory, much of this recent work has focused on the location of **high-benefit services.** The term **footloose industry** has come to describe businesses whose locations are not tied to resources, transportation, or consumer locations. In high-benefit services, a number of different activities are technically footloose and can be located anywhere executives desire. Here are a few examples:

- Corporate headquarters and regional offices
- Customer-service call centers
- Bill, claim, and records processing centers
- Research and development centers
- Software development centers
- Accounting and insurance service centers
- Business consulting service centers
- Architecture and engineering service centers

However, research has shown that there is not really such a thing as a completely footloose industry. As with manufacturers, there are a number of factors to consider before selecting a location to house a service-industry office. Often corporate executives are interested in a location for a number of particular qualities which compose a "best fit" for their **corporate culture.**

Economist Richard Florida has proposed that there is a **creative class** of high-benefit service industry firms and workers. **Local economic development** programs have become focused on the attraction of "creative" firms and laborers. Localities, states, and provinces in the United States and Canada are all competing to attract these creative-class employers. However, they also have to compete with other countries, especially English-language states like Ireland, Australia, and New Zealand.

Some of the local attributes that are in demand by high-benefit and creative service industries are as follows:

- Language of the workforce
- Availability of the workforce
- Education level of the workforce
- Climate and natural environment
- Recreation opportunities
- Entertainment venues
- Tolerant community
- "Cool" factor

Communities like Austin, Seattle, Portland, Vancouver, Toronto, Memphis, Atlanta, Boston, and San Francisco have all gained creative-class employment due to their amenable combination of local qualities. Internationally, city governments in Dublin, Glasgow, Auckland, Sydney, Melbourne, Brisbane, and Cape Town are in the business of attracting top service firms and young, cool, well-educated workers to their cities. These cities fall within the "cool" category. Unfortunately, coolness is something most social scientists have great difficulty defining, as so few of us have any idea what it is!

ADDITIONAL THEORETICAL PRINCIPLES AND EXAMPLES

In addition to the theories presented here, there are a few other theoretical and spatial principles of economic geography that you should know for the exam:

Agglomeration

In its most basic form, agglomeration refers to the concentration of human activities in a cluster or around a central place. **Agglomeration economies** are where firms with related or similar products locate together in clusters or regions. Together, the firms enjoy the advantages of a shared skilled-labor pool, specialized suppliers, and service providers and can share (or steal) technical knowledge on production or marketing. Normally, when one firm finds a cost-minimizing advantage of a location, other firms will move to that location to achieve the same savings. Likewise, when a location is known for a particular product, such as Detroit for automakers, related supplier and competing firms will attempt to locate there as well.

Deglomeration occurs when a location is overloaded with similar firms and services. If local resources or the labor pool are fully utilized or over-utilized, some firms may seek alternate locations to expand to or may move all operations completely. Again, in the case of automobile production, in the early 1980s Japanese firms looked to open factories in the United States to reduce transportation costs of moving new cars across the Pacific. The first company, Honda, looked at Detroit but found the labor force and land there too expensive. Instead, they went 165 miles south to rural Marysville, Ohio. Still close to many parts suppliers in Ohio, Marysville has proven to be an effective and inexpensive location.

The Foreign Auto Firms Move South

As Japanese firms looked into American production sites, they found further reduced-cost advantages as they moved south from Michigan and Ohio. These northern **unionized-labor states** had higher payroll and benefit costs which were ingrained into state workforce regulations. Southern locations were **right-to-work states** where regulation does not favor union and did not impact pay benefit costs.

The next Japanese plant opened during 1982 in Smyrna, Tennessee, for the Nissan Motor Company. This was followed in 1986 with the Toyota assembly facility in Georgetown, Kentucky. As these firms expanded operations at these sites, auto parts supply firms located in the surrounding region. In effect, this expanded the American auto parts manufacturing region from Ontario to the Gulf Coast states of Mississippi and Alabama.

In the 1990s, European automakers looked for similar locations to build affordable luxury-brand cars (an oxymoron). BMW opened its 3-series production plant in the Greenville-Spartanburg area of South Carolina in 1996. Tire supplier Michelin had moved its North American headquarters and several facilities to the area in the late 1980s. Mercedes, likewise, selected Vance, Alabama, to manufacture its E-class cars, which began production in 1997.

KNOW THE MAPS

Industrial Regions

In addition to understanding why agglomeration occurs, make sure to know the location and composition of the major industrial regions around the world:

North America
American Industrial Belt or "Rust Belt" following deindustrialization
Canadian Industrial Heartland or Canada's "Main Street"
Piedmont Industrial Region

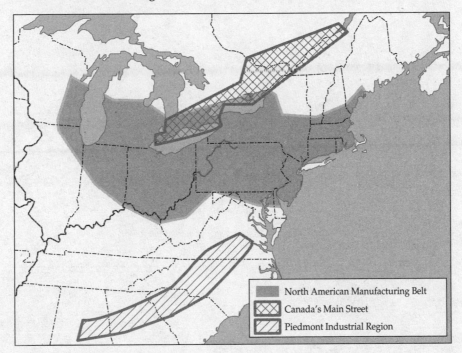

Europe
British Midlands
Ruhr Valley
Northern Italy or the "Third Italy"

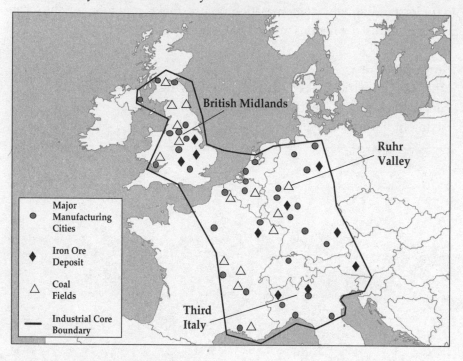

European Industrial Core

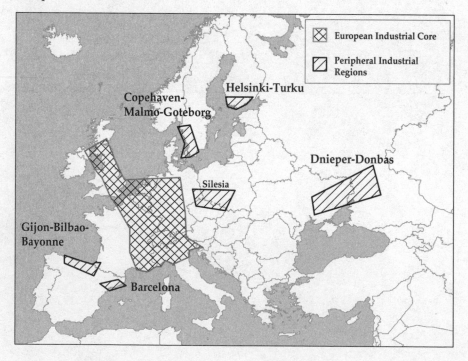

Asia
Japan, Korea, Taiwan, and China

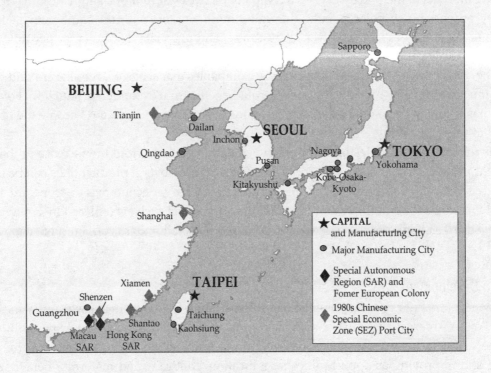

Sapporo

BEIJING ★

Tianjin
Dailan
Qingdao
Inchon
SEOUL ★
Pusan
Nagoya
TOKYO ★
Yokohama
Kitakyushu
Kobe-Osaka-Kyoto

Shanghai

Xiamen
Shenzen
Guangzhou
Shantao
Hong Kong SAR
Macau SAR
TAIPEI ★
Taichung
Kaohsiung

★ CAPITAL
and Manufacturing City

● Major Manufacturing City

◆ Special Autonomous
Region (SAR) and
Fomer European Colony

◆ 1980s Chinese
Special Economic
Zone (SEZ) Port City

Other World Industrial Regions

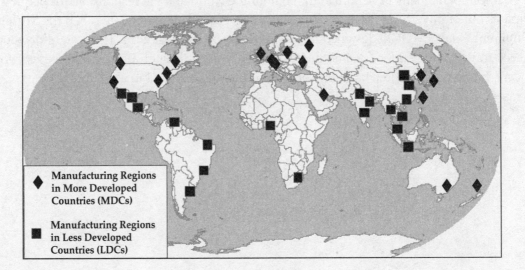

◆ Manufacturing Regions
in More Developed
Countries (MDCs)

■ Manufacturing Regions
in Less Developed
Countries (LDCs)

Economies of Scale

By definition, **economies of scale** are achieved when producers expand their operations but incur lower per unit costs in the process. When a company increases output of a single product, it can save money by purchasing supplies in bulk, managing more workers with the same management staff, financing larger sums of credit at lower interest rates, and negotiate discounts for per-mile transportation costs in larger bulk amounts. In addition, more goods are sold without increasing advertising, accounting, research, or other fixed service costs. Companies that achieve large size are said to receive "return from scale" as they reap the long-term profit benefits from expanded production. For example, Walmart has leveraged economies of scale for decades to offer low prices and become the ubiquitous retail outlet we know today.

This is related to **economies of scope,** where companies benefit from the increase in the number of different products under a larger brand name. For instance, several product lines can be marketed by a single sales staff, and produced in the same factories. Larger economies of scope are especially useful when one product at the end of its useful life, or **product cycle,** is replaced by a new model or alternative device. Apple's iPhone, iPod, and iMac products fall under economies of scope.

Women in Development

Women work more hours per day (in paid and unpaid labor) than men in every country in the world *except* in Anglo America and Australia. Women in the paid workforce are also growing in numbers across the world in both developed and developing countries and regions. Their role in society is changing and improving as opportunities for education, childcare, and maternity benefits open up. Improved access to microcredit such as the Grameen Bank microcredit loans in Bangladesh give women the chance to start their own small businesses and provide for their families. Practices similar to the Grameen Bank loans have spread throughout the world and are responsible for helping move participants out of poverty. In 2000, the United Nations developed a mandate called the **Millennium Development Goals** (**MDGs**) designed to erase poverty by the year 2015. These eight development goals seek to promote gender equality and empower women through provision of better women's healthcare, hunger eradication, basic universal education, and an end to abject poverty.

KEY TERMS

sectors
primary production
secondary production
manufacturing
tertiary production
services
quaternary production
quinary production
commodity chains
mining
energy extraction
resource-dependent country
fisheries
timber markets
nonrenewable products
renewable products
alternative energy
sustainable use
ecosystem
value-added processing
durable goods
non-durable goods
low-benefit services
high-benefit services
service firms
deindustrialized
foreign competition
off-shore locations
investment value
returns on investment
plow
steel
computer
microchip
uneven development
industrialized economies
service-based economies
Communist
restructuring
free-market reforms
agricultural economies
resource-based economies

underdeveloped states
economic crisis
more developed countries (MDCs)
less developed countries (LDCs)
newly industrialized countries (NICs)
infrastructure
rapid population growth
rapid rural-to-urban migration
foreign aid
foreign direct investment (FDI)
development loans
donor state
technology transfer
private investors
investment firms
World Bank
comparative advantages
off-shoring
North versus South analogy
Asian Tigers
market share
foreign competition
oil shocks of the 1970s
cheap labor
low-cost land and resources
few labor and environmental regulations
credit crisis
deindustrialization
guaranteed family employment
economic indicators
uneven development
gross domestic product (GDP)
total volume
gross national income (GNI)
exports minus imports
trade surplus
trade deficit
level of development comparisons
standard of living
gross national income purchasing power parity
  (GNI PPP)
Human Development Index (HDI)

Gini coefficient
income disparity
Gender-Related Development Index (GRDI)
gender equality
comparative advantage
colonial legacy
government corruption
capital flight
dependency theory
cycle of dependency
Prebisch thesis
transnational corporations (TNCs)
economic imperialism
economic risks
market stagnation
internal investment
capital accumulation
import substitution
nationalization of natural resource-based
  industries
profit-sharing agreements
technology development programs
tourist draw
ecotourism
free-trade zones
tariffs
maquiladoras
command economy
special economic zones (SEZs)
export processing zone
Alfred Weber
industrial location theory
weight-losing (bulk-reducing) manufacturing

weight-gaining (bulk-gaining) manufacturing
distance elastic
close proximity
transportation costs
mini-mills
shelf life
perishable products
decentralized network
ubiquitous industries
centralized production
supply chain
Fordist production (Fordism)
Post-Fordist era
outsourcing
just-in-time production
threshold
range
retail services
special margin of profitability
high-benefit services
footloose industry
corporate culture
creative class
local economic development
agglomeration economies
deglomeration
unionized-labor states
right-to-work states
economies of scale
economies of scope
product cycle
Millennium Development Goals (MDGs)

URBAN GEOGRAPHY

CHAPTER OUTLINE

This chapter is organized into the following three parts: Know the Theory, Know the Models, and Know the Concepts. The section on theory contains an explanation of central place theory and related concepts. The models section details the concentric zone model, the sector model, the multiple nuclei model, the galactic city or peripheral model, and the Latin American city model. The concepts section includes parts on suburbanization, gentrification, city types, urban change, economies, and sustainability issues.

KNOW THE THEORY

Central Place Theory

Central to spatial analysis and at the heart of all urban models is the basic concept of **central place theory**. Explained simply, central place theory holds that all market areas are focused on a central settlement that is a place of exchange and service provision.

The **market areas** of settlements, also known as **hinterlands,** overlap one another at different scales. Large settlements have larger market areas, but they are few in number, whereas small settlements have smaller, more numerous market areas. In terms of the size of market areas, large settlements have a larger number of services, for which consumers are willing to travel large distances to access. Small settlements have a smaller number of services, which are closer to consumers.

Research in the 1920s by German theorist **Walter Christaller** showed that there is a hierarchy of places (seven levels, from a small hamlet to the large regional service-center city) across the landscape that followed a regular pattern. Christaller used hexagons to represent individual market areas. Then, he overlapped smaller-scale patterns with larger scale layers of hexagonal market areas. The diagram below is a cutaway of three layers of this **urban hierarchy** as a basic example of Christaller's theoretical principles. In this example, the city's market area (or hinterland) contains three towns and five villages. One village and one town lie outside the city's market area.

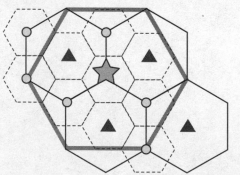

○	Village	---	Village Market Area
▲	Town	——	Town Market Area
★	City	▬	City Market Area

Use the market areas of food stores as an example to explain the principle. Describe the village with a convenience shop (such as a 7-11, Circle K, Wawa); then represent the town with a grocery store (Safeway, Kroger, Albertsons); and finally, define the city with a big-box warehouse store (Sam's

Club, BJ's, Costco). People are willing to travel different distances for the service of food retailing. These market areas are based on the number of goods available in the store and the volume discount received when purchasing in bulk.

Need a bottle of soda? Just go to the local convenience store for a 20-ounce bottle for $1.29. Head further to a grocery store, if you desire a 2-liter bottle for $1.09. And go all the way to the big-box warehouse store if you want a case of twenty-four 20-ounce bottles for $17.00.

Threshold and Range

The **threshold** of a service is the minimum number of people required to support a business. The **range** is the maximum distance that people are willing to travel to gain access to a service. Keep in mind that these concepts are modified by income and travel time, respectively. Threshold is partly calculated based on the earnings of the local population. For example, a luxury car dealership will have somewhat larger population requirements than a regular car dealer, but will exist in an area only if the population's income will support the business.

Range is calculated not in terms of distance but in **travel time** that a consumer needs to get to a service location. People are poor judges of actual distance, but they can tell you how long it takes to get somewhere. Sometimes traffic patterns become more important than distance in terms of how long it takes to reach a destination. Like the soda bottle example, decisions regarding access to a service are dependent on the amount of travel time and the necessity of the service. The convenience store is mainly for immediate consumption, the grocery store for the week's consumptive needs, and the warehouse store for the month's consumptive needs.

Agglomeration

Why then do we often find the same types of businesses in the same locations? **Agglomeration** is when similar business activities are found in a local cluster. In heavily populated areas, competition within markets is common. Also, planning and zoning rules often push some types of businesses with similar building space requirements into the same local areas. In the case of manufacturers and corporate services, firms will often locate near one another in search of technical knowledge and labor sharing. Likewise, there may be some local advantage for certain types of companies to all locate in one place.

The following are some examples of agglomeration:

- Computer hardware and software firms in the **Silicon Valley** area south of San Francisco: This is due to close proximity to the high-tech **growth poles** of Stanford University and the NASA Ames Research Center.
- Automobile companies in **Detroit**: This was originally due to manufacturing **cost advantages** of location on the Great Lakes for iron ore delivery by water, and proximity to coal in the Midwest and Appalachia.
- Banks in **South Dakota**: The state of South Dakota has **limited banking regulations** and no corporate taxes. Some national banks have facilities where large corporate and institutional accounts are held to avoid the high auditing costs and banking profit taxes of other states.

URBAN ORIGINS

Why do settlements form where they do? For this section, think back to when the cities we know today were just settlements. This section will review the spatial concepts related to central place theory that historically discuss why cities are located in a particular place and how they became prominent places among the mass of other similar settlements.

The origins of an urban place often have to do with one of two categorical factors: access to resources and access to transportation. Towns and cities that were founded due to access to natural resources are known as **resource nodes**. Similarly, places that were founded as settlements due to their location as intersections of two or more lines of transportation are known as **transport nodes**. Lines of transportation can include oceans, rivers, bays, trails, roads, and rail lines. Airports are also transportation nodes. Below is a basic diagram to help you better visualize this concept:

Resource Node   Transport Node

THE GOLD RUSH EXAMPLE: CALIFORNIA

Resource node: Transport node:
Sacramento, California (gold)   San Francisco, California (port)

In 1839, Sutter's Fort was established as a trading post in what is today downtown Sacramento. The site of the fort was right at the base of the Sierra Nevada Mountain foothills, where gold was discovered at Sutter's Mill in 1849. San Francisco, despite its historical association with the gold rush, had been founded in 1776 at the tip of the peninsula that separates San Francisco Bay from the Pacific Ocean. The literal transport node is the narrow natural canal between the bay and the ocean called the Golden Gate, hence the name of the bridge that spans it. From San Francisco Bay, riverboats moved people and goods inland to Sacramento and brought gold back, forming the resource node that later became the state capital.

Settlement Patterns

Patterns of rural settlements are generally described as being clustered or dispersed. **Clustered rural settlements** are communities in which all of the residential and farm structures of multiple households are arranged closely together. **Dispersed rural settlements** are where households are separated from one another by significant distances. Clustered communities are commonly seen in Europe and New England, where peoples of the same culture group or clan settled nearby one another for social interaction, use of common land-holdings, and security. In contrast, the farm regions of the American South, Midwest, and Great Plains generally have dispersed patterns of settlement, where large land holdings spread homes far apart. Here many settlers had no cultural or family relations on the agricultural frontier. Thus, they were less likely to settle near one another.

In addition, clustered patterns can have circular or linear settlements. **Circular settlements** are generally a circle of homes surrounding a central open space. Examples of these can be found in medieval-era German and English towns as well as the enclosed villages of tribal herding communities in Sub-Saharan Africa. **Linear Settlements** tend to follow along a road or a stream front, such as the French long-lots (see Chapters 3 and 5 for more on land survey patterns).

Site and Situation

The concept of **site**, in terms of urban origins, has to do with the physical characteristics of a place or its absolute location. In the same terms, **situation** has to do with a place's relationship with other locations, or its relative location.

Example: New York City

New York City's site characteristic is that it lies on a large, deep, enclosed water harbor at the end of the navigable Hudson River. Other colonial ports had large harbors but lay far inland (Baltimore or Philadelphia), or were not connected to inland waterways (Charleston, South Carolina, or Boston). This site characteristic gave New York an economic advantage during the colonial and postcolonial era.

The city's access to Albany gave traders in New York City a link to large volumes of natural resources and the early manufacturing centers of inland New England. Likewise, New York Harbor lies right on the open Atlantic Ocean with access to the wind-driven sailing trade routes coming from Africa, Latin America, and the Caribbean, and those ships heading back to northern Europe. Together site and situation help explain why New York City's optimal port location became the trade and financial capital of the United States by the early 1800s.

Economic Site Factors Today

Site and situation can still be used today to compare the economic prominence of cities. Economic site factors such as land, labor, and capital can be used to estimate the capacity of industry and services to develop in a particular place. Competition between cities for new business locations and new jobs are intense. How much land is developed, how educated the workforce is, and how much investment capital is available in a city are all important indicators of the potential for urban economic development.

Housing and the Built Environment

Over half of the people in the world live in urban settlements of some type now.

Very few North Americans spend more than 10 percent of their time outdoors. This fact means that the built environment (not the natural environment) has become the most important spatial environment for the majority of us. Structures such as houses, schools, stores, workshops, businesses, and recreational facilities make up the built environment. The cities, towns, villages, and suburbs are also our built environment on a larger scale. Most importantly, these places are not just our physical environment, they are our social environment, also called social space, where people meet and interact and carry on their daily activities.

Housing is shelter from the elements and wild animals but it also has another important function. The World Health Organization (WHO) has determined that housing is an important factor in human health. How safe and clean one's housing is directly impacts one's health. Housing needs to keep its residents dry, safe, and warm. Building codes and inspections ensure that safe buildings are built and maintained for home, school, and work use. They also protect us from building near floodplains or dirty, polluted rivers and industries. Housing must be clean and provide safe drinking water and adequate sewage and garbage removal systems. Housing must finally be attractive and well kept-up. It should provide us with a feeling of well-being and have safe places for our children to play and have fun. Other parts of the built environment—schools, stores, workplaces—must contain these necessary elements, too.

KNOW THE MODELS

For the AP Human Geography Exam, you will need to know a number of urban models. As with the other models in the course, knowing the structure of the model is only part of the process—that allows you to answer the "where" questions. You also need to be able to explain the "who, why, and how" behind the different parts of the model. And you'll need to give real-world examples of what these theoretical models represent.

If you can explain the different parts of the model and how they are related, then you will easily remember the shape. That is to say, spend more prep time understanding how the models work and what their parts represent, as opposed to trying to memorize the shape of the model, which will probably be included on the exam.

Another thing that will help you remember and better understand the models is knowing how the models have changed over time, both in terms of how cities have changed historically, and in the different ways geographers have looked at the city. As you go from the concentric zone model to the galactic city model, think of each as an evolutionary step along the way to better understanding the changing urban landscape.

CONCENTRIC ZONE MODEL

The **concentric zone model** was first published in 1923 by theorist Ernest Burgess. The model represents the Anglo-American city of the United States and Canada during the height of industrialization. Representations of the model vary but follow this general pattern:

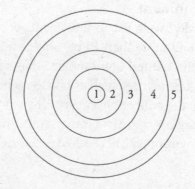

Practical Classifications	Alternate Terms
1. Central Business District	1. CBD, Downtown
2. Manufacturing and Wholesaling	2. Industrial Zone, Factory Zone
3. Lower-Class Housing	3. Working-Class, Blue Collar, Inner City
4. Middle-Class Housing	4. Professional-Class, White Collar, Suburbs
5. Upper-Class Housing	5. Country Estates, Exurbs

Theoretical Classifications	Density Classes
1. Central Business District	1. High-Density Commercial
2. Zone of Transition	2. Low-Density Commercial
3. Zone of Independent Workers Homes	3. High-Density Residential
4. Zone of Better Residences	4. Low-Density Residential
5. Commuter Zone	5. Very Low-Density Residential

The Model Explained

A number of different terms are used to describe the five concentric rings in the model, depending on the textbook or perspective of the researcher. Be familiar with the variations, since you never know how questions or potential answers could be worded. Also, keep in mind that it's a theoretical model and no city is perfectly laid out in nice, even rings. Let's go over some historical and current interpretations of each zone.

The CBD

All cities possess a **central business district,** or **CBD**. In all models, the CBD contains the highest density of commercial land use. This is characterized by **verticality** of buildings such as the tendency to build skyscrapers that maximize the use of one parcel of urban land. The CBD also contains the **peak land value intersection,** or **PLVI**, the downtown intersection surrounded by the most expensive pieces of real estate.

Industrial Zone

In the concentric zone model, the CBD is surrounded by an area of low-density commercial land that contains space-dependent activities such as factories, warehouses, rail yards, and port facilities. More recently in the era of **deindustrialization**, many American and Canadian cities have rebuilt former industrial areas into **festival landscapes**, converting the spaces and buildings into parks, museums, sports stadiums, arenas, convention centers, and outdoor concert venues. Examples include the Inner Harbor of Baltimore, Skydome in Toronto, and Centennial Olympic Park in Atlanta.

Inner City Housing

When the city model was first developed back in the early 1900s, the average worker did not have a car and some did not have access to public transportation. Since walking and streetcars were the main modes of transport, most people tended to live as close to work as possible. This is why high-density housing surrounds both the CBD and industrial zones.

The types of housing structures ranged from poor tenements and small apartments to row houses and townhouses for better-paid workers. Some of these areas today have been replaced or renovated through a process of **gentrification,** the economic reinvestment into existing buildings (discussed later in this chapter). However, most of these inner city neighborhoods retain their underdeveloped industrial-era housing or public housing projects and remain low-income areas.

The Suburbs

In the 1870s, the first planned developments with detached single-family homes began to appear on the periphery of American cities. One such place was Riverside, Illinois. Riverside was the design of Frederick Law Olmstead (the designer of Central Park in New York City), and is an example of the Victorian-era **garden city movement**. Homes were designed to look like European farmhouses with front lawns, and were built for the growing urban middle class of Chicago.

Although suburbs also contain garden apartments and townhouses, the detached single-family home has become the most common housing structure. Lots vary in size from a quarter acre to over an acre. We require a comparatively large amount of land for suburban housing. Suburbs continued to grow through the 1920s, but expansion ceased during the Great Depression and World War II.

It was following the war that American suburban growth really took off. The suburbs are home to a mostly middle-class to upper-class population. Today, just over 50 percent of the American population lives in suburban areas, compared to 30 percent in inner cities and 20 percent in rural areas. Redrawing the model for today's day and age, we would vastly expand the "zone of better residences" as the suburbs have pushed outward and become the largest of the concentric zones.

See the section on **suburbanization** later in this chapter.

The Exurbs

The "commuter zone" represents a wealthy area of people who own large tracts of land outside the city. Some of these could be described as country estates, while the owners of other exurban homes might be better described as **suitcase farmers,** who worked in the city but kept farms outside of town. Not only could these people afford large homes in the early 1900s, but they could also afford a personal vehicle or daily train ticket into town.

Today, many exurbs still retain the feel of the large country estate homes on multi-acre lots. However, many suburban and exurban areas in large cities have pushed well into traditional agricultural areas. This expansion has prompted the development of a number of regulations, including farmland protection laws, minimum-acreage zoning, and development boundary zones.

Related Topic: The Bid-Rent Curve

In addition to being a spatial model of the city, the concentric zone model has particular use as an economic model. The bid-rent curve represents the cost-to-distance relationship of real estate prices in the urban landscape. This is very similar to the land-rent curve related to von Thünen's model described in Chapter 7. The bid-rent curve is a cost function that shows the exponential increase in land prices as one moves closer toward the peak land value intersection (PLVI).

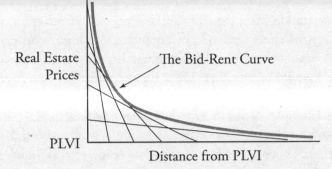

Real Estate Prices

The Bid-Rent Curve

PLVI

Distance from PLVI

One way to help remember the principle of exponential cost increase is that space for downtown commercial real estate is sold or leased by the square foot. By comparison, land in the suburbs is sold by the acre. Along the curve, you could plot different land uses. Land for a suburban home or space for a suburban apartment building are not that much different in price. However, land for that apartment building and land for building downtown is vastly different in price.

SECTOR MODEL

The **sector model** of urban structure was first proposed in 1939 by theorist Homer Hoyt. This model also applies to cities in the United States and Canada. In the model, the concepts of the industrial corridor and neighborhood are combined for practical purposes. These result in a much more realistic urban representation compared to the concentric zone model. The model is also used to depict ethnic variations in the city.

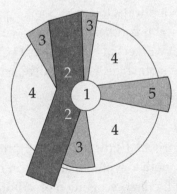

Theoretical Categories	Practical Descriptions
1. Central Business District	1. Central Business District, Downtown
2. Industrial Corridor	2. Rail Yards, Riverfronts, or Harbors
3. Lower-Class Housing	3. Ethnic Neighborhoods
4. Middle-Class Housing	4. Suburbs, WASPs
5. Upper-Class Housing	5. Elite Corridor or "The Boulevard"

The Model Explained

This is a standard central place model with the CBD at the center. Hoyt recognized that outside of the core business district, industrial space tended to be organized as a linear corridor surrounding a main transportation line. This could be a main rail line and parallel rail yard, a riverfront, or a harbor area. Warehouses and factories would be on either side of the corridor with equal access to transport.

In terms of residential space, Hoyt saw that a corridor of upper-class housing extended outward from the CBD of several cities. Examples of this include the Upper East Side in Manhattan, the Chicago North Shore, and Grosse Pointe in Detroit. Working-class neighborhoods also radiate out from the CBD along the industrial corridor. Other theorists recognized these lower-class housing areas as being generally **ethnic neighborhoods**, the result of immigration to industrial cities over previous decades.

By comparison, the middle-class areas of the city are broken into wide, separate areas radiating outward from downtown (remember that suburbs don't boom until after World War II). At the time, the socio-cultural makeup of these areas tended to be dominated by **WASPs**, white Anglo-Saxon Protestants. WASPs would continue to be the majority in suburban middle-class neighborhoods until the late 1960s, when middle-class inner city residents, including many white Catholics, began to move out in large numbers.

Related Topic: White Flight: Myth or Misnomer?

Many people including social scientists have described the phenomenon of people leaving inner city areas of the United States as **white flight**. In truth, not everyone that left the city was white, and not all whites left the inner city. Regardless of race, many inner-city residents with middle-class incomes moved out to suburban districts to escape the social unrest and economic blight of deindustrialization that characterized the 1960s and 1970s in the United States.

Although most non-white suburban migrants integrated into mostly white suburban neighborhoods in small numbers, this was not always the case. Some areas such as Prince George's County, Maryland, feature distinctly mixed suburban neighborhoods with large numbers of African Americans, many of whom are government workers in Washington, D.C. Conversely, inner-city areas in the United States still have large numbers of whites within a diverse mix of ethnicities.

MULTIPLE-NUCLEI MODEL

In 1945, geographers Chauncey Harris and Edward Ullman proposed the **multiple-nuclei model** of urban structure. This represents another evolutionary step in the conceptualization of the Anglo-American city. In the model, we see the first recognition of **suburban business districts** forming on the urban periphery. On the following page is a simplified graphic to explain the basic principles.

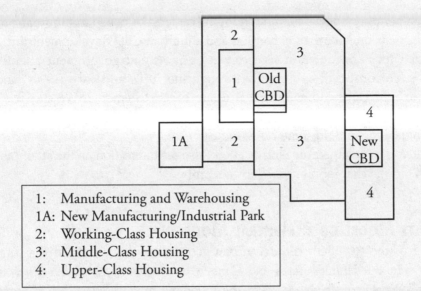

1: Manufacturing and Warehousing
1A: New Manufacturing/Industrial Park
2: Working-Class Housing
3: Middle-Class Housing
4: Upper-Class Housing

The Model Explained

Like the sector model, the multiple-nuclei model attempts to practically represent the urban landscape with neighborhoods and commercial corridors. However, the main difference is that instead of all commerce being focused on the center of the city as in the sector model, the term "multiple-nuclei" (the plural of nucleus or center) implies that there is more than one commercial center within the city landscape.

New **suburban CBDs** were emerging in post–World War II cities, and as suburbs spread outward, service industries followed. As will be discussed in the section on suburbanization later in this chapter, service providers came to the suburbs to be closer to their consumers and stay near members of the service workforce.

New areas of industrial development were also locating on the urban periphery. The area labeled 1A represents the new manufacturing locations that were added for war production and after the war. Expansion to the suburbs was necessary since many downtown factory districts had no room for expansion. The urban periphery offered large tracts of land for heavy industry such as aircraft production and new automobile plants.

Related Topic: The "Death of the American Downtown" in the 1970s

The Old CBD, as it is labeled on the diagram on page 276, was an area at risk in the last quarter of the twentieth century. "Deindustrialization" meant old factories and related industry and services in downtown areas closed down. As a result, the labor force moved away and capital investment into downtown real estate dwindled. Having lost many consumers (sources of income and investment), the CBD was no longer the most prominent place in the urban economy.

What was happening was that the country was moving away from a manufacturing-based economy to a service-based economy. As services migrated to the suburbs, so did the money to invest in commercial real estate. Soon the old CBD began to look run-down and dated. Prominent retailers that were once located on Main Street were replaced by discount stores or in many cases sat empty. City government efforts at downtown "urban renewal" projects had little impact. City downtowns had additional problems with crime and homelessness that cost money and diverted attention.

On the urban periphery, new malls and shopping centers flourished in suburban areas. Developers continued their focus on suburban expansion and suburban CBD development until the mid-1990s when a renewed focus on downtowns received business and government attention. Downtown property prices had dropped significantly through the 1980s and early 1990s, and cost-effective opportunities to reinvest in downtown real estate began to emerge. We still see many of these "urban redevelopment" projects in cities today and many have become successful as downtowns have become more appealing and, in some cases, trendy.

See more later in this chapter on gentrification. Also see the section on the attempts to create "cool" cities (page 257) in the chapter on economic geography.

GALACTIC CITY MODEL OR PERIPHERAL MODEL

In the last half of the twentieth century, urban geographers have noticed that many of the new suburban CBDs in the United States and Canada have become specialized toward a particular industrial or service sector. In many ways, the following model, regardless of what name is used, represents the **post-industrial city** with its several, dispersed business districts. Here is a simplified version:

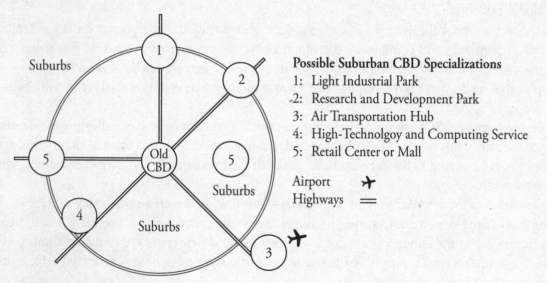

Possible Suburban CBD Specializations
1: Light Industrial Park
2: Research and Development Park
3: Air Transportation Hub
4: High-Technolgoy and Computing Service
5: Retail Center or Mall

Airport   ✈
Highways ═

The Model Explained

The model represents a distinct decentralization of the commercial urban landscape as the economy has transitioned to services as the leading form of production. It's not that manufacturing has disappeared; it has just declined significantly and become specialized. This specialization has meant that new manufacturing facilities tend to be much smaller and require low-cost land to afford to operate. Therefore, these new facilities tend to be in specially designated industrial parks on the urban periphery. They are often subsidized by local governments to reduce costs and increase employment opportunities.

Suburban retailing often occurs in multiple locations around the city. In the diagram on the previous page, the retail center closer to the old CBD is likely an older center from the 1950s or '60s among older neighborhoods. The retail center located at the intersection of the belt highway and the artery leading out from the old CBD is likely a newer center built late in the completion of the interstate highway in the 1970s or 1980s. The point to take away from this is that **transportation nodes** are common locations for suburban CBDs due to their high level of access. Other types of service specializations are found in suburban CBDs. Here are a few examples, including those shown on the diagram above:

High-technology and computing
Research and development
Transportation services
Bio-technology
Hospital centers
Telecommunications and call centers
Banking and finance
Suburban government centers
Universities or branch campuses

Related Topic: The Rise of Dulles

Commercial development around airports is as common as airports themselves. Hub airports, from which airlines service a large number of regional destinations, are especially important for local service and commercial land development.

For example, in the late 1990s, AOL and MCI Worldcom located large corporate headquarter facilities just north of Dulles International Airport in the northern Virginia suburbs of the Washington metropolitan area. These companies chose the D.C. area so they could be close to federal communication regulators and Internet service providers. However, their management workforce needed to travel the country and world on a frequent basis. The Dulles location proved very efficient for business travel.

The only problem was that these immense facilities were built on old farmland where no municipality or mailing address had previously existed. When AOL representatives went to the airport post office to figure out the company's new mailing address, they found out that no postal town or city was listed. The post office's suggestion was to just call it "Dulles." The name stuck and a new place was created.

LATIN AMERICAN CITY MODEL

Whereas the previous models depicted the Anglo-American cities of the United States and Canada, there are also models that depict the common urban landscapes of international locations. Only one of these appears commonly on the AP exam. The **Latin American city model** was first presented by Larry Ford and Ernst Griffin in 1980. The model was updated in 1996, but not all introductory textbooks show the changes.

Here is the model as it appeared in its original form:

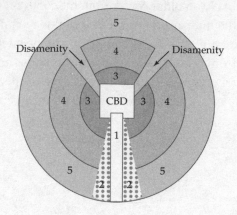

1: The Spine (or Commercial Spine)
2: Zone of Elite Residences
3: Zone of Maturity
4: Zone of *In Situ* Accretion
5: Zone of Peripheral Squatter Settlements

The Model Explained

This model is important as an example of the colonial city. The effects of European colonial rule on many cities in Latin America, Africa, and Asia are significant. Often colonial powers demolished old pre-colonial cities and rebuilt them in the European style. In other cases, new cities were built according to specific plans. The Latin American model tends to represent the latter. During the 1500s, the Spanish government in the New World enacted a number of colonial legal codes collectively known as the **Laws of the Indies**. One of these laws dealt specifically with the planning and the layout of colonial cities.

The CBD

Just as it is in Anglo-America, the CBD in Latin American cities is also at the center of the model. Historically, the Laws of the Indies stipulated that each settlement have a central square known as a **plaza**. This was to reproduce the style of European cities such as Madrid, which has at its center the *Plaza de Mayor*. Surrounding the plaza, the centers of government, religion, and commerce are located. Today, the CBD remains the primary location for businesses. This is unlike the United States and Canada, where numerous suburban CBDs dominate the economy. CBDs in Latin America are also vertically oriented and most large cities have a cluster of skyscrapers at their core.

The Commercial Spine

The Laws of the Indies also required that a main boulevard be constructed leading from the plaza to the outskirts of the city. In some large cities today, several boulevards radiate outward from the central square. For example, in Buenos Aires three main boulevards stretch outward from the central *Plaza de Mayo*. In the colonial era, the spine was often the location for the homes of the wealthiest merchants and landowners. Today, many of these old homes have been replaced by office towers and high-rise condominiums. As such, the spine is still an area of wealth and prestige.

The Zone of Elite Housing

Similar to the Sector model, an area of upper-class housing straddles the spine leading outward from the city center. In the colonial era, social status was gained by having your home along these main avenue districts. This remains true today. One of the primary differences between the urban models of Anglo-America and the Latin American model is that in Latin America, the wealthiest people tend to live close to the CBD, whereas in the United States and Canada, the wealthiest people tend to live on the urban periphery.

The Zone of Maturity

This area of middle- to upper-class housing surrounds much of the CBD. The Laws of the Indies segregated housing in Spanish colonial settlements. Only those who are of European descent were allowed to own homes and live within the city limits or walls. The name "maturity" comes from the type of European architecture and building materials used in homes of this zone. Today, many of the colonial era homes are being torn down and lost to commercial redevelopment as the CBD expands, or to the proliferation of high-rise apartment buildings surrounding the city centers.

The Zone of *In Situ* Accretion

In the colonial era, this was the area outside of the city limits or walls where people of indigenous or mixed descent made their homes. The name "*in situ* accretion" means growth over time (accretion) in the ground (the Latin, *in situ*). This is meant to describe the building materials and architecture of housing, which relied primarily on local timber and mud brick, known in some areas as *adobe*. Today, these are areas of middle-class and working-class housing. Many are single-family homes surrounded by walls or iron gates. The interiors of these homes may still contain parts of old colonial era homes that they were built on top of or next to.

The Zone of Peripheral Squatter Settlements

Squatter settlements on the urban periphery are home to most of the urban poor in Latin America. By comparison, in the United States, the peripheral suburbs are dominated by middle-class housing and the poor are generally in the inner city areas. These communities are known by several names such as *colonias* in Mexico, *barriadas* in Peru, or *invasiones* in Colombia and Ecuador.

Squatter settlements did not become a common feature of the Latin American urban landscape until the years following World War II. The rise of industrialization and the numerous civil wars fought in rural regions, among other **push and pull factors**, led to an increase in rural-to-urban migration in the region (See Chapter 4 for more on rural-to-urban migration). For most migrants new to cities, there was little to no available housing. Part of the reason for this is a lack of real estate investment for low-income housing in Latin American cities. This is different from the United States and Canada, where during the 1800s and early 1900s numerous inner city dwellings were built to house European immigrant workers.

Squatting and Land Tenure

In Latin America, rural to urban migrants have been forced to build their own squatter settlements on the urban periphery. **Squatters** are people who settle on land that they don't own. Often, the land available on the urban periphery is owned by either governments or agricultural landowners. Land that is sitting idle and unoccupied is most commonly targeted by communities of squatters. This is because in many countries, idle land, regardless of who owns it, can be legally squatted upon if the new residents make good use of it. This is the opposite of real estate laws in the United States that favor landowners, but is a common legal standard in many social democracies.

To avoid retributions from landowners and local police, squatters generally settle a new area overnight with a large number of families. This is known as a **land invasion**. A squatter camp can be quickly erected with makeshift homes using available building materials, such as scrap wood, plastic, and blue plastic tarps. These rudimentary homes may give squatters some legal protections, since in some places it is illegal for government to tear down housing of any type without court authority to do so.

Over time, the squatter homes are improved upon and utilize sturdier materials. A thirty-year-old squatter settlement may look like formal housing with brick walls and metal roofs, along with electric power or other utilities. However, as you move through to new squatter settlements farther out of the city, the quality of housing declines, as does the availability of utilities and other services such as bus lines.

Through these tactics, squatters attempt to achieve **land tenure;** that is, legal right or title to the land upon which they build their homes. It can take years if not decades to formalize property ownership. Until then, there is always the risk that squatters could be run off the land. To minimize this risk, squatter communities often pool their resources to pay off landowners, bribe local officials, or if money is short, promise local elected leaders the guarantee of votes in exchange for their protection. These political relationships are also important later on to gain government funding for schools, transit, clean water, or other public services.

Zones of Disamenity

These are squatter communities closer to the center of the city. They are built on land that is deemed unsuitable for standard homes and businesses, including steep hillsides, flood plains, old industrial sites, near airports, or on refuse dumps. They are settled because of their availability and due to their close proximity to work opportunities in the city center. For example, *favelas* in Rio de Janeiro rise up the steep hillsides of the city, some built partially on top of one another. The mountainous coastline leaves land available for low-income homes, as most of the flat land is taken for formal housing and commercial development. One problem with settling these areas is that they are often unstable, and a mudslide, flood, or fire can devastate the whole community.

Related Topic: The Updated Model

The updated model of the Latin American city contains a few additional parts that reflect the growth of the region's economy. In the Zone of Maturity, CBD expansion and the growth of high-rise apartments has caused city residents to be concerned that much of the old city character is being lost. In response, a number of cities have promoted the gentrification of the colonial era homes and neighborhoods that remain. Like historical preservation efforts elsewhere, these neighborhoods have value in their tourist appeal and the protection of local cultural heritage. The updated model adds a slice of the Zone of Maturity, which is labeled gentrification.

The Zone of Peripheral Squatter Settlements is expanded in the updated model to reflect the influx of rural-to-urban migration. Within this zone, three features have been added to the model. At the outer end of the commercial spine, shopping malls are common in Latin America; thus a mall is placed here on the updated model. Belt highways have been constructed around a number of major Latin American cities. Therefore, a circular *periférico*, or beltway, is added running through the middle of the zone. Lastly, opposite the mall on the other side of the model, is the industrial park zone. These zones are common and prolific on the outskirts of many Latin American cities, including the *maquiladoras* of northern Mexico, where manufacturing boomed following the passage of the North American Free Trade Agreement (NAFTA).

International Urban Diversity

Cities around the world have very different urban forms and structure. Even within a specific region or country, you find many interesting variations. Cities in Western Europe are much more compact in size than U.S. cities. They were developed for pedestrians and are smaller in area to permit residents to easily walk everywhere they need to go. Urban skylines don't generally contain the skyscrapers seen in other parts of the world. Public transportation is well-developed and most people live within walking distance of their schools, work, and shopping.

In Eastern Europe and countries of the former Soviet Union, the flavor of central planning reminds us of the Soviet era. There is a strict division between urban and rural zones and the overwhelming majority of residents live in apartments. The central part of the city (Central Cultural District or CCD) was not used for retail or commercial purposes but rather for government activities and recreational parks. Zones of uniform housing, called microdistricts, provided worker housing near the job site.

Cities in the developing world have widely divergent forms determined in large part by their religious make-up, colonial history, socialist influences, and many other cultural and urban land use influences. Some of these cities were established as colonial administrative centers: Mumbai (Bombay) and Kolkata (Calcutta), products of the British raj in India, and the French city of Dakar in Senegal. Other capital cities were built to serve as growth poles and were planned attract people and industry to that specific region of the country (Brasilia, Brazil).

Urban forms vary greatly even within a cultural realm. For example, in South Asia we find several different city types ranging from the traditional bazaar city and military installation to the colonial city and the resort city. There are some important characteristics that ALL developing-world cities possess: a large modern center of commerce, a massive immigrant population from rural regions, rapidly growing rates of natural increase, and huge outer rings of squatter settlements that lack even the most basic amenities.

KNOW THE CONCEPTS

A large number of urban geography concepts may be tested on the AP Human Geography Exam. Here are a few categories with examples included.

SUBURBANIZATION

We'll begin with suburbanization due to its many links to the material in the Know the Models section. As a quick review of what was covered in the models, keep these suburban concepts in mind:

- Though many people live in suburban apartments and townhouses, the detached single-family home is the dominant feature on the American suburban landscape.
- The suburbs are predominantly middle-class, economically. However many upper-class suburbs exist, as do some lower-class suburban neighborhoods.
- The first suburban single-family homes appeared in the 1890s. One early example is Riverside, Illinois, outside Chicago, which was designed by Frederick Law Olmstead.
- The original American suburbs were culturally populated by WASPs. This changed between the late 1960s and the 1980s when suburbs become more integrated with Catholic and non-white middle-class populations, who formerly lived in inner-city areas.
- In the 2010 census, just over 50 percent of the U.S. population lived in suburban areas.
- Suburbs continue to expand outward and are the largest zones within urban models.

Combine these facts and historical perspectives with the material in the following subsections.

Home Mortgage Finance and Suburban Growth

In post–World War II United States, homeownership increased significantly as a result of **federal home loan programs** such as the G.I. Bill. Several million war veterans and members of the Armed Forces were eligible for guaranteed federal home loans. Other federal programs such as the Federal Housing Administration and the public finance mortgage corporations Freddie Mac and Fannie Mae radically increased the number of mortgages available to the American public with regulated interest rates and limited processing fees.

The result was a massive influx in new home construction during the 1950s and '60s. Prior to World War II, rates of homeownership were limited. After the war, new large-scale housing developments were constructed. Demand was so high that factory-style housing construction methods—using prefabricated parts and specialized construction teams—became common. **Levittowns** were an example of this. In places such as Long Island; suburban Philadelphia; San Juan, Puerto Rico; and other cities, the Levitt Company built large communities of single-family homes in a short amount of time. New Levitt homes could be constructed start to finish in less than 18 days. Many companies copied the Levitt model, and similar communities were constructed around the country during the '50s and '60s.

Service Relocation in the Suburbs

The boom in suburban home construction prompted a number of small service providers to locate in suburban areas. As shown in the multiple-nuclei model, limited suburban business districts began to emerge from 1945 onward. These featured **basic services** like food, the family doctor, fuel, and auto repair, as well as **non-basic services** such as dry-cleaning and gift shops. Later, in the 1970s, the combination of **middle-class flight** from the inner city and the deindustrialization of urban manu-facturing economies prompted even more and larger service providers to **relocate** to suburban areas.

Two factors causing people to leave cities were at work. First, service providers realized much of their consumer base moved away from the old CBDs that had been the traditional service centers. Simply put, *companies brought the services to where the suburban consumers lived*. Large suburban retail centers and shopping malls became the places of service provision as the same services in the old CBD closed down.

Second, many service firms such as banks, insurance companies, and other white-collar businesses realized their labor force was moving farther and farther out from the old CBD. This influenced many corporate services offices to relocate to suburban CBDs. *Companies brought the service industry jobs to where the white-collar workers lived*. These two factors worked in concert to establish suburban central business districts as the central places of the post-industrial, service economy by the 1980s. As such, the suburban office park replaced downtown office buildings as the contemporary place of business and commerce.

Suburban Sprawl

Suburban **sprawl** is defined as the expansion of housing, transportation, and commercial development to undeveloped land on the urban periphery. In and of itself, suburban expansion is not necessarily a bad thing. The basic question is whether the expansion of suburbs is sustainable. Sustainability within the suburban context can be measured in both economic and environmental terms. Suburban sprawl has been cited as the cause behind a number of problems such as traffic congestion, shortfalls in public school funding, environmental degradation, and economic decline in farming.

A number of suburban political **anti-growth movements** have emerged in the United States and Canada. These groups push for new laws and regulations that slow suburban development and limit approval of new suburban roads and highways. Anti-growth sentiment is especially strong in places where the surrounding rural areas are environmentally sensitive or have historical significance.

An example is Loudoun County, Virginia, where in the 1990s, the county board of supervisors enacted a series of **growth boundaries** that set minimums for the lot sizes of new homes. Supporters were known to exclaim, "Don't Fairfax Loudoun!" in reference to neighboring Fairfax County, which has over a million people in roughly the same-sized area just to the east. On the other side of the argument were real estate agents, developers, and new residents who cited the rapidly increasing home prices in the Washington, D.C., metropolitan area as a reason to increase the local housing supply and loosen the development boundary regulations. Although there have been some changes to the original growth boundaries, much of central and western Loudoun County remains sparsely developed and retains its rural character.

Increased congestion in suburbs from suburban commercial development and sprawl has compelled some suburban residents to move even further away from the city. **Counterurbanization** is when inner-city or suburban residents move to rural areas to escape the congestion, crime, pollution, and other negative aspects of the urban landscape. To maintain their jobs, these people either endure long commutes or participate in the workplace by **telecommuting** and working from home. See more related to sprawl in the section on urban sustainability later in this chapter.

Edge Cities

The concept of the **edge city** was first put forward by journalist (and honorary geographer) Joel Garreau in 1991. Garreau recognized the importance of suburban central business districts to the new service-based economy in the United States and Canada. He also noticed that some suburban CBDs had grown to immense size and economic prominence. Many were built on former agricultural areas and lacked a municipal government, though some were built on towns that expanded into edge cities. To be considered an edge city, a suburban CBD would have the following characteristics:

- Minimum of 5 million square feet of office space
- Minimum 600,000 square feet of retail space
- No city government, except where built atop an existing town
- High daytime population, low nighttime population
- Located at transportation nodes or along commuter corridors

One effect that edge city growth has had in many large metropolitan areas is the large increase in **lateral commuting** between suburbs and edge cities. In some cases, significant amounts of **counter-commuting** have been detected from downtown residences to edge city locations. Traditionally, transportation planners have worked from a hub-and-spoke model of commuting in and out of the old CBD. Large amounts of lateral commuting and counter-commuting have made it necessary to construct transportation plans that have multiple hub-and-spoke traffic flow patterns centered on edge city locations in addition to the old CBD.

The Tyson's Corner Edge City

The quintessential edge city is Tyson's Corner, Virginia. Tyson's is located eight miles west of Washington, D.C., at the intersection of the Capital Beltway and Virginia Routes 7 and 123. The edge city complex of nearly 18,000,000 square feet of office space contains a number of government contracting and telecommunications firms, as well as the headquarters of the National Automobile Dealers Association, *USA Today*, and Freddie Mac.

At its core are not one but two large regional shopping malls, Tyson's Corner Center and the up-market Tyson's Galleria. In addition, a long string of big-box retail stores can be found along Route 7. Tyson's Corner has more office and retail space than downtown Miami, Florida (not to be confused with the Miami–Ft. Lauderdale metropolitan area).

This table provides examples of other edge cities in the United States and Canada:

Boston Area:	Toronto:	Washington (Maryland):
The Route 128 Corridor	Scarborough	Bethesda
Framingham	Markham	Rockville
Quincy-Braintree	Mississauga	Silver Spring
Waltham	Yorkville	New Carrollton

Chicago Area:	Houston Area:	Washington (Virginia):
O'Hare Airport	Clear Lake	Rosslyn
Northbrook	Greenpoint	Courthouse-Clarendon
Lombard	Greenway Plaza	Ballston
Naperville	Katy Freeway	Reston-Herndon
Oakbrook	Post Oak	Crystal City-National Airport
Schaumberg	Westchase	Dulles Airport

Numerous edge cities can be found in the areas surrounding New York, Los Angeles, and San Francisco. Other metropolitan areas with multiple edge cities include Detroit, Philadelphia, Baltimore, Montreal, Vancouver, Minneapolis, Seattle, San Diego, Dallas-Fort Worth, Phoenix, Atlanta, Orlando, and Miami.

City Types

In addition to edge cities, described in the previous section on suburbanization, there are a number of city types tested on the AP Human Geography course.

Colonial City

Cities with origins as centers of colonial trade or administration are classified together as **colonial cities**. In the postcolonial era of independence, many of these cities retained their European-style buildings and street networks.

However, newly independent governments have often changed street names and place-names to reflect local culture and social history. For instance, India has renamed the major cities of Mumbai, Chennai, and Kolkata from their respective British colonial names of Bombay, Madras, and Calcutta. Other countries such as Brazil have moved their national capitals away from former colonial capitals. In 1960, the Brazilian government moved from Rio de Janeiro to Brasilia, escaping the congestion of the old colonial capital and building a new modern city planned just for the country's government.

Fall-Line Cities

Larger colonial-era cities in the United States and Canada were most often port locations. The term **fall-line cities** is used to describe the ports that lay upstream on coastal rivers at the point where navigation was no longer possible by ocean-going ships. The fall-line is where a river's tidal estuary transitions to an upland stream at the first set of river falls.

As such, these were economic **break-in-bulk points** (or break-of-bulk) where ships were offloaded and then packed with outgoing trade. In the early part of the industrial revolution, the waterfalls on these rivers could be harnessed for hydropower. Waterwheels turned to drive industrial production of furniture, textiles, and food processing in these early American cities. Thus, many fall-line cities became both centers of trade and manufacturing in the 1800s.

Industrial Fall-Line Cities in the United States:

> Boston, Massachusetts
> Providence, Rhode Island
> Albany, New York
> Philadelphia, Pennsylvania
> Baltimore, Maryland
> Washington (Georgetown), D.C.
> Fredericksburg, Virginia
> Richmond, Virginia

In Canada:

Montreal, Québec, also lies on the fall-line of the St. Lawrence River. However, it is rarely listed with the other fall-line cities.

Medieval Cities

Medieval cities are urban centers that predate the European Renaissance, roughly 1400 C.E. In addition to Paris, Rome, and London, medieval cities in Europe include Cologne in Germany, Marseille in France, and York in England, all of which were originally settled during the Roman era and developed into significant centers of trade and population during the medieval period.

Outside of Europe, medieval cities include Istanbul, Turkey; Samarkand, Uzbekistan; Kyoto, Japan; and Beijing, China. These all became important centers of trade and governance during the medieval period.

Gateway Cities

Gateway cities are places where immigrants make their way into a country. As a result, gateway cities tend to have significant immigrant populations. Examples of gateway cities include New York City and Miami in the United States; Toronto and Vancouver in Canada; and ports in Europe such as Rotterdam and Hamburg.

Entrepôt

Entrepôt describes a port city in which goods are shipped in at one price and shipped out to other port locations at a higher price, resulting in profitable trade. This type of trade is made possible by the lack of customs duties (import and export taxes) that are common in most other port cities. Entrepôts tend to become large centers of finance, warehousing, and the global shipping trade. Examples include Singapore, Hong Kong, and Dubai.

Megacities

The definition of the **megacity** is a metropolitan area with more than 10 million people. About 20 cities qualify as megacities. You can probably think of the big ones like New York and Tokyo. However, you should keep in mind places like Jakarta in Indonesia (26.4 million), Dhaka in Bangladesh (16.3 million), Cairo (16.1 million), and Mumbai (21.4 million). Don't try to memorize it, but get to know examples:

Rank	City	Population (in Millions)
1	Tokyo	34.8
2	Guangzhou	31.7
3	Shanghai	28.9
4	Jakarta	26.4
5	Seoul	25.8
6	Delhi	24
7	Mexico City	23.8
8	Karachi	22.7
9	Manila	22.2
10	New York City	21.6
11	São Paulo	21.5
12	Mumbai	21.4
13	Beijing	19.3
14	Los Angeles	17.2
15	Osaka	16.8
16	Moscow	16.5
17	Dhaka	16.3
18	Cairo	16.1
19	Kolkata	16
20	London	15.5

Megalopolis

The definition of a **megalopolis** is when the urbanized areas of two or more cities merge together, generally through suburban growth and expansion. The name was given by French geographer Jean Gottmann following his travels through the Northeastern United States during the 1950s. Other megalopolises may form in coming decades, which may challenge Tokyo for the world's largest **conurbation**, or combined city.

Examples of Megalopolises:

> **Northeastern United States**: Boston, Providence, New York City, Philadelphia, Baltimore, Washington (also referred to as BosWash). Can also include Arlington, Richmond, and Norfolk, Virginia.
> **Ruhr Valley**: Essen, Dortmund, Duisburg, Bochum
> **Tokaido:** Tokyo, Yokohama
> **Randstad:** Amsterdam, The Hague, Rotterdam
> **Keihanshin:** Kobe, Osaka and Kyoto

Possible Future Megalopolises:

> **Pearl River Delta:** Guangdong, Shenzhen, Hong Kong, Macau
> **Southeastern Brazil:** São Paulo, Rio de Janeiro, Santos, Belo Horizonte

World City

The **world city** designation signifies a metropolitan area as a global center for finance, trade, and commerce. As such, world cities are ranked in levels of importance, and an example of **urban hierarchy** at the global scale. The **first-order world cities** include New York City, London, and Tokyo. The **second-order world cities** include Los Angeles, Washington, D.C., Chicago, Frankfurt, Paris, Brussels, Zürich, Hong Kong, São Paulo, and Singapore. A long list of the **third-order world cities** includes places such as Miami, Toronto, Seoul, Mumbai, Amsterdam, Buenos Aires, and Sydney.

Primate Cities

When the largest city in a country has at least twice the population of the country's next largest city, it can be designated as a **primate city**. In some cases primate cities are several times larger than the next largest city. The situation of **urban primacy** is sometimes blamed when there is uneven economic development within a country. Due to its high population, the primate city can receive a large majority of a country's economic development and investment.

For example, Bangkok, Thailand, is a rapidly developing industrial and service center with an improving quality of life for its residents. By comparison, much of the rest of Thailand remains a chronically underdeveloped rural region without access to many services. Here's another example: To counter the effects of urban primacy, the French government has regulated industrial investment for many years, directing portions of public industrial investment to locations away from metropolitan Paris. Regional manufacturing centers such as Marseille, Lyon, Lille, Clermont, and Bordeaux have benefited significantly from this purposeful **decentralization** of industrial development funding.

Examples of primate cities:

Asia/Oceana	North Africa/ Middle East	Latin America	Europe	Sub-Saharan Africa
Seoul, South Korea	Cairo, Egypt	Mexico City, Mexico	Paris, France	Dakar, Senegal
Bangkok, Thailand	Algiers, Algeria	Buenos Aires, Argentina	Lisbon, Portugal	Kinshasa, Dem. Rep. of Congo
Manila, Philippines	Amman, Jordan	Lima, Peru	Vienna, Austria	Nairobi, Kenya
Sydney, Australia	Beirut, Lebanon	Santiago, Chile	Warsaw, Poland	Luanda, Angola

The Rank-Size Rule

Related to the primate city concept is the theoretical notion of the **rank-size rule**. Population geographers have recognized an urban hierarchy of city populations, especially in countries with long social histories. Under the rank-size rule, a country's second largest city is half the size of its largest city; the third-largest city is one-third the size of the largest city; and so on, such that the eighth largest city is one-eighth the size of the largest city.

Be able to recognize the formulaic definition for the rank-size rule:

The nth largest city is $1/n$ the size of the country's largest city.

However, few countries have city populations that precisely follow the rule. The hierarchy of cities in the United States or in Russia is a close approximation of the rule.

URBAN SOCIETY

In addition to the ethnic and class-based comparisons within the urban models, a few other urban social concepts are important to know. Two significant areas of study are segregation and urban social change.

Segregation

Ethnic neighborhoods are, in some cases, areas of *de facto* **segregation** where no law requiring ethnic or racial segregation exists, yet they nonetheless remain zones of separation. Historically, legal or "*de jure*" segregation existed in the United States in a number of ethnic and racial situations. The segregation laws against African Americans in the "Jim Crow" American South are an example of *de jure* segregation. Asian immigrants in the 1800s were also segregated by law in cities across the country.

Today, **Chinatowns** are often seen as cultural districts, but many have their origins as zones where Chinese, Filipino, and Japanese migrants were forced to live.

African Americans have faced discriminatory real estate practices even in northern and western states. Although illegal today, banks and insurers historically engaged in **redlining,** designating neighborhoods on company maps where home mortgage and insurance applications would be automatically denied. The Federal Housing Administration now enforces rules against redlining and cases continue to be prosecuted.

Restrictive covenants were another means of racial discrimination through the real estate system. At the behest of neighbors and local politicians, homeowners added special covenants to their home real estate titles, restricting future sale of a home to white-only buyers. Some covenants also attempted to restrict Jews from buying homes. Such covenants are illegal today under federal fair-housing laws. However, title research often uncovers covenants in old titles during home sales—by law these must be ignored.

Even following the Civil Rights Act of 1964, some white urban communities openly engaged in **racial steering,** mainly through the use of real estate agents. When non-whites attempted to buy homes, real estate companies or their agents purposefully drove them to racially specific neighborhoods, regardless of their income or ability to pay for a house. This practice was banned in the Fair Housing Act in 1968, but cases have continued, including three lawsuits in 2006 by state attorneys general against realtors in Illinois, Michigan, and New York.

Urban Social Change

In many cities, a distinct social pattern of **invasion** and **succession** typifies the long-term turnover of neighborhood social and ethnic composition. Over time, one ethnic group or economic class leaves a neighborhood and is replaced by another.

Women and the City

Despite the job losses and outmigration caused by deindustrialization, remaining inner city populations have changed and adapted to the new urban economic landscape. Gender is an important factor in these changes. The percentage of **female-headed households** in urban areas has increased significantly in recent decades. Working mothers are an important demographic group and have been the subject of geographic research.

Geographer **Susan Hansen**, in particular, has focused on the urban transportation patterns of working mothers. Her work shows that the commuting patterns of female heads of household are different from male commuters. Specifically, female heads of household are likely to depend on public transportation and thus must live near bus and subway lines. Their patterns of commuting are not just from home into work. Women heads of household also must access food shopping, health care, and other services and plan their home location accordingly.

Overall, it's important to keep in mind that the **roles of women** in American and Canadian society have changed significantly in recent decades. Women make up half of the urban labor force. Women are increasingly equal (but not yet equal) to men in terms of pay, access to management positions, and political power. Educational statistics show that women are today outperforming men as university students, both in terms of numbers and overall grade performance.

As a result, two sectors of the service economy, health care and education, have seen women surpass men in terms of the number of positions and average pay. Many women hold senior management positions in these sectors, such as hospital administrators and university presidents. Furthermore, medical schools in the United States reported in 2008 that entering classes are 50 percent female for the first time.

URBAN ECONOMIES

Beyond those mentioned in the chapter on economic geography, there are some additional urban geography patterns directly related to economic development.

Gentrification

Gentrification is defined as the economic reinvestment in existing real estate. In recent history, deindustrialization left many older areas of cities neglected and economically depressed. Real estate prices in these neighborhoods devalued and many residents and businesses left. However, by the 1980s, prices had fallen to such a point that reinvestment in certain neighborhoods became profitable. Initially many gentrifiers, or "flippers," saw the opportunity to take old homes and storefronts and convert them into attractive modern accommodations.

This pattern began in many historic areas in the 1970s, when people in the **historical preservation** movement began renovating homes in places such as Greenwich Village in New York City and Georgetown in D.C. Many of the renovations were attempts to recreate homes and buildings near to their original form. But consumer demand for gentrified homes with modern amenities increased. By the 1990s, a whole **cottage industry** in gentrification had emerged where flippers bought old homes at low prices, renovated the homes to contemporary standards, and resold them at handsome profits. Preservation, in these cases, took a back seat to demand for hot tubs, granite countertops, and stainless steel appliances.

In addition to gentrified homes, **commercial gentrification** has occurred in many of the same areas. Formerly shuttered business places were rebuilt as coffee shops, art houses, bars, and restaurants. Mixed-use development is also common. Some old warehouses are converted into stores, office space, and loft apartments in the same building. The phenomenon of gentrification is so widespread that whole newly renovated districts have emerged in many cities.

This table shows a few examples of gentrified areas:

New York City:	Greenwich Village, SoHo, Williamsburg
Washington, DC:	Georgetown, Adams-Morgan
Chicago:	Wrigleyville, Hyde Park
Los Angeles:	West Hollywood, Silver Lake
New Orleans:	French Quarter, Garden District
Columbus, Ohio:	Short North-Victorian Village, German Village
Salt Lake City:	Sugarhouse, the Avenues-Federal Hill

In terms of urban social change, it is important to know that neighborhood-scale gentrification has a negative effect of driving out **low-income residents** from the community. As the number of gentrified homes increase, so does the price of even non-gentrified real estate in the area. For many urban poor people, rents increase to unsustainable levels. This is especially hard on elderly residents who have lived in these neighborhoods all of their lives. Finding new homes often becomes difficult, and **displaced elderly persons** can become a costly social welfare program issue for city governments.

Urban Economic Growth

In general, urban governments and investors are concerned with the **infrastructure requirements** of cities. Economic growth tends to occur only in urban areas where utilities, transportation, safety, health, and education needs are met in terms of access and capacity. As was mentioned in the chapter on economic geography, city leaders desire to create downtown areas with services such as specialty retailing, art, music, culture, nightlife, and other **cool city** amenities. All of this is done to attract investment to the city in the form of new businesses.

Much of this development is focused on revitalizing old central business districts that have suffered from deindustrialization. Attracting high-paying service industry jobs to old downtowns has become the focus of many city governments. By making the city attractive to young, educated businesspeople, the hope is that major service industry firms in high-paying fields such as technology, computing, research and development, and other **creative industries** such as media and advertising will relocate downtown.

Silicon Valley: Too Much Economic Growth?

Attracting new service firms is not easy, but some places have it easier than others. Companies tend to locate their offices near significant **growth poles** for their industry. Mentioned earlier in this chapter were the high-tech growth poles of Stanford University and the NASA Ames Research Center in the suburbs south of San Francisco. Economic **multiplier effects** around these centers have resulted in a multitude of companies and investment in computer hardware and software development.

The multitude of high-paying technology jobs in recent decades has driven local real estate prices to astronomical levels. As **rare commodities**, standard three-bedroom homes in Palo Alto can cost upwards of $1.6 million. A one-bedroom apartment can rent for over $2,000 a month.

Affordable housing for Silicon Valley residents who are not engaged in the technology economy has become a major urban social issue. This is true for a number of other cities in the United States where high pay and limited housing have created **inflated real estate prices**. Cities such as San Diego; Washington, D.C.; Seattle; Boston; New York; and Portland, Oregon, saw significant real estate price increases from the late 1990s until 2008. And while prices declined after the 2008 mortgage crash, they have bounced back, so affordable homes still remain out of reach for many urban residents, especially as unemployment has increased.

URBAN SUSTAINABILITY

The sustainability of urban growth and development is measured in economic and environmental terms. Questions of sustainability rarely have simple answers. Political attitudes and practical considerations often create a multitude of problems for urban government leaders and policymakers. Likewise, there tend to be several possible solutions to every sustainability problem. The trick for urban governments is to find solutions that are specific to local needs and that are affordable within the funding capabilities of the city.

Economic Sustainability

In addition to the problem of inflated real estate prices, city governments must address economic sustainability in terms of public services like transportation, utilities, health care access, public housing, and the most expensive: education.

Since deindustrialization, large city governments have had the difficult job of balancing depressed commercial tax revenues with the high cost of maintaining municipal services. One area of criticism lodged at city governments are large municipal payrolls. Eighty percent to 90 percent of municipal budgets go to pay the local public workforce. However, to lay off city workers would reduce public services and increase costs of social welfare programs for the unemployed and homeless. New sources of tax revenue are hard to come by. This is why there is development focus on projects like hotel and convention centers (hotel room taxes) and attracting new high-paying service jobs to the old CBD (local payroll taxes).

One approach to combat the high costs of running urban governments is to combine the municipal governments of the core city with the multiple town governments of the surrounding suburbs. The resulting regional municipality would have reduced administrative costs and increased cost efficiency for service delivery. The trick is to come up with a system of shared governance between the involved communities. Regional municipalities have been successful in Canada, where they are common around large cities. In the United States, examples of large regional municipalities include Lexington-Fayette County, Kentucky; Miami-Dade County, Florida; and a metropolitan Pittsburgh municipality is being considered in Pennsylvania.

The Expense of Schools

Suburban governments have similar financial problems. In several areas of the country, the property taxes collected on homes often do not meet the cost and demand for high-quality schools. Think about it; if the typical suburban home produces two children who go into the public education system, and if schools spend upwards of $8,000 per student annually to educate them, then property taxes must raise $16,000 per home each year or be provided by state income taxes. This doesn't include the additional costs of police and fire protection or other local government service programs.

Resistance by homeowners to increased taxes is often expressed by voting down school bond levies, which raise money by increasing property taxes. School systems are caught between a public that does not want to pay higher taxes and parents who demand higher-quality schools. As a result, local school districts are increasingly dependent on state governments to help meet funding needs or are forced to cut extracurricular programs and increase class sizes.

Environmental Sustainability

A number of environmental sustainability issues concern urban governments such as local air pollution, wetlands loss, watershed management, parkland creation, and solid waste management, as well as international issues such as global warming. The problems often center on the question of how urban development will impact the environment.

Urban Transportation

Urban transportation is a frequent topic of environmental sustainability discussion. **Traffic congestion** plagues many cities in the United States and Canada, and there is public pressure on local politicians to come up with solutions. Local leaders are often restricted in what they can do in terms of building highways because of the high cost of road construction and federal clean air regulations that limit emissions. Air pollution from cars has two scales of environmental impact. Locally, **smog** from vehicle emissions is harmful to public health and can create an unsightly haze. Globally, carbon dioxide emissions from cars are a significant source of **greenhouse gases** that contribute to the problem of global warming.

The benefits of **mass transit,** such as having fewer cars on the highway, reduced emissions, and increased accessibility for low income citizens, have become important for almost all cities. There are many public and political supporters of subways, dedicated busways, and street-level light rail networks. Although these systems use up less land than new highways, some property owners whose land is used for these projects complain about their losses. The cost of construction and vehicles is often more than what can be raised from rail and bus fees alone. Who should pay to subsidize mass transit is a contentious issue. It often falls to local governments to find other sources of tax revenue to pay for it.

New Downtown Housing

In addition to gentrified neighborhoods that add to the "cool" value of cities, many cities desire to add downtown housing. This is environmentally beneficial because it stops suburban housing sprawl from encroaching on farmland or sensitive environments such as wetlands, coastal zones, forests, or habitats of endangered species. By having workers live downtown close to their jobs, new downtown housing can also have the added environmental benefit of reducing transportation impacts, fossil fuel use, and air pollution.

City governments work with building developers to target idle downtown land like parking lots and former industrial sites for new construction. Occasionally, even old schools and library buildings are turned into loft apartment complexes. However, the most popular new approach is **mixed-use buildings** that contain both housing and commercial space. Several large mixed-use developments have been constructed in recent years. These types of developments have been referred to as the "New Urbanism."

Over the previous several decades, many cities have enacted zoning laws, which separate commercial and residential space. One of the significant effects of **New Urbanism** is that it has forced cities to re-examine the sustainability of their zoning codes. Many cities have added new zoning categories that allow for mixed-use development and special planning districts where housing, public transit, and office space is more spatially integrated.

The criticism of mixed-use downtown housing developments is similar to that of gentrification. The purchase and rental prices of many new downtown housing units are so high that only the upper middle-class income earners can afford to live there. To combat this issue, some cities require that a certain percentage of new construction be priced specifically for lower- to middle-income buyers and renters.

KEY TERMS

central place theory

market areas

hinterlands

Walter Christaller

urban hierarchy

threshold

range

travel time

agglomeration

Silicon Valley

growth poles

Detroit

cost advantages

South Dakota

limited banking regulations

resource nodes

transport nodes

clustered rural settlements

dispersed rural settlements

circular settlements

linear settlements

situation

concentric zone model

central business district (CBD)

verticality

peak land value intersection (PLVI)

deindustrialization

festival landscapes

gentrification

garden city movement

suburbanization

suitcase farmers

sector model

ethnic neighborhood

WASPS

white flight

multiple-nuclei model

suburban business districts

suburban CBDs

post-industrial city

transportation nodes

Latin American city model

Laws of the Indies

plaza

push and pull factors

squatters

land invasion

land tenure

federal home loan programs

Levittowns

basic services

non-basic services

middle-class flight

relocate

sprawl

anti-growth movements

growth boundaries

counterurbanization

telecommuting

edge city

lateral commuting

countercommuting

fall-line cities

break-in-bulk points

medieval cities

gateway cities

entrepôt

megacity

megalopolis

conurbation

world city

urban hierarchy

first-order world cities

second-order world cities

third-order world cities

primate city

urban primacy

decentralization

rank-size rule

segregation

Chinatowns

redlining

restrictive covenants

racial steering

invasion

succession

female-headed households

Susan Hansen

roles of women

historical preservation

cottage industry

commercial gentrification

low-income residents

displaced elderly persons

infrastructure requirements

cool city

creative industries

growth poles

multiplier effects

rare commodities

inflated real estate prices

traffic congestion

greenhouse gases

mass transit

mixed-use buildings

New Urbanism

PART ◆ V

THE PRINCETON REVIEW
AP HUMAN GEOGRAPHY
PRACTICE TESTS AND
EXPLANATIONS

10

PRACTICE TEST 1

AP® Human Geography Exam

SECTION I: Multiple-Choice Questions

DO NOT OPEN THIS BOOKLET UNTIL YOU ARE TOLD TO DO SO.

At a Glance

Total Time
60 minutes
Number of Questions
75
Percent of Total Grade
50%
Writing Instrument
Pencil required

Instructions

Section I of this exam contains 75 multiple-choice questions. Fill in only the ovals for numbers 1 through 75 on your answer sheet.

Indicate all of your answers to the multiple-choice questions on the answer sheet. No credit will be given for anything written in this exam booklet, but you may use the booklet for notes or scratch work. After you have decided which of the suggested answers is best, completely fill in the corresponding oval on the answer sheet. Give only one answer to each question. If you change an answer, be sure that the previous mark is erased completely. Here is a sample question and answer.

Sample Question   Sample Answer

The first president of the United States was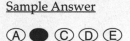
(A) Millard Fillmore
(B) George Washington
(C) Benjamin Franklin
(D) Andrew Jackson
(E) Harry Truman

Use your time effectively, working as rapidly as you can without losing accuracy. Do not spend too much time on any one question. Go on to other questions and come back to the ones you have not answered if you have time. It is not expected that everyone will know the answers to all of the multiple-choice questions.

About Guessing

Many candidates wonder whether or not to guess the answers to questions about which they are not certain. Multiple-choice scores are based on the number of questions answered correctly. Points are not deducted for incorrect answers, and no points are awarded for unanswered questions. Because points are not deducted for incorrect answers, you are encouraged to answer all multiple-choice questions. On any questions you do not know the answer to, you should eliminate as many choices as you can, and then select the best answer among the remaining choices.

GO ON TO THE NEXT PAGE.

This page intentionally left blank.

GO ON TO THE NEXT PAGE.

HUMAN GEOGRAPHY
SECTION I
Time—60 minutes
75 Questions

Directions: Each of the questions or incomplete statements below is followed by five suggested answers or completions. Select the answer that is the best in each case, and then fill in the corresponding oval on the bubble sheet.

1. Which of the following best describes a "push factor" that would cause rural people in the Third World to leave their farms and migrate away from their home community?

    (A) Guest worker policies in First-World countries
    (B) Civil war or armed conflict in the rural countryside
    (C) Job opportunities in manufacturing
    (D) Access to services and education opportunities in cities
    (E) Decreasing land costs for farmers

2. The concept where physical geographic factors such as soils, climate and resources shape a specific culture group's behavior and practices is known as

    (A) transhumance
    (B) cultural imperialism
    (C) convergence zones
    (D) environmental determinism
    (E) Tobler's law

3. An example of a nation without a representative state would be

    (A) Greeks
    (B) Egyptians
    (C) Panamanians
    (D) Indonesians
    (E) Kurds

4. As industrialized countries continue to develop economically, agriculture in these First World states tends to have the following characteristics

    (A) larger farm size and increasing corporate ownership of farms
    (B) larger farm size and more government ownership of farms
    (C) smaller farm size and a diversity of crops on each farm
    (D) smaller farm size and fewer family owned farms
    (E) larger farm size and increasing number of family owned farms

GO ON TO THE NEXT PAGE.

Use the map below to answer questions 5 and 6:

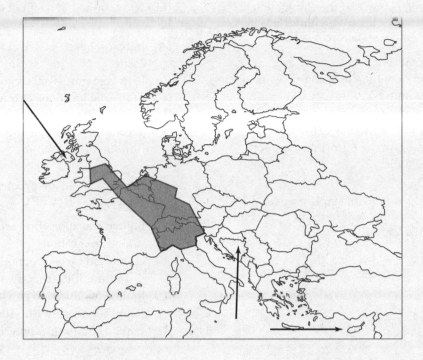

5. The shaded area on the map would be best described as the

   (A) European culture hearth
   (B) European industrial core region
   (C) European Union
   (D) Mackinder's Heartland
   (E) European population periphery

6. During the later part of the twentieth century, the three areas designated by arrows are places in Europe that

   (A) received large-scale in-migration from Africa and the Middle East
   (B) were original members of the European Economic Community or "Common Market"
   (C) became sovereign nation-states
   (D) transitioned from communism to free-market economies
   (E) experienced armed conflict based upon ethnic and religious differences

7. The long-term demographic effect of the One-Child Policy in China has been

   (A) large-scale out-migration of Chinese to foreign countries
   (B) reduction of the total fertility rate below the replacement rate
   (C) mass rural to urban migration
   (D) smaller total population of China
   (E) in-migration of foreign guest workers to fill low-paying service jobs

8. The effects of increasing worldwide use of the Internet, popularity of Hollywood movies and consumption of other English-language media would be examples of

   (A) cultural globalization
   (B) expansion diffusion
   (C) the Anatolian migration
   (D) contagious diffusion
   (E) vernacular regions

GO ON TO THE NEXT PAGE.

9. Workers freely moving between member states within the European Union and the elimination of customs inspections for cars, trucks and trains moving between EU member states are results of

   (A) the removal of tariffs
   (B) the development of the European Coal and Steel Community
   (C) open-border policies
   (D) the monetary union and use of the Euro
   (E) judicial decisions of the European Court of Human Rights

10. Which plant was the dominant staple crop for the culture hearths of Mesopotamia, ancient Egypt and the rest of the Fertile Crescent?

    (A) corn (maize)
    (B) potatoes
    (C) yams
    (D) wheat
    (E) rice

11. New factories located in less developed countries (LDCs) are often the result of corporations based in more developed countries (MDCs) that are seeking

    (A) industrial locations next to natural resource sites
    (B) least-cost industrial locations
    (C) industrial locations at transportation nodes
    (D) increased government regulation of industry
    (E) a technically trained and highly educated industrial workforce

12. All of the following are problems associated with suburban sprawl EXCEPT

    (A) limited transportation access and increasing road congestion
    (B) ethnic and racial segregation of suburban communities from the inner city
    (C) limited tax funds to pay for new public schools and services for the elderly
    (D) limited communications access and few utility services
    (E) destruction of natural landscapes and the elimination of farmland

GO ON TO THE NEXT PAGE.

Use the following diagram to answer Questions 13-16:

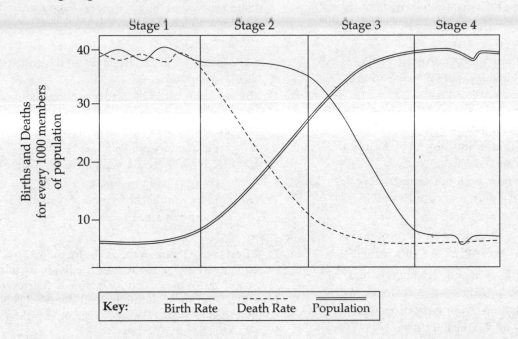

13. The diagram above displays the concept known as

    (A) Population Density
    (B) Demographic Transition Theory
    (C) Malthusian Theory
    (D) Rate of Natural Increase
    (E) Total Fertility Rate

14. As shown in Stage 4 of the model, birth rates can dip below death rates. A country that would be an example of this phenomenon would be

    (A) Sweden
    (B) Mexico
    (C) Brazil
    (D) United States
    (E) India

15. In countries that would fall into Stage 2 of the model, the economy would be best characterized as

    (A) service-based
    (B) heavy industrial
    (C) agricultural
    (D) high technology
    (E) post-industrial

16. In the diagram the point where population growth would at its highest rate would be

    (A) the beginning of Stage 1
    (B) the end of Stage 4
    (C) the line between Stage 1 and Stage 2
    (D) the line between Stage 2 and Stage 3
    (E) the line between Stage 3 and Stage 4

GO ON TO THE NEXT PAGE.

17. The large-scale mortality in the population of Native Americans during the decades following European settlement from 1492 onward was vastly the result of

    (A) warfare with invading European armies
    (B) changes in global climate which lead to crop failures and sea-level rise
    (C) slavery and forced labor in European-owned colonial plantations
    (D) infectious diseases introduced by European explorers and colonists
    (E) colonial government policies restricting the number of children in native families

18. One option for small family owned farms to increase the market value of their crops would be

    (A) eliminate irrigation and rely upon natural rainfall
    (B) switch to organic farming practices with no pesticides or chemical fertilizers
    (C) use biofuels such as vegetable-based diesel for their farm equipment
    (D) switch to growing traditional staple crops such as corn and use fertilizers
    (E) export their crops to Third World locations such as Sub-Saharan Africa

19. The forced expulsion and resettlement of culture groups through the use of fear and violence, such as the conflicts within the former Yugoslavia in the 1990s, is known as

    (A) insurgency
    (B) demilitarized zones
    (C) chain migration
    (D) relocation diffusion
    (E) ethnic cleansing

20. The deindustrialization process within First World countries where the national economy shifts away from manufacturing and toward services commonly leads to

    (A) decreased dependence on high technology and computers
    (B) large numbers of factory workers being laid-off and unemployed
    (C) increased dependence on agricultural production and fisheries
    (D) decreased need for workers with degrees from colleges and universities
    (E) smaller numbers of services available in suburban areas

21. Efforts were made in the 2000s by many First World city governments to increase the livability and "cool" factor of old central business districts (old CBDs) and surrounding industrial areas. This is intended to attract younger, educated residents and

    (A) creative or high-value service industries such as advertising and architectural firms
    (B) traditional basic services such as family shoe stores and children's clothing retailers
    (C) heavy industrial and other manufacturing firms such as steel plants and foundries
    (D) transportation terminals and break-in-bulk points such as ports and rail yards
    (E) sweatshops and other export-based production such as shoes and furniture

22. The borders of American South or "Dixie" as a culture region are

    (A) defined by the locations of all NASCAR races and county music radio stations
    (B) poorly defined fuzzy borders which overlap other American culture regions
    (C) a finite political boundary which surrounds the Civil War–era Confederate states
    (D) defined by the planting range of agricultural products like peanuts and cotton
    (E) a measurable transition zone of 10 miles along the Mason-Dixon line

GO ON TO THE NEXT PAGE.

23. The definition of United Kingdom (Great Britain) as a nation-state would be incorrect because of

    (A) the country's membership in the European Union
    (B) its physical location as an island nation
    (C) the large-scale fragmentation of the British Empire in the twentieth century
    (D) the widespread use of the English language in countries outside of the UK
    (E) the internal cultural differences between England, Wales, Scotland and Northern Ireland

24. The portion of an economy that is engaged in the production of natural resources such as fisheries, mining and timber is known as the

    (A) primary sector
    (B) secondary sector
    (C) tertiary sector
    (D) quaternary sector
    (E) quinary sector

25. Which group of locations below would be known as fall-line cities?

    (A) New York, NY; Norfolk, VA; Miami, FL; New Orleans, LA; New Haven, CT
    (B) Detroit, MI; Chicago, IL; Buffalo, NY; Cleveland, OH; Milwaukee, WI
    (C) St. Louis, MO; Memphis, TN; Baton Rouge, LA; Minneapolis, MN; St. Paul, MN
    (D) Los Angeles, CA; San Diego, CA; San Francisco, CA; Portland, OR; Seattle, WA
    (E) Richmond, VA; Washington, DC; Baltimore, MD; Philadelphia, PA; Albany, NY

26. One improvement that can increase the sustainability of large urban areas with sprawling suburbs is

    (A) converting larger areas of agricultural land to housing
    (B) constructing integrated public transit systems including bus, subway and rail
    (C) decreasing government spending on public schools
    (D) eliminating green spaces and using parkland to create more land for housing
    (E) creating incentives such as free parking downtown to encourage commuting by car

27. Nuclear power poses environmental risks due to the hazards associated with nuclear waste and power plant accidents. However, some environmentalists advocate nuclear power because

    (A) the low cost of building nuclear power plants
    (B) the simplicity of long-term underground storage of nuclear waste
    (C) the lack of carbon emissions from nuclear power plants
    (D) the ability to recycle nuclear fuel rods for reuse
    (E) the 12- to 13-year productivity of nuclear fuel rods

28. The concept of "place" in human geography can be best defined as

    (A) a location on the Earth's surface with a distinctive characteristic
    (B) a point formed by the intersection of two or more transportation lines
    (C) a point where a natural resource is located
    (D) a sub-unit of a region composed of villages or small towns
    (E) a location where people live and work

GO ON TO THE NEXT PAGE.

29. "Doubling time," or the number of years required for a population to double in size, can be estimated by

    (A) dividing the total population by the Total Fertility Rate
    (B) counting back the number of years to when the population was half the current size
    (C) multiplying the Total Fertility Rate by the Rate of Natural Increase
    (D) dividing 70 by the Rate of Natural Increase
    (E) multiplying the Rate of Natural Increase by the Total Life Expectancy

30. In the Third World, plantation crops like bananas, coffee and sugar are examples of

    (A) subsistence agriculture
    (B) import substitution
    (C) export-based agriculture
    (D) specialty agriculture
    (E) value-added agriculture

31. Which of the following place-name lists are characteristic of a French cultural landscape?

    (A) Boston, Albany, Burlington
    (B) San Juan, San Francisco, Los Angeles
    (C) Ste.-Anne de Bellevue, St.-Jean-Baptiste, Vincennes
    (D) Newark, Christiansted, Charlotte Amalie
    (E) Tallahassee, Miami, Chattanooga

32. A global religion founded on the principle of polytheism is

    (A) Judaism
    (B) Zoroastrianism
    (C) Christianity
    (D) Islam
    (E) Hinduism

33. Religious and belief systems in which items in nature such as animals, trees or mountains can have spiritual value or being can be classified as

    (A) animism
    (B) syncretic religions
    (C) infidel beliefs
    (D) tribalism
    (E) hybrid religions

34. The cultural and political ideas of nationalism can work to bond the social fabric of a state together. In this case nationalism can be seen as a

    (A) push factor
    (B) pull factor
    (C) centrifugal force
    (D) centripetal force
    (E) physical factor

35. The political geographic concept of the "state" is defined as

    (A) a population and defined area controlled by an organized government
    (B) a sub-unit of a federal system such as the United States or Brazil
    (C) a population represented by a singular culture
    (D) a population with a singular culture and single government
    (E) the equivalent of a nation or country

36. Two supranational organizations whose origins are primarily economic in origin are

    (A) NATO and the Warsaw Pact
    (B) NAFTA and the World Trade Organization
    (C) the UN and the International Committee of the Red Cross
    (D) the New York Stock Exchange and Tokyo Stock Exchange
    (E) the League of Nations and the UN

37. Two examples of value-added agricultural products produced on European farms would be

    (A) corn and wheat
    (B) rice and beans
    (C) cattle and hogs
    (D) chickens and farm-raised fish
    (E) cheese and wine

GO ON TO THE NEXT PAGE.

38. Which of the following population statistics would be commonly found in newly industrialized countries (NICs)?

    (A) slow population growth and rapid urban to rural migration
    (B) zero population growth and rapid rural to urban migration
    (C) high population growth and rapid rural to urban migration
    (D) high population growth and rapid urban to rural migration
    (E) slow population growth and rapid rural to urban migration

39. Singapore can be classified as all of the following EXCEPT

    (A) an entrepôt
    (B) an island state
    (C) a microstate
    (D) a dependent territory
    (E) a sovereign state

40. Which of the following cities is NOT part of a larger megalopolis?

    (A) New York
    (B) Paris
    (C) Tokyo
    (D) Osaka
    (E) Essen

41. Poor rural to urban migrants who settle in Latin American cities are most likely to have residences or homes

    (A) inside the abandoned buildings of downtown business districts
    (B) in government-provided public housing projects
    (C) in landlord-owned tenement buildings just outside the CBD
    (D) in squatter settlements on the urban periphery
    (E) in single-family detached houses within the suburbs

42. A financial factor that led to increased rates of home ownership and massive growth of suburbs in the United States after 1950 was

    (A) large decrease in the price of suburban land
    (B) the GI bill and similar government-guaranteed mortgage programs
    (C) increased availability and popularity of credit cards
    (D) the development of the interstate highway system and expanded street car networks
    (E) surplus agricultural production from farms in the United States

43. The Total Fertility Rate (TFR) can be defined as

    (A) the estimated number of children born to each father during a one-year period
    (B) the difference between crude birth rates and crude death rates divided by 10
    (C) the estimated number of children born to each female of birthing age (ages 15-45)
    (D) the total number of children each female given birth in the previous ten-year period
    (E) the number of children per family required to replace the previous generation

44. Popular resistance to the creation of a European Union citizen status and EU passports for the residents of EU member states can be attributed to

    (A) Western Europeans having higher wages than workers in Eastern Europe
    (B) security problems associated with the open borders between member states
    (C) concerns over higher taxes to pay for EU government programs
    (D) the popularity of high technology and communications systems which reduce barriers to the formation of social networks
    (E) the attachment to personal identity based upon nationality and regional uniqueness

GO ON TO THE NEXT PAGE.

Use the following diagram to answer questions 45-47:

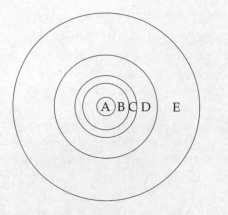

45. In von Thünen's model of the Isolated State the location of village, town or city would fall into the ring labeled

(A) A
(B) B
(C) C
(D) D
(E) E

46. In von Thünen's model the most time-intensive and labor-intensive agricultural activities would fall in

(A) rings D and E
(B) ring E
(C) rings A and B
(D) rings B and E
(E) rings C, D and E

47. In von Thünen's model the area that would be mainly used for grazing activities would be the ring labeled

(A) A
(B) B
(C) C
(D) D
(E) E

48. The concept of scale, in terms of the geographical analysis of population, would be divided upon levels such as

(A) private, business, government
(B) 1:24,000, 1:1,000,000, 1:6,000,000
(C) census tract, city, county
(D) male, female, dependents
(E) gender, age, ethnicity

49. The amount of energy resources known to be contained in a supply or deposit, such as the barrel volume of an oil field that has been explored by geologists, is known as a

(A) proven reserve
(B) potential reserve
(C) surplus
(D) consumption volume
(E) production volume

50. Pollution in the form of acid rain that can damage natural forest and lake environments is primarily the result of

(A) the combustion of natural gas for home heating and industrial production
(B) the burning of coal for electrical and industrial production
(C) the use of hydrochloric acid in factories
(D) airborne emissions from petroleum refineries
(E) water vapor from nuclear plant cooling towers

51. The industrial location of large steel manufacturing centers such as Pittsburgh would be most significantly determined by

(A) a high volume of steel consumers in the area
(B) nearby location of iron ore resources
(C) central location in retail networks
(D) nearby location of water, coal and limestone resources
(E) location as a break-in-bulk point

52. The identity of mestizos in Latin America is a mixture of culture and heritage from

(A) Africans and Native Americans
(B) multiple tribes from what is today California
(C) Europeans and Africans
(D) Native Americans and Europeans
(E) Asians and Africans

53. Two examples of absolute monarchies that exist today are

(A) United Kingdom and the Netherlands
(B) China and Japan
(C) Saudi Arabia and Brunei
(D) Iceland and Japan
(E) Turkey and Egypt

GO ON TO THE NEXT PAGE.

54. Improvements in health care systems, sanitation infrastructure and personal nutrition are factors that lead to

(A) increased total fertility rates and higher birth rates

(B) increased birth rates and decreased life expectancy

(C) decreased life expectancy and increased total fertility rates

(D) increased infant mortality rates and increased total fertility rates

(E) decreased infant mortality rates and increased life expectancy

55. In social geography the concept of race is best defined as

(A) differences based upon human physiological variations such as skin color and bone structure

(B) differences based upon linguistic variations such as the Indo-European language family versus Asiatic languages such as Mandarin or African Bantu languages

(C) differences based upon ethnic variation between different nations or culture groups

(D) differences based upon human-environmental factors such as how climates and resource availability can affect the prosperity of a region's population

(E) differences based upon the continent of a person's residence or origin

56. Friedrich Ratzel is noted as the geographer who

(A) established the concept of Heartlands and Rimlands in political geography in 1904

(B) devised the map and internal boundaries of colonial Africa at the Berlin Conference in 1884

(C) established contemporary human geography at the University of Berlin during the 1800s

(D) first proposed the Concentric Zone model of urban geographic form in the 1920s

(E) proposed German expansion into the Eurasian steppes as a strategy prior to World War II

Use the following image to answer questions 57 and 58:

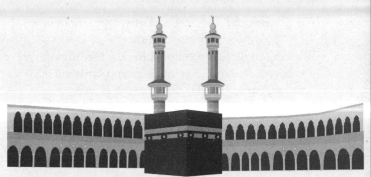

57. The place represented in the image is

(A) the Red Mosque of Islamabad

(B) the Al-Kaaba Mosque in Mecca

(C) the Hagia Sofia in Istanbul

(D) the Blue Mosque in Istanbul

(E) the Dome of the Rock (Al-Aqsa Mosque) in Jerusalem

58. The place represented in the image is

(A) the location of the five pillars of Islam

(B) a place of conflict between three major world religions

(C) the former political seat of the Ottoman Empire before the end of World War I

(D) the destination of the Hajj, a once-in-a-lifetime pilgrimage of all able Muslims

(E) located in the former Roman city of Byzantium

GO ON TO THE NEXT PAGE.

59. Gentrification in cities can be best described by which of the following processes?

(A) government funding and development of new downtown sports stadiums
(B) foreign direct investment in new factories
(C) corporate land development and building new suburbs
(D) corporate land development and building Edge Cities
(E) private investment and reconstruction in existing residential buildings

60. The notion that Christopher Columbus was the first European to "discover" America can best be characterized as

(A) a historical inaccuracy that has nonetheless become folklore strongly tied to the national history of the United States
(B) a historical fact that been established by archaeological and archival evidence in Florida and Spain
(C) a myth that never actually occurred and has been removed from all textbooks in the Americas
(D) a turning point in the technology of navigation where longitude was accurately calculated at sea
(E) a historical fact that has been woven into the multicultural identity of the United States

61. The Prime Meridian is

(A) located in Greenwich, Connecticut
(B) 0° longitude
(C) a meridian that cannot be divided by a whole number
(D) 23°30' N latitude
(E) 180° longitude

62. Places such as Silicon Valley in California and Hyderabad, India, are areas of economic development in

(A) automobile parts manufacturing and vehicle assembly
(B) finance and corporate stock trading
(C) mining of silica and production of silicon
(D) high-technology equipment and software
(E) vineyards and wine production

63. Two examples of current "hard-line" Marxist-socialist states are

(A) Nicaragua and Grenada
(B) Russia and Belarus
(C) Cambodia and Laos
(D) Czech Republic and Slovakia
(E) North Korea and Cuba

64. Which of the following lists are New World agricultural products that came to Europe in the Columbian exchange after 1492?

(A) horses, cattle, wheat
(B) maize (corn), potatoes, turkeys
(C) yams, melons, chickens
(D) noodles, mushrooms, geese,
(E) coffee, sugar, hogs

GO ON TO THE NEXT PAGE.

Use the image below to answer questions 65-67:

65. The agricultural system represented in the image would be most often found in

(A) Fourth or Fifth World states
(B) Newly Industrialized Countries (NICs)
(C) Third World states only
(D) Lesser-Developed Countries (LDCs)
(E) First and Second World states

66. The type of crop farmed using the equipment employed in the image would be

(A) tubers (root vegetables)
(B) paddy rice
(C) grains
(D) summer vegetables
(E) fruits

67. Which source of energy is the type of agriculture production depicted in the image most dependent?

(A) coal
(B) geothermal
(C) natural gas
(D) hydropower
(E) petroleum

68. The following are all factors in the Green Revolution EXCEPT

(A) pesticides
(B) chemical fertilizers
(C) low-cost human labor
(D) plant hybridization
(E) mechanized irrigation

69. The existence of Hindu Indian communities in places such as Guyana, Fiji, and South Africa is the result of

(A) relocation diffusion
(B) colonial-era labor migrations
(C) religious conversions
(D) migrants to high-technology development zones
(E) rural to urban migration

70. A decrease in trade or interaction between different places as the distance between places increases is defined as

(A) elasticity
(B) friction of distance
(C) distance decay
(D) segregation
(E) terminal costs

GO ON TO THE NEXT PAGE.

71. The caste system in Hindu India is a social structure based upon

    (A) a social hierarchy in which a person is born into a caste and cannot change castes during their lifetime
    (B) an economic class which poor people can work and earn money to raise their position in society
    (C) a political party system strongly tied to economic class divisions such as blue-collar and white-collar workers
    (D) regional cultural divisions dominated by Hindi-speakers from northern India
    (E) a colonial social structure created by British rulers and imposed from the 1800s through the 1940s until independence

72. Major population centers in Canada are mainly located on waterways, ports and

    (A) agricultural production areas, especially for wheat and corn
    (B) land borders with the United States
    (C) natural resource locations, especially for minerals and oil
    (D) animal resource locations, especially bison and fur-bearing species such as mink and beaver
    (E) hydropower production sites

Use the diagram below to answer questions 73-75:

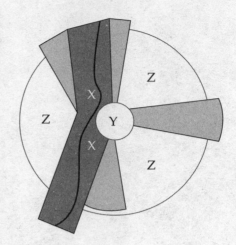

73. The urban model depicted in the diagram best resembles

    (A) the Galactic City model
    (B) Burgess' Concentric Zone model
    (C) Hoyt's Sector model
    (D) Mackinder's Heartland-Rimland model
    (E) Cohen's Shatterbelts

74. In the twentieth-century North American city if area Y is the CBD then area X is most likely

    (A) a new CBD
    (B) an area of forest, parkland or pasture
    (C) a sprawling suburb
    (D) an industrial corridor with a river, port, or rail yard
    (E) squatter settlements

75. In the twentieth-century North American city if area Y is the CBD then area Z is most likely

    (A) an ethnic neighborhood with a single culture-group such as Irish-Catholic, Italian or an African-American community
    (B) an area of forest, parkland or pasture
    (C) an area of manufacturing development
    (D) a Chinatown or Japantown
    (E) a neighborhood dominated by middle-class white Anglo-Saxon Protestants (WASP's)

END OF SECTION I

HUMAN GEOGRAPHY
SECTION II
Time—75 minutes
Percent of total grade—50

Directions: You have up to <u>75 minutes</u> to answer all three of the following questions. It is recommended that you spend approximately one-third of your time (25 minutes) on each question. It is suggested that you take up to 5 minutes of this time to plan and outline each answer. While a formal essay is not required, it is not enough to answer a question by merely listing facts. Illustrate your answers with substantive geographical examples where appropriate. Be sure that you number each of your answers, including the individual parts, in the answer booklet as the questions are numbered below.

1. Using the map above address the following:

   A. Explain how the concept of arithmetic density is expressed on the map.

   B. Describe how the concept of physiologic density can be used to describe the pattern on the map until the 1950s.

   C. Using one historical example, explain how the pattern on the map changes after the 1950s.

GO ON TO THE NEXT PAGE.

2. Explain the shift in manufacturing locations from the First World to Third World during the 1970s to the present. Comparing the conditions between MDCs and LDCs, give **TWO** examples from each of the following factors to illustrate your answer:

A. Labor

B. Government regulations

GO ON TO THE NEXT PAGE.

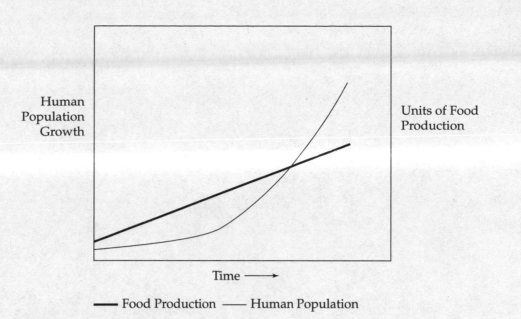

Food Production —— Human Population

3. Summarize the theoretical process described in the graph as it was presented by Thomas Malthus. Using the graph and historical examples, explain why Malthus's prediction has not occurred. What arguments do neo-Malthusians make as a warning?

STOP

END OF EXAM

11

Practice Test 1:
Answers and Explanations

MULTIPLE CHOICE QUESTIONS

1. **B** In this question, the key is to compare *push* versus *pull* factors in human migration. The question requires you to identify a factor related to rural agricultural life that would push someone to move off the farm, such a war or conflict in the countryside. The distractors (A), (C), and (D) are pull factors, or things that are a part of urban life that attract people to cities. Choice (E) is the opposite of an expected push factor, in that *increasing* land costs (as opposed to decreasing) are what often push people off their farms and into cities.

2. **D** This reverse definition question is sort of like watching *Jeopardy!* "What is environmental determinism? Alex, I'll take human geography for 500." In this type of question you must match the question material to the keyword definitions you have learned. Transhumance is used to describe seasonal migration in search of natural resources or pasture animals. Cultural imperialism is when a dominant state expresses its culture in colonies or other parts of the world. Convergence zones are physical geographic areas, where one climate transitions to a different climatic zone. Tobler's law is a spatial analysis principle describing how all places are related, and closer places are more related than others.

3. **E** The cultural geographic notion of the *nation* is a population represented by a singular culture. As a culture group, the Kurds are a nation and population, which span the borders of Iraq, Iran, Syria, and Turkey, but are not incorporated into the governments in these states—Kurds control an autonomous region in northern Iraq, but are still under the sovereignty of the new Iraqi government. The other answers are all national identities based on a representative sovereign state—Greece, Egypt, Panama, Indonesia.

4. **A** This question requires you to identify multiple characteristics for agriculture in a nonspecific category. Consider agriculture in the United States and Canada. Small family farms are not able to earn a profit and are being replaced by large corporate farms. The United States and Canada are First World countries. Of course, we've also seen the growth of small specialty agriculture focused on organics and fruit crops. However, the question asked you to generalize; the word "tends" means "usually." Thus, you have to filter out some of the exceptional or new trends that have emerged in First World agriculture and rely on the typical image of the First World industrial farm. A related fact that will help you remember is that industrialized states have already experienced large-scale rural-to-urban migration. Therefore, rural areas have depopulated and family owned farms are increasingly rare.

5. **B** The first step to identifying the shaded area on the map is to visualize which regions are a part of the shaded area. Notice that portions of countries such as the British Midlands, northern Italy, western Germany, and northeastern France are shaded. The second step is to recognize which of the answers would or would not include these regions. Using POE, you can immediately eliminate (C), as this would include multiple whole states. Reading the other answers reveals that you have a couple of core-periphery examples to examine. Mackinder identified his Heartland core region as being the steppes of Eastern and Central Europe. A number of areas in Europe are identified as culture hearths to some degree. Typically, the classical Mediterranean cultures of Rome and Greece are identified as the European culture hearth. In some ways, the location of the industrial and population core of Europe can be equated regionally. Imagine where there is a high concentration of large cities in Western Europe, and you could, at minimum, locate London and Paris within the shaded region.

Thus, the shaded region is more likely to be the European population core as opposed to the periphery. Consider also that northern Italy, the Rhine River Valley, and the British Midlands are all important industrial regions.

6. **E**   The areas identified by the arrows include Northern Ireland, Bosnia, and Cyprus. Choice (A) is very general and applies to all of Europe. Thus, you can eliminate it as a continental scale issue. Choices (B), (C), and (D) each have flaws, with at least one of the areas identified. None of the three areas were original 1957 members of the EEC—Great Britain joined in 1973. In the question of sovereignty, Northern Ireland has been granted limited autonomy through its own parliament but is still part of the United Kingdom. And only Bosnia, of the three identified, was under Communism during the twentieth century.

7. **B**   There are many population dimensions to the one-child policy in China. This question asks you to relate the one-child policy to other population geography issues. The key here is to figure out which population issue fits into the one-child policy story. Eliminate (A), as there has been out-migration by Chinese to other parts of the world, but we cannot show a direct cause-and-effect relationship between the policy and outmigration because there are other political and economic reasons for which people leave China. Choice (C) is not possible because rural-to-urban migration is the result of industrialization in China. Choice (D) seems like a possibility; however, China's population is still growing (despite the policy), with an RNI of 0.7 percent—recall that the only countries with negative rates of natural increase are in Europe. Likewise, (E) is incorrect because foreign guest workers are common in First World countries and in the Persian Gulf oil states, where there is a combination of low birth rates, wealth, and higher education standards. Thus, (B) fits best, even if you don't know that China's total fertility rate is around 1.8 (and the statistical replacement rate is 2.1). Do the math. If most couples in China have only one child, then a large proportion of the population is not replacing itself. China's population may one day shrink. However, compared to (D), it will take a few generations and some time for negative population growth to occur.

8. **A**   The majority of the world's Web sites are in English, as are all Hollywood movies. Thus, other cultures and governments in non-English-speaking countries often complain about the globalizing effects of exported English-language media. Choices (B) and (D) are specific types of diffusion. Diffusion questions would describe some sort of pattern. And the Internet has diffused globally in a hierarchical pattern from technologically advanced First World states to other parts of the globe. Choices (C) and (E) are unrelated to the topic of globalization. The Anatolian migration is one of two theories used to explain the geography of Indo-European language migration routes. Vernacular regions are culture regions self-identified and recognized by their inhabitants.

9. **C**   The establishment of the European Union has a number of geographic implications. It is primarily a free-trade zone where tariffs have been eliminated. However, a number of enhancements have been added to make free-trade more effective, such as open borders and the single common currency, the Euro. Likewise, the EU has created a large regulatory and legal system to its federal governance of its member states. By allowing EU citizens to work anywhere within the union and by removing customs stations on the borders between EU states, the internal borders of the Union are not eliminated but are opened for the purposes of labor and trade. Choice (A) might be seen as referring to the elimination of customs controls,

but it has no relationship to the workforce movement. Choice (B) is incorrect because the European Coal and Steel Community (ECSC) was the 1950s forerunner of the EU. You can get rid of (D) because the introduction of the Euro in 2000 came after the elimination of border controls, which began in 1985. Choice (E) is a new legal aspect of the EU that can be considered a non-economic aspect of the union.

10. **D** Ancient history? Yes, but we're talking about an important concept in cultural geography, *culture hearths*. Wheat is thought to have been domesticated in Mesopotamia (present-day Iraq) 4,000 to 5,000 years ago. The ancient Egyptians used wheat to make two staples, bread and beer, which fed the empire. The Fertile Crescent is the curved strip of arable land that connects Mesopotamia and Egypt through to the Levant (present day Lebanon, Israel, eastern Syria, eastern Jordan, and southern Turkey. Corn, the Amerindian maize, was planted in the culture hearths of Central America, including the Aztec and earlier Maya, Toltec, and Olmec cultures. The potato was the staple food crop of the Inca in the highland Andes. Yams (ones bigger than those you see today) were grown by the civilizations of West Africa such as the Songhai, in places such as Gao and Timbuktu. Rice was domesticated several thousand years ago in the Irrawaddy valley of present-day Burma (Myanmar) and later spread to the ancient culture hearths of China, Southeast Asia, and India.

11. **B** "Off-shoring," or the process in which companies move factories and facilities to foreign LDC locations, is most often the result of the need for cost reductions. The main cost factor is labor, which can eat up as much as 85 percent of the overall production costs. LDCs offer a primary advantage over MDCs in terms of far lower labor costs. Transportation access and access to natural resources, choices (A) and (D) respectively, can be important factors; however, these do not impact profitability as much as the cost of labor does. Choices (D) and (E) are opposite distractors when talking about LDCs. LDCs generally have far less regulation of industry and have much lower rates of technical skill and education in the workforce than MDCs.

12. **D** Suburban sprawl is a multifaceted problem with many geographical aspects. In this question, you must identify the one aspect that is opposite to the real world situation. Transportation access is a problem due to congestion and a lack of public transit. A social problem seen in suburban sprawl is the lack of diversity in the communities, which can further ethnic tensions in a country. Generally property taxes do not fully cover the cost of public services such as public education. Utility and communication access is far improved in suburban areas (the opposite of "limited"). Another complaint with suburban sprawl is the elimination of natural areas and animal habitat caused by new housing developments.

13. **B** The diagram shows the model known as the demographic transition theory. Population density would be shown in a dot-density map format. Malthusian theory would be a graph showing the relationship between food production and population growth. The rate of natural increase would be shown as percentage data, which is found by subtracting the death rate from the birth rate and dividing by 10. The total fertility rate will also be numerical data and will estimate the average number of children born to each female of birthing age in a population.

14. **A** First, look at the data in Stage 4 only. There, birth rates and death rates are very low and population has reached a plateau. Countries in Stage 4 would be First World countries only. Using POE, you can then eliminate Mexico, Brazil, and India. The two remaining answers, Sweden

and the United States, are similar in terms of economic development. However, Sweden is a much smaller country, and shows more of the population effects of postindustrial society. That is, with most Swedish women in the highly educated labor force, very few remain at home as traditional housewives raising children, as is more common in the United States (despite the fact that many American women are full-time workers).

15. **C**   Countries that would fall within Stage 2 have very high birth rates and declining death rates. This is characteristic of Third World countries, whose economies are mainly agricultural production, with limited mechanization. In these countries, children are seen as necessary farm labor—the more children you have, the more agricultural work that can be done, and thus the more food and money produced. Historically this was also the case in First World countries prior to the industrial revolution. Service-based economies are found in Stage 4, as they are "post-industrial" states. Heavy industry would be found in newly industrialized countries (NICs), Second World states (Stage 3), and First World states (Stage 4). High technology-based economies are often at the same time service-based economies, in Stage 4.

16. **D**   Population growth is measured by the rate of natural increase, sometimes known as the natural increase rate. The simple formula for this is birth rate minus death rate divided by 10. Thus, the highest rates of population growth would be where first rates are the farthest from death rates at the same point on the diagram. Therefore, what you are looking for is the point where the birth rate line and the death rate line are the farthest apart vertically. This falls right on the border line between Stage 2 and Stage 3.

17. **D**   More than anything else, the post-Columbian decline in population of Native Americans is the direct result of disease epidemics. European explorers and settlers brought with them Old World diseases to which Native Americans had no natural immune defense. Most Native Americans who contracted pathogens such as influenza, smallpox, and measles died because their immune systems had not been exposed previously, and therefore they had no genetic or immune resistance. Choices (A) and (C) were causes of mortality; however, the numbers of deaths combined pale in comparison to the impact of Old World diseases. Choice (B) was not a cause of Native American mortality at the time. Choice (E) is incorrect because government policies restricting fertility were more commonly imposed on African slave communities.

18. **B**   Small family owned farms face great difficulty competing with large-scale corporate agriculture in terms of being able to produce large quantities of crops at low cost and therefore remain profitable. By switching to specialty crops such as organics, farmers can vastly increase prices and thus remain competitive and profitable. Choices (A) and (D) are opposite from the reality of small family farming, as irrigation is a necessity in many areas and staple food crops do not bring high prices and they depend on expensive chemical inputs. Choice (C) sounds positive, as it is an environmentally wise decision, but it may not necessarily bring higher prices for the crops grown using this method. Choice (E) is incorrect because Third World countries will not be able to afford higher prices and are thus dependent on imports from large agro-industry corporations.

19. **E**   The ethnic conflicts that emerged in the former Yugoslavia during the 1990s brought the issue of ethnic cleansing to the political and cultural forefront. In this case, ethnic groups often forced minority ethnic groups out of their homes and towns at gunpoint. Those who resisted paid with the destruction of their homes or with their lives. Insurgencies occur when there is

armed resistance to a controlling government or military. Demilitarized zones are established to create a buffer between two belligerent states. Chain migration is where immigrants choose to move to a location where there are people of similar nationalities or backgrounds. Relocation diffusion occurs when an idea culture or technology relocate across a significant physical barrier such as an ocean or mountain range.

20. **B** This question requires you to identify the effects of deindustrialization on the labor force. The most commonly cited impact of deindustrialization is large numbers of layoffs, which occur in factories as manufacturing is moved from the First World to foreign locations. The other answers (A), (C), (D), and (E) are all opposites of the effects of deindustrialization. In reality, emerging service economies are highly dependent on technology and computers; agriculture continues to be important, but contributes comparatively minimal value to the overall economy (or, agriculture is a very small percentage of the GDP); the work requires higher education; and the number of available services increases due to their comparatively higher value and profitability compared to manufacturing.

21. **A** The revitalization of old central business districts after the "death of the American downtown" has been an important urban policy issue for the last few decades. Part of this is the gentrification of existing old industrial buildings into office space and residential units. To fill downtown office space, and to attract tenants who can pay for gentrified apartments and homes, city governments attempt to bring high-value service industries "back from the suburbs." Traditional retailers such as groceries and restaurants are needed as part of this revitalization. However, the younger, educated residents tend not to be starting families and would not need the services listed in this answer choice. Younger, educated residents are not interested in working in manufacturing fields. Likewise, their labor is not required for transportation terminals.

22. **B** As a culture region, the American South, or "Dixie," is just like any other culture region, which is typified by fuzzy border characteristics. Where the American South ends and the North begins is not so easily decided by political boundaries such as the Mason-Dixon Line, as in (E). Likewise, in the case of (C), political boundaries are poor indicators of a culture region boundary. Civil War–era border states such as Maryland and Virginia have taken on more northern cultural characteristics, whereas West Virginia, a union state, has increasingly gained Southern cultural characteristics over time. Choice (A) is incorrect because country music radio stations are found in all 50 states, and two of the largest attended NASCAR events are in California and Wisconsin. Choice (D) is incorrect because although peanuts and cotton are historically identified with the South, the largest cotton-producing states today are California and Arizona, which are decidedly not Dixie.

23. **E** The definition of a nation-state is a singular culture represented by a single government. Internally, the United Kingdom of Great Britain and Northern Ireland, as it is officially known, is made up of a number of indigenous culture groups or nations—English, Welsh, Scots, Irish, Manx, and other smaller groups. Too often, the United Kingdom is incorrectly associated only with England due to English being the common and official language. Although the United Kingdom is a member state of the EU and the concept of European Union citizenship threatens the identity of its citizens, this external situation does not threaten the internal concept of a nation-state. Nation-states are common in island countries such as Iceland, Tonga, and Japan. Historically, the British Empire has had a diversifying effect on the United Kingdom,

as many immigrants have come from Commonwealth countries (former colonies) such as Nigeria, India, Pakistan, and Jamaica. The widespread use of the English language outside the United Kingdom does not threaten the internal possibility of a nation-state.

24. **A** This reverse-definition question requires you to place natural resource extraction with the traditional sector of the economy. Since mining natural resources is the first and initial step to producing goods, it is referred to as the primary sector. The resources are processed in the factories of the secondary sector, transported wholesale, and then sold in the tertiary sector. Quaternary and quinary sectors provide corporate business and professional services to other parts of the economy.

25. **E** This definition-example question requires you to know that fall-line cities lie at the point on a river where oceangoing ships cannot sail further upstream due to upland waterfalls or rapids. The fall-line also marks the end of the estuary or tidal waterway leading to the ocean. Not only were these locations important transportation nodes as break-in-bulk points, but waterfalls also provided a source of kinetic waterpower for early factories at the start of the industrial revolution (prior to electrification). Choice (A) refers to large coastal port cities. The cities in (B) are important industrial cities of the twentieth century Rust Belt or American Manufacturing Belt. The places in (C) are all river ports on the Mississippi. Choice (D) are all coastal ocean ports on the Pacific.

26. **B** The question asks which actions can increase the sustainability of large cities with sprawling suburbs. Or, what can be done to reduce transportation and housing congestion and reduce government costs? There are a number of major issues associated with sprawl, including land use, transportation, schools, recreation, and the revitalization of old downtowns. Constructing public transit increases the sustainability, or livability, of a suburban area. The other answers are all opposite—ones that decrease sustainability. Sustainable land use would use less agricultural land and less parkland. Even over the long-term, the costs of education programs and new school construction generally exceed the property taxes collected on new homes. Downtown parking would be counter to sustainability, as this would increase the number of cars on the road.

27. **C** Despite the risk of accidents and costs associated with nuclear waste, there are two positives to the use of nuclear power. One is that nuclear plants do not release carbon emissions into the atmosphere, and therefore have limited impact on global warming. The second is that nuclear fuel can be reprocessed and is thus considered a renewable, long-lasting energy. The problem with reprocessing fuel is that it often creates weapons-grade plutonium, which can present a security risk. Thus, (D) and (E) are plausible answers, but *not the best* answer for this question. Nuclear power plants are extremely expensive to build. Underground storage as a possibility for nuclear waste has yet to be proven viable either from an engineering or policy standpoint.

28. **A** This question requires you to know the technical geographic definition for the term "place." Although all the answers could be a common definition for place, (A) most closely represents the generalized textbook definition. Consider that there are many different types of places and that the non-specific definition may work best when there is little specificity in the question. Choice (B) is transportation-specific. Choice (C) is environmentally specific. Choice (D) is focused on urban geography. Choice (E) refers to settlement and labor, and nothing else. There are places where people don't live or work.

29. **D** The question provides you with both the term and the technical definition, but asks you for the formulaic definition from a basic mathematical standpoint. Actual doubling times can be calculated using complex formulas that resemble inflation calculations. However, the easier way to get a rough estimate of doubling time is to divide 70 by the rate of natural increase. The other answers are merely speculative and none of them represent a formulaic definition for any population statistic.

30. **C** Plantation agriculture almost always means producing food for wholesale processors and for export. Subsistence agriculture is farming solely for the household or local community. Import substitution is the manufacture of goods internally instead of purchasing them from foreign producers. Specialty agriculture requires growing highly specialized crops in generally smaller quantities, such as organics, delicacies, and special varieties. Value-added agriculture is the processing of raw agricultural goods on the farm, such as cheese and wine, to give them additional value.

31. **C** All the cities listed in the answers are from the United States and Canada. Each is a set of three place names from the same linguistic origin. Choice (A) gives all places in New England, which have English place names. Choice (B) gives all places on the West Coast; all have Spanish place names. In (C), the first two locations are in Québec, and the third is in Illinois. Choice (D) gives all Scandinavian place names from Delaware and the Virgin Islands. Choice (E) gives all Native American place names.

32. **E** By definition, polytheistic religions are belief systems based on multiple supreme gods. Of those on the list, only Hinduism qualifies by having a small number of supreme deities, such as Vishnu, Shiva, and Brahma. Each of the other answers have lesser supernatural deities (such as angels or saints) in their cosmography but only one supreme deity, making them monotheistic.

33. **A** Animistic religions such as those found in Native American cultures and in West African voodoun are based on items in nature having spiritual value. Syncretic religions are ones that have integrated the beliefs of two or more other religions. An example would be Sikhism in India, drawing from both Hinduism and Islam, or the Druze of the Levant, whose beliefs draw from both Christianity and Islam. *Infidel* is a derogatory term used to describe those who do not share the belief system of the main group. Although many of the world's tribal groups have animistic beliefs, they are identified as a social unit, not a religion. Hybrid religious practices can describe the syncretic or involve the worship of two or more religions simultaneously.

34. **D** Nationalism for many groups creates a social bond between the group's many individual members. From a political geography standpoint, centripetal forces are those that hold the social fabric of the state together. Thus, a singular nationalist ideology is a centripetal force, as opposed to a centrifugal force, which tears apart the social fabric of the state. Note the way the question is worded; it does not introduce the possibility of competing culture groups (nations) within the state. Choices (A) and (B) are factors that play a role in rural-to-urban migration. Physical geographic factors can play an effective role in nationalism, such as natural disasters, and are often centrifugal forces at the same time.

35. **A** Like the term *nation*, the *state* is a political geographic term with a specific definition, different from how it is used in common everyday speech. The state implies not only a level of

government but also a defined territory of land. Choice (B) is incorrect because federations or confederations like the United States or Brazil are made up of a number of states under a unitary federal state or an umbrella government. Choice (C) is the definition for nation. Choice (D) is a definition for a nation-state. Choice (E) is a distractor meant to catch people who have not been trained on the technical definitions of these seemingly common terms.

36. **B** This definition-example question requires you to know the definition of a supranational organization and be able to identify examples of supranational organizations that are mostly economic in purpose. These supranational organizations are primarily military or strategic in their purpose. The UN is a multipurpose organization with some economic responsibility, and the Red Cross serves mainly as a relief organization. Stock exchanges are purposefully economic organizations. However, they serve the national economic interests only of the countries in which they are located. The League of Nations, like the UN, was a multipurpose organization with only a limited economic role.

37. **E** This definition-example question requires you to know the concept of value-added agriculture and to apply the proper examples. All of the examples in (A) through (D) are standard forms of primary agricultural products that are most often sent to secondary facilities to process the foodstuffs. Cheese and wine, by contrast, are made from products that are most often harvested or collected on the farm and then processed into secondary goods on the farm, thus adding financial value to the farm's output.

38. **C** The population characteristics of newly industrialized countries (NICs) can be visualized in the demographic transition model as falling on the border of stage two and stage three. That is, NICs are moving from a primarily agricultural to a manufacturing-based economy. At this point on the demographic transition model, birth rates are high and death rates are low. As a result, the rate of natural increase is at its highest. In other words, these countries have very high population growth rates. Another aspect of NICS is that manufacturing develops mainly in cities. Therefore, many people are moving from rural areas to cities to find jobs. All NICs experience rapid rural-to-urban population shifts, much like what was experienced during the 1980s and '90s in Mexico or presently in India.

39. **D** In this EXCEPT question, you find that Singapore can be classified as many things, but you have to identify what it cannot be classified as. This type of question is almost the reverse of a definition-example question, and requires you to know the definitions of several terms to apply to a single example. As an entrepôt, Singapore has the economic purpose of importing goods and then re-exporting them at a higher price to other parts of the world. Singapore is an island that sits off the coast, very close to, but not on, Malaysia. Despite its economic importance, Singapore is a very small piece of land, and like Monaco or Brunei, it is considered a microstate. Although Singapore was once part of the British Empire, it has since received its independence (1965), and thus can no longer be considered a dependent territory of the British Crown—an example of a British dependent territory would be the Falkland Islands, St. Helena Island, or Anguilla (Hong Kong was a dependent territory prior to its reintegration with China in 1997).

40. **B** This NOT question is a slightly different version of the definition-example question. Here you have to visualize the map in your mind. New York is part of the northeastern megalopolis the United States, which is an urban and suburban landscape that stretches from southern

New Hampshire to Richmond, Virginia. Paris is the center of a large metropolitan area, but has not met the definition of the megalopolis because it has not merged its urban landscape with any other larger metropolitan areas. Another giveaway is that Paris is a primate city, and thus is much larger than the next largest city in France, Lyon, which is far to the south. Tokyo is also a large city in its own right, and has merged its metropolitan area with neighboring Yokohama and thus qualifies as a megalopolis. Likewise Osaka has merged with neighboring Kobe. Over a hundred years ago, Essen merged with the neighboring city of Dortmund during the height of urban industrial growth in late-1800s Germany.

41. **D** The question here asks you to visualize the Ford Griffin model of the Latin American city. Think about the difference between the Latin American city and the Anglo-American city in the United States and Canada. In the Latin American city, the wealthy tend to live in the center of the city due to historical reasons, like the Laws of the Indies, which segregated the inner city for Europeans and required non-Europeans or people of mixed descent to live on the outskirts. Today, wealthy urban Latin Americans also find social status by living close to the center of the city, or on the "spine" boulevards leading away from the city center. By comparison, in the Anglo-American city models (such as the concentric zone model), the wealthier residents tend to live on the outskirts; that is the periphery. Again, the theme of core and periphery is important here. When poor Latin Americans migrate from rural areas to cities, they commonly find that there is no available housing for them once they arrive. Thus, it is necessary for them to establish their own squatter settlements on the urban periphery.

42. **B** In the post–World War II American housing boom, a number of factors came together that increased the overall percentage rates and home ownership within the general population. One often-cited reason is the mass production techniques used to produce large numbers of homes, such as what was seen in the Levittowns. However, to pay for all this, the U.S. federal government guaranteed home loans to returning war veterans and established a number of other federal programs that increased access to credit for first-time homebuyers. (A) Think of land prices in First World countries as continuously rising over time. Rarely do land prices ever decline significantly. (C) Even though credit cards became widely available in the 1970s and 1980s, they have no practical use in purchasing homes. (D) The interstate highway system was another post–World War II development in the United States. Although some highways made access to suburbs much easier, the highways themselves were not a "financial factor"; they are instead considered *infrastructure*. (E) Likewise, high levels of farm production created little access to capital in the post–World War II era. The booming number of manufacturing and white-collar jobs meant much more to the financial success of the American middle class, who led the suburban migration.

43. **C** This pure definition question uses several similar distractors. These test your ability to weed out the finite details within the multiple-choice answers. When you hear fertility, think mothers, not fathers so eliminate (A). Choice (B) is the definition for the rate of natural increase, which is an annual statistic that uses data from one-year periods. By comparison, the total fertility rate is more of a running estimate, or a snapshot of fertility at a given time. In (D), the term *the total number* should turn you away from this answer. This would not imply a "rate," which would be represented more by an average or index. Choice (E) is a verbal definition of the replacement rate, which would be a total fertility rate of 2.1.

44. **E** Resistance to the creation of the EU has been limited and is better represented by a series of complaints from EU citizens about this new form of supranational governance. These issues include higher taxes like the value added tax (VAT), the loss of government sovereignty, and the *loss of local identity*. The concepts of citizen status and passports are symbolic to the national identity of European nation-states like France, Italy, or Germany. Others are concerned that smaller nations such as Wales in Great Britain, Breton in France, or Friesland in the Netherlands will be further covered up and disintegrated by the notion of Europeanism. Choice (A) describes a labor economics issue, as opposed to the cultural issues in the question. Likewise, Choice (B) is more of a political geographic category. Choice (D) is in some way parallel with the concept of the supranational state, as networking tends to further erode national borders. Choice (C) would be an economic complaint.

45. **A** Keep in mind that von Thünen's model follows the general pattern of the central place theory and shows core-periphery relationships. Like the similar concentric zone model, von Thünen's model is economic in nature, and places the economic center—the town, village or city—at its core.

46. **C** The economic part of von Thünen's model is based on a labor-intensive nature of agricultural land use. The most intensive labor—the types of crops that require the most attention—must be located close to the place of residence. For example, perishable foods such as dairy products, which required the daily milking cows and that were also perishable, were often located next to the place of residence to minimize loss from spoilage. Vegetable gardens, as opposed to staple plant crops like wheat, had to be tended almost daily to remove pests such as weeds or insects, and needed to be picked fresh from the vine or tree. Therefore, market gardens would be inside, or just outside, the town village or city.

47. **E** The least intensive agriculture requires minimal human labor inputs. Grazing took place on the farthest and least productive lands. Animals also needed to move from pasture to pasture. Think of a shepherd sleeping with his flock. The young men in this role were often too far from town to go home at night. However, they were not alone. For centuries, herding dogs aided shepherds and thus reduced the need for human labor inputs and provided additional protection for livestock from predators. In this regard, one person could raise and harvest a single product.

48. **C** In the geographical or *spatial* analysis of a population, we use different *scales of analysis*, also known as *levels of aggregation*. When examining a quantitative population issue, ask what scale of analysis is being used. Is it a county, state, or something smaller such as a census tract? Scale matters, because we cannot numerically compare data from different scales; data analyzed using one scale may produce different numerical results than when analyzed using another scale. Choice (A) shows different classifications of financial capital. Choice (B) has examples of ratio-based map scales. Choices (D) and (E) refer to gender, age, or ethnicity categories, which are not related to scale.

49. **A** Any quantity of mineral or energy resource that is underground is a *reserve*. The difference between *proven* reserves and *potential* reserves is that a proven reserve has been explored and scientifically analyzed by geologists, who can then give a more accurate estimation of the resource contained within. By comparison, the potential reserve is a known resource that has not been fully analyzed for its volume or quantity. "Surplus" generally refers to an available

good or resource that has already been extracted. Consumption volumes would be measured on the resource-usage end. Production would be measuring a natural resource as it is being extracted from that reserve resource area.

50. **B** This cause-and-effect question gives you the effects and asks you to identify the cause. All the potential answers are related to air pollution to some degree. Acid rain is a specific form of air pollution, which generally is the result of burning coal that contains sulfur impurities—like much of the coal mined in Appalachia. If the sulfur is not removed by expensive scrubbing devices or if the coal does not come from low sulfur deposits, such as those in Wyoming and Montana, then sulfur emissions from smokestacks can mix with water vapor in the air to create sulfuric acid. In cloud layers, this sulfuric acid can form a solution with water and form rain droplets, which then deposit the acid in forest and in lakes. The increased acidity can then harm vegetation and small animal species. Choices (A), (C), and (D) are all forms of pollution that increase carbon emissions and contribute to global warming. Choice (E) is incorrect because water vapor emissions from the cooling towers of any type of electrical plant (coal, nuclear, or geothermal) can also produce water vapor, which contributes to the greenhouse effect and thus, global warming.

51. **D** Traditional *industrial location theory* applied to manufacturing examines the location of factories in relation to resource deposits. The least-cost location for a multiple-resource factory is in terms of its relationship to natural resources. Factory location is most highly influenced by the location of resources that are mostly lost in the production process. In the case of steel manufacturing, Pittsburgh is an optimal location due to the ready availability of water from the city's three rivers; the limestone geology of the local area; and the nearby coal deposits of the Appalachian Mountains. Iron as a "low-loss good" is the most valuable resource in the production process, and can thus be transported over a much greater distance, such as the iron fields of northern Michigan, Wisconsin, and Minnesota.

52. **D** The notion of cultural identity changes from region to region around the world. In Anglo-North America, individualized race and ethnicity are the most common means of identification. However, in Latin America, mixed identities are far more common. Understanding the origins and the degree to which an individual is mixed play an important role in cultural identification and position in Latin American society. The most common mixture in Latin America is the mestizo, which is derived from a mix of European and Native American. Choice (A) would most likely be represented by a group like the Garifuna of the southern Caribbean and Central American coasts, who are a mix of Carib Native American and African. Choice (B) is a distractor that attempts to focus you on the large Hispanic population in California. Choice (C) would be identified as mulatto. Choice (E) is not a particular ethnic mixture found in Latin America.

53. **C** The concept of absolute monarchy is part of understanding the political economy of feudalism. Absolute monarchies are characterized by a supreme ruler who does not share power with a parliament or legislature, and few exist today. The United Kingdom and the Netherlands are both constitutional monarchies, where power is shared between the monarch and the parliament. Japan was a monarchy prior to World War II. Also prior to World War I, Turkey and Egypt were both formally part of the Ottoman Empire, which was part absolute monarchy, part theocracy. Today, these two countries have no monarchy.

54. **E** This cause-and-effect question is directed toward the study of age structure in the population, as well as the factors that influence infant mortality. As a population becomes healthier, their environment becomes cleaner, and nutrition improves. People live longer and are less likely to have complications during pregnancy. You can eliminate (A) because fertility rates increase and birth rates are relatively higher in Third World countries where health care, sanitation, and nutrition tend to be comparatively low. You can cross out (B) and (C) because increases in health care systems alone would lead to increased life expectancy. Likewise, in (D), these improvements lead to decreased infant mortality; that is, fewer newborn children dying of disease and malnutrition.

55. **A** Race is an often-discussed concept, that has many difficult dimensions to it. However, the concept of race in scientific terms is purely physiological, based on the genetic, not geographic, origin of an individual person. For instance, whites born in South Africa and Namibia consider themselves "African," though we would racially call them Caucasian. Likewise, Persians, Bangladeshis, and Japanese are all geographically Asian. The terms *Caucasian* (European), *Mongoloid* (Asian), and *Negroid* (African) were developed in 1800 by physical anthropologists in an attempt to classify the human species. Unfortunately, this science was based on the ideology of environmental determinism, which led people to reinforce (the now-considered negative aspects of) racism.

56. **C** Ratzel is credited for bringing the science of geography into the modern (contemporary) era by going beyond the old traditions of exploration and mapping. He formalized human geography as a scientific study of peoples and places in the late 1800s. Choice (A) would be the answer if you are asked about the British geographer Halford Mackinder. Choice (B) is incorrect because the Berlin conference (a distractor for Ratzel's German name) was convened by a group of diplomats. Choice (D) would be correct if you were asked about E. W. Burgess. Choice (E) was a military strategic goal of the Nazi party in the 1930s.

57. **B** Here's one of those cultural geographic questions that ask you to know something about symbolic architecture and religious holy places. In the picture, you know there is a mosque of some sort. This one happens to be an open-air mosque with a large black structure in the middle. This is unique only to the Al-Kaaba in Mecca, which is considered the most holy place in Islam. For this type of question, also be able to recognize the Dome of the Rock in Jerusalem, which is an eight-sided building with a central dome and sits atop the Temple Mount and next to the Al-Aqsa Mosque building.

58. **D** This question tests your ability to recall the five pillars of Islam. The five pillars are a moral code (in some ways similar to the Judeo-Christian "Ten Commandments"). One of the five pillars requires all Muslims to make the Hajj, a pilgrimage to Mecca, at least once in their life. (A) is a distractor that tests the detail of your knowledge of the five pillars. Choice (B) would best describe the Temple Mount in Jerusalem. Choices (C) and (E) are distractors that attempt to trap you had you chosen Istanbul on question 57.

59. **E** This definition question uses the term "best," so you need to be careful as you examine the possible answers. Choice (A) would be better described as "urban renewal," as it is government-led development of stadiums—or infrastructure. Choice (B) describes industrial investment. Choices (C) and (D) describe developments in suburban areas, which is generally not where gentrification happens. Gentrification is still most likely to happen in old

neighborhoods close to the center of the city. Choice (E) best describes gentrification, as it is most likely privately funded development, and regardless of where it occurs, basically involves reinvestment and reconstruction of existing buildings.

60. **A** This is a cultural geography question that deals with both factual history and the construction of mythic folklore. As you should know, Columbus was not the first European to explore the Americas. Take, for example, the Viking settlements in Newfoundland, around 1000 C.E.; thus, this is a historical mistake and not a fact, as in (B) and (E). Choice (C) is incorrect in that Columbus's voyages did occur, and were not myths. Choice (D) is historically inaccurate because longitude was not accurately calculated at sea until the late 1700s, after the development of accurate chronometers, or clocks which used gears instead of pendulums to keep time precisely at sea. Focus on the facts in the answers.

61. **B** This is a basic geography and mapping question. Choice (A) is a distractor, as the Prime Meridian is derived from Greenwich, a suburb of London where the Royal Naval Observatory is located and which was used as a point of origin for navigation by the Royal Navy. Choice (C) is a distractor using the prime concept of mathematics. Choice (D) is the Tropic of Cancer. Choice (E) is the line opposite the Prime Meridian, which is used as the international dateline.

62. **D** This question tests your understanding of the geography of service industries and high technology. Silicon is an element, and silicon oxide is what sand, glass, and the structural frame of microchips are made of. Silicon Valley is the area south of San Francisco, which includes places such as Palo Alto, where Stanford University is located, and is home to several high-tech firms such as Hewlett-Packard and Google. Hyderabad, India, in the south of the country, has likewise become the technology development center of South Asia. It is home to many companies that provide customer service call centers for consumers in MDCs.

63. **E** This definition-example question does not use the term *Communism*, and instead utilizes the political-economic term *Marxist socialist*. Note also that the modifiers "current" and "hard-line" are used as well. All of the countries listed in (A), (B), (C), and (D) are former Marxist-socialist states. The only two remaining true "hard-line" Marxist-socialist (or communist) states are North Korea and Cuba. By exception, the People's Republic of China and Vietnam are states controlled by Communist parties, but are not considered hard-line as both have accepted free-market economic reforms.

64. **B** This definition-example question regarding the "Columbian exchange" asks you to specify which products went from the New World (the Americas) to the Old World (Europe) after permanent settlement was established by the Spanish on the mainland Americas in the early 1500s. All the other answer choices are incorrect: There were no horses or chickens in the Americas prior to the 1500s. The noodle was developed in China. Coffee was domesticated in the Middle East.

65. **E** The picture depicts mechanized agriculture, which implies large-scale production typically found only in First and Second World states. The picture shows a combine harvester, which is used to collect crops such as wheat, corn, and soybeans that are typically grown in the United States and Canada (First World) and in the former Communist states of Russia, Belarus, and Ukraine (Second World or *former* Second World). The typical agriculture found in LDCs remains today focused on human labor for the harvest of staple food crops.

66. **C** Combine harvesters, which have large paddle wheels on the front, are used to harvest grain crops, which grow on stalks. Tubers, such as potatoes, would require a harvester to have several row plows used to dig up spuds from under the soil. Paddy rice would be harvested from drained ponds where the rice was grown—dry-land rice (like what is grown in the United States) can be harvested using a combine. Summer vegetables and fruits tend to be gathered by hand, even in the First World.

67. **E** An environmental impact associated with mechanized farming is its dependency on petroleum-based fuels, namely gasoline and diesel, to power machinery. When combusted, these fuels produce carbon-based emissions that lead to global warming. Choices (A) and (D) are energy sources primarily used to produce electricity. Choices (B) and (C) are energy sources that are increasingly used in vehicles and mechanized equipment, but still make up a very small proportion of the overall vehicle fuels used in mechanized agriculture.

68. **C** The Green Revolution represents a historical turning point away from archaic agriculture in the Third World and toward the incorporation of modern First World agricultural techniques, namely pesticides, fertilizers, hybrids, and mechanization. Low-cost human labor is a part of Third World agriculture (on a decreasing basis, yet still a critical element, as it has been historically), but not a component of the Green Revolution.

69. **B** This question asks about migration within the British Empire between the early 1800s and early 1900s, when the British controlled India. Skilled and educated Indian laborers were sent to other parts of the empire to fill shortages in engineering, rail, and mining operations. (A) This could be seen as a type of relocation diffusion, but the question asks what the communities are a *result* of, not an example of. (C) Hindu religious expansion would be better shown in places such as Bali in Indonesia, not far-off places such as Guyana in South America. (D) is incorrect, as Guyana and Fiji are not high-tech development zones. (E) Rural-to-urban migration is not generally responsible for migration to countries as a whole, but instead applies to specific cities.

70. **C** This definition question requires you to identify a term among similar-sounding concepts. Choice (A) is incorrect because elasticity from a spatial perspective would describe an ability to stretch out contact over variable distances. Choice (B) refers to impediments and barriers that increase the relative distance between two points. Choice (D) refers to the separation of people based on their characteristics, such as ethnicity. Choice (E) refers to expenses incurred for the on-loading and off-loading of goods, imports, or other break-in-in-bulk points.

71. **A** Although there are a number of caste-based societies around the world, the largest and most commonly discussed are the Hindu in India. Caste is different from economic *class* as it is based on birth into a particular level of society, in which one stays for the remainder of their life. In Hindu beliefs the caste system is based on multiple levels of existence to which humans can be reincarnated, based on an individual's level of karma. In basic terms, if you live a good and moral life (collecting good karma), when you die and are reincarnated, then you can be born into a higher caste in your next life.

72. **C** Population centers (cities) in Canada tend to be located on ports and waterways. However, this does not explain other population centers such as Edmonton, Alberta, or Sudbury, Ontario, which lie landlocked in the middle of their provinces. These are resource node locations for petroleum and mineral extraction, respectively. As for (A) and (E), grain production

and hydropower dam sites tend to be in sparsely populated regions. Choice (B) is incorrect because it is a common misunderstanding in the United States that Canadians want to live close to the U.S. border, when in reality, the physical geography of waterways and resource locations are a better explanation for population location in Canada. Choice (D) might explain the early frontier settlements such as trading posts, but are not related to the origins of cities in Canada.

73. **C** The diagram shows the city landscape divided into geometric sectors, but these lack nodes on the urban periphery necessary for the galactic city model or other multiple-nuclei models or edge cities. Choice (B) would represent and divide the city into multiple rings. Choice (D) would at minimum show a map of Europe and Asia. And (E) would be centered on Europe and Asia but show the whole earth's surface.

74. **D** Industrial zones are mainly located next to the central business district, and realistically are long, column-shaped areas that follow transportation corridors such as rivers or railways. A new CBD, suburb, or Third World squatter settlement would be on the outer part of the model, the *periphery*. Urban models tend not to show forest or parkland—this would be found solely on von Thünen's model.

75. **E** It is important to notice that area in question, Z, is the largest of the polygons in the model. The largest culture group in North America (and for that matter, North American cities, including their suburbs) are white Anglo-Saxon Protestants, otherwise known as WASPs. Ethnic neighborhoods would hold a similar position on the model. However, it would be much smaller in comparison to area Z. As in question 74, urban models tend not to show forest or parkland—this would be found on von Thünen's model.

SCORING AND SAMPLE ESSAYS FOR SECTION II

Do yourself a favor and don't read this section until you have completed the practice test.

You will now have a chance to take a look at the scoring rubrics, the answer key for the essays, and sample essays for the questions that you completed. After showing you the rubric, we will show you what an average essay looks like; that is, a typical low-scoring essay. Then we'll show you the same essay, slightly modified, that scores much higher on the rubric.

Once you've read the rubric, the average essay, and the improved essay, go through both essays and write a shorthand outline of the material that you see. Compare these two outlines to see what different keywords and example sections are added to the improved essay. Then do this for each of the other essays. This should give you a sense of the detail necessary in your shorthand outlines to write high-scoring essays on the AP Human Geography Exam.

BE THE RUBRIC

Afterward, do the same with the essays that you wrote during the timed exam. Rewrite the same essays, adding the additional elements you gained from the rubric, and construct essays that earn full points. By knowing what top-scoring essays look like and training yourself to write more detailed essays, you will score well above average.

SCORING RUBRICS FOR FREE-RESPONSE QUESTIONS

1. Using the map above, address the following:

   A. Explain how the concept of arithmetic density is expressed on the map.

   B. Describe how the concept of physiologic density can be used to describe the pattern on the map until the 1950s.

   C. Using one historical example, explain how the pattern on the map changes after the 1950s.

Rubric

1 + 3 + 3 = 7 Points

A. 1 point for the definition of arithmetic density (population per unit of land), must reference graph
OR 1 point for the concept of the population centroid (weighted center of the population distribution within the boundary of the state), must reference map

B. Physiologic density—the population per unit area of arable (farmable) land
Examples below must be pre-1950:
0 points for no description of physiologic density
1 point for a basic definition of physiologic density, or pattern of westward expansion
2 points for definition incorporated into basic description of westward expansion
3 points for definition incorporated into complex explanation of the changing patterns of American agriculture into the available land west of the Appalachian Mountains
OR
Immigrants moving into Midwest/plains to farm in numerous historical waves.

C. Frostbelt to Sunbelt shift
0 points for no description of post-WWII internal migration
1 point for a basic description of post-WWII internal migration
2 points for description of post-WWII internal migration with one cause or basic factor
3 points for complex description of post-WWII internal migration with multiple causes or factors that influence migrant's decision-making.
Better climate; health reasons (allergies, arthritis); higher pay opportunities in service industries or aerospace manufacturers; loss of manufacturing jobs in Frostbelt; retirement locations such as Florida and Arizona; defense industries and military concentrated in Sunbelt states after WWII; companies move to Sunbelt to find cheaper non-union labor and decreased environmental and labor regulations.

2. Explain the shift in manufacturing locations from First World to Third World during the 1970s to the present. Comparing the conditions between MDCs and LDCs, give **TWO** examples from each of the following factors to illustrate your answer:

A. Labor

B. Government regulations

Rubric

4 + 4 = 8 Points

For each section (a) and (b):

0 points for no valid factors

1 point for a simple factor statement or keyword

2 points of a cause and effect-type discussion of each factor's impact on facility relocation

+

0 points for no additional valid factors

1 point for a second simple factor statement or keyword

2 points of another cause and effect-type discussion of each factor's impact on facility relocation

= 4 points per section, maximum

A. Labor factors: Companies sought lower cost locations in LDCs for

Factor	Causation
Salaries	High in MDC, low in LDC
Benefits	High in MDC, low in LDC
Unionization	High in MDC, low in LDC
Skills/knowledge/automation	Jobs were de-skilled making them possible for less-educated workers and highly educated workers were over-qualified or redundant.
Economic Imperialism	Labor in LDCs were less likely to challenge corporate management; were seen as more pliable and willing to work under more severe conditions.

B. Government Regulation factors: Companies sought less-regulated and, therefore, lower-cost locations in LDCs for

Factor	Causation
Labor Rules	Age (youth labor) and workday rules not enforced.
Environment	Pollution regulations not enforced.
Safety Regulation	Workplace and highway safety rules not enforced.
Corruption	Companies could pay off foreign officials to ignore regulations or negotiate taxes.
Trade restrictions	Companies could avoid tariffs and other restrictions by using suppliers in favored LDCs

3. Summarize the theoretical process described in the graph as it was presented by Thomas Malthus. Using the graph and historical examples, explain why Malthus's prediction has not occurred. What arguments do neo-Malthusians make as a warning?

Rubric

1 + 4 + 3 = 8 points

A. Summary (1 point)
Malthus's proposition was that increasing global population would exceed the global ability to produce food (1 point).

B. Malthusian Data Analysis (4 points)
Example 1 (2 points) + Example 2 (2 points)
Possible explanations: (only 2 points per line)
1. Increased use of mechanization to increase food production or transport food
2. Use of chemical fertilizers to increase food production
3. Use of pesticides to increase food production
4. Use of hybrids to increase food production
5. Use of genetic engineering to increase food production
6. Expanded areas of irrigation to increase food production
7. More ecologically friendly farming practices (soil conservation, erosion controls, crop rotations) that increase food production (organics do not count as it causes a decrease)

C. Neo-Malthusian Arguments (3 points)
1. Identification of neo-Malthusian ideology as a modern iteration of Malthus's ideas. (1 point)
2. Possible warnings (2 points possible). One from each of the following (one point each):
   a. Continuation of potential food crisis in the face of overpopulation; or, population exceeding the global carrying capacity.
   b. An energy crisis as the result of the inability to meet the global population for energy resources.
   c. Destruction of the earth's natural habitats as a result of a global over-dependency on natural resources.
   d. Armed conflicts as a result of food, resource or land limitation or crisis as a result of over-population

FREE-RESPONSE QUESTION SCORE SHEET

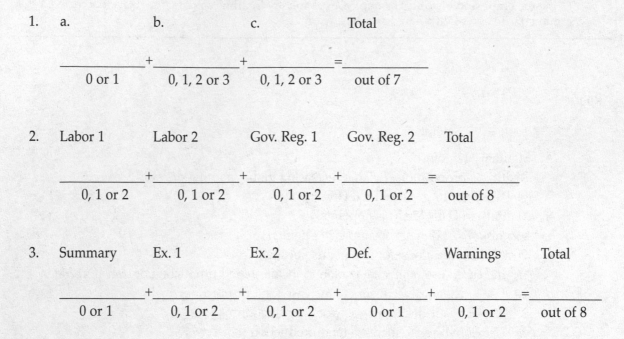

Total Points out of a possible 23, with a goal of at least 14 points (60.8 percent).

SAMPLE ESSAY 1

1. The map above of US Population Centroids illustrates the westward movement of the center of the population of the United States. In particular, the concept of arithmetic density is expressed on the map at each individual spot on the map at a particular time in history. Each dot represents the "center" of the population in each decade from 1790 until 1990—that is by averaging the population along both lines of longitude and latitude, one is able to pinpoint a specific spot on the map. For example, the map shows the arithmetic density of the population in 1880 to be at the junction of Indiana, Ohio, and Kentucky. This does not mean that the majority of the nation's people live in this location. On the contrary, this spot means that in the year 1880, half of the population of the United States lives north of this point and half lives to the south. In addition, half of the population lives to the east of the Ohio/Indiana border and half lives to the west.

The US Population Centroids map also illustrates the more fluid concept of how the physiologic population density has changed over the past 200 years. On its most basic level, there is a clear westward movement of the center of population as the years progress. Until the 1950s, this westward movement appears to be in a straight horizontal line. Although there is clear migration westward, there does not appear to be any major changes in north to south population density. There is a significant change in the map after 1950, however. The center of population shows a definite west southwest movement beginning in 1960, which is interpreted to mean that not only are more and more people moving west but also to the south. Historically, this coincides with the development of the "Sunbelt" which occurred in the years following World War II. Improving economic conditions and international relations following the war led to a general positive feeling among Americans.

Let's see how this essay scored from the rubric:

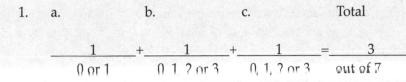

1. a.   b.   c.   Total

$$\frac{1}{0 \text{ or } 1} + \frac{1}{0, 1, 2, \text{ or } 3} + \frac{1}{0, 1, 2, \text{ or } 3} = \frac{3}{\text{out of } 7}$$

Now let's look at a higher-scoring version of this essay:

1. The map above of US Population Centroids illustrates the westward movement of the center of the population of the United States. In particular, the concept of arithmetic density is expressed on the map at each individual spot on the map at a particular time in history. Each dot represents the "center" of the population in each decade from 1790 until 1990—that is by averaging the population density from across the country. For example, the 1880 point at the junction of Indiana, Ohio, and Kentucky does not mean that the majority of the nation's people lived in this location. On the contrary, this spot means that in the year 1880, this is where the spatial average of the population from across the country was located.

The US Population Centroids map also illustrates the more fluid concept of how the physiologic population density has changed over the past 200 years. On its most basic level, there is a clear westward movement of the center of population as American history progressed. Until the 1950s, this westward migration was the result of people settling from the Midwest, and further westward over time, to settle on available farmland. As physiologic density measures people per square mile of farmland, the map not only represents arithmetic density but also the physiologic influence of farmland to westward expansion in the United States.

There is a significant change in the map after 1950, however. The center of population shows a definite west southwest movement beginning in 1960, which is interpreted to mean that not only are more and more people moving west but also to the south. Historically, this coincides with the development of the "Sunbelt" which occurred in the years following World War II. Many people and companies sought to move southward with the decline of manufacturing in the northeastern "Frostbelt." Many new service industry firms and high-tech manufacturers located in places such as Atlanta, Phoenix and the San Francisco Bay area. Along with this economic change a desire by many Americans to live in a more comfortable southern climate.

ESSAY 2

2. There has been a clear shift in manufacturing locations from First World to Third World countries in the past 40 years. There are many reasons for this shift, but the differences in both labor and in governmental regulations between the more and less developed nations allow goods to be produced more inexpensively in the LDC's. This drop in production cost is at the core of the shift in manufacturing locations.

Labor is both more available and less expensive in Third World locations. Manufacturing jobs in general do not require a high level of education to perform. After minimal on the job training, most people are able to perform the simple tasks required of manufacturing jobs. As a result, these jobs are not seen as particularly desirable, especially among more educated populations, and are often difficult to fill. Labor—particularly unskilled labor—is more available in lesser developed nations where population numbers are higher in general and education is not as available. In addition to greater availability, labor is much less expensive in Third World locations. This is due to a number of factors—among them are the lower cost of living and the lack of a nationally regulated "minimum wage" in lesser developed countries.

In addition to the differences in the availability and cost of labor between First and Third World nations, there is also a significant difference in the regulations which has led to the outsourcing of manufacturing jobs to lesser developed areas. More specifically, labor regulations are much less controlled, which allows goods to be manufactured at a lower cost in LDC's compared to MDC's. Minimum wage laws (which were mentioned above) and also laws regarding child labor and the maximum number of hours per week an employee is allowed to work are absent or only loosely enforced in LDC's. Incidentally, the goods from LDC's are often of inferior quality as well, but quality is often secondary to a lower bottom line in today's particularly competitive manufacturing economy.

2. | Labor 1 | | Labor 2 | | Gov. Reg. 1 | | Gov. Reg. 2 | | Total |
|---|---|---|---|---|---|---|---|---|
| 2 | + | 1 | + | 2 | + | 0 | = | 5 |
| 0, 1 or 2 | | 0, 1 or 2 | | 0, 1 or 2 | | 0, 1 or 2 | | out of 8 |

Now let's look at a higher-scoring version of Essay 2:

2. Reductions in production cost is the root cause of the shift in manufacturing locations. Labor is both more available and less expensive in Third World locations. Manufacturing jobs in general do not require a high level of education to perform. After minimal on the job training, most people are able to perform the simple tasks required of manufacturing jobs. As a result, these jobs are not seen as particularly desirable, especially among more educated populations, and are often difficult to fill. This unskilled labor is more available in lesser developed nations where population numbers are higher in general and education is less available. In addition to greater availability, labor is much less expensive in Third World locations. This is due to a number of factors among them, a national-scale lower cost of living. Workers need less to live on in the Third World and, as a result, are willing to work for far less while maintaining a reasonable quality of life. These factory jobs pay far better than farming in the Third World.

In addition to the differences in skills and cost of labor between First and Third World nations, there is also a significant difference in the regulations which has led to the outsourcing of manufacturing jobs to lesser developed areas. More specifically, both labor regulations and occupational and material safety regulations are much less controlled which allows goods to be manufactured at a lower cost in LDC's compared to MDC's. Minimum wage laws (which were mentioned above) and also laws regarding child labor and the maximum number of hours per week an employee is allowed to work are absent or only loosely enforced in LDC's. Finally, both occupational safety and material safety are much less regulated in LDC's. Without having to worry about OSHA safety regulations or whether or not there is lead in the paint used to coat their finished products, companies are able to produce goods at a lower cost.

ESSAY 3

3. In the late 18th Century, Thomas Malthus proposed a theoretical process whereby the human population of the earth grows in an exponential curve where the food production grows in a straight line. At some point in time, the population growth will exceed the available food supply and widespread famine will result. History and present conditions show us that Malthus's prediction has not yet come to fruition. The population of the earth has continued to grow exponentially, but so far the food supply has been able to keep pace. This is in part to the development of new farming techniques, and manufacturing processes whereby food can be grown, harvested, and packaged more efficiently and with less waste. With the dawn of the industrial age, the human population curve has remained the same, but the curve of food production has been able to grow exponentially as well. This is on contrast to what Thomas Malthus predicted.

In recent years, Neo-Malthusians have warned that in spite of recent industrial advancements, Thomas Malthus's theory of food production not being able to keep pace with population growth can still happen. One of the reasons food production has increased is that we have developed rainforests into rangeland to produce beef. In addition, much of this land is not being used as effectively as it could be because of the recent increase in demand for meat. Meat-based diets, which are less common in LDC's, are becoming more and more popular as the world industrializes. This puts a much greater strain on the agricultural resources, however. It takes approximately 20 times the resources (land, water, and labor) to produce 1 pound of meat as it does to produce the same weight of grain. At this rate, Neo-Malthusians warn that there is no way the earth can continue to sustain its ever-growing population.

Let's see how it scored:

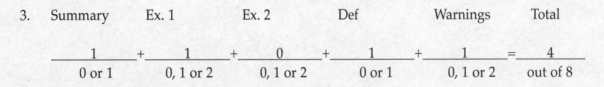

3.	Summary	Ex. 1	Ex. 2	Def	Warnings	Total
	1	+ 1	+ 0	+ 1	+ 1	= 4
	0 or 1	0, 1 or 2	0, 1 or 2	0 or 1	0, 1 or 2	out of 8

Now let's look at a higher-scoring version of Essay 3:

3. In the late 18th Century, Thomas Malthus proposed a theoretical process whereby the human population of the earth grows in an exponential curve where the food production grows in a straight line. At some point in time, the population growth will exceed the available food supply and widespread famine will result. History and present conditions show us that Malthus's prediction has not yet come to fruition. The population of the earth has continued to grow exponentially, but so far the food supply has been able to keep pace. New crop hybrids have made a significant impact in the amount of food grown as new varieties have been bred to be more productive and drought resistant. In addition, the development of mechanized planting and harvesting equipment and manufacturing processes whereby food can be grown, harvested, and packaged on a much larger scale. With technical advances such as these, the curve of food production has been able to grow exponentially ahead of population demands, in contrast to what Thomas Malthus predicted.

In recent years, neo-Malthusians have warned that in spite of recent industrial advancements, Thomas Malthus's theory of food production not being able to keep pace with population growth can still happen. There are physical limits to the land available for agriculture. Much of this land is not being used as effectively as it could be because of increased global demand for meat, particularly beef. Meat-based diets, which are less common in LDC's, are becoming more and more popular as the world industrializes. It takes approximately 20 times the resources (land, water, and labor) to produce 1 pound of meat as it does to produce the same weight of grain. A second example is the destruction of rainforests to create more farmland. Rainforests are the earth's lungs, reducing the carbon load in the atmosphere and therefore reduce global warming. If forests continue to be cut for food production, the global average temperature could rise significantly, leading to a global environmental crisis. For these reasons, many meo-Malthusians warn that there is no way the earth can continue to sustain its ever-growing population.

HOW TO SCORE PRACTICE TEST 1

SECTION I: MULTIPLE-CHOICE

$$\underline{\hspace{3cm}} \times 0.8000 = \underline{\hspace{3cm}}$$

Number of Correct (out of 75)　　　Weighted Section I Score (Do not round)

SECTION II: FREE RESPONSE

(See if you can find a teacher or classmate to score your essays using the rubics in this chapter.)

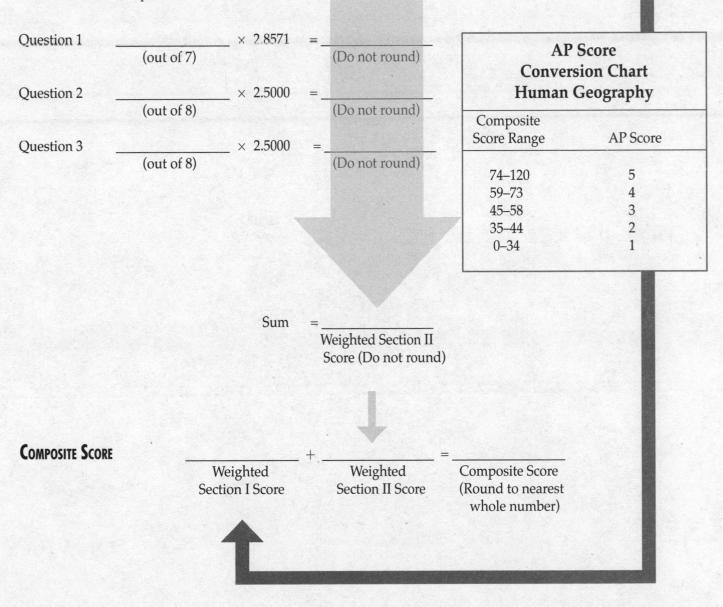

Question 1　$\underline{\hspace{2cm}}$　$\times$ 2.8571　= $\underline{\hspace{2cm}}$
　　　　　(out of 7)　　　　　　　(Do not round)

Question 2　$\underline{\hspace{2cm}}$　$\times$ 2.5000　= $\underline{\hspace{2cm}}$
　　　　　(out of 8)　　　　　　　(Do not round)

Question 3　$\underline{\hspace{2cm}}$　$\times$ 2.5000　= $\underline{\hspace{2cm}}$
　　　　　(out of 8)　　　　　　　(Do not round)

AP Score Conversion Chart Human Geography

Composite Score Range	AP Score
74–120	5
59–73	4
45–58	3
35–44	2
0–34	1

Sum　= $\underline{\hspace{3cm}}$
　　　Weighted Section II Score (Do not round)

COMPOSITE SCORE

$$\underline{\hspace{3cm}} + \underline{\hspace{3cm}} = \underline{\hspace{3cm}}$$

Weighted Section I Score　　Weighted Section II Score　　Composite Score (Round to nearest whole number)

12

PRACTICE TEST 2

AP® Human Geography Exam

SECTION I: Multiple-Choice Questions

DO NOT OPEN THIS BOOKLET UNTIL YOU ARE TOLD TO DO SO.

At a Glance

Total Time
60 minutes
Number of Questions
75
Percent of Total Grade
50%
Writing Instrument
Pencil required

Instructions

Section I of this exam contains 75 multiple-choice questions. Fill in only the ovals for numbers 1 through 75 on your answer sheet.

Indicate all of your answers to the multiple-choice questions on the answer sheet. No credit will be given for anything written in this exam booklet, but you may use the booklet for notes or scratch work. After you have decided which of the suggested answers is best, completely fill in the corresponding oval on the answer sheet. Give only one answer to each question. If you change an answer, be sure that the previous mark is erased completely. Here is a sample question and answer.

Sample Question   Sample Answer

The first president of the United States was   Ⓐ ● Ⓒ Ⓓ Ⓔ
(A) Millard Fillmore
(B) George Washington
(C) Benjamin Franklin
(D) Andrew Jackson
(E) Harry Truman

Use your time effectively, working as rapidly as you can without losing accuracy. Do not spend too much time on any one question. Go on to other questions and come back to the ones you have not answered if you have time. It is not expected that everyone will know the answers to all of the multiple-choice questions.

About Guessing

Many candidates wonder whether or not to guess the answers to questions about which they are not certain. Multiple-choice scores are based on the number of questions answered correctly. Points are not deducted for incorrect answers, and no points are awarded for unanswered questions. Because points are not deducted for incorrect answers, you are encouraged to answer all multiple-choice questions. On any questions you do not know the answer to, you should eliminate as many choices as you can, and then select the best answer among the remaining choices.

GO ON TO THE NEXT PAGE.

This page intentionally left blank.

GO ON TO THE NEXT PAGE.

HUMAN GEOGRAPHY

SECTION I

Time—60 minutes

75 Questions

Directions: Each of the following questions or incomplete statements below is followed by five suggested answers or completions. Select the answer that is the best in each case, and then fill in the corresponding oval on the bubble sheet.

1. The effect of Internet connectivity on global communication and business is that it

   (A) increases the absolute distance between places
   (B) decreases the absolute distance between places
   (C) increases the friction of distance between places
   (D) decreases the relative distance between places
   (E) decreases the Euclidean distance between places

2. The theory of environmental determinism generalizes a region's culture as being shaped by

   (A) the combined influences of the physical geography of the region
   (B) access to waterways for transport
   (C) the population's choice of a staple food crop
   (D) the dominant religion of the region
   (E) people's ability to live sustainably and prevent population pressure

3. All of the following are branches or denominations of Islam EXCEPT

   (A) Shia
   (B) Sunni
   (C) Sufism
   (D) Quranism
   (E) Hinduism

4. The staple crop of the Andean culture hearth of the Inca peoples was

   (A) maize (corn)
   (B) potatoes
   (C) yams
   (D) manioc
   (E) wheat

GO ON TO THE NEXT PAGE.

Use the following map to answer questions 5-7:

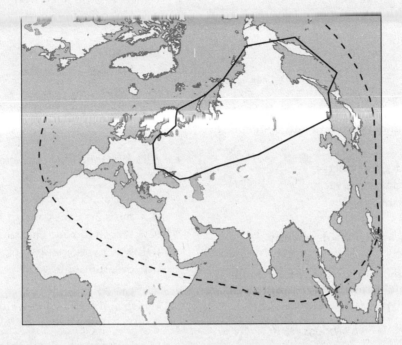

5. The model presented in the map is

   (A) the division between Roman Catholic and Eastern Orthodox religious dominance
   (B) Northern and Southern economies separated by the Brandt Line
   (C) world map as prescribed during the Berlin Conference of 1884
   (D) Mackinder's Heartland-Rimland model
   (E) the Russian and British Empires in 1904

6. The Pivot Area as depicted on the map is important because it contains

   (A) valuable land resource regions such as the Eurasian Steppe and Siberia
   (B) the political heart of Communism during the twentieth century
   (C) the region connected by the Trans-Siberian Railway
   (D) the extent of the Russian empire before the rise of Communism in 1917
   (E) the area devoid of British and American cultural and political influence

7. Cohen's Shatterbelt theory predicted that armed conflicts after 1950 would likely occur in areas

   (A) within the Pivot Area
   (B) along the borders of the Pivot Area and Inner Crescent
   (C) within the Inner Crescent
   (D) along the borders of the Inner and Outer Crescents
   (E) within the Outer Crescent

GO ON TO THE NEXT PAGE.

8. Fisheries, mining, and timber are types of economic production that are part of the

    (A) primary sector
    (B) secondary sector
    (C) tertiary sector
    (D) quaternary sector
    (E) quinary sector

9. The political-economic system found in Communist states is known as

    (A) free-market federal democracy
    (B) free-market social democracy
    (C) Marxist-Socialism
    (D) feudalism
    (E) free-market parliamentary democracy

10. In addition to employment and increased pay opportunities, poor rural to urban migrants in LDCs can be influenced by pull factors such as

    (A) entertainment and increased access to services in cities
    (B) armed conflicts and disasters in rural areas
    (C) decreased political corruption and increased police protection in cities
    (D) increasing land costs for agriculture in rural regions
    (E) lack of clean water and sanitation availability in new urban settlements

11. By calculating the size and agricultural productivity of former Native American farming areas, geographer William Denevan has estimated the size of the population of the Americas in 1492 as being in the range of

    (A) 5 million to 6 million
    (B) 10 million to 12 million
    (C) 50 million to 60 million
    (D) 180 million to 200 million
    (E) 400 million to 420 million

12. New suburban CBDs that have developed into large centers of commercial office space and are often located at major transportation nodes or retail centers are known as

    (A) entrepôts
    (B) break-in-bulk points
    (C) edge cities
    (D) export processing zones
    (E) greenbelts

13. All of the following are factors that contribute to the greenhouse effect EXCEPT

    (A) volcanic eruptions
    (B) methane emissions
    (C) carbon dioxide emissions
    (D) water vapor emissions
    (E) desertification

14. Which of the following would indicate sustainable resource utilization?

    (A) Disposal of solid municipal waste in an open landfill at a rural location
    (B) Commercial fishing only in open oceans beyond the continental shelf
    (C) Paving roads and highways with recycled automobile tire and glass waste
    (D) Heating and cooking in Third World homes with wood from local forests
    (E) Increased cattle farming in dry grasslands where commercial crops will not grow

15. The geographic concept of "nation" can be best described as

    (A) a population and defined area controlled by an organized government
    (B) a federal system such as the United States or Brazil
    (C) a population represented by a singular culture
    (D) a population with a singular culture and single government
    (E) the equivalent of a state or country

GO ON TO THE NEXT PAGE.

16. Which of the following countries were former Communist states and are now members of the European Union?

    (A) Finland and Kazakhstan
    (B) Austria and Switzerland
    (C) Serbia and Albania
    (D) Russia and Belarus
    (E) Lithuania and Poland

17. The traditional method of farming in woodland areas that has been practiced for centuries but now poses an environmental problem in tropical rainforest regions is

    (A) raised-field agriculture
    (B) slash and burn agriculture
    (C) multi-cropping
    (D) aquaculture
    (E) factory farming

18. Which one of the following lists are ALL renewable energy resources?

    (A) natural gas, coal, hydropower
    (B) solar, geothermal, wind power
    (C) petroleum, hydrogen, coal
    (D) nuclear, petroleum, ethanol
    (E) coal, lignite, peat

19. The border characteristics of political regions are

    (A) considered fuzzy
    (B) overlapping other regions
    (C) measurable transition zones
    (D) finite delineations
    (E) vernacular in popular definition

Use the diagram below to answer questions 20–23:

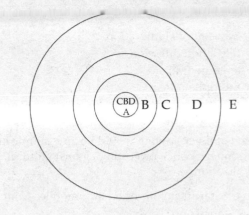

20. This urban model best resembles a

    (A) concentric zone model
    (B) von Thünen's model of the Isolated State
    (C) sector model
    (D) multiple nuclei model
    (E) galactic city model

21. In this urban model, land prices would be highest in the area labeled

    (A) A
    (B) B
    (C) C
    (D) D
    (E) E

22. In the United States following World War II, the ring that would expand most significantly in size would be the area labeled

    (A) A
    (B) B
    (C) C
    (D) D
    (E) E

23. Using the diagram, a model of urban realms that more realistically represents commercial land values can be created by inserting

    (A) rivers and trails
    (B) roads and railways
    (C) airports and schools
    (D) power plants and ports
    (E) banks and hospital

GO ON TO THE NEXT PAGE.

24. The use of the English language by all commercial airline pilots worldwide for the purpose of air-traffic control safety would be an example of

    (A) transnational migration
    (B) relocation diffusion
    (C) a lingua franca
    (D) multiplier effects
    (E) a footloose industry

25. Which of the following would be an example of a government policy protecting against cultural globalization?

    (A) U.S. tariffs on imported automobiles from Japan and Germany
    (B) French and Canadian government funding for production of French-language movies
    (C) French and Japanese trade limitations on beef produced in Great Britain
    (D) South African government-sponsored "peace and reconciliation" committees
    (E) Chinese establishment of Special Economic Zones in coastal port areas

26. Which of the following lists are ALL primate cities?

    (A) Tokyo, Beijing, Djakarta
    (B) New York, Chicago, Los Angeles
    (C) Mexico City, Buenos Aires, Lima
    (D) Rio de Janeiro, Miami, New Orleans
    (E) Mumbai, Shanghai, Karachi

27. Which of the following examples would best represent the concept of map scale?

    (A) private land, commercial land, government land
    (B) 1:24,000, 1:1,000,000, 1:6,000,000
    (C) census tract, city limits, county boundaries
    (D) Washington, New York, Springfield
    (E) line coloration from blue to green and then to red

28. The concept of "space" in human geography can be defined as

    (A) areas of the earth's surface bounded by objects, real and imagined
    (B) a point on the earth's surface with a meaningful characteristic
    (C) areas outside of planetary atmospheres
    (D) the amount of human population that can be supported by the resources in the area
    (E) an area with a common homogeneous characteristic

29. Jerusalem is considered a holy place by all of the following religions EXCEPT

    (A) Catholicism
    (B) Protestantism
    (C) Islam
    (D) animism
    (E) Judaism

GO ON TO THE NEXT PAGE.

30. A small family-run farm in an LDC that produces a variety of crops including corn, vegetables, eggs, and milk would most likely be an example of

    (A) crop rotation
    (B) subsistence farming
    (C) export-based agriculture
    (D) monoculture
    (E) plantation farming

31. The North American Free Trade Agreement (NAFTA) is considered a free-trade zone between Canada, the United States, and Mexico because of

    (A) the elimination of border control stations and customs inspections
    (B) the adoption of the dollar as the common currency
    (C) the free movement of labor across international borders without visas
    (D) the elimination of tariffs on goods and services traded across borders
    (E) the free shipping of goods between countries provided by postal services

32. The Russian Baltic Sea port of Kaliningrad (Koenigsberg) is separated on land from Russia by Lithuania and Belarus. In this regard it is a political example of an

    (A) entrepôt
    (B) enclave
    (C) ethnic neighborhood
    (D) enterprise zone
    (E) exclave

GO ON TO THE NEXT PAGE.

Use the map below to answer questions 33-36:

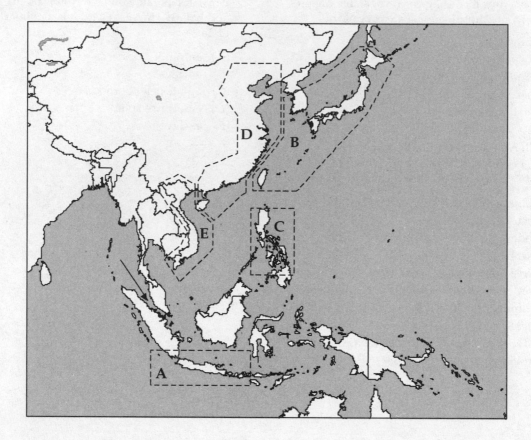

33. Which of the regions in the map would contain the older "Asian Tigers" that experienced large-scale industrial redevelopment in the 1950s and '60s?

    (A) A
    (B) B
    (C) C
    (D) D
    (E) E

34. Which of the regions in the map would contain areas known as special economic zones (SEZs)?

    (A) A
    (B) B
    (C) C
    (D) D
    (E) E

35. The economically important sea lane designated by the arrow on the map is the

    (A) Straits of Hormuz
    (B) Panama Canal
    (C) Suez Canal
    (D) Straits of Magellan
    (E) Straits of Malacca

36. The areas that have large Catholic religious populations are

    (A) A and B
    (B) C and D
    (C) C and E
    (D) B and C
    (E) A and D

GO ON TO THE NEXT PAGE.

37. Spain, Morocco, and Pakistan share commonalities in cultural landscape features such as architecture, vocabulary, and place names due to the influence of _____ culture.

    (A) French
    (B) British
    (C) Spanish
    (D) Arabic
    (E) Roman

38. The musical styles of reggae and ska, along with the religion of Rastafarianism, have their origins in

    (A) the United States
    (B) Great Britain
    (C) Ethiopia
    (D) Trinidad
    (E) Jamaica

39. The countries of Belgium, Luxembourg, and the Netherlands are considered all of the following EXCEPT

    (A) founding members of the European Economic Community (later the EU)
    (B) states with high Total Fertility Rates (TFR)
    (C) the Benelux countries
    (D) states with high per capita gross national products (GNP)
    (E) founding members of the North Atlantic Treaty Organization (NATO)

40. The time frame of decolonization in Africa during which most states became independent of European control was

    (A) 1810s–1830s
    (B) 1890s
    (C) 1914–1918
    (D) 1945–1948
    (E) 1960s–1990s

41. The amount of energy resources estimated to be contained in fossil fuel deposits, but have not been explored and analyzed by geologists, is known as a(n)

    (A) proven reserve
    (B) potential reserve
    (C) energy deficit
    (D) energy surplus
    (E) production volume

42. The type of manufacturing which involves the coordinated assembly of products as supplies and parts are received, and thus reduces production costs and decreases inventory space is known as

    (A) footloose industries
    (B) tertiary production
    (C) just-in-time production
    (D) craft manufacturing
    (E) cottage industries

43. A place, such as a port or rail yard, where goods are transferred from one mode of transportation, subdivided and then sent on another transport system is known as a(n)

    (A) resource node
    (B) export processing zone
    (C) break-in-bulk point
    (D) PLVI
    (E) transport node

GO ON TO THE NEXT PAGE.

44. The primary concern of Thomas Malthus's theory of population was that

(A) human populations would eventually shrink to sizes where industrial economies could not be sustained

(B) human populations would grow at rates that would exceed their ability to produce food and resources

(C) human populations would eventually stabilize in size, and that demand for new food and resource supplies would subside

(D) human populations would become fully urbanized, leaving no one to perform agriculture in rural areas

(E) human populations would reach densities where eventually epidemic disease would become impossible to control

45. In a country where the rate of natural increase (RNI) is a negative number, an expected secondary effect of this population situation would be

(A) a decrease in the per capita gross national product

(B) fewer women entering management, scientific and political positions

(C) a repeal of open-border policies

(D) decreased government protection of natural environments

(E) an increase in foreign guest workers immigrating to fill jobs

46. The replacement rate is a Total Fertility Rate (TFR) of

(A) 0.1
(B) 1.1
(C) 2.1
(D) 3.1
(E) 4.1

47. The study of the movement of disease across space is known as

(A) epidemiology
(B) technical diffusion
(C) contagious diffusion
(D) redlining
(E) geomorphology

GO ON TO THE NEXT PAGE.

Use the map below to answer questions 48-50:

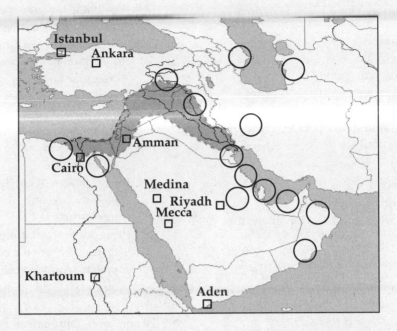

48. The shaded region of ancient civilizations which spanned from the Nile River valley through and to the Tigris and Euphrates Rivers is known as the

    (A) Arabian Peninsula
    (B) Fertile Crescent
    (C) Anatolian Migration
    (D) Maghreb
    (E) Kingdom of Heaven

49. The circled areas on the map are all areas which

    (A) are under the control of al-Qaeda from 2001 to present
    (B) were under the control of the U.S.-led military coalition as of 2003
    (C) are home to the Kurdish peoples
    (D) are production zones of proven oil reserves
    (E) have large-scale irrigated agriculture

50. The cities labeled on the map all share which of the following characteristics

    (A) all are national capitals
    (B) all have majority Sunni Muslim populations
    (C) all are located in *Sharia* states
    (D) all are theocracies
    (E) all are located in secular states

GO ON TO THE NEXT PAGE.

51. The political economy of Canada would be best described as a

    (A) British colony
    (B) dependent territory
    (C) Marxist-socialist state
    (D) supranational organization
    (E) free-market parliamentary democracy

52. Mediterranean agricultural products are grown in the United States primarily in

    (A) Hawaii
    (B) the Upper Midwest
    (C) Central and Southern California
    (D) the New York–New Jersey metropolitan area
    (E) the Atlantic Coastal Plain

53. In the states of the former Soviet Union and Eastern Europe, the shift from communism to free-markets is referred to as

    (A) socialization
    (B) economic restructuring
    (C) nationalization
    (D) containment theory
    (E) the Cold War

54. The process of soil salinization is most likely to occur in areas where there is

    (A) excessive irrigation in dry-land agricultural zones
    (B) deforestation in temperate climate zones
    (C) irrigation near ocean or sea coasts
    (D) plowing of loess soils
    (E) long-term use of fertilizers and pesticides

55. Secondary industries such as fish canneries and lumber mills where manufacturing is dependent on a single natural resource tend to be located

    (A) dispersed near consumer retail locations in a decentralized pattern
    (B) centralized close to natural resource locations
    (C) centrally within consumer market regions
    (D) dispersed near wholesale distribution centers
    (E) centralized near international airport hubs

56. The process of gerrymandering is best described by

    (A) the establishment of new city, county or state governments more favorable to business interests and wealthy citizens
    (B) the creation of new voting districts that have irregular boundaries designed to favor a particular candidate or political party
    (C) the delineation of areas where insurance companies do not wish to sell policies to homeowners due to race, ethnicity or income differences
    (D) the expansion of city limit boundaries to include new suburbs and areas of city utility infrastructure
    (E) the random overlapping of public service districts where the boundaries of school systems, public utility services and political boundaries do not match

57. The development indicator which uses a combination of factors including life expectancy, education rates and income to measure a country's level of development is known as the

    (A) Human Development Index (HDI)
    (B) Gross Domestic Product (GDP)
    (C) Gross National Product (GNP)
    (D) Gross National Income Purchasing Power Parity (GNI PPP)
    (E) Consumer Price Index (CPI)

58. The process by which a national economy shifts away from manufacturing to production dominated by services and high technology development is known as

    (A) a newly industrialized economy
    (B) Fordism
    (C) the Industrial Revolution
    (D) deindustrialization
    (E) market capitalism

GO ON TO THE NEXT PAGE.

59. In the post–World War II United States, the locational shift of commercial offices and services from downtown CBDs to suburban areas can be attributed to

(A) the shift in government locations from downtowns to new suburban locations

(B) decreased environmental regulations in suburban areas that did not limit water pollution and air emissions

(C) the demand for more industrial land for factories in inner city areas pushing out other commercial activities

(D) the availability of low-cost immigrant workers in suburban areas which decreased corporate labor costs

(E) the shift in commercial service workers and consumer residences from inner cities to the suburbs

60. The area off the coast of a country that extends 200 nautical miles across the water, where that country controls all natural resource extraction including fisheries, energy and minerals, is established under the United Nations Conference of the Law of the Seas (UNCLOS) as

(A) international waters
(B) the special economic zone
(C) the exclusive economic zone
(D) territorial seas
(E) sovereign territory

Use the following diagram of the Latin American city model to answer questions 61-64:

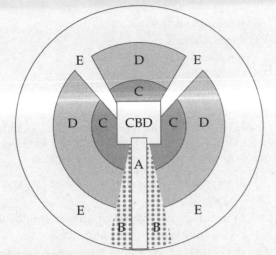

61. The elite residential sector of the city is found in the areas labeled

(A) A
(B) B
(C) C
(D) D
(E) E

62. The CBD labeled on the map historically is centered around a colonial-era

(A) plaza
(B) port or embarcadero
(C) temple complex
(D) castle or fort
(E) coliseum

63. Squatter settlements near the center of the city, situated in areas such as river banks, steep hillsides, or abandoned industrial lands, are known as

(A) Zona Rosa
(B) cordon sanitaire
(C) zone of maturity
(D) peripheral squatter settlements
(E) zones of disamenity

64. The zone of *in situ* accretion is the area labeled

(A) A
(B) B
(C) C
(D) D
(E) E

GO ON TO THE NEXT PAGE.

65. To increase agricultural productivity and increase the pest-resistance of many crops, in recent decades agroindustry firms have developed

   (A) heirloom varieties
   (B) organic farming
   (C) genetically engineered foods
   (D) value-added agriculture
   (E) chemical fertilizers

66. Prior to the rise of steam power and the electrification of industry, manufacturing centers of the early Industrial Revolution were mainly located

   (A) along roads with large amounts of cart and wagon traffic
   (B) in forest regions where wood was abundant
   (C) on waterfalls of streams and rivers
   (D) in national capitals with government funding
   (E) at university research and development centers

67. Which of the following is a list of newly industrialized countries (NICs)?

   (A) Brazil, Mexico, India
   (B) Kenya, Zambia, Tanzania
   (C) Russia, Ukraine, Poland
   (D) United States, Great Britain, France
   (E) Japan, South Korea, Taiwan

68. NATO and the Warsaw Pact can be best described as

   (A) regional organizations based on economic cooperation
   (B) early attempts at free-trade zones in Europe
   (C) partners in combating irredentism in the former Yugoslavia
   (D) military allies during World War II
   (E) supranational organizations based on military cooperation

69. The point in the urban landscape with the highest real estate prices is known as the

   (A) transport node
   (B) resource node
   (C) central place
   (D) peak land value intersection
   (E) breaking point

70. Population density in the United States since the 1940s has

   (A) shifted toward the northern and western states
   (B) decreased overall
   (C) remained high in the agricultural Midwest
   (D) rapidly increased in downtown CBDs
   (E) shifted toward the southern and western states

GO ON TO THE NEXT PAGE.

Use the following diagrams to answer questions 71-73:

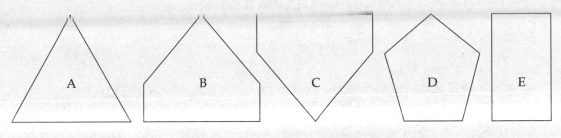

Diagrams of Population Pyramid Shapes

71. The diagrams with the highest dependency ratios are

(A) A and E
(B) A and C
(C) B and C
(D) C and D
(E) D and E

72. The diagram that most resembles the population structure of the United States is

(A) A
(B) B
(C) C
(D) D
(E) E

73. The diagram that most resembles the population structure of Germany is

(A) A
(B) B
(C) C
(D) D
(E) E

74. The Creole culture found in and around the Caribbean and Gulf of Mexico is a mix of the following influences:

(A) Anglo-American and Mexican
(B) Asian, African, and European
(C) Native American, African and European
(D) Native American and Asian
(E) European, Asian, and Native American

75. Low-profitability manufacturing, in goods such as clothing or shoes, tends to be located in LDCs that have all of the following EXCEPT

(A) low real estate prices
(B) high-level government environmental rules
(C) low labor costs
(D) high numbers of available labor
(E) high amounts of foreign direct investment

END OF SECTION I

HUMAN GEOGRAPHY
SECTION II
Time—75 minutes
Percent of total grade—50

Directions: You have up to 75 minutes to answer all three of the following questions. It is recommended that you spend approximately one-third of your time (25 minutes) on each question. It is suggested that you take up to 5 minutes of this time to plan and outline each answer. While a formal essay is not required, it is not enough to answer a question by merely listing facts. Illustrate your answers with substantive geographical examples where appropriate. Be sure that you number each of your answers, including the individual parts, in the answer booklet as the questions are numbered below.

1. Explain **TWO** push factors and **TWO** pull factors that affect rural-to-urban migrants in newly industrialized countries (NICs). For new rural-to-urban migrants, describe the conditions of housing found in most industrial cities within NICs.

GO ON TO THE NEXT PAGE.

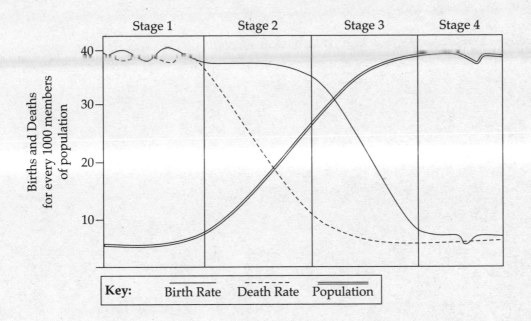

Key: Birth Rate — Death Rate — — — Population ═══

2. Use the diagram to answer the following questions:
   A. Use generalized examples to explain the changes in birth rates and death rates across the Demographic Transition. Be sure to describe how these changes affect total population over time.

   B. Using social and economic characteristics, describe where you would place the following two counties in the model:
      Sweden

      India

3. Describe the advantages and disadvantages posed by nuclear power in comparison to fossil fuel resources. Address the following issues in your comparison:
   A. air pollution

   B. environmental safety

   C. waste management

STOP

END OF EXAM

13

PRACTICE TEST 2:
ANSWERS AND EXPLANATIONS

MULTIPLE CHOICE QUESTIONS

1. **D** The effect of new technologies like the Internet (or historically, trains) is that they reduce the relative distance in time traveled between places as opposed to the absolute distance, which remains a constant length. The trick is to think that your "relatives" come to visit you and thus reduce the time and distance between you and them, whereas you "absolutely" can't change the distance in road miles from their house to your home. Use POE to eliminate (A) and (B). You can eliminate (C) because the friction of distance is concerned with things that slow down the transit of something in between two fixed points—think of a rough road as friction that slows down a car. Choice (E) is incorrect because Euclidean distance is the linear fixed distance between two points; "as the crow flies" is a term your teacher may use, or he or she may show you this concept by holding a ruler across a map, showing the straight-line distance between places.

2. **A** Simply put, the old scientific ideology or paradigm of environmental determinism was that "nature shapes culture." The idea that physical geography—the combination of landforms, plants, soils, animals, oceans, climate, and weather—was different everywhere and resulted in different human adaptations to nature. Thus, cultures were different from place to place as a result. Choice (B) is referring to "site" characteristics. Choice (C) is pointed toward the "culture hearth" concept of a specific staple food to feed a large empire. Choice (D) is wrong because religion is one of many elements that compose the concept of culture. Don't be fooled by (E). Just because the word "sustainably" is here doesn't mean that it's automatically linked to the word *environmental*.

3. **E** The part of the course on culture has a large section of global religions. The key to this question is not the knowledge that (A), (B), (C), and (D) are all forms of Islam: Instead, the key is knowing that Hinduism is very old (over 5,000 years) and that Islam is an Abrahamic religion.

4. **B** This example question asks you to match the staple food crop to its historical example—in this case, the Inca who fed their empire many varieties of potato. Maize or corn was the staple crop of the Aztec in what is today Mexico. Yams were the staple crop of several West African empire states including the Songhai. Manioc (also called yuca—not to be confused with yucca) is a root vegetable and is thought to have been the staple of pre-Columbian civilization in the Amazon Basin. Wheat has its origins in the culture hearth of Mesopotamia in present-day Iraq.

5. **D** Halford Mackinder's Heartland-Rimland model was the first major theoretical model of geopolitics in the twentieth century, and it has been used to predict areas of conflict since the world wars. If the labels such as "Pivot Area" don't clue you in to the definition of Heartland-Rimland, use POE to cross off the other choices. Eliminate (A) as Catholicism is not dominant in Asia. Get rid of (B) since the Brandt line is an economic division of the world into Northern (developed) and Southern (less developed) economies; the United States would be above the line. Choice (C) is incorrect because the Berlin conference set the political boundaries of Sub-Saharan Africa. You can cross off (E); the British Empire would have some gaps in it, such as Thailand and Vietnam (French Indochina) as well as much of central and southern Europe.

6. **A** This question asks you to explain the components of the Heartland-Rimland model. All of the answers are spatially true, but only (A) is true in relation to the model. Land was the commodity that Mackinder was mainly concerned with in his theories. And some lands, such as the Eurasian Steppes (the Russian–Ukrainian) breadbasket, and the timber and mineral rich expanse of Siberia, were more valuable than others.

7. **C** Here is another place where you need to know how the models have changed over time. After Mackinder's death in 1947, Saul Cohen picked up where he left off and applied the same land and conflict principles to the post–World War II era. With "Shatterbelts" identified as the areas of tension between the USSR and the USA, Cohen predicted many of the Cold War conflicts such as Vietnam, Malaya, Greece, India and Pakistan, and the Middle East that were just beginning to brew. These latter twentieth century conflict zones all fall in the Inner Crescent.

8. **A** Think of the primary sector as being where raw natural resources are produced and thus are the primary or first components in a supply chain that are processed by secondary industries (factories). Choices (C), (D), and (E) are all parts of the service economy.

9. **C** Marxist-socialist political economies are found only in states that are controlled by ruling communist parties. The term communism arises from the communal farms and collective ownership of industry which Karl Marx and Friedrich Engels envision in the *Communist Manifesto*. POE should eliminate the "democracy" answers, (A), (B), and (E). Feudalism predates all of the other answers and is represented by land, money, and resources being under the control of a small but powerful aristocracy and the majority of the population being landless peasants.

10. **A** The question asks for a valid pull factor, which is different from push factors when discussing migration. The pull factors are things specific to cities that draw migrants toward urban settlements. One way to organize this in your mind is to remember that the opposite of a positive rural factor cannot be a pull factor. For example, that lack of good pay for farmers is a push factor, whereas available, well-paying jobs in urban factories is a pull factor.

11. **C** This question requires you to know that the pre-Columbian (that is, before Columbus came to the Americas in 1492) population of North and South America was significant and larger than you might think. William Denevan collected archaeological findings to estimate the total area covered by agriculture in 1492. Multiply this number by the amount of people that could be fed per acre by this agriculture (about 40 million). The product was added to an estimated size of hunting and gathering and fishing communities thought to be in existence at that time. The total came out to be around 52 million people.

12. **C** Edge cities are suburban central business districts that have grown into large centers of commercial office space. In the book *Edge Cities*, Joel Garreau stated that to qualify as an edge city, the density of a suburban central business district has to have in excess of 5,000,000 square feet of office space; occur at a transportation node; and have a high daytime population and a low nighttime population. Most edge cities tend not to have their own form of municipal government. Entrepôts are ports that import products and then sell them as exports at higher prices. Break-in-bulk points are locations where goods are transferred from one line of transportation to another. Export processing zones are areas in which factories typically make goods for foreign markets. Greenbelts are areas of forest or suburban parkland that surround cities.

13. **A** Volcanic eruptions can eject extremely large amounts of ash into the atmosphere. The ash suspended in the air then prevents some solar heat energy from entering the earth's atmosphere, and thus can cool the air, creating a global shade effect. The noticeable cooling occurs after large volcanic eruptions. Methane emissions are a lesser-known form of greenhouse gas, similar to carbon dioxide emissions, which are the more commonly known source of global warming. Water vapor emissions from power plants and motor vehicles can also create greenhouse effects in the atmosphere and thus lead to global warming. Desertification is a result of human action, such as deforestation or vegetation removal, which turns a natural environment into a desert-like state. The result is a condition where the earth's reflection surface or *albedo* is increased. Thus, more solar energy is reflected from the surface to the atmosphere and increases the potential greenhouse effect.

14. **C** Using recycled materials such as tires and melted glass to pave roads instead of natural resources such as the tar or asphalt produced from petroleum refining is considered a sustainable means of resource utilization. Old tires are processed into a tar-like substance that can replace asphalt, which comes from petroleum refining. Landfills are often not sustainable because they require a great deal of open land, and rarely are the materials in a landfill ever recycled. Open ocean fishing on the continental shelf may seem like an "elastic" resource, but it has proven to be an unsustainable process using current fishing methods. For example, mile-long microfiber drift nets can easily ensnare and endanger other marine life. In the Third World, wood is a common source of household cooking fuel and heating energy. However, fuelwood supplies are considered threatened in most Third World forests. This is because these forests are not used in a sustainable manner and many cut forests are not being replanted, but being turned into additional agricultural production zones. Using natural dry grasslands for animal grazing is a common agricultural practice, especially where grain and vegetable crops will not grow. However, in most cases, grasslands are being too intensively utilized and are under threat from desertification.

15. **C** Although the term *nation* is used in common speech synonymously with country and sometimes the word state, in the field of geography *nation* specifically refers to a culture group, or a population that is represented by a single culture. Choice (A) is a definition that can be used for the term *state*. Choice (B) refers to confederations like the United States or Brazil or even Mexico that are unitary federal states made up of a multitude of local or regional states. Choice (D) is the technical definition for the term *nation-state*. Think of the concept of the pure nation-state, such as Iceland or Japan, where there is one single culture, and one representative government. (E) feeds back on the common language synonym with nation and is attempting to trick you with the non-technical context.

16. **E** In 2007, the European Union fully admitted a number of former Eastern Bloc states, including Estonia, Latvia, Lithuania, and Poland and the Czech Republic, Slovakia, and Slovenia. Finland is already a member of the European Union and has been so since the 1980s. Kazakhstan is not a member. Switzerland is not a member of the European Union, even though it's in the center of Europe geographically. The Swiss pride themselves on their political independence and neutrality. Thus, Switzerland and Norway, along with Iceland, are the only Western European countries that are not EU members. Serbia (part of the former Yugoslavian republic) and Albania are former parts of the communist Eastern Bloc. However, these two countries

face significant political and financial difficulty, and are far from being considered for EU membership. Russia and Belarus, former parts of the Soviet Union, are the least likely former communist states to be considered for EU membership. Both countries have strong dictatorial like presidencies. Despite their transition to free-market style economies, EU membership would require a distinct shift toward more democratic forms of governance in these countries.

17. **B** Slash and burn agriculture, also known as "swidden," is a type of farming that has been used since the pre-Columbian period in rainforest regions. However, in the twentieth century, population pressures, especially in countries such as Brazil and Indonesia where many poor people have been encouraged by their governments to move into wooded regions and settle, have created problems, especially the destruction of rainforests. Attempts to permanently settle rainforest farmland—given the low quality of rainforest soils—presents long-term sustainability problems. Raised-field agriculture is the type of farming which William Denevan recognized as the primary form of agriculture in the Americas before 1492. Multi-cropping is agriculture that integrates more than one type of plant and farming practice. Aquaculture is the raising of marine species such as seaweed or kelp, or animal species such as oysters for food or other purposes. Factory farming, such as the use of hydroponics, is most common in First World countries. Remember that tropical rainforests exist almost exclusively in the Third World.

18. **B** Solar energy, geothermal energy (the use of the earth's heat energy to create steam or other forms of heat), and wind power are all sources of energy that are naturally related without significant human inputs, other than the equipment used to collect it. Natural gas and coal are both fossil fuels and are not renewable. Petroleum, otherwise known as oil, is also a fossil fuel resource.

19. **D** Political boundaries must be finite, because it's difficult for states to share land or territory. "Fuzzy" borders are what are found at the edges of culture regions, which easily overlap one another. "Overlapping" is not specific enough to answer the question. Measurable transition zones are characteristic of the borders between bioregions. These bioregion borders are often referred to as *ecotones*. Choice (E) tries to trick you by confusing political with culture regions. Remember that a vernacular region is a type of culture region that is named and identified by its inhabitants.

20. **A** The bull's-eye shape model can be one of the two major models in a human geography course. The other bull's-eye shape model is the von Thünen model, which deals specifically with agriculture and the types of land use in relation to cost of labor and distance from a central town. Choices (C), (D), and (E) are all models that will have irregular shaped parts, but you will not see the circular rings, as you do in the concentric zone model.

21. **A** Burgess was one of the primary designers of this model, and his name is often associated with it (don't forget the names of people who developed the models; these names have been asked on the AP Human Geography Exam previously). Burgess saw the city not for its neighborhoods, but as an economic surface. Land costs across the surface are highest the center, the model shows the highest value in the central business district (CBD), which exponentially decreases as one moves out toward the suburbs.

22. **D** The area of single-family homes in the suburbs, or the *zone of low-density residential space* would expand most significantly in the second half of the twentieth century. Recall the relevant American history; veterans returning from World War II received guaranteed home loans from the Department of Veterans Affairs. These and other government home loans made ownership of single-family homes possible for hundreds of thousands of American families who had not previously held property. In the 50s, the growth of suburbs, especially Levittown-style developments, greatly expanded the suburban landscape. Thus, the ring labeled (D) would grow significantly and expand outward.

23. **B** Access to transportation will increase the value of commercial land space more than anything else. There are several different types of urban realms models that you can find in textbooks. You may see some that look like a concentric zone model has been turned into a large octopus. The arms of the octopus stretch out along transportation lines and show you the effect of transportation more realistically on an expanse of commercial land. Rivers could also be incorporated into this urban realms expansion of commercial land space. However, trails would not. Airports play a significant role in transportation, but schools themselves would not increase commercial land values in the surrounding area. Ports likewise have a significant transportation effect, yet power plants do not. Banks and hospitals are themselves commercial land space. Although they can create *multiplier effects*, they do not appear in any of the major urban models. This is because they are not considered significant characteristics, despite being important services.

24. **C** A *lingua franca* is defined as a common language used as a bridge between people of different linguistic groups. All airline pilots speaking English for air traffic control safety is such an example. Transnational migration is basically the movement of people across international borders. Relocation diffusion deals with the movements of ideas or technology across a significant physical barrier. Multiplier effects are what are seen around *growth poles*, or locations that create significant economic development in the surrounding area. Footloose industries are corporate firms that are not tied by their location to either consumers or natural resources. Thus, footloose-type locations can appear just about anywhere that corporate decision-makers choose.

25. **B** The spread of American culture in the form of movies and television, for example, is seen as potentially harmful to other linguistic cultures around the world. Many foreign governments see linguistic and cultural diffusion as a threat, and some have created policies to protect their linguistic heritage and cultural institutions. Tariffs are an active economic protection in the United States. They do not apply to culture. Trade limitations on beef, say, in response to mad cow disease, are agricultural and public health provisions. Peace and reconciliation commissions, such as those seen in South Africa or Rwanda, have more to do with the healing social rifts within countries. Special economic zones (SEZs) in China are another economic structure. Again, these do not protect the national culture from foreign influence.

26. **C** A primate city by definition is a city that is the least four times larger than the next largest city in the country (some sources use different multipliers for size. Mexico City is vastly larger than Guadalajara. Buenos Aires, again, is much larger than Mendoza. Lima is also vastly larger than the next largest city in Peru, Cusco.) Although Jakarta could be labeled a primate city, urban primacy is not the case in Japan or China, which have multiple large cities. There is no primate city in the United States. Likewise, Brazil has several very large cities; even São Paulo does not qualify as a primate city. There is also no urban primacy in India or Pakistan.

27. **D** Map scale is expressed as a ratio of the relationship between distance on a map and distance in the real world. 1 : 24,000 means that 1 inch on the map would equal 24,000 inches in the real world. Choice (A) refers to different types of land use and has no relationship to scale. Choice (C) represents different scales within population analysis. Choice (D) shows different orders of magnitude used in cartography to represent the population and importance (such as national capitals) of cities. Similarly, what is described in (E) would be a cartographic tool to differentiate values on a chloropleth map.

28. **A** Like the term *place*, "space" is an important theoretical term used in human geography. It can refer to the planar or two-dimensional surface of the earth, or refer to different types of space, both real and imagined, such as *commercial space* or *spaces of fear*. Choice (B) is the definition for the term "place." Choice (C) attempts to make you think about physics or common uses of the term space in everyday language. Choice (D) is the definition, roughly, for the term *carrying capacity*. Choice (E) is the basic definition for the term *region*.

29. **D** Animism is a belief system based upon *natural spirituality*, where items in nature such as trees, animals or mountains, can have spiritual meaning or being. Choices (A) and (B) are both denominations in Christianity. Islam considers Jerusalem its third-most holy place, after Mecca and Medina. Judaism, like Christianity, is spiritually centered in Jerusalem.

30. **B** Small farms in LDCs or lesser developed countries tend to be operated by families who are farming with the primary purpose of feeding themselves or, in part, the local village. These families subsist on the animals and crops which they tend to personally and rely little on the outside world. This is the opposite of "cash-cropping," export-based agriculture or plantation farming. Crop rotation deals with the changing annual selection of plants on farm plots to take advantage of different characteristics, such as alternating planting soybeans and corn. Soybeans will replenish the nitrogen that corn leaches from the soil. Monoculture refers to the farming of a single crop.

31. **D** The concept of free trade is centered on the removal of trade restrictions, primarily tariffs that are basically taxes on goods and services that cross international borders. NAFTA is intended to strengthen the Canadian, U.S., and Mexican manufacturing economies by eliminating these tariffs and reducing the cost of production for manufacturers in this three-country region. Choice (A) is not true, as there are still border control stations between the three countries, despite the fact that removing these controls would make trade more efficient. These are a result of concerns about illegal immigration and contraband freely moving across the borders. Likewise, free movement of labor would be problematic in the current context. A common currency for NAFTA has been discussed but is not considered a serious possibility due to the poor state of the Mexican economy. Free shipping service might also reduce costs, but someone (taxpayers) would have to pay for the shipping.

32. **E** Kaliningrad is a part of Russia, but is separated by land from the main body of Russia. This is the definition of an "exclave." Technically, Alaska is an exclave of the United States by the same definition. Entrepôts are ports where goods are shipped in and exported to foreign locations for a profit. An enclave would be an area inside of a country that had a different culture group within it. Ethnic neighborhoods are technically types of enclaves. Enterprise zones are special tax districts used for economic development to attract new manufacturing firms.

33. **B**   Japan, Korea and Taiwan (what one textbook refers to the *Jakota triangle*) is the area in Asia that was first to develop or redevelop manufacturing following World War II.

34. **D**   Special economic zones are a major component of the free market economic reforms in the People's Republic of China (mainland China).

35. **E**   The Straits of Malacca is an extremely important sea lane near the major port of Singapore. Oil from the Middle East headed to East Asia passes through the Straits; and manufactured goods from East Asia travel to the sea lane headed for Europe.

36. **C**   This is a historical geography question about European colonialism. Catholic populations would be expected in countries that had a colonial history under the rule of southern European countries. Vietnam was once part of French Indochina, and prior to the Spanish-American war, the Philippines was a colony of Spain.

37. **D**   Spain, Morocco, and Pakistan together all share historical influences of Islam, Arabic language and culture. Despite being on the European mainland, Spain was invaded in the tenth century C.E. by Muslim North African Moors. The Iberian Peninsula was under the control of Muslims until the late 1400s, when they were expelled. Their culture left an impression on Moorish architecture and Arabic language on the Spanish and Portuguese landscapes. Spain shares the Arabic heritage with Morocco across the Straits of Gibraltar, and Pakistan, an Islamic country in South Asia.

38. **E**   New forms of culture in the twentieth century emerged as a result of the Pan-Africanism movements, which culturally connected displaced Africans around the world with their cultural forebears. As a result, the creation of Rastafarianism, a modified form of African Christianity or the Coptic Church, emerged in the Caribbean island of Jamaica in the 1960s. Rastafarianism achieved international notoriety through the musical missionary work of artists such as Bob Marley. The United States and Great Britain are both recipients of migrants and musical culture from Jamaica. Ethiopia is seen as the spiritual origin of the Rastafarian faith as the birthplace of their messiah, Haile Selassie (birth name: Ras Tafari Makonnen). Trinidad is used as a distractor to try to get you to second guess the selection of Jamaica.

39. **B**   This question asks you to characterize Belgium, Luxembourg, and the Netherlands as being First World nations. One of the characteristics of First World service-based economies is the relatively low birth rates and fertility rates of the population. Remember: A low rate of natural increase, or negative growth rate, is a major policy problem for some European governments. Benelux is an acronym for Belgium, Luxembourg, and the Netherlands together—they are also known as the *Low Countries*. All three are highly valuable economies with small populations, and less have high per capita GNP. All three were founding members of the European Economic Community and NATO.

40. **E**   It is important to remember that Africa was the last part of the world to achieve independence from European colonial powers. Thus, (E) is the correct answer as it represents this recent period of decolonization. The 1810s to 1830s would be the historical timeframe for independence and South America. The 1890s is a random distractor. Nineteen fourteen to 1918 is the time period of the First World War. 1945 to 1948 is the timeframe of decolonization of many non-African British and Dutch colonies such as India, Indonesia, and Palestine.

41. **B** There are many areas of the earth where energy resources are known to be but have not been studied in detail in terms of the actual volume contained in, for example, a natural gas field. Thus, the term "potential reserve" is used to designate areas which *potentially* have large amounts of future resources which are uncalculated. Proven reserves are known when the volume of resources have been studied and scientifically estimated for their volume. An energy deficit is when a country consumes more energy than what it produces. This is the opposite of energy surplus, where countries produce more energy than they use. The production volume of a country is the actual amount of energy produced, but has nothing to do with consumption or reserves.

42. **C** Newer forms of manufacturing rely upon very sophisticated and *flexible* systems of inventory supplies and parts assembly. Having just-in-time production means that manufactures can reduce costs by not storing large inventories of spare parts. Footloose industries are firms that are not tied to supply chains, natural resources, or consumer locations. Tertiary production refers to service industries, which wholesale, transport or retail manufactured goods. Craft manufacturing uses minimal mechanization and incorporates handmade products to create cultural goods. Cottage industries are the types of manufacturing which take place in homes or residences.

43. **C** Break-in-bulk points are exactly what they say they are. For instance, an oceangoing ship carrying wheat is off-loaded, in port, to a waiting train. The bulk of the wheat from the ship's hold has to be broken up into smaller units to fit into the several rail hopper cars. Resource nodes are where natural resources are connected to lines of transportation to extract them. Export processing zones are manufacturing districts where goods are made specifically for export to foreign countries. The PLVI is the *peak land value intersection*, the highest-priced piece of land in the CBD or *central business district*. Transport nodes are where two or more lines of transportation intersect.

44. **B** Thomas Malthus, the father of Malthusian and neo-Malthusian theories regarding population growth, was concerned in the early 1800s that human populations would one day outgrow their ability to feed themselves. In contemporary terms, what neo-Malthusians are saying is that human populations will exceed the global *carrying capacity*—the earth's environmental ability to provide food, clean air and water, and other resources such as energy, sustainably to people.

45. **E** A country that has a shrinking population (negative RNI) is most likely a First World service-based economy such as those found in Western Europe. In this situation, there is a highly educated population that has few new workers entering the workforce for jobs that require lower education levels—a deficit of low-skill service laborers to work in less-desired jobs. Therefore, it is necessary to bring in labor from the outside (guest-workers or *gastarbeiter*) to do the work the highly educated population does not care to do; for example, sanitation workers, cleaners, and restaurant workers. Relate what you know about rates of natural increase, the difference between birth rates and death rates, to the demographic transition model. Countries with low RNI are most likely in stage four. These same countries have high GNP per capita. In First World countries we see an increase in women entering management, scientific, and political positions. Open border policies are not relevant, and are a distractor here. Likewise (D) is a distractor in a way like (B), where you should expect an increase in environmental laws in countries that have low RNI.

46. **C**   The replacement rate is a total fertility rate of 2.1. For a population to replace itself, you must have two offspring, plus you must add an error factor of 0.1 to account for children who will not live to adulthood; those who die of childhood disease, accidents, and so on.

47. **A**   As a science, epidemiology is a meeting place between geography and medicine. Look at the roots of the word, epidemic, and -ology. The main distractor answer is (C), contagious diffusion; this term describes the movement of ideas or technology in a pattern that is similar to disease, but not disease itself. Technological diffusion describes the pattern in which technologies move across space. Redlining is an illegal technique once used by insurance companies to designate areas where people would not be insured. Geomorphology is the science in which geology meets geography as a study of landforms.

48. **B**   The Fertile Crescent is a region that spans the ancient civilizations of the Middle East. It is the curved area from the Nile through the Levant and over to the Tigris and Euphrates rivers, where land could be cultivated. Choice (A) is the broad peninsula that includes Saudi Arabia, Yemen, Oman, Qatar, and the United Arab Emirates. The Anatolian migration is believed to be one of the two possible routes of the Indo-European population and language traditions from Asia and Europe. Choice (D), the Maghreb, is the region of northwestern Africa, including Morocco, Algeria, Tunisia and Libya. Choice (E) was a movie starring Orlando Bloom about the end of the Third Crusade.

49. **D**   Oil and gas are produced in three major areas in the Middle East. One is North Africa (not pictured), the Persian Gulf, and the Caspian Sea region. Al-Qaeda does not control any territory. U.S.-led military coalitions exist only in Iraq and Afghanistan. The Kurdish people exist in the borderlands of northern Iraq, Eastern Turkey and Northwestern Iran. (E) Irrigated agriculture exists in the Tigris and Euphrates River systems, and in areas where there has been groundwater pumped to the surface for agriculture in this region.

50. **B**   All of the cities on the map are located in countries with majority Muslim populations. While both Sunni and Shia sects of Islam exist, the Sunni sect makes up 85% of Islam's population. The countries with a Shia majority include Iraq, Iran, Bahrain, and Azerbaijan, none of which have cities labeled on the map. Mecca and Medina are not national capitals, so eliminate choice (A). While *Sharia* law is fully implemented in Saudi Arabia (Medina, Riyadh, and Mecca), Sudan (Khartoum), and Yemen (Aden), *Sharia* law does not apply in the secular state of Turkey (Istanbul and Ankara). The variety of Islamic states should lead you to eliminate choices (C), (D), and (E).

51. **E**   This definition-example question asks you to recall the concept of political-economy; then identify a form of political economy, free-market parliamentary democracy; and finally, related to the given example, Canada. Canada is a member state of the Commonwealth of Nations, signifying its former status as a British colony. Canada still recognizes the British monarch as its titular *head of state*. Canada is not however, a "dependent territory" of its former colonizer, the United Kingdom. An example of a British dependent territory would be a place such as Gibraltar, the Turks and Caicos Islands, or Ascension Island. Despite Canada having a strong government-led social welfare program influenced by socialism, Canada's political economy is not guided by a Marxist ideology. Supranational organizations are collection of sovereign states working together toward a common goal.

52. **C**   This definition-example question requires you to apply a principle from one part of the world to that of the United States. Mediterranean agricultural products such as lemons, olives, avocados, artichokes, and almonds, are specialty crops grown in central and Southern California

in its warm, temperate climate. Despite its northern latitude Hawaii sits in the middle of the Pacific Ocean; it has a very tropical climate with significant moisture. The upper Midwest sits in a temperate climate. The Garden State vegetable-growing areas around New Jersey and New York are similar in climate and moisture to the Atlantic Coastal Plain.

53. **B** Economic restructuring is when a state shifts from one type of economy to another. Since the 1980s and '90s, as the former member states of the Soviet Union and countries in Eastern Europe have abandoned communism, free-market capitalism has come to replace the old communist command-economy system. Socialization is a distractor in that is a sound-alike term for socialism, which was part of the former Soviet Union's political economy. Nationalization is when governments take privately owned business and make them government-owned entities, the opposite of what is happening in the former communist Europe. Choices (D) and (E) are both terms used as distractors as they refer historically to the time before the transition to free markets.

54. **A** Soil salinization occurs when irrigation in arid regions causes the accumulation of mineral salts on the surface of soils. When irrigation water is spread on crops, the high daytime temperatures evaporate much of that water. This process of evaporation causes minerals in the soil to rise to the surface. The evaporated mineral salts can "poison" the plants farmers are trying to grow. Deforestation can lead to things like desertification and damage soil quality. There is not enough information in this answer to determine whether soil salinization will be a direct result. Loess soil is very rich in nutrients, and excessive plowing in these regions may cause soil erosion, but may not deplete the high-nutrient quality of soils. Build-up of fertilizers and pesticides over time may also be harmful to the environment, but does not salinize soils.

55. **B** Secondary industries, where industrial production depends on a single natural resource, tend to be located close to that resource. Perishable goods are things that have a short shelf life and need to be close to the consumer retail locations. Products that are distributed through a chain of retailers are located centrally amongst the market areas of those retailers. With the onset of online retailing, many warehousing operations are commonly located at airports, where shipping companies have large distribution facilities. In this way they can get their products to consumers within a short time after the products are ordered.

56. **B** Gerrymandering, in the case of U.S. congressional districts, occurs when state-level politicians redraw the boundary lines of voting districts and create areas that can be long and slender or spread apart, connecting different clusters of similar voters. Some suburban municipalities have been created to serve wealthier residents or specific industrial firms. Choice (C) is *redlining*. Choice (D) is the process of municipal annexation, where outlying areas would be added to cities and their services, such as sewers and water systems. Overlapping public-service areas is seen as a public administration problem for many communities the United States.

57. **A** The Human Development Index (HDI) was a statistic created by the United Nations to compare rates and levels of a country's combined social and economic development. Quality-of-life issues such as life expectancy and education rates, which could be quantified, were integrated with economic indicators (like GNP *per capita*) to get a better picture of the overall *standard of living*. The other answers in this question are all quantitative measures, which incorporate the value of goods and services produced in the country as a means of determining a country's economic volume or productivity.

58. **D** Deindustrialization is what the United States, Western Europe, and the old Asian Tiger economies such as Japan have experienced economically over the last few decades. Their economies have shifted away from manufacturing as the primary source of economic production, and toward services, specifically those driven by high technology as the new force behind development. Newly industrialized countries (NICs) are those shifting away from agriculture and toward manufacturing. Fordism represents the mode of production during the manufacturing era of American industry. The industrial revolution can be thought of as a time period when Western Europe and the United States were themselves newly industrialized countries, historically. Market capitalism is a constant means of accumulation of wealth within free-market societies.

59. **E** Much of the drive during the 1960s, 1970s, and 1980s in the United States to develop commercial office space in suburban central business districts was from the realization by businesses that much of the consumers and labor force for the emerging service economy were located in suburbs. Thus, it made sense on a regional scale to locate new businesses close to these consumers and workers instead of in the traditional old downtown central business district (CBD).

60. **C** The United Nations Conference on the Law of the Seas (UNCLOS) established and codified international boundaries systems at sea. One boundary system was the 12-nautical-mile territorial sea within which all the laws of that country apply. At 200 nautical miles (nm) a second boundary exists within this exclusive economic zone (EEZ); that country controls all of the natural resources within that zone. Beyond this 200 nm limit are *international waters* or the *high seas*. SEZs are a sound-alike distractor, and are export processing zones in China. Sovereign territory mainly includes land, but can also include a 12-nautical-mile territorial sea.

61. **B** The elite residential sector falls on either side of the spine, where the main boulevard leads out of the city center. These boulevards were dictated by the Laws of the Indies, Spanish colonial laws, which included details on how cities should be laid out. These wide main boulevards symbolize wealth and status and thus became locations for the elites and wealthy of the community.

62. **A** The Laws of the Indies dictated that the center of the city have a plaza, usually a square marketplace, around which would be located the centers of governance, commerce, and religion, symbolized by a Catholic cathedral or Basilica. These features mimic the central squares found in Spanish cities in Europe, such as the Plaza Mayor in Madrid.

63. **E** Most squatter settlements in the Latin American city model are located on the outer part of the city, or *urban periphery*. However, some squatter settlements exist in areas close to the center of the city where more people traditionally would not build housing, such as river banks, steep hillsides, and polluted areas such as industrial parks and trash dumps. The "zones of disamenity," despite the many social problems that exist in them, provide their poor residents with much closer access to downtown areas and jobs than those living in peripheral squatter settlements.

64. **D** The zone of *in situ* accretion is the second ring outside of the central business district and lies immediately outside the zone of maturity. Under the Laws of the Indies, only those of European descent were allowed to live inside the city walls. The housing in this segregated area is known as the zone of maturity, because of its more European-style architectural

elements. The zone of *in situ* accretion is outside of this, where people of mixed or indigenous descent settled during the colonial era. The resulting housing in this area used mainly local materials like mud brick (hence the "*in situ*" or "in the ground" reference) and architectural elements, and thus has a very different structure and look than the urban landscape.

65. **C** Agroindustry firms have focused the latest in genetic engineering technology to create plant and animal varieties that are resistant to a number of pests, which include insects and fungus. Heirloom varieties are older *cultivars* (subspecies), which are not popular in the modern market, and are grown mainly by specialty farmers. Organic farming accepts that some crops will be lost to pests, but also incorporates crop rotation strategies, which minimize the impact of one pest type on a specific crop. Farmers do this by not growing the exact same plant varieties year after year. Value-added agriculture is the processing of raw agricultural goods on the farm, to add additional value, such as cheese and wine. Artificial fertilizers provide nutrients for improving only the soils. Don't confuse fertilizers with chemical pesticides that do kill bugs, fungi, rodents and the other things that destroy crops.

66. **C** Kinetic hydropower (waterwheels as opposed to electric hydropower) was the main source of energy for early industrial production in Europe and North America. Transportation is an important aspect of production, but alone does not determine industrial location. Timber, as fuelwood, was an important energy source in the pre-electricity era. However, wood was never cultivated in a large centralized fashion to provide for manufacturing energy needs. Choices (D) and (E) are both concepts of *growth poles*, which become important factors for industrialization in the twentieth century, but not during the early industrial revolution.

67. **A** Newly industrialized countries (NICs) are those which are shifting away from agriculture toward manufacturing, as the primary source of economic production. The list of states with NIC status includes Brazil, Mexico, India, China, Vietnam, Malaysia, Thailand, Indonesia, Singapore, Nigeria, Gabon and a few other states that could be considered "borderline" such as the Philippines. Choice (B) are states in Africa identified as potential NIC states over the long-term. Choice (C) are former communist states going through economic restructuring. Choices (D) and (E) are, today, postindustrial states, whose economic development is mainly focused on services and are experiencing a decline in manufacturing productivity.

68. **E** The North Atlantic Treaty Organization (NATO) and the Warsaw Pact, adversaries during the Cold War, are examples of a supranational organization; a group of states aligned for a common purpose, in this case, military operations. Supranational organizations focused on economic cooperation would be groups like NAFTA or the European Union. Free trade also refers to economic cooperation. By the time irredentism lead to armed conflict in the former Yugoslavia, the Warsaw Pact was defunct. NATO and the Warsaw Pact existed after World War II.

69. **D** The peak land value intersection (PLVI) is generally the main intersection in a central business district, around which can be found the highest real estate prices in the metropolitan area. One thing to keep in mind is that the high prices in CBDs exist because commercial office space is leased by the square foot, whereas homes are sold on land units in acres. Choices (A) and (B) are both spatial concepts that explain the likely origins of a city, or why an urban place was originally settled, but they aren't the part of town where prices are highest. Central place theory is useful in understanding why a place became prominent economically compared to other like places.

70. **E** This question refers to the Frostbelt to Sunbelt shift in population, that is the internal migration within the United States that has been seen since World War II. From the traditional population centers of the northeastern United States since the 1940s, Americans tended to migrate to the quickly growing cities of the South, Southwest, and Pacific Coast regions of the United States, such as Atlanta, Phoenix, and the San Francisco Bay area. Choice (A) is the opposite of the Frostbelt to Sunbelt shift. With areas staying the same and population growing, mathematically *population density* would have to increase overall. Although the population centroid, or the center population density of the United States, is located in the Midwestern states, the states are less densely populated than the coastal regions. From the 1960s onward, population density around central business districts has declined on average.

71. **C** Dependency ratios are defined as the proportion of the population that is not in the labor force, that is, those age 15 and under and those age 65 and above. The *dependent* population is those ages 0 to 15 and over 65. Therefore, you should look at the pyramids that have the largest bases and/or large top areas.

72. **E** As a postindustrial country in stage four of the demographic transition, the United States has both low birth rates and low death rates and a population which is growing slightly. Therefore, you would expect to see a column-shaped population pyramid that is only slightly larger at the bottom that it is at the top.

73. **D** Germany is an example country where there is a negative rate of natural increase (RNI). Thus, the German population is shrinking ever so slightly each year. Like the United States, the German population pyramid will be column shaped. Unlike the U.S. pyramid, the bottom of the German column will be smaller than layers at the top, due to the larger older population.

74. **C** Like many other mixed cultures in Latin America, the Creole culture combines different ethnicities. In the Caribbean region, the mixture includes both the genetic and cultural heritage of Native Americans, Africans, and Europeans. These are all groups from the pre-colonial and colonial periods, which have since intermarried. Likewise, these cultures have been integrated into one another, creating new cultural forms that show influences from each of the different groups. For examples, look to Louisiana's Creole cooking traditions and Mardi Gras traditions and costumes.

75. **B** This EXCEPT question requires you to discern which high or low category is incorrect in this case. Manufacturing firms seek out the least-cost factory locations for low-profit-goods manufacturing. These locations tend not to be in areas that have stringent environmental regulations. Environmental controls to reduce air and water pollution or solid waste tend to increase the costs of production for manufacturing firms. Therefore, countries that enforce environmental laws tend to not attract companies working on narrow profit margins.

SCORING RUBRICS AND SAMPLE ESSAYS

Again, please do yourself a favor and don't look at the following section until you have completed the essays in Practice Test 2.

As mentioned in the previous section, in this part you will have a chance to take a look at the scoring rubrics, the answer key for the essays, and the sample essays for the questions that you completed. After showing you the rubric, we will show you what an average essay looks like; that is, a typical, lower-scoring essay. Then we'll show you the same essay, slightly modified, that scores far better according to the rubric.

Once you've read each rubric, the average essay and the improved essay, go through both essays and write a shorthand outline of the material that you see in each. Compare these two outlines to see what different keywords and example sections are added to the improved essay. Then do this for each of the other essays. This should give you a sense of the detail necessary in your shorthand outlines to write high-scoring essays on the AP Human Geography Exam.

BE THE RUBRIC, AGAIN

Afterward, do the same with the essays that you wrote during the timed exam. Rewrite the same essays adding the additional elements you gained from the rubric, and construct essays that earn full points. By knowing what the top-scoring essays look like and training yourself to write more detailed essay, you will score well above average.

SCORING RUBRICS FOR FREE-RESPONSE QUESTIONS

1. Explain **TWO** push factors and **TWO** pull factors that affect rural-to-urban migrants in newly industrialized countries (NICs). For new rural-to-urban migrants, describe the conditions of housing found in most industrial cities within NICs.

Rubric

$4 + 4 + 2 = 10$ points
For each of the A (push) and the B (pull) sections:
    0 points for no valid factors
    1 point for a simple factor statement or keyword
    2 points for a cause-and-effect-type discussion of factor's impact on migration

+

    0 points for no additional valid factors
    1 point for a second simple factor statement or keyword
    2 points for a second cause-and-effect-type discussion of factor's impact on migration
=   a total of 4 points per section
Note: The opposite of a push factor cannot count as a pull factor and vice versa.

  A. Push factors (4 points total. Maximum of 2 points per factor.)
    1. Armed conflict or civil war, narcotics production
    2. Increased cost of land, rent or agricultural inputs (seed, chemicals, and so on.)
    3. Effects of environmental pollution, water contamination, chemical poisoning
    4. Natural disasters
  B. Pull factors (4 points total. Maximum of 2 points per factor.)
    1. Availability of industrial and service jobs
    2. Jobs in cities tend to provide year-round (as opposed to seasonal) work with consistent pay

3.   Access to public services (medical, schools, utilities—do not accept "clean water" or housing as examples of public services)
4.   Proximity to entertainment, sport facilities
5.   Increased communication and social networking activities

C.   Housing Conditions (2 points)

0 points for no condition of the quality of housing or low availability of services

1 point for basic condition of poor housing quality or low service availability.

2 points for basic condition of poor housing quality AND low service availability.

Poor housing conditions: cramped and expensive available housing; many people forced to exist in squatter settlements and provide their own housing materials; settlements in hazardous and unsafe areas; settlements far from city centers in urban periphery.

Low service availability: Limited public health facilities for poor migrants as there is often little access to electricity, clean water, sanitary sewers, energy supplies for heating and cooking fuel; poor access to public transit, and public safety agencies tend to not serve squatter communities.

---

2. Use the diagram to answer the following questions:

A.   Use generalized examples to explain the changes in birth rates and death rates across the Demographic Transition. Be sure to describe how these changes affect total population over time.

B.   Using social and economic characteristics, describe where you would place the following two counties in the model:

Sweden

India

Rubric

$(2 + 2 + 2 + 2) + (1 + 1) = 10$ Points

A. Four Stages (2 points per stage)
Must explain birth and death rates for 1 point and population change for the second point.

Stage One

Birth Rates:	High due to more children being seen as additional labor; or increased fertility due to high infant mortality.
Death Rates:	High due to poor nutrition, epidemics, war, or lack of food trade; seasonal migrations for resources take a toll on population.
Total Population:	Remains low overall.

Stage Two

Birth Rates:	High due to more children being seen as additional labor; or increased fertility due to high infant mortality.
Death Rates:	Decreasing due to better nutrition, education, food trade networks, less warfare, location stabilization (no need to migrate seasonally).
Total Population:	Increases as a result of comparatively high birth rates.

Stage Three

Birth Rates:	Decreasing fertility due to rural-to-urban migration, less need/time/space for children. Increased mechanization on farms.
Death Rates:	Decline and bottom-out due to better medical care, attention to sanitation, nutrition or education.
Total Population:	Continues to increase due to higher birth rates.

Stage Four

Birth Rates:	Bottom out due to large numbers of women active in the labor force; contraception availability; decreased marriage/increased divorce/single parent household rates.
Death Rates:	Continue to stay low due to medical care, attention to sanitation, nutrition or education.
Total Population:	Levels off, can decrease.

B. Locations on the Model

Sweden: Must be in stage four where birth rates are below death rates due to negative rate of natural increase (RNI).

India: Can be on the intersection of stage two and stage three or early in stage three due to its status as a newly industrialized country (NIC).

---

3. Describe the advantages and disadvantages posed by nuclear power in comparison to fossil fuel resources. Address the following issues in your comparison:

A. air pollution

B. environmental safety

C. waste management

Rubric

3 + 3 + 3 = 9 Points

For each of the three sections (no more than 3 points available per section):

0 points for no valid advantages or disadvantages

1 point for an advantage or disadvantage basic statement

2 points for a strong comparison; or two basic statements (one advantage and one disadvantage)

3 points for a strong comparison with an example; or two basic statements with example

Do not accept arguments associated with nuclear weapons (except in C. Disadvantage 3)

A. Advantages of nuclear:
   1. Eliminates carbon emissions
   2. Reduces greenhouse gas emission
   3. Eliminates acid rain pollution
   4. Reduces smog and potential for respiratory diseases in the local population

Disadvantages of nuclear:
   1. Risk of radioactive steam leaks
   2. High cost of nuclear plants compared to coal powered plants
   3. Radioactive dust pollution at uranium mining sites

B. Advantages:
   1. Uranium has smaller mining impacts; strip mining of coal is destructive to the natural landscape on a large scale. Uranium mining requires much smaller volumes to produce same amount of energy.
   2. Coal mining leads to water pollution near mine sites.
   3. Particulates from fossil fuel burning can cause asthma and other respiratory diseases to plant workers and local residents; coal miners can suffer from "black lung" disease.
   4. Cost of safety features to prevent and clean up oil spills, gas leaks, and coal mine accidents.

Disadvantages:
   1. High cost of safety features and monitoring at nuclear plants
   2. Risk of plant accidents, e.g. core meltdown (you may not accept nuclear explosions) or fire to the region around a nuclear plant
   3. Risk of nuclear plants as targets for terrorist activity

C. Advantages:
   1. Students may state that there are few to no solid waste products from the combustion of fossil fuels other that the aforementioned air pollutants or oil spills. (They may not leave this blank.)
      or
   2. Fossil fuels can create hazardous materials as byproducts of refining petroleum.

Disadvantages:
   1. Long-term storage of spent nuclear fuel requires several thousand years of managed underground storage.
   2. Short-term storage of spent nuclear fuel requires on-site storage at plants where they are at risk for fire or terror attack.
   3. Reprocessing of spent uranium fuel creates weapons-grade plutonium, which can be used to create nuclear weapons.

Free-Response Question Score Sheet

1. push 1   push 2   pull 1   pull 2   housing   Total

_____ +	_____ +	_____ +	_____ +	_____ =	_____
0, 1 or 2	0, 1 or 2	0, 1 or 2	0, 1 or 2	0, 1 or 2	out of 10

2. stage one   stage two   stage three   stage four   i.   ii.   Total

_____ +	_____ +	_____ +	_____ +	_____ +	_____ =	_____
0, 1 or 2	0, 1 or 2	0, 1 or 2	0, 1 or 2	0 or 1	0 or 1	out of 10

3. a.   b.   c.   Total

_____ +	_____ +	_____ =	_____
0, 1, 2 or 3	0, 1, 2 or 3	0, 1, 2 or 3	out of 9

Total Points out of 29 possible, with a goal of at least 17 points (58.6 percent).
Let's go to the examples.

SAMPLE ESSAY 1

1. Newly Industrialized Countries (NIC's) are characterized primarily by a shift from an agricultural economy to one based on manufacturing. As a result, increased numbers of people are moving from the rural countryside into developing urban areas. Several factors contribute to this rural to urban migration and can be categorized as either "push" or "pull" factors. Push factors are essentially those that make rural life more difficult, including decreased value of crops and poor access to healthcare. "Pull" factors, or those that make urban life more attractive, include availability of manufacturing jobs at increased wages and decreased cost of living.

In general, people who have made a living based on agriculture for generations are used to fluctuating economic conditions and resistant to urban migration. However, in many of the NIC's, including Brazil and Mexico, several factors have pushed people into more densely populated areas. The first "push" factor is the decrease in the global prices of agricultural crops. Farmers in NIC's are finding it more and more difficult to make a living off the land and are therefore choosing to move into the cities in greater numbers. In addition, poor access to healthcare (including doctors and medication) has pushed urban migration in Newly Industrialized Countries.

By contrast, there are also several factors that "pull" migrants into cities. As the general economy of the NIC's moves from agricultural to manufacturing based, more factory jobs become available. These jobs are quite attractive to former farmers who are no longer able to make a living off their land. Also, the cost of living in the cities is decreased compared to that of the countryside. Housing and groceries are more affordable in urban areas. People who used to have a difficult time making ends meet in rural areas are suddenly finding access to amenities like recreation and luxury goods. All of these factors "pull" migrants from rural into urban areas.

Both Mexico and Brazil are good examples of Newly Industrialized Countries. At present time, there is a fundamental shift in these countries from an agricultural based economy to a manufacturing based one. This shift has created a situation where rural homes are less attractive and better quality homes in urban areas are more attractive to citizens. Both "push" and "pull" factors described above are responsible for the increased rural to urban migration that essentially defines the Newly Industrialized Countries.

1.

push 1	push 2	pull 1	pull 2	housing	Total
2	0	2	1	0	4
0, 1 or 2	0, 1 or 2	0, 1 or 2	0, 1 or 2	0, 1 or 2	out of 10

Now let's look at a higher-scoring version of this essay:

1. In many NICs, increasing numbers of people are moving from the rural countryside into developing urban areas. Several factors contribute to this rural to urban migration and can be categorized as either "push" or "pull" factors.

In general, people who have made a living based on agriculture for generations are used to fluctuating economic conditions and resistant to urban migration. However, in many of the NICs, including Brazil and Mexico, several factors have pushed people into more densely populated areas. The first "push" factor is the decrease in the global prices of agricultural crops. Farmers in NICs are finding it more and more difficult to make a living off the land and are therefore choosing to move into the cities in greater numbers. Likewise in Mexico, many farmers are caught up in the decision to farm drugs like opium or marijuana versus less-profitable food crops. Those who choose not to farm drug crops are often scared-off their land by narco-traffickers. These poor people often have no choice but to move to cities for safety.

By contrast, there are also several factors that "pull" migrants into cities. As the general economy of the NICs moves from agricultural to manufacturing based, more jobs at higher wages become available. These jobs are quite attractive to former farmers who are no longer able to make a living for their families off the land. Most migrants are eager for a regular paycheck compared to the seasonal pay the received farming. With the increase in factory job availability in NICs there is a high demand for low-cost workers. These jobs, despite paying far less that factory jobs in MDC's pay far better than farming and therefore draw many people, both men and women to the cities.

Both Mexico and Brazil are good examples of Newly Industrialized Countries where people moving into cities from rural areas find that there is little available housing in cities. Often migrants are forced to provide for their own home in squatter settlements of the urban periphery. People collect scrap wood, metal and plastic to quickly construct "houses" until they can come up with something better. These "shanty towns" often have no services or utilities like clean water or flush toilets. Disease outbreaks are a problem in these areas the health of children in these areas is often poor.

Essay 2

2. The first stage of the Demographic Transition model represents a prehistoric or hunting/gathering type of society. Both the birth and death rates are particularly high and remain about the same in relation to one another. People in this time period had a very difficult time meeting their basic needs for food and shelter. The "name of the game" is one of survival. People did not live very long. Therefore multiple children were essential to the survival of the species but resulted in little population growth and change overall.

Stage 2 of the Demographic Transition model illustrates the differences that an agricultural based economy has on the birth and death rates. As people settle down and begin to farm the land and domesticate animals to meet their basic needs for food, the death rates begin to decline down into the range of 10-30 per every 1000 people. Basic needs are being met more efficiently than in the hunting/gathering societies and thus quality and length of life improves. Children are still seen as a sign of prosperity so the birth rates remain high. India is a good example of a county that falls into stage 2 on the Demographic model. Although it is slowly becoming more industrialized, the majority of India's population still farms for a living and produces very little excess to export and build monetary wealth.

The transition of a population into an industrialized economy is shown in stage 3 of the Demographic model. This stage is characterized primarily by a decline in birth rates down into the range of 10-30 per 1000 people. There is an interesting lag in the fall of the birth rates behind the fall in death rates (as seen in stage 2). In an industrializing economy, wealth is produced in excess of what is needed to provide for basic food and shelter. Monetary wealth now becomes an important measure of success rather than multiple offspring. There is less time and need for having children. All of this contributes to the falling birth rate. This stage is certainly one of great transition for a population.

Stage 4 of the Demographic model shows a post-industrial or modern society. The birth and death rates are similarly low (around 8 per 1000 people). Modern standards of healthcare and economic success contribute to these low birth and death rates. The interesting characteristic of stage 4 is that the birth rate can occasionally fall below that of the death rate. This represents a very significant change from the previous 3 stages. Sweden is a prime example of a post-industrialized nation that falls well within stage 4 of the Demographic Transition model.

2.	stage one	stage two	stage three	stage four	i.	ii.	Total
	$\underline{\quad 2 \quad}$ +	$\underline{\quad 0 \quad}$ +	$\underline{\quad 0 \quad}$ +	$\underline{\quad 1 \quad}$ +	$\underline{\quad 0 \quad}$ +	$\underline{\quad 0 \quad}$ =	$\underline{\quad 3 \quad}$
	0, 1 or 2	0, 1 or 2	0, 1 or 2	0 or 1	0 or 1	0 or 1	out of 10

Now let's look at a higher-scoring version of Essay 2:

2. The first stage of the Demographic Transition Model represents a prehistoric or hunting/gathering type of society. Both the birth and death rates are particularly high and remain about the same in relation to one another. People in this time period had a very difficult time meeting their basic needs for food and shelter. The "name of the game" is one of survival. People did not live very long. Therefore multiple children were essential to the survival of the species but resulted in little population growth and change overall.

Stage 2 of the model illustrates the difference that an agricultural based economy has on the birth and death rates. As people settle down and begin to farm the land and domesticate animals to meet their basic needs for food, the death rates begin to decline down into the range of 10-30 per every 1000 people. Basic needs are being met more efficiently than in the hunting/gathering societies and thus quality and length of life improves. Children are seen a source of agricultural labor so the birth rates remain high. This difference between high birth and lowering death rates results in an expanding population. India is a good example of a county that falls into latter part of stage 2 on the model. Although it is becoming more industrialized, the majority of India's population still farms for a living and produces very little excess to export and build monetary wealth.

The transition of a population into an industrialized economy is shown in stage 3 of the Demographic model. This stage is characterized primarily by a decline in birth rates down into the range of 10-30 per 1000 people. Birth numbers decline as a result of urbanization of the population. In cities compared to farming areas, there is less time and need for having children. The death rate declines due to better healthcare for people and better sanitation in cities which increases lifespan. The difference in births and deaths continues to cause population growth, but it slows down later in stage 3.

The final stage of the model shows a post-industrial or modern society. The birth and death rates are similarly low (around 8 per 1000 people). Modern standards of healthcare and economic success contribute to these low birth and death rates. As a result population growth plateaus with little growth, if any, The interesting characteristic of stage 4 is that the birth rate can occasionally fall below that of the death rate. Sweden is a prime example of a post-industrialized nation that falls in this negative growth period in stage four of the Demographic Transition Model.

Essay 3

3. Nuclear power has been touted by supporters as the "magic bullet" of sorts that will solve both the planet's current energy crisis and environmental calamity. On the surface, nuclear energy appears to be an obvious "clean" replacement for fossil fuel resources. However, it is important to note that nuclear energy is not without significant risks to the environment. With respect to the issues of air pollution, environmental safety, and waste management, both nuclear energy and fossil fuels have significant advantages and disadvantages.

Nuclear power definitely has an advantage over fossil fuel resources when it comes to air pollution. Carbon emissions are virtually eliminated in the production of nuclear energy. Compare that to the burning of fossil fuels, which is the primary contributor to the air pollution that is responsible for global warming (according to Al Gore, of course). Replacing fossil fuel energy with nuclear power stands to have a significant positive impact with respect to global climate change.

Environmental safety is an important concern with both nuclear power and with fossil fuel resources. Nuclear power plants are risky to operate because of the potential for accidents that can leak radioactive materials into the surrounding air and groundwater. This poses a major environmental and health risk for the community. Fossil fuels also pose a risk to the community with respect to environmental and occupational safety. Coal mines, for example, are on par with nuclear power plants as particularly treacherous places to earn a living.

Waste management appears to be the primary concern with nuclear power. Much in the same way that fossil fuel burning contributes to air pollution, the routine production of nuclear power contributes to "earth pollution" by generating radioactive waste that must be managed. In fact, finding a solution to the problem of nuclear waste may be the deciding factor on whether or not nuclear power will replace fossil fuel resources as a primary source of energy for the planet.

3. A.   B.   C.   Total

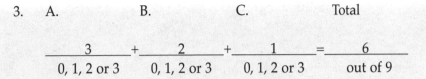

3	+	2	+	1	=	6
0, 1, 2 or 3		0, 1, 2 or 3		0, 1, 2 or 3		out of 9

Now let's look at a higher-scoring version of Essay 3:

3. Nuclear power has been touted by supporters as the "magic bullet" of sorts that will solve both the planet's current energy crisis and environmental calamity. On the surface, nuclear energy appears to be an obvious "clean" replacement for fossil fuel resources. However, it is important to note that nuclear energy is not without significant risks to the environment. With respect to the issues of air pollution, environmental safety, and waste management, both nuclear energy and fossil fuels have significant advantages and disadvantages.

Nuclear power definitely has an advantage over fossil fuel resources when it comes to air pollution. Carbon emissions are virtually eliminated in the production of nuclear energy. Compare that to the burning of fossil fuels, which is the primary contributor to the air pollution that is responsible for global warming (according to Al Gore, of course). Replacing fossil fuel energy with nuclear power stands to have a significant positive impact with respect to global climate change.

Environmental safety is an important concern with both nuclear power and with fossil fuel resources. Nuclear power plants are risky to operate because of the potential for even minor accidents that can leak radioactive materials into the power plant. This poses a major environmental health risk for workers and their families. Fossil fuels also pose a risk to the community with respect to environmental and occupational safety. Coal mines, for example, are on par with nuclear power plants as particularly treacherous places to earn a living, due to oil fires and cave-ins at coal mines. However, safety features at nuclear plants are much more expensive than at fossil fuel-fired plants.

Waste management appears to be the primary concern with nuclear power. Much in the same way that fossil fuel burning contributes to air pollution, the routine production of nuclear power contributes to "earth pollution" by generating radioactive waste that must be managed. By comparison fossil fuels produce far less problematic waste products. For example, ash from coal burned in power plants can be landfilled. In fact, finding a solution to the problem of nuclear waste may be the deciding factor on whether or not nuclear power will replace fossil fuel resources as a primary source of energy for the planet.

HOW TO SCORE PRACTICE TEST 2

SECTION I: MULTIPLE-CHOICE

_____ × 0.8000 = _____
Number of Correct   Weighted
(out of 75)   Section I Score
                        (Do not round)

SECTION II: FREE RESPONSE

(See if you can find a teacher or classmate to score your essays using the rubrics in this chapter.)

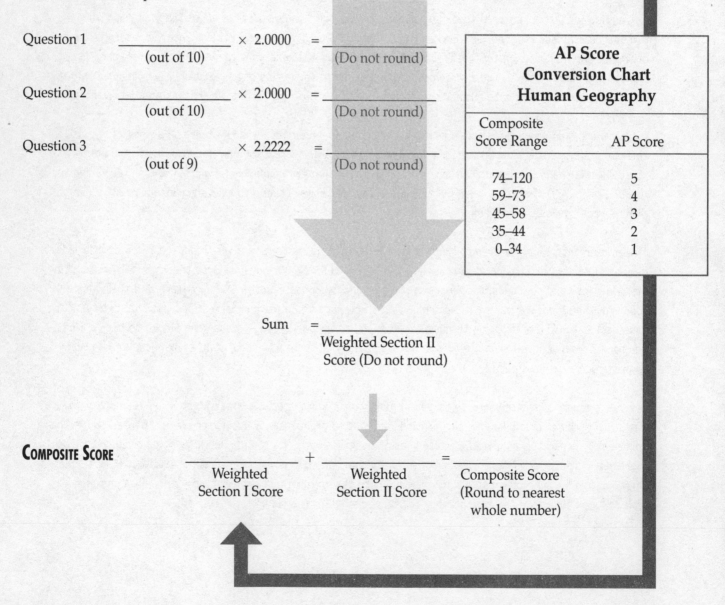

Question 1   _____ × 2.0000 = _____
                  (out of 10)   (Do not round)

Question 2   _____ × 2.0000 = _____
                  (out of 10)   (Do not round)

Question 3   _____ × 2.2222 = _____
                  (out of 9)   (Do not round)

Sum = _____
      Weighted Section II
      Score (Do not round)

AP Score Conversion Chart Human Geography

Composite Score Range	AP Score
74–120	5
59–73	4
45–58	3
35–44	2
0–34	1

COMPOSITE SCORE

_____ + _____ = _____
   Weighted   Weighted   Composite Score
Section I Score   Section II Score   (Round to nearest
                                      whole number)

ABOUT THE AUTHOR

Jon Moore is Assistant Professor of Geography at the University of Akron in Ohio. He has been writing AP Human Geography Exam questions for nine years and has been an exam reader since the first test in 2001. He is currently a Question Leader for the AP Human Geography Exam reading. After majoring in geography as an undergraduate at The George Washington University, he obtained a master's degree in geographic sciences from George Mason University and a Ph.D. in geography from The Ohio State University. Dr. Moore is an avid alpine skier and spends warmer weekends refereeing rugby.

The Princeton Review®

1

YOUR NAME: _____
(Print)
　　　　　　　　Last　　　　　　　　First　　　　　　　　M.I.

SIGNATURE: _____　　　DATE: __/__/__

HOME ADDRESS: _____
(Print)
　　　　　　　　Number and Street

　　　　City　　　　　　State　　　　　　Zip Code

PHONE No.: _____
(Print)

IMPORTANT: Please fill in these boxes exactly as shown on the back cover of your test book.

2. TEST FORM

3. TEST CODE

4. REGISTRATION NUMBER

5. YOUR NAME

First 4 letters of last name				FIRST INI	MID INIT
A	A	A	A	A	A
B	B	B	B	B	B
C	C	C	C	C	C
D	D	D	D	D	D
E	E	E	E	E	E
F	F	F	F	F	F
G	G	G	G	G	G
H	H	H	H	H	H
I	I	I	I	I	I
J	J	J	J	J	J
K	K	K	K	K	K
L	L	L	L	L	L
M	M	M	M	M	M
N	N	N	N	N	N
O	O	O	O	O	O
P	P	P	P	P	P
Q	Q	Q	Q	Q	Q
R	R	R	R	R	R
S	S	S	S	S	S
T	T	T	T	T	T
U	U	U	U	U	U
V	V	V	V	V	V
W	W	W	W	W	W
X	X	X	X	X	X
Y	Y	Y	Y	Y	Y
Z	Z	Z	Z	Z	Z

6. DATE OF BIRTH

Month		Day	Year
JAN			
FEB			
MAR	0	0 0	0 0
APR	1	1 1	1 1
MAY	2	2 2	2 2
JUN	3	3 3	3 3
JUL		4 4	4 4
AUG		5 5	5 5
SEP		6 6	6 6
OCT		7 7	7 7
NOV		8 8	8 8
DEC		9 9	9 9

Test Code bubbles: 0 A 0 0 0 0 0 0 0 0 0; 1 B 1 1 1 1 1 1 1 1 1; 2 C 2 2 2 2 2 2 2 2 2; 3 D 3 3 3 3 3 3 3 3 3; 4 E 4 4 4 4 4 4 4 4 4; 5 F 5 5 5 5 5 5 5 5 5; 6 G 6 6 6 6 6 6 6 6 6; 7 7 7 7 7 7 7 7 7; 8 8 8 8 8 8 8 8 8; 9 9 9 9 9 9 9 9 9

7. SEX

MALE　　FEMALE

The Princeton Review®

Start with number 1 for each new section. If a section has fewer questions than answer spaces, leave the extra answer spaces blank.

1 A B C D E	21 A B C D E	41 A B C D E	61 A B C D E
2 A B C D E	22 A B C D E	42 A B C D E	62 A B C D E
3 A B C D E	23 A B C D E	43 A B C D E	63 A B C D E
4 A B C D E	24 A B C D E	44 A B C D E	64 A B C D E
5 A B C D E	25 A B C D E	45 A B C D E	65 A B C D E
6 A B C D E	26 A B C D E	46 A B C D E	66 A B C D E
7 A B C D E	27 A B C D E	47 A B C D E	67 A B C D E
8 A B C D E	28 A B C D E	48 A B C D E	68 A B C D E
9 A B C D E	29 A B C D E	49 A B C D E	69 A B C D E
10 A B C D E	30 A B C D E	50 A B C D E	70 A B C D E
11 A B C D E	31 A B C D E	51 A B C D E	71 A B C D E
12 A B C D E	32 A B C D E	52 A B C D E	72 A B C D E
13 A B C D E	33 A B C D E	53 A B C D E	73 A B C D E
14 A B C D E	34 A B C D E	54 A B C D E	74 A B C D E
15 A B C D E	35 A B C D E	55 A B C D E	75 A B C D E
16 A B C D E	36 A B C D E	56 A B C D E	76 A B C D E
17 A B C D E	37 A B C D E	57 A B C D E	77 A B C D E
18 A B C D E	38 A B C D E	58 A B C D E	78 A B C D E
19 A B C D E	39 A B C D E	59 A B C D E	79 A B C D E
20 A B C D E	40 A B C D E	60 A B C D E	80 A B C D E

DO NOT MARK IN THIS AREA

The Princeton Review®

1

YOUR NAME: _____
(Print)　　　　Last　　　　First　　　　M.I.

SIGNATURE: _____　　　DATE: ___/___/___

HOME ADDRESS: _____
(Print)　　　　Number and Street

_____
City　　　　State　　　　Zip Code

PHONE No.: _____
(Print)

IMPORTANT: Please fill in these boxes exactly as shown on the back cover of your test book.

5. YOUR NAME

First 4 letters of last name				FIRST INIT	MID INIT
A	A	A	A	A	A
B	B	B	B	B	B
C	C	C	C	C	C
D	D	D	D	D	D
E	E	E	E	E	E
F	F	F	F	F	F
G	G	G	G	G	G
H	H	H	H	H	H
I	I	I	I	I	I
J	J	J	J	J	J
K	K	K	K	K	K
L	L	L	L	L	L
M	M	M	M	M	M
N	N	N	N	N	N
O	O	O	O	O	O
P	P	P	P	P	P
Q	Q	Q	Q	Q	Q
R	R	R	R	R	R
S	S	S	S	S	S
T	T	T	T	T	T
U	U	U	U	U	U
V	V	V	V	V	V
W	W	W	W	W	W
X	X	X	X	X	X
Y	Y	Y	Y	Y	Y
Z	Z	Z	Z	Z	Z

2. TEST FORM

3. TEST CODE

	A									
0	A	0	0	0	0	0	0	0	0	0
1	B	1	1	1	1	1	1	1	1	1
2	C	2	2	2	2	2	2	2	2	2
3	D	3	3	3	3	3	3	3	3	3
4	E	4	4	4	4	4	4	4	4	4
5	F	5	5	5	5	5	5	5	5	5
6	G	6	6	6	6	6	6	6	6	6
7		7	7	7	7	7	7	7	7	7
8		8	8	8	8	8	8	8	8	8
9		9	9	9	9	9	9	9	9	9

4. REGISTRATION NUMBER

6. DATE OF BIRTH

Month	Day	Year
JAN		
FEB		
MAR	0 0	0 0
APR	1 1	1 1
MAY	2 2	2 2
JUN	3 3	3 3
JUL	4	4 4
AUG	5	5 5
SEP	6	6 6
OCT	7	7 7
NOV	8	8 8
DEC	9	9 9

7. SEX
- MALE
- FEMALE

The Princeton Review®

© 2006 The Princeton Review, Inc
FORM NO. 00001-PR

Start with number 1 for each new section. If a section has fewer questions than answer spaces, leave the extra answer spaces blank.

1 A B C D E	21 A B C D E	41 A B C D E	61 A B C D E
2 A B C D E	22 A B C D E	42 A B C D E	62 A B C D E
3 A B C D E	23 A B C D E	43 A B C D E	63 A B C D E
4 A B C D E	24 A B C D E	44 A B C D E	64 A B C D E
5 A B C D E	25 A B C D E	45 A B C D E	65 A B C D E
6 A B C D E	26 A B C D E	46 A B C D E	66 A B C D E
7 A B C D E	27 A B C D E	47 A B C D E	67 A B C D E
8 A B C D E	28 A B C D E	48 A B C D E	68 A B C D E
9 A B C D E	29 A B C D E	49 A B C D E	69 A B C D E
10 A B C D E	30 A B C D E	50 A B C D E	70 A B C D E
11 A B C D E	31 A B C D E	51 A B C D E	71 A B C D E
12 A B C D E	32 A B C D E	52 A B C D E	72 A B C D E
13 A B C D E	33 A B C D E	53 A B C D E	73 A B C D E
14 A B C D E	34 A B C D E	54 A B C D E	74 A B C D E
15 A B C D E	35 A B C D E	55 A B C D E	75 A B C D E
16 A B C D E	36 A B C D E	56 A B C D E	76 A B C D E
17 A B C D E	37 A B C D E	57 A B C D E	77 A B C D E
18 A B C D E	38 A B C D E	58 A B C D E	78 A B C D E
19 A B C D E	39 A B C D E	59 A B C D E	79 A B C D E
20 A B C D E	40 A B C D E	60 A B C D E	80 A B C D E

DO NOT MARK IN THIS AREA